Conflict and Coop[eration]
in Cyberspac[e]

The Challenge to National [Security]

OTH[ER]

Asset Prot[ection]
Tyler Justin
ISBN 978-1

Automatic
Polymorph[ic]
Networks
Mohssen M
ISBN 978-1

The Comp[lete]
From Plan[ning]
Balaji Ragh
ISBN 978-1

The Comp[lete]
Paul R. Bak
ISBN 978-1

Conflict a[nd]
The Chall[enge]
Panayotis A
(Editors)
ISBN 978-1

Cybersec[urity]
and Resp[onse]
Kim J. And
ISBN 978-1

The Defin[itive]
HIPAA/HI[TECH]
John J. Tri
ISBN 978-

Digital Fo[rensics]
Greg Gogo
ISBN 978-1

Digital Fo[rensics]
Eamon P. D
ISBN 978-

Effective
Balancing
Francesco
Francesch
ISBN 978-

Electroni[c]
The Com[plete]
Understa[nding]
Search, a[nd]
David R. N
ISBN 978-

Enterpris[e]
Assuranc[e]
James A.
ISBN 978

www.au[erbach]

Conflict and Cooperation in Cyberspace

The Challenge to National Security

Edited by
Panayotis A. Yannakogeorgos
Adam B. Lowther

Taylor & Francis
Taylor & Francis Group
Boca Raton London New York

Taylor & Francis
Taylor & Francis Group
6000 Broken Sound Parkway NW, Suite 300
Boca Raton, FL 33487-2742

© 2014 by Taylor & Francis Group, LLC
Taylor & Francis is an Informa business

No claim to original U.S. Government works

Printed on acid-free paper
Version Date: 20130620

International Standard Book Number-13: 978-1-4665-9201-8 (Hardback)

Library of Congress Cataloging-in-Publication Data

Conflict and cooperation in cyberspace : the challenge to national security / editors, Panayotis
A Yannakogeorgos, Adam B Lowther.
    pages cm
Includes bibliographical references and index.
ISBN 978-1-4665-9201-8 (hardcover : alk. paper)
    1. Information warfare--Prevention. 2. Cyberspace--Security measures.
3. Cyberspace--Security measures--Government policy--United States. 4.
Cyberterrorism--Prevention. 5. National security--United States. I. Yannakogeorgos,
Panayotis A., editor. II. Lowther, Adam, editor.

U163.C625 2013
355.4'1--dc23   2013020070

Visit the Taylor & Francis Web site at
http://www.taylorandfrancis.com

and the CRC Press Web site at
http://www.crcpress.com

Contents

FOREWORD ix

ACKNOWLEDGMENTS xiii

INTRODUCTION xv

EDITORS xxv

CONTRIBUTORS xxvii

PART I KEY CONSIDERATIONS

CHAPTER 1 THE FUTURE OF THINGS CYBER 3
MICHAEL V. HAYDEN

CHAPTER 2 TAMING THE "21ST CENTURY'S WILD WEST"
OF CYBERSPACE? 9
LYNN MATTICE

CHAPTER 3 CYBERSPACE SUPERIORITY CONSIDERATIONS 13
FRED TAYLOR, JR. AND JERRY CARTER

CHAPTER 4 TWO, MAYBE THREE CHEERS FOR AMBIGUITY 27
MARTIN C. LIBICKI

CHAPTER 5 THE ESSENTIAL FEATURES OF AN ONTOLOGY
FOR CYBERWARFARE 35
RANDALL R. DIPERT

CHAPTER 6   THE PROSPECTS FOR CYBER DETERRENCE:
             AMERICAN SPONSORSHIP OF GLOBAL NORMS   49
             PANAYOTIS A. YANNAKOGEORGOS AND
             ADAM B. LOWTHER

PART II   TECHNOLOGY

CHAPTER 7   CHALLENGES IN MONITORING CYBERARMS
             COMPLIANCE   81
             NEIL C. ROWE, SIMSON L.
             GARFINKEL, ROBERT BEVERLY, AND
             PANAYOTIS A. YANNAKOGEORGOS

CHAPTER 8   DIGITAL POLICY MANAGEMENT: A FOUNDATION
             FOR TOMORROW   101
             NATIONAL SECURITY AGENCY (NSA),
             ENTERPRISE SERVICES DIVISION, IDENTITY AND
             ACCESS MANAGEMENT BRANCH

CHAPTER 9   ON MISSION ASSURANCE   107
             KAMAL JABBOUR AND SARAH MUCCIO

CHAPTER 10   STUXNET: A CASE STUDY IN CYBER WARFARE   127
             ERIC P. OLIVER

CHAPTER 11   THE INTERNET AND DISSENT IN
             AUTHORITARIAN STATES   161
             JAMES D. FIELDER

PART III   ETHICS, LAW, AND POLICY

CHAPTER 12   CAN THERE BE AN ETHICAL CYBER WAR?   195
             GEORGE R. LUCAS, JR.

CHAPTER 13   PERSPECTIVES FOR CYBERSTRATEGISTS ON
             CYBERLAW FOR CYBERWAR   211
             CHARLES J. DUNLAP, JR.

CHAPTER 14   A NEW NORMAL? THE CULTIVATION
             OF GLOBAL NORMS AS PART OF A
             CYBERSECURITY STRATEGY   233
             ROGER HURWITZ

CHAPTER 15 CYBERDEFENSE AS ENVIRONMENTAL
PROTECTION—THE BROADER POTENTIAL
IMPACT OF FAILED DEFENSIVE COUNTER
CYBER OPERATIONS 265

JAN KALLBERG AND ROSEMARY A. BURK

CHAPTER 16 CYBER SOVEREIGNTY 277

STEPHEN K. GOURLEY

CHAPTER 17 AMERICAN CYBERSECURITY TRIAD:
GOVERNMENTWIDE INTEGRATION,
TECHNOLOGICAL COUNTERINTELLIGENCE, AND
EDUCATIONAL MOBILIZATION 291

SUNGHYUN KIM

INDEX 311

Foreword

Cyber publications generally seek to provide the reader a methodology to address the challenges of cyberspace based on their experience or research. The editors of this compilation take a different approach, reminding their readers that cyberspace is complicated and the breadth of opportunities yet unknown, proposing instead that an understanding of cyberspace's multidimensional complexities is necessary to overcome its associated challenges. This book is intended to provide readers with the views from a diverse set of experts and offer insights into the direction they are moving the discussion in their particular areas of expertise. Rather than provide answers or solutions, it seeks to draw readers, regardless of their field, into the larger debate, which focuses on national and economic security. As the authors note, the implications of this debate are critically important for the United States.

The book's editors argue the need for common ground among the disciplines involved in today's cyber debates and discussions. The Air Force Research Institute conducted several workshops and numerous small group discussions to facilitate the crossflow of information among subject matter experts across a wide variety of relevant subject areas. The result is a rich cyberspace dialogue with multidimensional insights that have not been previously highlighted in other published works.

Consider the diversity of cyberspace perspectives this volume addresses: to many, cyberspace is a means to collect private information or intelligence, or prevent others from doing so. In a military context, it is viewed as a contested domain that must be controlled to ensure freedom of action for joint operations. To yet others, cyberspace is a way to achieve global effects for both strategic and regional stability, but at the same its capabilities can be used to foment regional instability leading to international crises. Cyberspace has reduced the cost of entry to participate in global commerce, international diplomacy, social networking, targeted message delivery, and organizational recruiting; however, these same attributes also enable adversary nations, international crime syndicates, transnational extremist organizations, and terrorist groups to undermine the public and private interests of the United States at very low cost. Furthermore, the absence of legal frameworks for maintaining law and order in cyberspace, exacerbated by the difficulties of attribution, allow actors to conduct illegal operations against the United States and its population with very low risk of retribution. Not surprisingly, these different perspectives on cyberspace drive widely divergent views regarding appropriate policies, strategies, and courses of action to protect the United States and advance its global interests. This underpins the authors' desire to find common ground for these discussions and debates.

This book is different. Its purpose is not an attempt to sell a product, concept, or organization. It does not claim to have all the answers to the questions posed by the rapid growth of cyberspace. Instead, it seeks to help its readers ask key questions that are relevant to their own organizations and missions. To support this aim, it begins with a number of thoughtful discussions about the attributes and importance of cyberspace to the future American way of life. It then examines the challenges and opportunities inherent in the technologies on which cyberspace exists. The book concludes with chapters that examine the topics of cyber ethics, law, policy, and strategy. This treatise is not only informative and stimulating, but also a valuable reference on the disciplines comprising the national and economic security aspects of cyberspace.

The authors' individual insights and perspectives provide important contributions to the ongoing debate over cyberspace. Collectively they offer a powerful cross-disciplinary appreciation of cyberspace that enables practitioners to balance their focus between the exploitation of cyber-related opportunities and the mitigation of its challenges. Cyberspace has broken many of the barriers imposed by time and space; it's up to the users of cyberspace to break the organizational and disciplinary barriers that prevent us from fully leveraging its benefits. Facilitated by the exceptional handiwork of the editors, this book significantly advances the effort to achieve common ground in the debates regarding cyberspace; national security and cyber-related professionals will find it equally useful in their work.

Lt. Gen. Bob Elder, USAF (Ret.)

Acknowledgments

This book summarizes research that was conducted by a network of many individuals and institutions around the world. Several people contributed directly or indirectly to an ongoing Air Force Research Institute project on cyber power, national security, and military operations, but the most important hosting and funding organization for this work was the United States Air Force Research Institute (AFRI), where we serve as research professors. The institute and its devoted team serve us both as a home and a family and continue to be a great source of support.

Many individuals among the institute's staff deserve our gratitude, but we would like to first single out General John Shaud, AFRI's founding director. General Shaud was a source of guidance. Others at the institute who greatly assisted us include Dale Hayden, John Geis, Steve Hagel, Chad Dacus, Scott Johnson, Tony Gould, and Billy Barth. Grateful acknowledgement is also made to the leadership of Air University; Lieutenant General David Fadok, Commander of Air University, and former Air University Commander Lt. Gen. Al Peck, for supporting AFRI's cyber research endeavors that led to this volume.

We would also like to thank our contributors, whose insights were indispensable. Finally, we would like to thank Rich O'Hanley and his team of editors, typesetters, and marketing personnel for making the book you are holding possible.

Introduction

In recent years, large-scale cyber threats that include the Stuxnet worm, the emergence of hacker networks, and the militarization of cyberspace have been raising the awareness of government decision makers and the private sector to the vulnerability of a networked and digital world. The risks such threats pose to vital systems and infrastructures—upon which societies and economies depend—are beginning to receive the serious attention they deserve. While there is widespread understanding that cyber security is important for the public and private sectors, key players in government and industry often offer a collective shrug of the shoulders when asked who bears responsibility for the defense of American networks and the information they contain. Within the government and the Department of Defense (DoD), in particular, a lively debate is underway. Many within the military wonder what role they may be asked to play in defending the nation's cyber assets in coming years—some advocating an expanded role and some advocating limiting DoD's efforts to its own network defense. In an effort to address this and related questions, actors across the national security system are actively seeking to develop legal and policy solutions that protect the nation while limiting government regulation and intrusion into what is largely a privately owned and operated domain.

Within the DoD, the US Air Force (USAF) is a key player in cyberspace. Given the service's technology focus, it should come as no surprise that the "organize, train, and equip" function of the Air Force—in cyberspace—is taking center stage. In recent years, the service activated 24th Air Force (2009) as its dedicated cyber component, created a career specialty for cyber specialists, developed the cyber corps tactical school, and made a number of additional changes to better address its cyber needs. This continues a long tradition of Air Force involvement in cyberspace starting from the mid-1990s when Air Force Office of Special Investigations (OSI) investigator Jim Christy tracked down an East German cyber espionage ring, which became the stuff of hacker legend in *The Cuckoo's Egg*. The Air Force was the first service to stand up a Computer Emergency Response Team (CERT) as well as to develop an information warfare doctrine. However, the complexity and changing nature of the domain creates an environment that appears unsettlingly new, when indeed it should be familiar.

In order to assist the service in grappling with some of the complex questions that must be answered before the Air Force can best serve the nation, on 26–27 October 2011, the Air Force Research Institute (AFRI) convened. "Cyber Power: The Quest towards a Common Ground" at Maxwell AFB was the first in a series of conferences and workshops focusing on contemporary cyber challenges. The objective was to open avenues of dialogue and shared understanding among cyber stakeholders, while advocating a "whole of society" approach to cyber security.

As part of its mission, AFRI seeks to enhance the unity of cyber efforts across the military, government, industry, academia, and international communities. Through its conferences and workshops the organization is creating a forum for the exchange of ideas and experiences among cyber professionals from all sectors. Recent events gave particular attention to articulating and anticipating the need to foster a common methodology on which to base new-style partnerships among relevant cyber security stakeholders. The quest for common ground, with respect to cyberspace, refers to the lack of accepted standards for definitions, data structures, threat assessments, and policies both within and across communities that employ cyber—a central challenge in the short term.

The Quest for a Common Ground

When practitioners and scholars discuss the air, land, sea, and space domains, there is little confusion as to what they mean. Common definitions and an accepted lexicon are the foundation of any debate. Thus, it is rare for individuals to talk past one another or enter a discussion with very different assumptions about the domain under discussion. With cyberspace the same cannot be said.

To illustrate this point, it is interesting to point out that Daniel Kuehl, of the National Defense University, identifies at least 13 definitions of cyberspace in circulation.[1] Since the United States, its allies, and other nations invest vast sums of treasure into cyberspace, a domain that is identified not only as part of the nation's critical national infrastructure—with myriad vulnerabilities—but also a warfighting domain, it should come as no surprise that developing widely accepted concepts and norms is of central interest to both the public and private sectors. With the Air Force playing a greater role in the domain, it is also natural for the service to take the lead in facilitating such agreement and collaboration.

Recent Efforts

The purpose of this book is to expand the formal debate that began at AFRI in 2011 as AFRI and the USAF continue to discuss and debate the service's role in cyberspace. As part of this effort, forging common cyberspace terms, definitions, and methodologies that will eventually lead to more coherent cyberspace policy, strategy, and doctrine is important. This is not a topic of mere academic semantics, but necessary for reaching a common framework that those involved in the debate and decision making can employ when operating in a dangerous world.

In a recent *Strategic Studies Quarterly* article, Gen. Michael Hayden writes:

> Rarely has something been so important and so talked about with less clarity and less apparent understanding than this phenomenon. But few of us (myself included) have created the broad structural framework within which to comfortably and confidently place these varied phenomena. And that matters. I have sat in *very* small group meetings in

Washington, been briefed on an operational need and an operational solution, and been unable (along with my colleagues) to decide on a course of action because we lacked a clear picture of the long-term legal and policy implications of *any* decision we might make.[2]

The interdisciplinary nature of cyberspace and the challenges it poses are unique when compared to national security challenges in other domains. The way in which AFRI has sought to examine the many questions under investigation reflects a whole-of-society approach, rather than an airpower-focused approach. Although the Air Force is on the cutting edge of cyber, the service cannot solve cyberspace challenges alone. Without the help of joint, interagency, and private-sector partners, key variables that must be considered are likely to go unnoticed.

A variety of topics have received attention over the past two years of meetings. Data needs and structures—focusing on how to share data for common situational awareness of vulnerabilities and threats—are of particular importance, because reducing national vulnerability to cyber attacks requires a common situational awareness among internal and external stakeholders that defend the cyber domain. Thus, identifying data needs and influencing the eventual creation of shared common data structures are essential.

Another area of interest has been common analytical methodologies (i.e., the best approach to studying hackers). With cyber situational awareness proving a challenge that hinges on the ability to analyze complex data, significant debate has focused on this issue. While the shape of a common analytical methodology that emphasizes critical and creative thinking for understanding, visualizing, and describing complex and ill-structured problems remains unclear, there is common agreement that it is necessary so operators can offer decision makers the best approaches to resolving those problems.

In moving from discussions of technical issues to the need for improved policy, bringing technical and policy experts together has proven important. All too often they do not understand one another or the challenges the other faces. In bringing these groups together, some of the nation's best and brightest thinkers on cyber policy issues have informed fruitful discussions between the broader technical and policy communities. As part of the policy discussion, topics such as cyber incidences that can be for criminal, espionage, military, and other purposes are of importance. A common understanding of what constitutes criminal, espionage, military, and other cyber activities assists in assigning the appropriate authorities, resources, and type of response to each incident. This common understanding and methodology will help analysts across all services, government, industry, and allies identify threats and trends—and appropriate target sets from which threats emanate. The lack of a common cyber understanding, methodology, and lexicon has policy and strategic implications. Achieving commonality, at least among US equities, should contribute to improved policy and strategy.

For readers of this volume, it is important to understand the context in which each chapter is offered. As you read, imagine each author sitting in AFRI's conference room—where many of the discussions occurred—along with two dozen other experts. In a lively give-and-take, participants from academia, industry, government, and the military are exchanging ideas concerning the topics listed above and found in these pages. While not every contributor participated in these discussions, most played an important role in informing the debate and shaping the thinking of other participants. The chapters reflect that discussion and are often written from the perspective of a practitioner rather than an academic, although some chapters are written by academics. Thus, the style and length of each chapter varies in accordance with each author's approach to writing about the challenge or issue he or she was asked to discuss with the group. Where chapters written by academics are often longer and thoroughly noted, chapters written by government and industry participants are often shorter and focus on more tangible problems and solutions. With this in mind, a brief description of the book's format and each chapter is useful.

Format

This book is divided into three sections: Key Considerations; Technology; and Ethics, Law, and Policy. Part 1 takes a broad look at many of the challenges facing the public and private sector in cyberspace, with a particular focus on those areas where national security is a concern. Part 2 examines the technical challenges of improved cyber security and focuses on possible solutions. Finally, Part 3 looks at the larger ethical, legal, and policy challenges facing government as it seeks to provide improved cyber security across the public and private sectors.

Key Considerations

General Michael V. Hayden (Ret.), former director of the National Security Agency and the Central Intelligence Agency, opens Part 1 with "The Future of Things Cyber." Given his long career and significant experience at senior levels in government, Hayden suggests that the nation, particularly those working on cyber issues, must come to understand the policy implications of a rapidly developing cyber technology before seeking to solve the security challenges that are increasingly evident. In many ways, Gen. Hayden's brief chapter poses very strategic questions that later chapters attempt to address in greater detail.

Lynn Mattice then follows with "What's Wrong with Cyberspace?" Here, Mattice argues that early software and hardware designers neither envisioned the interconnected world of today, nor was there commercial or legal imperative to develop products that were free from "bugs" or secure from hacking. Thus, according to the author, a culture of accepting flawed products exists. Mattice argues that this must change and that through a harmonization of laws and international treaties, threats in cyberspace can be mitigated more effectively.

Fred Taylor and Jerry Carter, in "Cyberspace Superiority Considerations," suggest that the Department of Defense is inadequately prepared to gain and maintain cyber superiority now or in the foreseeable future. They advise that DoD must overcome critical limitations related to four factors: capability, capacity, cognizance, and governance. To meet this need, the authors offer a series of more technically focused, but policy relevant, solutions.

In "Two, Maybe Three Cheers for Ambiguity," Martin Libicki discusses some of the most prescient issues in the debate over the applicability of deterrence to cyberspace. Focusing his discussion on deterministic versus probabilistic deterrence policy, Libicki weighs the pros and cons of such policies. With cyberspace possessing a number of unique characteristics that make it distinct from other domains, the author demonstrates that comparisons to nuclear deterrence have their limits. In the end, Libicki suggests that the determinism of a policy should not exceed the determinism of the domain over which the policy applies.

Randall Dipert shifts course in "The Essential Features of an Ontology for Cyberwarfare," where he examines the reasons for creating an applied cyberwarfare ontology and its required characteristics. As he suggests, a cyberwarfare ontology would systematically organize and allow inference on all data relevant for the conduct of offensive and defensive cyberwarfare. Dipert explains that it will have some distinctive characteristics when compared with other ontologies. With information sharing about malware and vulnerabilities rapidly increasing, the author argues for ontologies using widely accepted best practices, making a single, robust, and extensible framework for sharing data possible.

Part 1 ends with "The Prospects for Cyber Deterrence: American Sponsorship of Global Norms." Panayotis Yannakogeorgos and Adam Lowther argue that calls for cyber deterrence are premature. Instead, they posit that cyberspace must become sovereign territory of nation-states before cyber deterrence is possible. It will then become possible for the United States to hold nations responsible for their actions or inactions within the tenets of global norms and behavior in cyberspace. They offer a framework for developing a deterrence strategy based on US sponsorship of embryonic global norms.

Technology

Part 2 opens with Neil Rowe, Simson Garfinkel, Robert Beverly, and Panayotis A. Yannakogeorgos' "Challenges in Monitoring Cyberarms Compliance." Rowe and his colleagues argue that the technical means exist, or are in development, to enable cyberarms control and monitoring. Where some scholars suggest that international cyberarms agreements are not technically feasible, the authors offer illustrations of technologies that will enable the very agreements many states desire but believe are not technically possible. While some of the approaches offered would likely face challenging political obstacles, the options discussed are certainly thought provoking.

The National Security Agency's (NSA) Enterprise Services Division, Identity and Access Management Branch succinctly describes the challenges posed in today's networked world in "Digital

Policy Management: A Foundation for Tomorrow." Not only do the authors describe current challenges facing all Internet users, but they briefly describe NSA efforts to build an open standard based on digital policy management capability for the Department of Defense and the US government at large.

Kamal Jabbour and Sarah Muccio give their take on "On Mission Assurance" in a brief and direct discussion. With the US Air Force increasingly relying on cyberspace to perform its mission, the generation, storage, processing, dissemination, consumption, and destruction of information are increasingly occurring in a contested and denied environment. Here, Jabbour and Muccio present mission assurance in a contested cyber environment comparing and contrasting approaches to cyber security with the requirements for mission assurance. Within this discussion, they offer a view of the dichotomy between security and reliability, drawing parallels between system safety and system security.

In "Stuxnet: A Case Study in Cyber Warfare," Eric Oliver examines the truths and myths surrounding Stuxnet and industrial control systems more broadly. Oliver suggests that the offensive employment of cyber weapons can be consistent with US national security strategy but is also accompanied by risks. Because of these risks, the author argues that the United States should show restraint and seek international agreements to limit and outlaw the most damaging effects of attacks on industrial control systems. To this aim, Oliver offers specific steps the United States can take to improve its defense against such attacks.

James D. Fielder's "The Internet and Dissent in Authoritarian States" asks the relevant question: does the Internet facilitate anti-regime dissent within authoritarian regimes? By examining a number of variables related to Internet use in authoritarian regimes, Fielder finds that Internet use in authoritarian regimes does facilitate protest and anti-regime activities, even if the regime attempts to censor dissent. His work stands to illuminate current discussion of social media's role in the Arab Spring and beyond.

Ethics, Law, and Policy

George Lucas opens Part 3 with "Can There Be an Ethical Cyber War?" In asking an interesting question, Lucas posits that there have, in fact, been examples of ethical war, consistent with international law. Further, he suggests that cyber can play an ethical role in warfare. The author also offers some innovative ways to wage ethical cyber war, explaining his rationale for the means he describes.

"Perspectives for Cyberstrategists on Cyberlaw for Cyberwar," Charles Dunlap's contribution to the volume, delves into the many intricacies and considerations cyberstrategists must contemplate before they engage in cyber war. General Dunlap (Ret.) clearly highlights the US military's growing role in defending American networks and in responding to attacks. He also identifies the substantive legal challenges that come with such a role. In the end, Dunlap warns that allowing intelligence agencies and the military to assist in the defense of private networks may pose unexpected legal and political challenges.

Roger Hurwitz's detailed discussion of the prospects for achieving international cyber norms in "A New Normal? The Cultivation of Global Norms as Part of a Cybersecurity Strategy" offers a variety of options available to the international community. While the author acknowledges the tension between liberal democracies, which seek to advance the free flow of information, and more authoritarian regimes, which see social media and other web outlets as a threat, there is common ground between the two. Hurwitz makes an interesting contribution that spans the many differing perspectives.

In Jan Kallberg[3] and Rosemary Burk's "Cyber Defense as Environmental Protection—The Broader Potential Impact of Failed Defensive Counter Cyber Operations" the authors examine the potential environmental damage that can result from a cyber attack, which is often overlooked or marginalized. Kallberg and Burk argue that a cyber attack against an industrial control system in the energy, chemical, and waste treatment industries, for example, can lead to serious environmental damage and pose a significant economic cost. In the end, they advocate considering such risks when thinking about cyber security.

Stephen Gourley takes a similar position in "Cyber Sovereignty" to that of the previous chapter. He argues that since cyber is a man-made domain, it is appropriate for cyberspace to fall under the same regulation of other human activities. Contrary to those who seek the unfettered flow of data on the Internet, Gourley believes that cyber, like the air, land, sea, and space domains, must be recognized as a nation-state's sovereign territory, based on the principal of territoriality. While the author acknowledges that authoritarian regimes will seek to use sovereignty over cyberspace to their advantage, Gourley argues that national security imperatives require the state to exert control over the cyber domain.

In examining the Comprehensive National Cybersecurity Initiative (2008), Sunghyun Kim's "American Cybersecurity Triad: Governmentwide Integration, Technological Counterintelligence, and Educational Mobilization" takes an interesting look at one recent policy initiative. In creating a "cybersecurity triad," Kim offers a framework for thinking about the best way to tackle the cyber challenges facing the United States. Her construct is one not seen previously.

Conclusion

In bringing together an array of academic, government, and private sector cyber experts, a number of relevant cyber security challenges are brought to light. Efforts to address those challenges, by offering policy and technical solutions, may bear fruit in the future, but only if common ground is achieved and norms are broadly accepted. To that end, this work seeks to inform readers of where some experts seek to move the discussion. It also attempts to draw readers into the larger debate, which because of its implications for national security, is an important one.

Endnotes

1. See Daniel T. Kuehl, "From Cyberspace to Cyberpower: Defining the Problem," in Franklin D. Kramer, Stuart H. Starr, and Larry K. Wentz (eds.), *Cyberpower and National Security* (Washington, DC: Potomac Press, 2009), 26–27.
2. Gen. Michael Hayden, "The Future of Things Cyber," in *Strategic Studies Quarterly* Vol. 5, No. 1 (Spring 2011), 3.
3. Jan Kallberg is co-author, with Bhavani Thuraisingham, of the forthcoming book, *Digital National Security: Cyberdefense and Cyber Operations.*

Editors

Panayotis "Pano" A. Yannakogeorgos is a research professor of Cyber Policy and Global Affairs at the Air Force Research Institute. His expertise includes the intersection of cyberspace, national security, and military operations; cyber international relations; cyber arms control; violent non-state actors; and Eastern Mediterranean studies. He has recently authored articles and chapters including "Internet Governance and National Security" (*Strategic Studies Quarterly*), "Challenges in Monitoring Cyber Arms Control" (*Journal of Information Warfare and Terrorism*), "Pitfalls of the Private-Public Partnership Model" in *Crime and Terrorism Risk: Studies in Criminology and Criminal Justice* (Routledge, New York), and "Cyberspace: The New Frontier and the Same Old Multilateralism" in *Global Norms: American Sponsorship and the Emerging Pattern of World Politics* (Palgrave Macmillan, New York). He has also published in *The Atlantic*, *The National Interest*, and *The Diplomat*. Prior to his current position, Yannakogeorgos taught graduate-level courses on globalization, security, and intelligence at Rutgers University's Division of Global Affairs (Newark, New Jersey), where he also served as senior program coordinator, and led the Center for the Study of Emergent Threats in the 21st Century. He has participated in the work of global cybersecurity bodies including the High Level Experts Group of the Global Cybersecurity Agenda of the International Telecommunications Union. In 2006 he served as an advisor within the United Nations Security Council on issues related to nuclear nonproliferation, the Middle East (including Iran), Al-Qaida, and Internet misuse. He holds a PhD and MS in global affairs from Rutgers University, and an ALB in philosophy from Harvard University (Cambridge, Massachusetts).

Adam Lowther (BA, Arizona State University; MA, Arizona State University; PhD, University of Alabama) is a research professor at the Air Force Research Institute (AFRI), Maxwell Air Force Base (Montgomery, Alabama). His principal research interests include deterrence, nuclear weapons policy, airpower diplomacy, and terrorism.

Lowther is the editor of *Deterrence: Rising Powers, Rogue Regimes, and Terrorism in the Twenty-First Century* (Palgrave Macmillan, New York), co-editor of *Terrorism's Unanswered Questions* (Praeger Security International, Westport, Connecticut), and the author of *Americans and Asymmetric Conflict: Lebanon, Somalia, and Afghanistan*. He has published in the *New York Times, Boston Globe, Joint Forces Quarterly, Strategic Studies Quarterly,* and elsewhere.

Prior to joining AFRI, Lowther was an assistant professor of Political Science at Arkansas Tech University and Columbus State University. Early in his career Lowther served in the US Navy aboard the USS *Ramage* (DDG-61). He also spent time at CINCUSNAVEUR-London and with NMCB-17.

Contributors

Robert Beverly
Naval Postgraduate School
Monterey, California

Rosemary A. Burk
Arkansas Tech University
Russelville, Arkansas

**Lieutenant Colonel
Jerry Carter**
US Marine Corps
Washington, DC

Randall R. Dipert
University at Buffalo
Buffalo, New York

**Major General Charles J.
Dunlap, Jr. USAF (Ret.)**
Duke University
Durham, North Carolina

Major James D. Fielder
Air Force ISR Agency
JBSA-Lackland, Texas

Simson L. Garfinkel
Naval Postgraduate School
Monterey, California

Stephen K. Gourley
Gourley Consulting, LLC
Aurora, Colorado

**General Michael V. Hayden
USAF (Ret.)**
Chertoff Group
Washington, DC

Roger Hurwitz
Massachusetts Institute of
    Technology
Cambridge, Massachusetts

Kamal Jabbour
Air Force Institute of
  Technology
Wright-Patterson Air Force
  Base, Ohio

Jan Kallberg
Arkansas Tech University
Russelville, Arkansas

Sunghyun Kim
EWHA Woman's University
Seoul, Korea

Martin C. Libicki
Rand Corporation
Santa Monica, California

Adam B. Lowther
US Air Force Research Institute
Maxwell Air Force Base
Montgomery, Alabama

George R. Lucas, Jr.
Naval Postgraduate School
Monterey, California

Lynn Mattice
National Economic Security
  Grid
Vienna, Virginia

Sarah Muccio
Air Force Research Lab
Rome, New York

**Lieutenant Colonel
Eric P. Oliver**
US Air Force

Neil C. Rowe
Naval Postgraduate School
Monterey, California

**Lieutenant Colonel Fred
Taylor, Jr.**
US Air Force
Colorado Springs, Colorado

Panayotis A. Yannakogeorgos
US Air Force Research Institute
Maxwell Air Force Base,
  Alabama

PART I
KEY
CONSIDERATIONS

1

The Future of Things Cyber[*]

MICHAEL V. HAYDEN

Years ago, when I was an ROTC instructor, the first unit of instruction for rising juniors dealt with communication skills. Near the beginning of the unit, I would quote Confucius to my new students: "The rectification of names is the most important business of government. If names are not correct, language will not be in accordance with the truth of things." The point had less to do with communicating than it did with thinking—thinking clearly. Clear communication begins with clear thinking. You have to be precise in your language and have the big ideas right if you are going to accomplish anything.

I am reminded of that lesson as I witness and participate in discussions about the future of things "cyber." Rarely has something been so important and so talked about with less clarity and less apparent understanding than this phenomenon. Do not get me wrong. There are genuine experts, and most of us know about patches, insider threats, worms, Trojans, WikiLeaks, and Stuxnet. But few of us (myself included) have created the broad structural framework within which to comfortably and confidently place these varied phenomena. And that matters. I have sat in *very* small group meetings in Washington, been briefed on an operational need and an operational solution, and been unable (along with my colleagues) to decide on a course of action because we lacked a clear picture of the long-term legal and policy implications of *any* decision we might make.

US Cyber Command has been in existence for more than a year, and no one familiar with the command or its mission believes our current policy, law, or doctrine is adequate to our needs or our capabilities.

---

[*] Reprinted with permission from *Strategic Studies Quarterly*, Volume 5, No. 1, Spring 2011.

Most disappointingly—the doctrinal, policy, and legal dilemmas we currently face remain unresolved even though they have been around for the better part of a decade. Now it is time to think about and force some issues that have been delayed too long. This edition of *Strategic Studies Quarterly* therefore could not be more timely as it surfaces questions, fosters debate, and builds understanding around a host of cyber questions. The issues are nearly limitless, and many others will emerge in these pages, but let me suggest a few that frequently come to the top of my own list.

> *How do we deal with the unprecedented?* Part of our cyber policy problem is its newness, and our familiar experience in physical space does not easily transfer to cyberspace. Casually applying well-known concepts from physical space like deterrence, where attribution is assumed, to cyberspace where attribution is frequently the problem, is a recipe for failure. And cyber education is difficult. In those small group policy meetings, the solitary cyber expert often sounds like "Rain Man" to the policy wonks in the room after the third or fourth sentence. As a result, no two policy makers seemed to have left the room with the same understanding of what it was they had discussed, approved, or disapproved. So how do we create senior leaders—military and civilian—who are "cyber smart enough"?
>
> *Is cyber really a domain?* Like everyone else who is or has been in a US military uniform, I think of cyber as a domain. It is now enshrined in doctrine: land, sea, air, space, *cyber*. It trips off the tongue, and frankly I have found the concept liberating when I think about operationalizing this domain. But the other domains are natural, created by God, and this one is the creation of man. Man can actually change his geography, and *anything* that happens there actually creates a change in someone's *physical* space. Are these differences important enough for us to rethink our doctrine? There are those in the US government who think treating cyber as an independent domain is just a device to cleverly mask serious unanswered questions of sovereignty when conducting cyber operations.

They want to be heard and satisfied before they support the full range of our cyber potential.

Privacy? When we plan for operations in a domain where adversary and friendly data coexist, we should be asking: what constitutes a twenty-first-century definition of a reasonable expectation of privacy? Google and Facebook know a lot more about most of us than we are comfortable sharing with the government. In a private-sector web culture that seems to elevate transparency to unprecedented levels, what is the appropriate role of government and the DoD? If we agree to limit government access to the web out of concerns over privacy, what degree of risk to our own security and that of the network are we prepared to accept? How do we articulate that risk to a skeptical public and who should do it?

Do we really know the threat? Former Director of National Intelligence Mike McConnell frequently says we are already "at war" in cyberspace. Richard Clarke even titled his most recent cautionary book, *Cyber War*. Although I generally avoid the "at war" terminology, I often talk about the inherent insecurity of the web. How bad is it? And if it is really bad, with the cost of admission so low and networks so vulnerable, why have we not had a true cyber Pearl Harbor? Is this harder to do than we think? Or are we just awaiting the inevitable? When speaking of the threat, citizens of a series of first-world nations were recently asked whom they feared most in cyberspace, and the most popular answer was not China or India or France or Israel. It was the United States. Why is that and is it a good thing? People with money on the line in both the commercial and government sectors want clear demonstrable answers.

What should we expect from the private sector? We all realize that most of the web things we hold dear personally and as a nation reside or travel on commercial rather than government networks. So what motivates the private sector to optimize the defense of these networks? Some have observed that the free market has failed to provide an adequate level of security for the net since the true costs of insecurity are hidden or not understood. I agree. Now what: liability statutes that create the incentives and disincentives the market seems to be lacking? Government intervention, including a broader DoD role to protect critical infrastructure beyond .mil to .gov to .com? The statutory responsibility for the latter falls to the Department of Homeland Security, but does it have the "horses" to accomplish this? Do we await catastrophe before calling for DoD intervention or do we move preemptively?

What is classified? Let me be clear: This stuff is overprotected. It is far easier to learn about physical threats from US government agencies than it is to learn about cyber threats. In the popular culture, the availability of 10,000 applications for my smart phone is viewed as an unalloyed good. It is not—since each represents a potential vulnerability. But if we want to shift the popular culture, we need a broader flow of information to corporations and individuals to educate them on the threat. To do that we need to recalibrate what is truly secret. Beyond this tactical concern, our most pressing need is clear policy, formed by shared consensus, shaped by informed discussion, and created by a *common* body of knowledge. With no common knowledge, no meaningful discussion, and no consensus... the policy vacuum continues. This will not be easy, and in the wake of WikiLeaks it will require courage, but it is essential and should itself be the subject of intense discussion. Who will step up to lead?

What constitutes the right of self defense? How much do we want to allow private entities to defend themselves outside of their own perimeter? Indeed, what should Google appropriately do *within* its own network when under attack from the Chinese state? I have compared our entry into cyberspace to mankind's last great era of discovery—European colonization of the Western Hemisphere. During that period large private corporations like the Hudson Bay Company and the East India Tea Company acted with many of the attributes of sovereignty. What of that experience is instructive today for contemplating the appropriate roles of giants like Google and Facebook? We probably do not want to outfit twenty-first-century cyber privateers with letters of marque and reprisal, but what should be the relationship between large corporations and the government when private networks on which the government depends are under sustained attack?

Is there a role for international law? It took a decade last century for states to arrive at a new Law of the Seas Convention, and that was a domain our species had had literally millennia of experience. Then, as a powerful seafaring nation, we tilted toward maritime freedom rather than restraints. Regulating cyberspace entails even greater challenges. Indeed, as a powerful cyber faring nation, how comfortable are we with regulation at all? After all, this domain launched by the DoD has largely been nurtured free of government regulation. Its strengths are its spontaneity, its creativity, its boundlessness. The best speech given by an American official on macro net policy was given late last year by Secretary of State Clinton when she emphasized Internet freedom, not security or control or regulation. But there are moves afoot in international bodies like the International Telecommunications Union to regulate the Internet, to give states more control over their domains, to Balkanize what up until now has been a relatively seamless global enterprise. How and when do we play?

Is cyber arms control possible? As a nation, we tend toward more freedom and less control but—given their destructiveness, their relative ease of use, and the precedent their use sets—are distributed denial-of-service attacks *ever* justified? Should we work to create a global attitude toward them comparable to the existing view toward chemical or biological weapons? Should we hold states responsible if an attack is mounted from their physical space even if there is no evidence of complicity? And, are there *any* legitimate uses for *botnets*? If not, under what authority would anyone preemptively take them down? These are questions for which no precedent in law or policy (domestic or international) currently exists. If we want to establish precedent, as opposed to likely unenforceable treaty obligations, do we emphasize dialogue with like-minded nations, international institutions... or multinational IT companies?

Is defense possible? At a recent conference I was struck by a surprising question: "Would it be more effective to deal with recovery than with prevention?" In other words, is the web so skewed toward advantage for the attacker that we are reaching the point of diminishing returns for defending a network at the perimeter (or even beyond) and should now concentrate on how we respond to and recover from inevitable penetrations? This could mean more looking at *our* network for anomalous behavior than attempting to detect every incoming zero day assault. It could mean concentrating more on what is going out rather than what is coming in. It could mean more focus on operating while under attack rather than preventing attack. Mike McConnell and I met with a group of investors late last year, and we were full-throated in our warnings about the cyber threat. One participant asked the question that was clearly on everyone's mind, "How much is this going to cost me?" At the time I chalked it up to not really understanding the threat, but in retrospect our questioner may have been on to something. At what point do we shift from additional investment in defense to more investment in response and recovery?

There are more questions that could be asked, many of them as fundamental as these. Most we have not yet answered or at least have not yet *agreed* on answers, and none of them are easy. How much do we really want to empower private enterprises to defend themselves? Do we want necessarily secretive organizations like the NSA or CyberCom going to the mats publicly over privacy issues? At what point does arguing for Internet security begin to legitimate China's attempts at control over Internet speech? Do we really want to get into a public debate that attempts to distinguish cyber espionage (which all countries pursue) from cyber war (something more rare and *sometimes* more destructive)? Are there any cyber capabilities, real or potential, we are willing to give up in return for similar commitments from others?

Tough questions all, tougher (perhaps) but not unlike those our airpower ancestors faced nearly a century ago. As pioneer air warriors grappled with the unfamiliar, so must we. Until these and other questions like them are answered, we could be forced to live in the worst of all possible cyber worlds—routinely vulnerable to attack and self-restrained from bringing our own power to bear.

2

TAMING THE "21ST CENTURY'S WILD WEST" OF CYBERSPACE?

LYNN MATTICE

Today's complex and interdependent global economy relies heavily on an Internet infrastructure that is wrought with risks, threats, and hazards of which the average computer user or small and medium-sized enterprise (SME) and many major corporations are unaware, unprepared, or simply choose to ignore. Confidence in the ability to effectively, efficiently, and securely conduct commerce and business processes over the Internet and through emerging mobile device applications are vital fundamental elements to ensure vibrant and stable economies around the globe. The world faces unprecedented risks across the Internet in what has become known as "The 21st Century's Wild West," where attacks on computer systems and networks are generally conducted with the complete anonymity and impunity for those perpetrating these acts.

The generally unsecure nature of our interconnected environment can be traced to several factors:

1. For over 40 years universities have taught courses on designing and writing computer coding. When these college-level courses were first established, we lived in a world where no one ever imagined the interconnectivity that would evolve and become so central to our lives today. Computer systems were stand-alone and not networked to third parties that performed various services or support. As the interconnectivity of the Internet evolved, few people realized the inherent flaws and lack of sound security measures in legacy systems or new systems that were developed utilizing legacy-style programming methodologies.

2. Legacy computer hardware, middleware, and network designers also overlooked or outright ignored building in security measures as they were viewed as negatively affecting performance, output, or throughput and were generally deemed unnecessary.

3. Both software developers and hardware manufacturers established an environment from the beginning where they accepted no liability or responsibility for any loss, delay, disruption, or any other action that could have an effect on the purchaser/user community whether caused directly or indirectly by the systems, hardware, or software supplied. This "use at your own risk" disclaimer to liability has manifested itself into a patch management nightmare. Every new release of software or hardware is regularly followed with periodic security patches. These patches deal with flaws that the "rush-to-market" mentality of the manufacturers and producers created by failing to take a duty-of-care philosophy in product design and delivery. Early on in the evolution of software, hardware, and networks people became accustomed to "computer bugs" and other design flaws that they simply accepted as the norm. Rarely has a single industry benefited from such a desensitized consumer population which has allowed the producers and manufacturers to skirt responsibility and liability for the flawed products and systems they produce.

4. Individuals, corporate executives, and elected officials have very little understanding of the scope of the risks and threats they face through computer systems and networks that are ultimately linked through the Internet today. To further highlight this point, a joint study on cyber-based crime conducted by Verizon and the US Secret Service indicated that in 65% of the data breach cases they reviewed, a third party notified the unsuspecting victim that they had been subjected to a breach in their computer system or network. A recent study indicated that the on average breaches went undetected for over 400 days. Additionally, a report issued by the White

House in 2009 conservatively estimated the value of the loss of US intellectual property, as a result of cyber hacking alone, at in excess of $1 trillion in 2008 alone.

When resourceful individuals, organized criminals, extremist groups, hacktivists, and activists and ultimately nation-states started to exploit these inherent weaknesses in computer programs, networks, and hardware a cottage industry was formed. These new companies focused on measures to counter computer attacks with firewalls and anti-virus protection. Software developers also provide a continuous flow of patches to fix the flaws that contribute to these exploitations. It wasn't until the arrival of the 21st century that universities started to include preventative security measures into their coursework as a key basis of design for software and hardware.

A patchwork of state and federal laws and regulations has developed across the United States and around the globe to begin to deal with computer-related crime. Issues such as conflicting state laws and requirements to notify individuals if their personally identifiable information has been subjected to a computer breach have created confusion and excessive costs of compliance. The complexity of the privacy protection laws across the European Union, as well as individual countries in the European Union having their own set of complex laws and regulations dealing with privacy and data breaches, has also created dramatic levels of complexity in establishing compliance regimes.

To instill trust and order in the Internet as a key facilitator of global commerce, a number of things must be accomplished:

- Laws and regulations dealing with computer software, hardware, and networks must be harmonized to ensure that compliance is increased and non-compliance can be easily identified and dealt with swiftly.
- Software producers, hardware manufacturers, and network providers should be held liable for delivery of flawed products and services that contribute directly or indirectly to the losses, disruption, or denial of services of those using the systems, hardware, or networks. Liability exposure will force these producers, manufacturers, and providers to ensure in-depth security is built into their products before they are delivered to market and maintained after they are operational.

- Treaties must be established to ensure that no individual, organized criminal, hacktivist or activist, extremist group, or nation-state can operate with anonymity or impunity on the Internet and held accountable for their actions. Nation-states must be held responsible for rooting out, stopping, and bringing to justice any individual, group, or entity committing any illegal act against another over the Internet.
- Governments should not classify data they uncover on the methodologies that are utilized to attack mobile devices, computer systems, and networks. This information should be openly and broadly published. Broadcasting the methodologies utilized by these attackers and providing information on how to detect, prevent, and mitigate the specific types of attacks will quickly reduce the opportunities for the attackers. As each new attack methodology is uncovered the same process should be handled utilizing this vital information sharing process.

Establishing a robust system of monitoring, controls, and sanctions to ensure that the Internet functions as a trusted and heavily defended environment that fosters cooperation, collaboration, and commerce will have a dramatic effect on the stability, viability, and resilience of our interconnected global economy.

3

CYBERSPACE SUPERIORITY CONSIDERATIONS*

FRED TAYLOR, JR.

JERRY CARTER

Contents

Enhance Capacity	14
Capacity Recommendations	15
Improve Capability	15
Capability Recommendations	16
Increase Cognizance	16
Cognizance Recommendations	17
Strengthen Governance Structure	18
Governance Recommendations	20
The Next Stuxnet Attack Is Only a Day Away	20
Assessment of the DoD's Ability to Achieve Cyberspace Superiority	21
Endnotes	25

As cyberspace becomes more essential to the execution of a wide range of military missions, achieving strategic cyberspace superiority is a concept that demands critical analysis. The Department of Defense (DoD) defines cyberspace superiority as "the degree of dominance in cyberspace by one force that permits the secure, reliable conduct of operations of that force, and its related land, air, sea and space forces at a given time and sphere of operations without prohibitive interference by an adversary."[1] For the US DoD to achieve cyberspace superiority, critical factors including capability,

---

* The views expressed are those of the authors and do not reflect the policy or position of the US government, the Department of Defense, or Harvard University.

capacity, cognizance, and governance must be considered. The military has limited ability to address the first three factors unless comprehensive changes in governance and prioritization are made across all sectors to enable the military to find, fix, and finish threats in cyberspace. To this end, the DoD requires significant attention from across the US government and non-governmental actors to improve capacity, advance capabilities, and expand cognizance. In addition, financial and knowledge capital will be needed to develop revolutionary technologies, specific to DoD applications, to offset a progressively sophisticated threat. At present, the DoD is unable to achieve strategic cyberspace superiority.

Enhance Capacity

Adequate capacity is a necessary factor in any DoD cyberspace operation, but there are inherent systemic vulnerabilities that may prevent the DoD from achieving cyberspace superiority. DoD has limited control of critical infrastructure, including lines of communication, utilities, hardware, software, and supply chains, which makes cyberspace superiority questionable. Added to this, the reliance on private infrastructure coupled with the inability to control the flow of data over shared lines of communication is problematic.

The DoD needs to establish resilience in infrastructure, software, hardware, supply chains, and lines of communication. Government-prescribed regulatory standards and controls should ensure the safety and security of these key areas. Single points of failure and vulnerabilities continue to pose risks to achieving cyberspace superiority. To offset these risks, the United States must mitigate them through investing in more secure, diversified infrastructure. Additionally, separate infrastructure and controlled supply chains for military use are needed for greater security and confidence that key infrastructure is available for mission operations.

Software drives the cyber enterprise, but there are minimal controls, standards, and oversight of software development and implementation. The US government should exact greater oversight over software. Establishing standards and enacting legislation, similar to the "lemon laws" in the automotive industry, will drive improvements in software and better protect users.[2] This action would help the DoD achieve cyberspace superiority by reducing vulnerabilities in mission applications and key infrastructure.

Capacity Recommendations

- Establish greater resilience in infrastructure through the development of software and security standards.
- Develop a more secure and reliable supply chain along with more protected lines of communication.
- Partner with private industry to invest in increased resiliency, redundancy and diversification in infrastructure, software, hardware, supply chains, and lines of communication by building robust control measures and advanced technology.

Improve Capability

Advanced capability is another factor required for strategic cyberspace superiority. The United States may not have an enduring technical advantage in cyberspace. Specifically, the DoD uses the same protocols, hardware, software, and suppliers for many of its missions as well as many other users. This is the same technology used by many other non-governmental organizations and private entities to include other nations and adversaries. Inherent flaws and weaknesses in software and hardware can be exploited since cyber capabilities are widely available to a multitude of actors and because technical diffusion is rapid. This capability disadvantage is prevalent across DoD systems.

The DoD should continue to build operational plans and procedures for informed decision making, in order to achieve objectives in a contested environment, across all levels of conflict, where cyberspace superiority is not guaranteed. Operational plans should be developed to provide the Joint Force Commander adequate mission assurance so that defensive and offensive cyberspace capabilities, and associated systems, will be available to achieve the desired effects.

Furthermore, the DoD must strengthen partnerships with private industry and international supporters to protect and improve infrastructure, software, hardware, and supply chains. This symbiotic relationship will require new levels of cooperation, sharing, and trust to ensure cyberspace capabilities are available and that there is sufficient broad support to mitigate deficiencies or attacks. The President's February 2013 Executive Order is a good example of steps the government should take domestically to develop a cybersecurity framework and increase information sharing with industry.[3] Agreements and policy should be further defined to formalize the level and type of cooperation and support.

Capability Recommendations

- Continue to build operational plans for informed decision making in order to achieve objectives in a degraded environment where cyberspace superiority is not guaranteed.
- Increase knowledge and education by cultivating an innovative workforce.
- Strengthen partnerships with private industry to protect and improve infrastructure, software, hardware, and supply chains and to create revolutionary technological capability solely for military use.

Increase Cognizance

The military has limited situational awareness due to incomplete visibility into US networks in order to identify vulnerabilities and threats. Further complicating the DoD's ability to achieve cyberspace superiority is the result of limited insight into a potential adversary's networks, infrastructure, or capabilities.

The DoD must continue to improve situational awareness and protection—internally, nationwide, and of potential adversaries—by developing revolutionary technical tools in a new Internet construct. In cyberspace, advantage is gained through the knowledge and skill of cyber professionals. The United States must place more attention on developing technically trained citizens, and the DoD must increase investment in recruiting, training, and retaining skilled cyber personnel. Recent efforts to build up the cyber workforce are crucial and must be accelerated.

Recognizing that the Internet tools used today are ubiquitous, the US technological advantage is challenged. The US military should develop revolutionary information technology tools using a new construct. The DoD in partnership with industry and other government agencies must research and develop new cutting-edge technologies for military applications that are more secure. This will require significant investment, years of research and development, and a protected environment to create an infrastructure not based on current technology and protocols. The DoD must become a leader in this domain versus a market follower or laggard. The 2011 DoD Strategy for Operating in Cyberspace suggests that a new infrastructure be developed, but it must be implemented with sufficient resources and with haste.[4]

First, in order to overcome technological and situational awareness limitations that impede DoD's ability to achieve cyberspace superiority, the military must have the necessary tools to determine attribution in the cyber domain. One such tool might be an automated system capable of monitoring one's own Command and Control (C2) infrastructure while probing an adversary's capabilities.

Although this task is controversial, it is essential to establish an active defense. It would require technical engineering of C2 systems across the government, which would require the political will of the people and of US policymakers. Such a system would need to be able to detect intrusions, disruptions, and attacks while also providing commanders viable options to counter threats. Other features would include a capability to assess an adversary's ability to use its own infrastructure and systems. Offensive intrusion capabilities along with tools to manipulate the adversary's perception would be useful to commanders, especially in the face of a technologically sophisticated adversary. Likewise, it is necessary to be cognizant of DoD capabilities and operational status to detect, deter, and defend against hostile attack through decisive coordinated action across the DoD and beyond.

Cognizance Recommendations

- Continue to improve situational awareness and protection by developing revolutionary technical tools in a new Internet construct.

- Gain greater situational awareness of US and potential adversarys' networks and capabilities through the application of new advanced technology and development/retention of a skilled workforce.

Strengthen Governance Structure

The US government must have a unified effort to advance cyberspace capabilities through national priority, policy, legislation, and organization. The effort should be in partnership with the private sector and must establish a clear national strategy, with supporting policy guidance, for rules of engagement at home and abroad. It must also obviate legal, political, and organizational constraints for cyberspace security. Recent domestic and international policy and legislation, such as the DoD Strategy for Operating in Cyberspace and the International Strategy for Cyberspace, have made significant progress clarifying the US position on cyberspace, but additional work needs to be done government-wide to delineate organization, roles, responsibilities, authorities, and military action to support strategic objectives for cyberspace superiority. Identification and priority must be given to mission essential systems within and outside of DoD to facilitate continuity of operations and cyberspace superiority. President Obama's Executive Order on Improving Critical Infrastructure Cybersecurity is an important step but broad legislation must be passed to enable DoD's cyberspace superiority goals.

The United States must have an agreed upon position across government on how it will deal with conflict in cyberspace and how it will enable the Internet to fuel economic growth and openness while offering a reasonable level of security. National leaders must define the US position and articulate that position at home, as has been done to some degree internationally. Appropriate legal, policy, and economic decisions and resource allocations must be made in line with a coherent national security strategy on cyberspace.

Finally, the modernization of authorities to enable both offensive and defensive military cyberspace operations must be applied to advance cyberspace superiority objectives. Rear Admiral Jerry Burroughs, Navy Program Executive Officer for Command, Control, Communications, Computers, and Intelligence, points out that the cyber picture is further complicated by layers of technology and bureaucracy, and we need agility and robustness.[5] Cyberspace has evolved continuously and rapidly since 1990, and this rapid pace calls for the need for more flexible but decisive cyber operations in and through cyberspace. Current authorities to conduct cyber operations are more oriented on the defensive component based on Cold War threat models. To address the global cyberspace challenges, strict legal and budgetary authorities must be provided to US Cyber Command (USCYBERCOM) to find, fix, and finish threats to US national security interests across the threat spectrum. Any recommendation authorizing military cyberspace operations in the public-private arena rightfully raises important privacy and civil liberties issues among Americans but should be considered in the context of overall national security and prosperity.

The establishment of new and expanding mission areas is not unique to the military. In fact, our most recent operational domain—space—encountered many similar challenges in its infancy. Some of those issues have yet to be resolved.[6] However, there is value in looking to Air Force Space Command and the intelligence community, notably the National Reconnaissance Office, models for space operations, and its interaction with other areas of government and the private sector for lessons on how we can better mature military operations in the cyberspace domain. Any action must be done in concert with the private sector and other governmental agencies for a comprehensive, synchronized approach for full-spectrum cyberspace operations.

To be successful, modernization of authorities and organizational relationships must provide security while protecting privacy and civil liberties at home and abroad. The US Special Operations Command (USSOCOM) construct is a successful military model on authorizations that should be weighed. As the Functional Component Command for Special Operations, USSOCOM has adequate funding and policy emphasis for low-intensity conflict and special operations. Major Force Program-11 (MFP-11) for Special Operations Forces (SOF) provides USSOCOM a unique funding line to advance research and development, influence acquisition, and control fielding of SOF systems. USSOCOM is also responsible for contingency plans for specific missions. A Unified Component Commander is also on par with the other combatant commands. This unique structure and associated authorities make the USSOCOM an effective instrument of national power. Some aspects of USSOCOM may be worthy of emulation.

Similar consideration should be given to USCYBERCOM to enable the force to meet the cyber challenges of the twenty-first century. In addition, with increased cooperation across government, USCYBERCOM authorities should be carefully expanded to give the Command greater power to address threats in and through cyberspace. Secretary of Defense Panetta stated in October 2012 that DoD had developed the capability to conduct operations to counter threats to our national interests in cyberspace and was producing new rules of engagement to make the Department more agile and able to confront major threats quickly.[7] However, this may require additional changes to current laws to allow the DoD more latitude to act in more nontraditional roles. New thinking on interagency, civil-military, and private-sector roles, responsibilities, and authorities has been undertaken but must be further developed and implemented to support DoD cyberspace superiority objectives.

Governance Recommendations

- Develop and implement a comprehensive national security strategy for cyberspace and move public and private actors toward a shared cyberspace vision at home and abroad.
- Continue to establish clear policy guidelines and define authorities to delineate roles and responsibilities for a national strategy and investment in cyberspace security at home and abroad.

The Next Stuxnet Attack Is Only a Day Away

The dawn of the twenty-first century presents strategic challenges for the United States, and achieving superiority in cyberspace will be a bold endeavor. Our national approach to cyberspace must adapt to meet these rapidly changing challenges as recognized by Leon Panetta, outgoing Secretary of Defense, who asserted that a cyberattack perpetrated by nation states or violent extremist groups could be as destructive as the terrorist attack on 9/11, virtually paralyzing the nation.[8] Sophisticated threats will require innovative solutions and demand new approaches in order to mitigate risk. In essence, the cyber threat environment will demand a new mindset to ensure agility in adapting to new challenges.

Achieving strategic cyberspace superiority means different things to different people. From a doctrinal perspective, strategic cyberspace superiority can be considered a measure beyond parity but less than total dominance in which joint warfighters can operate at a given time and in a given sphere without prohibitive interference by an adversary.[9] Like air and maritime superiority, cyberspace superiority is a condition that warfighters need to establish in order to gain an operational advantage and to minimize risks associated with an overall campaign.

The 2006 National Military Strategy for Cyberspace Operation's Strategic Goal is for the US military to have strategic superiority in cyberspace.[10] This goal is ambitious given the challenges with capacity, capability, cognizance, and governance. When considering these factors, the DoD cannot currently achieve its goal of strategic superiority in cyberspace. Subjectively measured, the DoD is at a disadvantage with respect to capacity and cognizance, and may only achieve parity in governance and capability when measured against competitors and their assessed potential.

Assessment of the DoD's Ability to Achieve Cyberspace Superiority

For the DoD to have a better chance of achieving strategic cyberspace superiority, it must overcome limitations and shortfalls in four critical areas: capability, capacity, cognizance, and governance (Table 3.1). Cyberspace is a complex environment that integrates private and

Table 3.1   Assessment of DoD's Ability to Achieve Cyberspace Superiority

FACTORS	CONSIDERATIONS	ASSESSMENT
Capacity	Private industry reliance/vulnerabilities Open access	●
Capability	Protocols, h/w, s/w Investment/workforce	○
Cognizance	Threat environment Identification/attribution	●
Governance	Policy Authorities Investment	○

Assessment Criteria: US advantage ◎; no US advantage/parity ○; U.S. disadvantage ●.

operational environments much more than has been seen in other domains. The DoD must consider how it looks at cyberspace and incorporate civil-military resources for full spectrum operations in cyberspace. Although the establishment of USCYBERCOM has placed the DoD firmly on the path to address a number of these factors, the help of the US government will be required to more fully address other elements. Senior leaders must broaden their view on the strategic importance of cyberspace. This will aid in the development of a comprehensive national strategy to shape US policy in accordance with national interests. Once US goals are implemented and US actions in cyberspace are in consonance with stated objectives, concerted effort can be made to increase capacity, improve capability, increase cognizance, and solidly establish an effective governance structure.

The United States can increase capacity through the development of more robust infrastructure, utilities, hardware, and software. The need for security, redundancy, and resilience is a priority to improve capacity for military operations. The United States has broad capacity that strengthens operations but also provides for more opportunities for malicious actors. The diversification of hardware and software from trusted, certified providers across multiple lines of communication strengthens national security and provides for greater DoD mission assurance.

Likewise, military capability requires a strong investment in technology and people. The technology undergirding cyberspace needs to be advanced through a public-private partnership such that the military is able to operate revolutionary tools guided by a skilled and trained workforce. The government should promote and participate in developing advanced cyber technology for military use. The scope and scale of investment in research and development should be increased substantially in order to maintain our technical edge but also to strengthen national security. Recognizing there are significant budget constraints across the US government, cyberspace technological investment should still be given an increased level of funding to counter a growing threat environment. Investment in military-specific capabilities and infrastructure and hiring and retaining the best and brightest workforce will provide greater DoD capability while a military-unique infrastructure will better enable the military to execute operations with greater mission assurance. It should be a national imperative to train and retain personnel today and for tomorrow in technical fields, with increased emphasis on information technology.

Last, the DoD must increase its understanding of the threat environment and the capabilities of actors in order to assure a high degree of mission assurance and the ability to achieve desired effects in cyberspace. However, before embarking on understanding an adversary's motives and capabilities, the DoD must gain a higher degree of situational awareness of friendly capabilities to successfully deter attacks. The International Strategy for Cyberspace is a move in the right direction, to partner with like-minded states to increase cognizance of the cyberspace environment and to have a degree of collective security founded on existing treaties and agreements to thwart aggression. But more must be done at home and abroad to implement this strategy. This goal will be challenging because according to Alec Ross, Special Technical Advisor to the Secretary of State, the United States has a low level of credibility and trust in the international community.[11] To reverse this perception the United States must take a strong leadership role to establish norms, build partnerships, and promote cyberspace security at home and abroad. Military cooperation has been beneficial and should be sustained and expanded as indicated in the DoD Strategy for Operating in Cyberspace. Overall, the United States must encourage like-minded states to cooperate, while discouraging adversaries, whether they are nation-states or rogue groups, by making them believe that the benefits they hope to gain are not worth the risk or that they will not be able to achieve their objectives.

These steps support the DoD's efforts to move toward cyberspace superiority. The US government and the DoD must sustain focus on cyberspace security and take significant action as not only a medium of commerce but, more importantly, for national security. The interdependencies between the public and private sectors are integral to cyberspace security and national defense, requiring a strong partnership and adequate oversight to maintain our ideals for peace and security. The growing reliance on cyberspace requires that US interests be defended using all instruments of national power and that all citizens may play a role.

Victory in competitive decision cycles requires one side to understand what is happening and act faster than the other. A cyber dimension that is driven by ingenuity, encourages initiative and is decentralized by its very nature, gives a distinct advantage to the adversary. Additionally, the preponderance of cyber maneuvers happen in "machine time" and are neither observable nor easily attributable. The tyranny of computing cycles means that important actions taken by our forces will have to be pre-approved—rules of cyber engagement—and that at least some of the decision making to "act" will have to be decentralized.

The requirement to find, fix, and finish a threat in the current operating environment is essential to centralize approvals and authorities under a single commander to gain and maintain freedom of action in the operating environment. The need to identify a lead agency to address a threat is based on the global nature of the problem, the ability to communicate and exercise control forces, the magnitude of the stakes in a cyber conflict, and uncertain collateral effects of cyberspace activities.

Until the US government establishes an effective comprehensive cybersecurity framework, implements policy, grants authorities, and provides resources to address limitations in capacity, capability, and cognizance, DoD strategic cyberspace superiority will be limited. It may not be the next "cyber Pearl Harbor" as described by Richard Clarke, former White House counterterrorism czar, but it is very conceivable to see the United States fall prey to an attack similar to Stuxnet. Considering our shortfalls, the United States could be only a day away from a debilitating Stuxnet-like type of attack resulting from a "death of a thousand cuts" unless we take immediate action.[12,13]

The 2006 National Military Strategy for Cyberspace Operation's Strategic Goal is for the US military to have strategic superiority in cyberspace.[14] This goal is ambitious given challenges with capacity, capability, cognizance, and governance. The latest cyberspace policy documents add recognition of the many challenges in cyberspace with which the United States and DoD must contend. There has been increased attention on cyberspace security but investment and legislation must follow. In the context of cyberspace superiority, these documents minimally advance this goal. Without sustained emphasis across the whole of government, strategic cyberspace superiority will remain beyond our grasp. Taken in total, the DoD cannot currently achieve its goal of strategic superiority in cyberspace.

Endnotes

1. Cartwright, James E., memorandum, "Joint Terminology for Cyberspace Operations," Department of Defense, Washington DC, 2010.
2. Taylor, Fred, Software: The Broken Door of Cyberspace, *National Security Journal*, February 2011, http://harvardnsj.com/2011/02/software-the-broken-door-of-cyberspace-security/.
3. Obama, Barack, Executive Order on Improving Critical Infrastructure Cybersecurity, Washington DC, Feb 2013.
4. Department of Defense Strategy for Operating in Cyberspace, July 2011.
5. Corrin, Amber, Dominance in Cyberspace Might Not Be Possible, AFCEA cyber warfare panel, January 27, 2011, http://defensesystems.com/articles/2011/01/27/AFCEA-West-cyber-warfare-panel.aspx.
6. Interview at Maxwell Air Force Base, John Sheldon, Air University, April 16, 2011.
7. Austin, Greg, America's Challenging Cyber Defense Policy, *The International Policy Digest*, October 2012 (http://www.internationalpolicydigest.org/2012/10/15/americas-challenging-cyber-defense-policy).
8. Panetta, Leon, Text of Speech by US Secretary of Defense Leon Panetta, *Defense News*, 12 October 2012 (http://www.defensenews.com/article/20121012/DEFREG02/310120001).
9. Interview at Army Space and Missile Defense Command, Dr. Frank Gray, Army SMDC, Colorado Springs, CO, December 2011.
10. National Military Strategy on Cyberspace Operations, Chairman of the Joint Chiefs of Staff, Washington DC, Dec 2006.
11. Interview at Department of State, Alec Ross, US Department of State, Washington, DC, January 6, 2011.
12. Clayton, Mark, How Stuxnet Cyber Weapon Targeted Iran Nuclear Plant, *The Christian Science Monitor*, November 16, 2010, http://www.csmonitor.com/USA/2010/1116/How-Stuxnet-cyber-weapon-targeted-Iran-nuclear-plant.
13. Rosenbaum, Ron, Richard Clarke on Who Was behind Stuxnet Attack, *The Smithsonian*, April 2012, http://www.smithsonianmag.com/history-archaeology/Richard-Clarke-on-Who-Was-Behind-the-Stuxnet-Attack.html.
14. Ibid.

4

TWO, MAYBE THREE CHEERS FOR AMBIGUITY

MARTIN C. LIBICKI

Contents

Conclusions   34

Civilization, we have all been taught, advances when societies make the transition from rule of man (think *gemeinschaft*) to rule of law and contract (think *gesellschaft*). Life is more predictable. People can govern their conduct with the expectation that if they stay within the lines, their life and property are safe. These rules, in turn, are established by a sovereign, preferably but not necessarily democratic. In the twentieth century, this tenet has been introduced into international relations: rules are a way of moderating the behavior of states that otherwise exist in an inherently anarchic environment. Rules, of course, are only hortatory unless there are ways to monitor compliance and enforce against—which, essentially means punish—noncompliance.

Deterrence policies in general, and nuclear deterrence policies in particular, constitute an extension of these rules, in the sense that a state declares that a particular behavior is unacceptable and, if observed, will be met with punishment. The extension of nuclear deterrence doctrine into cyberspace has been mooted. Pessimism over how much good it would do rests on several grounds, the most salient being the difficulty of ascertaining with sufficient confidence who carried out a cyberattack, unless the attacker is bold enough to volunteer such information. Conversely, though, few in the national security community would argue against retaliation of some sort if attribution could be made with sufficient confidence and the damage crossed some high threshold. To argue that deterrence should not be a centerpiece of US cybersecurity policy and even that a deterrence posture is unlikely to do much good is not the same as saying retaliation should be completely foresworn.

The question this essay poses is whether a deterrence policy should be deterministic—*if you do this we will do that*—or probabilistic—*if you anger us enough by your behavior we will strike back*. The latter policy does not have to be explicitly declared as such; it is the default for all sufficiently self-empowered states. US history provides a basis for believing that the United States will take a great deal of injury until it has had its fill, after which point it becomes bent on destroying the source of its injuries. This lesson was most recently demonstrated in the wake of the September 11 attacks, when the United States, in righteous anger, destroyed the Taliban regime, not for carrying out attacks, but for condoning al Qaeda's doing so (and refusing to yield al Qaeda's leadership after the 1998 embassy bombings). In the run-up to World War II, the United States stayed out of combat as long as it could despite the clear moral asymmetry between the Axis powers and their victims—until Pearl Harbor; total war and nuclear weapons followed. In World War I the United States, "too proud to fight," tolerated submarine attacks (e.g., the Lusitania) until the Zimmerman telegram and Germany's announcement of unrestricted submarine warfare. Before that war was the popular reaction to the sinking of the USS Maine. Indeed, in a democratic society like the United States, responses are often driven or at least strongly supported by popular sentiment, a strength from the viewpoint of deterrence. All this should suggest to potential adversaries that the United States would respond harshly to sufficient provocation even if the exact nature of the provocation was not pre-specified. To paraphrase *The Treasure of The Sierra Madre*, "Red lines? We don't need no stinkin' red lines."

One way to envision the choice is provided in Figure 4.1. The black line is a binary provocation-response curve—no possibility of response until a red line is crossed and then a certain response. The gray line is an analog provocation-response curve—a small probability of response, which grows larger as the provocation increases to the point where a response is a near certainty. It is important to this argument to note that in Figure 4.1, the x-axis represents not the degree of response but its likelihood. As far as the attacker is concerned—and

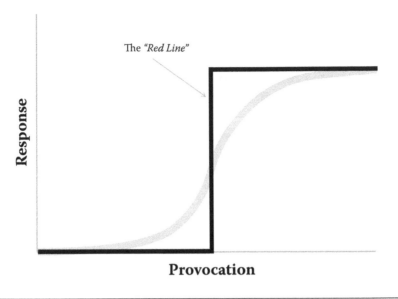

The *"Red Line"*

Response

Provocation

Figure 4.1   Deterministic and probabilistic responses to incidents.

deterrence exists only if it exists in the mind of the attacker—it does not matter if the United States had a probabilistic red line (i.e., it declared fixed probabilities of response and then tossed the dice after each provocation) or if the United States did have a red line but the attacker was uncertain of where it lay. Either way, the perceived likelihood of a response rises as the seriousness of the contemplated attack does.

A policy of determinism, to be sure, has advantages. It tends to promote stability in the sense that it assures adversaries that certain conduct can be carried out safely, creates an enormous penalty for stepping over the threshold and thereby inducing self-restraint by the adversary as the threshold is approached, and legitimizes the subsequent reaction as foretold rather than arbitrary. One problem with determinism even outside cyberspace, however, is that, in practice, it is not deterministic, even if the relationship between the provocation and the red line is known. The nuclear weapons use that Cold War deterrence was based on was expected to be unmistakable (not only was radiation a tell-tale sign, but the smallest nuclear weapon was more powerful than the biggest conventional weapon). However, the likelihood that the United States would respond in kind to a nuclear attack, particularly one that was singular and not followed up, was never one hundred percent. Schelling's famous deterrence that "left something to chance" was a way of creating a deterrence policy that suggested to the Soviet Union that there was always *some* likelihood that the United States would respond to something that crossed a line, even if the United States faced a devastating counter-retaliation by doing so.

Determinism for cyberattacks is harder to justify than it is for conventional, much less, nuclear attacks. The relationship between effort and outcomes, for instance, is chancy. A full-throated cyberattack may be stopped or substantially weakened by unexpected defenses (the headlines say what attacks succeeded; they rarely report those that have failed completely, and only occasionally report those that go in but got nothing out). Conversely, a cyberattack may overachieve in the sense that a precision attack meant to disable a capability (e.g., power to a radar) may create cascading effects. An attacker's painstaking observation of a target system may reveal the source of all of its inputs, but say nothing about which processes depend on the target system's outputs. So, if these outputs are corrupted, those processes will be harmed accordingly. In cyberspace, there are also disjunctions between actual effects and perceived effects. Many attacks (e.g., Stuxnet) are meant to corrupt systems so that they produce incorrect results rather than render them useless and permit their owners to seek correct results elsewhere. From a military perspective, there is considerable value in breaking a system in ways that are not obvious until the system is used; this way the victim is likely to under-react to such attacks. Again, conversely, if that particular corruption is obvious to the user, the user may suspect that many other systems have been corrupted even if the adversary knows it did not strike them. So the target's damage estimate may be much higher than facts warrant.

The advantages of a deterministic policy are vitiated by the indeterminism of cyberspace. The chances of an inadvertent war may be less, in the sense that the red line is clear. Yet, they are not zero because the relationship between intent and effect is uncertain, and so is the relationship between effect and perception. A state can think it is in the safe zone because its intent stayed left of the red line, but its target thinks otherwise because the perceived effect wandered to the right of the red line. Hence, retaliation lands on the table and, with a hit, the risks of an all-out confrontation.

The second advantage of determinism is that the inhibition from crossing the red line is higher if the red line is clearly marked; hence, deterrence is greater. But that inhibition can be eroded by difficulties in attribution. Granted, attribution should be a neutral factor in comparing a deterministic versus a probabilistic deterrence policy. They both reduce the odds of retaliation by the same amount. Similarly, difficulties in attribution ruin the credibility of both. Yet, credibility is far more important to a deterministic policy than it is to a probabilistic policy. One state declares a red line and avers that punishment would follow its crossing. Another state crosses it but attempts to hide who did it. Punishment never comes. The attacker would be justified in asking: Did I hide well enough, or did the target, knowing who did it, nevertheless refuse to respond (perhaps for fear of starting a nasty fight)? If the latter, how credible is the threat in cyberspace? Worse, the attacker may be asking, how credible are all the other threats? The same scenario played out against an ambiguous deterrence policy may cause the attacker to wonder if it did hide well, or it was found out but the provocation-response curve lies to the right (greater provocation needed) of where it was previously thought to be. The major difference is that the probabilistic deterrence strategy did not depend on credibility; furthermore, if the target state had deterministic deterrence policies for other types of attacks (e.g., nuclear), the credibility of the latter would not be damaged by the ambiguities of its policy in cyberspace.

Beyond that, a probabilistic deterrence policy has many advantages in an uncertain world.

It establishes no safe zone. Since there is no red line, there's no area left of the red line where attackers can play without consequences. Everything that rises above some noise level risks retaliation in the same way that walking in a mine field is not safe even if the first footfall is unremarkable. Indeed, if Americans determine that the accumulation of injuries (e.g., the continual theft of intellectual property by one often-named country) had excited the population enough to demand a response, the fact that such behavior had passed muster before would be beside the point.

It does not make the world safe for cyberwar. A stated red line may also raise the question of what an appropriate punishment would be. The declaring state has a choice. If it says it will react with violence to a cyberattack, it may enhance deterrence, but if tested, such a policy may drag the state into a very costly war when perhaps a less costly response in kind might have sufficed to give teeth to deterrence. If it says it will react *only* in kind, then it sets a top limit on the amount of damage the attacker can expect. And if the attacker, say, by dint of having less infrastructure at stake, determines it can outlast the target in an all-out tit-for-tat, it may not be deterred at all. The optimal solution, *if the means of retaliation is specified*, is to make the punishment fit not only the crime but the criminal. Discriminate deterrence, however, sends a very mixed message and may evoke the Melian dialogue (the strong do as they will, and the weak suffer what they must), which is anathema in a rules-based world. Ambiguity in specifying the means of retaliation has its virtues.

It weakens counter-deterrence. Many a deterrence policy fails or leads states to danger when the potential recipients of such warnings threaten to strike back if struck, even if in retaliation. In theory, counter-deterrence should work the same way regardless of what triggered retaliation. However, if the impetus for retaliation is not calculation and measurement but the outrage of the population, the recipient of the warning may want to think twice if it believes that it can ward off punishment by the counter-threats. The population is unlikely to understand the requisite nuances. If they are driven by anger, they may not be in a mood for fine calculation, anyway. The leaders of the target country can plead to the attacker: "I'd like to hold my fire, but I fear more from my own people than I do from anything you can do to me." Incidentally, the basis for retaliation need not be public ire, if calculation coupled with public acquiescence suffices. But the fact that it *could* be public ire suffices to neutralize what the attacker *thinks* will be the effect of the counter-deterrence strategy.

It creates less need to explain. Any explicit deterrence policy creates the risk that its intended recipients will not take it at face value. Instead, they will try to infer the state's underlying posture by asking why the policy was declared at a particular point in time, and why the red line was set as it was. Such questions could undermine not only the legitimacy of a policy but its credibility. By contrast, if retaliation follows the expression of popular anger—as it would in a *de facto* policy—everyone from friend to foe can determine its rationale based on ostensible evidence freely available to all (although, in practice, there may be residual suspicions of manipulation and selective amplification).

It permits time for contemplating a proper response. The more deterministic a deterrence policy, the greater the pressure is to respond quickly if an attack crosses some line, lest the target's credibility be called into question (not only in cyberspace but across the board, as noted above). The excuse that the target is gathering the means and looking for an opportunity may not be credible for a state that has announced a deterrence policy, especially if it is the United States, which is perceived as having the means and having explored all the opportunities for retaliation (even in cyberspace). But, an instant response may be inappropriate while information is being gathered that validates attribution, assesses the degree of damage, and weighs the various alternatives. If the government deems the attack serious enough, it can strike back on its own. Alternatively, it can release (or leak) material in ways that create popular pressure to force or at least excuse retaliation. If the government chooses, ultimately, not to respond, all it signals by inaction is that the attack did not cross the red line at that point and in that context.

It reduces the moral hazard. Effective cyberattacks require both an undeterred attacker and a feckless victim. Remove either, and the cyberattack fails, in whole or in large part. A deterministic posture creates a moral hazard by instilling a false confidence among system owners that they need not protect their systems (over and above what is required to ward off criminals and other nonstate actors), because the responsibility to deal with state attackers has been assumed by their own government. This is a step in the wrong direction, since it results in greater vulnerability and greater damages from any given cyberattack—hence greater odds that a red line has been crossed. An ambiguous policy does not provide such certainty, leaving system operators little choice but to defend themselves.

It permits a sub rosa *response.* The target state may want to strike back but fears sparking an all-out series of exchanges forced upon both governments via public pressures. The *sub rosa* option allows retaliation but in ways that do not necessarily excite the attacking state's public (e.g., by disabling systems owned by the attacking state that serve, say, the security services but not the public at large). Such responses are designed to catch the attention of the attacking state's leaders and let them know that continuation of the aggression would be unwise. Those leaders, acting without pressure from what would otherwise be a population that was injured and aggrieved (from having suffered retaliation) could concede the point without losing face in front of their people. An ambiguous deterrence policy preserves that option; the target state does not have to justify its inaction very strenuously. A deterministic deterrence policy makes such an option difficult to pursue since the apparent lack of response will be taken by almost everyone (except the leadership of the attacking state) as no response at all, calling its credibility into question.

Conclusions

As a general rule, the instinct that a rules-based world is safer than one ruled by emotion is a sound basis for policy. Such instinct assumes a world of sufficient black and white. When faced with the gray fog of cyberwar, ambiguity has many attractions. No sane state will harm the United States without fearing the consequences of having angered this country. That being so, the absence of a deterrence strategy should not be confused with the absence of deterrence. All this suggests the following rule: The determinism of a policy should not exceed the determinism of the domain over which the policy applies.

5

THE ESSENTIAL FEATURES OF AN ONTOLOGY FOR CYBERWARFARE

RANDALL R. DIPERT

Contents

Using Biomedical Ontologies for Method and Content 39
Existing Military Ontologies 41
Conclusion 46
Endnotes 46

This chapter examines the reasons for creating an applied ontology for cyberwarfare and gives an outline of what such an ontology would look like. A cyberwarfare ontology would systematically organize and allow inference on all data relevant for the conduct of offensive and defensive cyberwarfare operations. The key features of such an ontology are: (1) humanly understandable definitions using controlled vocabularies, (2) an upper-level ontology using widely accepted categories and principles of organization, (3) representation in the best available formal system such as in Ontology Web Language (OWL) or Common Logic, and (4) application of methodologies for building a mid-level domain ontology and annotating instance-level data. An ontology for cyberwarfare will have some distinctive entities when compared with other (including other military) ontologies, such as a categorization of information-theoretic entities and the key notion of functioning, and impaired functioning, of information systems. There will soon be a rapidly expanded effort, both voluntary and as a product of regulation, to share information about malware and information system risks and vulnerabilities among private cybersecurity experts and companies, and cybersecurity departments of large government agencies, the military, and corporations. To date there has only been slight movement toward standardization of data in this domain. A principled ontology, using widely accepted best practices, offers the only tool to construct a single, robust, extensible framework for sharing data.

In this chapter I am going to sketch how one would develop an ontology for cyberwarfare: this would amount in practice to a systematic way of collecting, storing, and then utilizing all the data that would be relevant to the conduct of cyberwarfare, as well as for cybersecurity in general. To an extent, some of the classification of entities and their relationships can be taken from existing upper-level ontologies and the relatively few existing military ontologies. However, cyberwarfare has some distinctive features, most notably that its primary notion of an attack involves the disruption of an information processing system rather than the killing of human beings or the permanent destruction of physical objects. It crucially involves harm to the functioning of systems but not necessarily with permanent (hardware) destruction. Cyberwarfare *could* involve the intended or foreseeable deaths or destruction, but it need not.[1] Of the four most talked about probable acts of cyberwarfare, Estonia in 2007, Georgia in 2008, the Israeli incapacitation of Syrian air defense while attacking a reactor in 2007, and Stuxnet in 2010, only Stuxnet involved the intentional destruction of physical objects by cyberoperations alone, and apparently none have involved intended or foreseeable deaths.[2]

Since cyberwarfare is by its very nature information warfare, an ontology of cyberwarfare would necessarily include ways of specifying information objects (including information content and physical storage of information content), the destruction or corruption of data, and the nature and properties of malware. This would be in addition to what would be required of a domain-neutral upper-level ontology, which addresses the types and characteristics of the most basic categories of entity that are used in virtually all sciences and domains: material entity, event, quality of an object, physical object. A cyberwarfare ontology would also go beyond or employ variants of types of entity of a military ontology, such as agents, intentional actions, unintended effects, organizations, artifacts, commands, attacks, and so on. A piece of malware is in essence an algorithm, and an algorithm is not a physical object in the usual sense, although its storage, transmission, and effect necessarily involve processes and events within physical objects.[3] The identity and nature of algorithms have been understood and clearly talked about only since the late 1930s, and the quantitative theory of information dates from the early post World War II period. So the ontology of cyberwarfare would extensively involve what most people would think are very exotic components. Some might also call these entities, such as information-theoretic entities, "abstract," although this is not, strictly speaking, correct.[4]

Ontology, or more precisely applied ontology, is a newly emerging field intended to provide a solution to two of the most severe problems facing those who would fully utilize the vast stores of data our information systems have gathered.[5] The first is the integration of data from diverse sources using differing systems of classification or tagging. This is frequently described as the "interoperability" problem. The second is a problem of access to this data. Is there a best way to classify and categorize all data so that the data become optimally accessible and can be searched and reasoned over?

One solution to these problems is typically described as the "semantic web." One uses natural languages to store and retrieve data but incorporates connections among the meanings of terms in a language, such as English. This may be supplemented by an ontology specified in, for example, the Ontology Web Language (OWL). At its most superficial level, this is making WWW search engines such as Google or Bing perform "intelligent" searches. So if I search for "hound," the most visited sites that are retrieved are not just those with the literal string 'hound', but also sites that are semantically linked to it, such as those that deal with dogs, greyhounds, canines, and perhaps even Elvis, the Baskervilles, and Conan Doyle. The search engine "knows" subjects that are semantically related to the expression I typed and incorporates background knowledge most human beings would know in its search. The largest-scale project using these methods is the Cyc Project of Douglas Lenat and his co-workers at CyCorp. However, because this project was begun well before principles of applied ontologies (and languages for expressing them) had been developed, its own ontology has more of the character of data- and conceptual modeling techniques discussed below. It has many links between entity types but lacks a clear hierarchy of basic entities and a short list of basic ontological relations, and thus lacks a single, clear, upper-level ontology.

Rather than using an off-the-shelf tool such as a database program to store and access information, another approach is to engineer a "conceptual model" that incorporates some of the useful features of data into a complete multipurpose software tool that prompts a user to enter certain crucial information and retrieves, and can reason over, just the kind of data for which the program is designed. In the last 20 years many computer scientists and engineers have categorized data in this way and used *ad hoc*, "homemade" categorizations in programs and databases in this way. This approach is typically called conceptual or data modeling, and its most telltale features are an emphasis on human concepts (rather than external reality) and relations between these entities that follow semantic relations. These efforts are mostly incompatible, and there would be little agreement between what one group of computer scientists would come up with and what another group would devise. Examples of such efforts within the US federal government include the National Information Exchange Model (NIEM) for the Department of Justice and Department of Homeland Security and most applications of the federal government's UCore initiative. The original aim for NIEM was to extend a data standard to the Department of Defense (DoD) and the various intelligence agencies. An older effort was the data model, and the software supporting it, of NATO's Joint Consultation, Command and Control Information Exchange Data Model (JC3IEDM). Both have had some limited success, and the JC3IEDM is remarkable for the shear number of entities that it classifies—in some cases down to the level of models of vehicles and parts for those models.

By the most advanced standards in applied ontology that are now being developed, these efforts have severe flaws. First, for help with human understanding, these projects have used definitions taken straight from dictionaries and lexicons, including various DoD lexicons and manuals. When one follows this practice, one rapidly creates cases of circularity and contradictions and ends up with only as much ability to access information and make inference as is possible using natural language understanding processing (in other words, only with great difficulty). A modern applied ontology should be usable both by human beings and by information systems. Today's best practice in ontology instead uses a controlled vocabulary (limited to hundred or thousands of words and limited grammatical structures) that closely parallels—ideally, can be parsed into—whatever the "logical" representations of facts about entities are in the data representations. The proof of concept for the use of controlled English was developed by John Sowa, and has been further developed in Common Logic Controlled English.[6] A successful example of this method is the miniature prototype for a larger-scale, mid-level ontology for the DoD, UCORE-SL.

Second, none of these conceptual-modeling efforts uses similar "upper-level" categorizations of entities other than at the top or next-to-the-top levels of generality. However, there is agreement on what these should be among the existing major upper-level ontologies that have been developed in the last 15 years, such as the Suggested Upper Merge Ontology (SUMO), the Descriptive Ontology for Linguistic and Cognitive Engineering (DOLCE), and the Basic Formal Ontology (BFO). These ontologies all give us a coherent, tree-like structure of entity types, axioms governing standardized properties such entities have, as well as axioms governing relations that different entity types may find themselves in. For example, it is inconceivable that an event could occur without the existence of continuants (such as physical objects) that take part in these events. Continuants are all those kinds of entities that endure through time and often change some features over time: this category includes human beings and physical objects.

Using Biomedical Ontologies for Method and Content

To date the most extensive use of applied ontologies has been in biomedical research and development. Estimates of the money invested in these ontologies is in the tens or even hundreds of millions of dollars—in addition to the billions or trillions of dollars invested in biomedical, including pharmaceutical, research, and development that are now using them. There are hundreds or thousands of biomedical researchers who are practicing ontologists, with increasingly large yearly conferences and self-organized communities that set standards.[7] Within biomedical research one of the first subfields that extensively used ontologies was in genetics. The Gene Ontology (GO) is now a worldwide standard for collecting data on genetic information, proteins, and connections between them, as well as classifications of biochemical processes, diseases, and anatomical features that depend on them. As with other subfields within the biomedical realm, such as the Protein, Cell, and Disease Ontologies, a consortium of users was founded with one or more websites that serve as open source clearinghouses for the controlled vocabulary (a list of terms), the actual ontology, and tools for accessing and making inferences on stores of data encoded in this standardized way.[8] The older (>10 years) biomedical ontologies have gone through a number of cycles of revisions and extensions that were motivated by shortcomings of an earlier proposed ontology. One might speak of what were originally philosophical ontologies being molded by applicability and the scientific method—testing ontologies in the field. It is obvious to everyone that tremendous progress has been made in genetic theory and technology. What is less noticed is that these successes have required development in information technology, and specifically in applied ontologies.

An ontology is a hierarchy of entity types and axioms relating them. They are typically represented in the Ontology Web Language (OWL) with some movement toward representation in standard first-order predicate logic (FOPL), especially now that there is a standard ISO notation for FOPL.[9] Separate from this would be the instance-level data, which would be (for example) data about an individual human being and events in his or her medical history. In many cases, instance-level data can be incorporated from standard databases or other representations into an ontology by writing transformation rules. A simple way of regarding an ontology is that it is a systematic classification system for all entities these data talk about.

While a biomedical ontology would seem like an unlikely place to look for help in building a military or cyberwarfare ontology, this is not so. For one thing, the entities used in one field are, at a top level, the same in every ontology. So one can build upon ontologies developed for other domains: physical entities, physical events, etc. The biomedical ontologies have the most extensively tested upper-level ontologies, and remarkably few phenomena are now encountered that cannot easily be classified by existing entity types and relations. Furthermore, there are deep similarities between a cyberwarfare and the biomedical domain. The biomedical ontologies have a subontology of "adverse events" (itself a part of an event ontology). Biomedical ontologies have wrestled for some time with problems in representing the notion of function—either of natural entities such as the heart, or of engineered ones, such as measuring devices. There are other deep similarities, such as the idea of a vector for the spread of disease, the notions of reproduction, transmission, and modification, which have straightforward application to malware. Finally, the gene ontology, and specifically the Sequence Ontology within it, has developed a theory of information and encoding of that information (as nucleic acid sequences) that offers an almost straightforward carryover: just as one looks for markers and distinctive sequences in genetic material, one can similarly screen for distinctive binary code signatures in malware. In biology, this has resulted in the creation of a new field, bioinformatics. Sequence patterns (genes) express themselves in molecular (usually protein) synthesis and then in cellular structures and processes. Similarly, a piece of malware has varied effects on its host information system, depending on its environment. It might affect a SCADA system, or result in other actions on its environment, and may change its sensors. Some malware suppresses the desired effect of anti-virus software, just as some diseases suppress the immune system. Although the original word chosen for one type of malware, "virus," was probably chosen as a loose analogy, it has been extended into deep metaphorical similarities between disease and malware.

Existing Military Ontologies

The broad effort to implement a data standard for all federal agencies was first focused on the development of the Universal Core (UCore) now in version 2.0. UCore's governance and user base are now primarily the Department of Defense, Office of the Director of National Intelligence, the Department of Justice, and the Department of Homeland Security. Its main features were to be extensible—expandable without changing central features—and to use a widespread system of encoding data, XML. The effort was guided by a number of DoD directives and implementation goals such as in *Guidance for Implementing Net-Centric Data Sharing* (2006).[10] While there was some effort to make UCore compatible with best practices in applied ontology (as described above), UCore's upper-level ontology is much weaker than any of the developed upper-level ontologies we have discussed, and it lacks a specific and sophisticated methodology for extending it into various domains. Application on different domains has been pursued by suborganizations in diverse and often incompatible ways (except insofar as all use XML and XML schemas stipulated as conventions by UCore directives).

Before UCore's development, there seems not to have been research into how best to design interoperable data representation systems in general, but instead just an awareness that one was needed. Perhaps more lamentably, UCore's project managers and the various federal agencies still pursuing diverse data standardization strategies seem unaware of the scientific successes of applied ontologies, with their very demanding users and extensive processes of revision, as described above. In the last few years there is also considerable interest in sharable ontologies for the financial and corporate management sectors. They are looking not to failed government efforts (except for some at the National Institute of Standards and Technology [NIST]) but to robust upper-level ontologies and success stories in biology and medicine. The biomedical and financial sectors have numbers of users, data quantities, and economic factors that are as large, or larger, than the federal government, especially since the biomedical and financial ontology efforts are international in scope. One striking sociological difference between the biomedical field and the behavior of government agencies in pursuing data interoperability is that the initiative for information representation in biological and medical research has arisen from, and been developed by, practitioners. The more data there are, and abilities to analyze the data, the better for them. (The field of medical records has, in contrast, not moved rapidly to standardization, with patients lodging privacy concerns, and insurance and other agencies resisting compulsory standardization. It remains to be seen whether pending changes in the US medical system will push practitioners toward rational systems of data organization.) The desire to hold on to distinctive terminology is legendary within the military services, and within other federal agencies, although it can scarcely be contested that they are dealing with the same basic entities in reality: human beings, physical objects, computer programs, computer hardware, etc.

One effort to graft onto UCore a more sophisticated ontology as described above was UCore SL ("SL" meaning "Semantic Layer"). This was developed with funds from the Department of the Army and built upon the upper-level ontology BFO (the most widely used ontology in biomedical research). UCore SL could be described as a middle-level ontology, since it goes beyond the specification of types of entities and relations common to all fields and sciences, as a true upper-level ontology does. It sketches how an upper-level ontology can be extended into classifying the types of entities and relations that are common to all human activity (agent, action, artifact, organization). It is thus a bridge between an upper-level ontology and what would be required to build an intelligence[11] or defense ontology.

Among the military ontologies that are under development are:

- Ontology of Command and Control (C2, Department of the Army) 2009
- Counter-terrorism Ontology (Air Force Research Laboratory) 2011
- Biometrics Ontology 2009
- Ontology for IEDs: Joint Improvised Explosive Device Defeat Organization (JIEDDO)
- Electronic Warfare Ontology: Space and Naval Warfare Systems Command (SPAWAR) 2010
- An Ontology of Information Operations[12]

Except for the last two, all were developed within the framework of the Basic Formal Ontology.[13] There is also an effort directed by LTC William Mandrick to develop a general military ontology as an extension of BFO and UCore SL.[14]

I am not aware of any unclassified ontology of, or ontology related to, offensive cyberwarfare. Defensive cyberwarfare is of course equivalent to cybersecurity, and here there are many proposals.[15] With the introduction of numerous legislative proposals and the likelihood that something along the US Senate's S-2105, The Cybersecurity Act of 2012, will be enacted, there will probably soon be intense demand for an interoperable language and ontology of cybersecurity. This (and several other proposals) mandates close cooperation between critical infrastructure and DHS, and proposes a cybersecurity information exchange that shares information about attacks and mitigation efforts among government and industry. For these efforts to work, there must be agreement on a shared standard of nomenclature. The amount of raw data (especially involved in attacks that have not been fully analyzed) would be huge, and there is a need for real-time reaction to these intrusions; this would require not just sorting through massive amounts of data but doing it in a fully automated way.[16]

Currently the NIST maintains a National Vulnerability Database (NVD)[17] whose major component is the Common Vulnerability and Exposures (CVE) list. Take for example two entries including from a specific buffer overflow (CVE) vulnerability when running the Explorer web browser and from a description of a generic weakness, buffer overflows in general, #3 of the most common weaknesses on the Common Weakness Enumeration (CWE) list.[18]

Currently there is little or no attempt to categorize the various terms according to the different kinds of entity they represent, or to characterize them in a controlled vocabulary and grammar. The condition of a "buffer overflow" is an event-type, whose main continuant participant is the hardware processing system. But also involved are other event-types such as the running of a program and the operating system (OS, usually referred to in cybersecurity as the "platform"). Invisible but implicit in the description of this vulnerability is the agent targeting the vulnerability, the vector by which this is accomplished (typically the Internet, software implemented for managing communication traffic on the hardware of the network itself), the intended and unintended consequences (other events or event-types) on the information system, and the malicious agent's wider intended effects on the owner of the affected information system (such as root access), or, beyond the information system, malicious effects on company or agency's operations, such as diverting resources or interference with military command and control.

The beginning of categorization of malware is offered by another NIST initiative, Mitre's Malware Attribute Enumeration and Characterization (MAEC), but it is similarly little more than extensive but disorganized lists of characteristics that groups of computer and cybersecurity experts think are significant. These files are not searchable or manipulable except as strings of text.[19]

In the private sector, Symantec offers a list of malware (in its own nomenclature and without referencing NIST's classification system). A glossary is offered, but without following standards of controlled vocabulary and grammar, or following other lexicographic principles that might support a systematic ontology.[20] A definition of adware from Symantec is "programs that facilitate delivery for advertising content to the user and in some cases gather information from the user's computer, including information related to Internet browser usage or other computer habits."

The signatures (suspicious lengths of code in specific memory locations) are presumably available through the software product Symantec markets (Norton Anti-Virus). Risks are classified by Symantec as "Spyware | Adware | Dialers | Hack Tools | Joke Programs | Remote Access | Hoaxes | Trackware | Misleading Applications | Parental Controls | Potentially Unwanted Applications | Security Assessment Tools | Other."

What Symantec calls risks appear to be tools or methods for corrupting an information system. A vulnerability is the flaw or characteristic of the attacked system. In ontological terms these are reciprocal dispositions: one is part of the function of the corrupting software tool (or more precisely a function of a hardware system running the software tool) while the other is the feature of the attacked system that permits it to be corrupted. A function is a designed, created, or selected-for disposition, and dispositions in general are dependent continuants in BFO.

Fortunately, once a more robust ontology for cybersecurity is created, this is simultaneously part of an ontology for offensive cyberweapons. That is, once one can categorize malware by signature, effects, and means of achieving those effects, one also has a list of characteristics—which would have to be far more detailed than these—that can be applied to all malware, including one's own cyberweapons. Of special concern in the development of cyberweapons is careful consideration of the likely and possible effects of their deployment on civilian information systems (including financial and other business software) and their likely and possible effects on third-party nations. To determine these, one would have to infiltrate this software into various configurations in tests (a "sandbox"). There are hundreds of settings for operating systems and application software listed in NIST's Common Configuration Enumeration (CCE), in addition to considering effects on a variety of operating systems and non-targeted applications.[21]

Conclusion

A common data standard for cyberwarfare defense, cybersecurity in general, and for cyberwarfare offense will be essential for tracking the diverse characteristics and effects, intended and unintended, of malware; detection and mitigation of malware attacks; and development, use, and effectiveness rating of cyberweapons. This effort is becoming necessary for sophisticated sharing of data among government, military, and private organizations. The chapter proposes that the only long-term solution to severe problems of data interoperability, as well as real-time access to and the ability to perform inferences over massive amounts of data, is the development of a cyberwarfare ontology. To be effective and truly extensible, it has to avoid the segmented, *ad hoc* practices of many previous efforts in the federal government. The chapter has argued that there are powerful reasons to pursue what are increasingly regarded as "best practices" for applied ontologies, and that success of this approach has been demonstrated by the methodologies used in biomedical ontologies on similarly massive stores of data.[22]

Endnotes

1. I use a narrow definition of a cyberwarfare operation, such that it is an intentional state-on-state act targeting information systems that does harm within the targeted state for political purposes. Excluded would be acts of cyberespionage and theft of intellectual property.
2. For details of these cyberwarfare operations, an examination of the kinds of cyberattacks, and a survey of ethical and legal issues see Randall R. Dipert, The Ethics of Cyberwarfare, *Journal of Military Ethics* 9: 4, 384–410.
3. I here ignore denial-of-service (DoS) and distributed denial-of-service (DDoS) attacks, because they are not intrusive with respect to the affected information system, occur in a public or open context (the Internet and access to websites), and are typically supported by botnet malware. Detection of DoS attacks is rather simple—a spike in activity—and there are now a number of well-known ways of mitigating or defeating such an attack.
4. In philosophy, an abstract object is one that lacks spatio-temporal characteristics and does not causally interact with physical objects and events. Information-theoretic entities are however represented, communicated, and manipulated in physical objects and processes.

5. In the rest of this chapter, I will use "ontology" to refer to an *applied* ontology. The field of pure or theoretical ontology is a branch of philosophy going back to the ancient Greeks (especially to Aristotle) and is often referred to as "metaphysics." The applied ontologies were developed utilizing some of this philosophical work and also using modern logical tools and practices in computer science.

6. See Sowa, John F., Controlled English, accessed March 2012, from http://www.jfsowa.com/logic/ace.htm.

7. The conference is the International Conference on Biomedical Ontology (ICBO). There is also a cross-domain yearly conference, the (International Conference on) Formal Ontology in Information Systems (FOIS). An example of self-organized standardization is the Open Biomedical Ontology (OBO), and various domain ontologies organized according to the principles of the OBO Foundry. This includes a limited number of basic ontological relations between entities, such as part_of.

8. The Gene Ontology's site is at http://www.geneontology.org/. Serious research on the ontologies for genetic research can be dated to approximately the date for the copyright on "Gene Ontology," 1999.

9. ISO/IEC 24707:2007 Common Logic (CL): a framework for a family of logic-based languages. Technically, the main part of this document is not a single notational standard but a framework for artificial languages that would be easily and mechanically inter-translatable. The single notation that is most likely to dominate the field will be CLIF (Common Logic Interchange Format).

10. Department of Defense Guide, Information Management Directorate Assistant Secretary of Defense for Networks and Information Integration, DoD CIO, April 12, 2006.

11. The intelligence community has embraced state-of-the-art ontologies with more zeal than the defense community. A yearly conference, Ontology for the Intelligence Community, was begun in 2007.

12. LTC Timothy Clark (USMC), *An Ontological Approach to Developing Information Operations Applications for Use on the Semantic Web*, Masters Thesis, Naval Postgraduate School, Monterey, California, 2008, accessed March 13, 2012, from http://oai.dtic.mil/oai/oai?verb=getRecord&meta dataPrefix=html&identifier=ADA489120.

13. I was a paid consultant on the C2 Ontology (Department of the Army) and have participated in the development of UCore SL and all of the above ontologies except for the SPAWAR project.

14. William Mandrick, *The Ontology of War*, PhD dissertation, University at Buffalo, New York, 2004.

15. Ashley Brinson, Abigail Robinson, Marcus Rogers, "A cyber forensics ontology: Creating a new approach to studying cyber forensics"; Ashley Brinson, Abigail Robinson, and Marcus Rogers, *Digital Investigation* (2006), pp. 37–43; Mary C. Parmelee, "Toward an Ontology Architecture for Cyber-Security Standards," October 28, 2010.

16. My colleagues and I working on cyberwarfare issues at the Stockdale Center at the US Naval Academy believe that much more intervention is necessary at the level of ISPs (especially at the Tier 1 level that would handle international Internet traffic) and even at the level of individuals who connect to their local ISP. Upper-tier ISPs should be more energetically engaged in detecting malware and anomalies, and perhaps in filtering them or blocking certain IP addresses. A residential or business system should ideally not be permitted to connect to the Internet unless its ISP examines their system and determines that there was anti-virus software and that it had recently been run (perhaps even in the last 12 hours). If under the control of a botnet or other malware, it is "polluting" the Internet data stream and endangering other users.

17. Currently version 2.2 located at National Vulnerability Database, accessed March 13, 2011, from nvd.nist.gov. See also NIST's effort, the National Initiative for Cybersecurity Education (NICE), http://csrc.nist.gov/nice/framework/.

18. Common Vulnerabilities and Exposures, http://cve.mitre.org/.

19. Malware Attribute Enumeration and Characterization, http://maec.mitre.org/.

20. Symantec, Glossary, accessed March 14, 2012, http://www.symantec.com/security_response/glossary/.

21. Common Configuration Enumeration, http://cce.mitre.org/.

22. My thanks for help in the preparation of this chapter go to Barry Smith, Director, NCOR, University at Buffalo, main author of BFO and UCore-SL; LTC Bill Mandrick (US), Military Ontology, C2 Ontology; Ron Rudnicki, C2 Ontology, Counter-terrorism Ontology, Biometrics Ontology; Alan Ruttenberg, Assistant Director, NCOR, University at Buffalo, Information-artifact ontology, OBO (consortium of biomedical ontologies), W3C Committee on OWL2; and Fabian Neuhaus, National Institute of Standards and Technology (NIST).

6

THE PROSPECTS FOR CYBER DETERRENCE

American Sponsorship of Global Norms

PANAYOTIS A. YANNAKOGEORGOS

ADAM B. LOWTHER

Contents

Introduction	50
Deterrence Framework	52
Attribution	55
Broad Solutions	56
Multi-Stage, Multi-Jurisdictional Attacks	57
Spoofing Machines to Mask Geography	58
Wrongful Acts in Cyberspace	60
A Framework for Development, Diplomacy, and Defense	62
Development, Diplomacy, and Defense Responses	62
Development	63
Diplomacy	64
Defense	65
Linking It All Together	66
Legislative Language for "Victims of Trafficking of Malicious Code"	67
Legislation	67
Leading by Example: US-Based Entities Responsibility	70
US-Based Internet Intermediaries	70
Where Do We Go from Here?	71
Endnotes	73

Introduction

Defending America's vital national interests in cyberspace requires the United States to develop the ability to deter adversaries from misusing the domain. This necessitates going against the accepted paradigm that cyberspace is not tied to geography, and recognizing that it is a domain which in its entirety is connected to the territorial jurisdiction of some country. Even the governance of the Internet, cyberspace's most potent global manifestation, is centralized in a hierarchical structure, such as the Domain Name System, and within international organizations, such as the Internet Corporation for Assigned Names and Numbers (ICANN). Current US policy is forged on the misperception that cyberspace is a virtual environment, and as such, eliminates discussion of territory and sovereignty in that debate. Such a mistake undermines cyber deterrence. Correcting this view and creating the norms and laws that are required will improve attribution (the central problem for cyber deterrence), which will allow for better deterrence strategies.

As Joseph Nye notes:

> Cyber war, although only incipient at this stage, is the dramatic manifestation of the potential threats. Major states with elaborate technical and human resources could, in principle, create massive disruption as well as physical destruction through cyber attacks on military as well as civilian targets. Responses to cyber war include a form of interstate deterrence (though different from classical nuclear deterrence), offensive capabilities, and designs for network and infrastructure resilience if deterrence fails. At some point in the future, it may be possible to reinforce these steps with certain rudimentary norms, but the world is at an early stage in such a process.[1]

Offering a solution to the attribution challenge through the creation of global norms and state responsibility is the objective of this chapter. In creating the framework described, it is believed that deterrence, as Nye suggests, can then play an effective role in deterring large-scale cyber attacks.

Currently, malicious cyber actors exploit gaps in technology and international cybersecurity cooperation to launch complex attacks against often unsuspecting or unprepared targets. Rather than considering technical attribution the challenge, a more accurate argument holds that "solutions to preventing the attacks of most concern, multi-stage multi-jurisdictional ones, will require not only technical methods, but legal/policy solutions as well."[2]

The current focus of attribution efforts within the national security context concentrates on law enforcement paradigms aiming to gather evidence to prosecute an individual attacker. This is usually dependent on technical means of attribution.[3] In a malicious cyber action, it is more often the case that spoofing or obfuscation of an identity can and will occur. It is therefore not easy to know who conducts malicious cyber activity. Thus, preventing or deterring such attacks is proving extremely difficult.

While conventional wisdom suggests that cyber deterrence is difficult, if not impossible, in large part due to the attribution problem, there is hope for success. However, attempts to draw close analogies between cyber deterrence and nuclear deterrence make the development of effective cyber deterrence less likely. Where nuclear deterrence is effective largely because adversaries understand the capabilities of one another and possess a strong understanding of an adversary's "red lines," such is not the case in cyberspace.[4] Here, exploiting vulnerabilities in an adversary's software is what makes a cyber attack possible. Therefore, an incentive to demonstrate capability does not exist since once a vulnerability is known and patched, an exploit for that vulnerability will no longer work. Patching vulnerabilities in industrial control systems (ICS) and medical devices, where the virtual and the physical merge, is not so straightforward. Thus, the opposite incentive structure as nuclear deterrence exists with the critical software on which our industry, utilities, and public health sectors rely.

Furthermore, private sector reports have proven that it is possible to determine the geographic reference of actors to varying degrees.[5] Our view is that rather than individual accountability, nation-states should be held culpable for the malicious actions and other cyber threats originating in or transiting information systems within their borders, or owned by registered corporate entities therein. If this premise is accepted, cyber deterrence becomes a viable option but not a guarantee for success.

Engaging the global community to develop a global culture of cybersecurity is required to begin mitigating the risk of a country from being used as a transit or origin point for a malicious cyber act. In order for such engagement to be considered legitimate, the United States will need a framework based on articulated norms of responsible state behavior in cyberspace.[6]

It is not the technical challenges that hinder global cybersecurity cooperation; rather, the latter suffers from a lack of national-level cybersecurity policies that employ the technology, management procedures, organizational structures, law, and human competencies that exist—for national security.[7] As reported in the *Quadrennial Defense Review* (2010), *National Security Strategy* (2010), *International Strategy for Cyberspace* (2010), and the *DoD Strategy for Operating in Cyberspace* (2011), strengthening international partnerships to secure the cyber domain requires an understanding of what technical, legal, and defense challenges international partners face.[8] Appealing arguments for state responsibility in cyberspace exist, but a convincing deterrence framework to support these recommendations is lacking.[9] This chapter aims to fill this gap by providing policymakers with the toolbox they need to guide the US's international engagement and Department of Defense (DoD) operations in cyberspace.

Our proposed framework aims to support America's partners in strengthening their cybersecurity—contributing to a safer cyber environment. It will also aid the judgment of DoD and US policymakers as they contemplate escalation of diplomatic and military responses when countries do not behave responsibly.

Deterrence Framework

Cyber conflict activities constitute a critical form of coercive power. Effects can range from disruption to destruction. The loss of electrical power for extended periods of time, inability to conduct commerce due to networking failures, and incapacity of military organizations to command and control their forces are credible threats. In the past, the United States has faced adversarial states and violent nonstate actors organized in relatively hierarchical structures. However, today the evolution of information and communication technology (ICT) such as those that make up the Internet, and the intensification of reliance on these vulnerable technologies provide US adversaries with the opportunity to organize themselves as decentralized networks with no clear evidence of state control.[10] One expert notes:

> The question is who is responsible for these things, even if you trace it back to China, is if they are bored hackers or PLA members or criminals with ties to the PLA or PLA divisions acting criminally? We don't really know. I suspect that the majority of the attacks and espionage on the criminal side are by patriotic hackers that have some sort of connection, maybe financial, to the PLA or the State Security Ministry. In the cases of power grids and other cases like that, I suspect PLA affiliation, but there is no way to know.[11]

This highlights the blurred lines between state and nonstate actors who may initiate a cyber conflict. It is a line that states hide behind when confronted over attacks originating within their territory.

In addition to its principal aim, this work reframes the question of attribution from one that asks who exploited US information systems to which state did the exploitation originate from, and what state was it filtered through? By doing so, states are incentivized to actively prevent the use of their territory for cyber attack. Thus, host-nation accountability increases the desired deterrent effect. It is useful to point out that when it comes to deterrence, credibility equals capability plus will. If states are held accountable for what originates from their territory and/or what passes through it, their will to prevent such an attack should increase—improving deterrence credibility.

Although hackers might not be officially controlled by the Chinese government—allowing the PLA plausible deniability—evidence of indirect control should be enough to hold China responsible. Several recent studies of cyber espionage and the publicized results of corporate investigations traced several attacks against the US's commercial infrastructure to China.[12] Denying its official involvement, the government of China bemoaned its fate as the greatest victim of cyber crime.[13]

A recent report to Congress by the US–China Economic and Security Review Commission observed that China's "[p]rofessional state sponsored intelligence collection not only targets a nation's sensitive national security and policymaking information, it increasingly is being used to collect economic and competitive data to aid foreign businesses competing for market share with their U.S. peers."[14] The same report noted that the Chinese are aware of the gaps in US cyber strategies and may be exploiting "U.S. policymaking and legal frameworks to create delays in U.S. command decision making." The major flaw in US policy is focusing on individual responsibility for an act of cyber espionage, crime, or conflict. The policy gaps that currently exist are those of formulating response frameworks to cyber events that do not rely on a law enforcement paradigm. Michael Levi, in a discussion of state-sponsored nuclear terrorism, writes, "By threatening states with retaliation should a nuclear terrorist attack be traced back to them, it may be possible to deter them from transferring nuclear materials in the first place."[15] Much the same is true for state actors in cyberspace.

Weak domestic law enforcement cybersecurity capabilities in both developed and developing nations create virtual safe havens from which perpetrators of cyber crime operate (either physically or virtually) to spoof their true identity and operate with near impunity. It is this "spoofing" that has come to dominate the discussions around responses to cyber attack with a law enforcement paradigm of attribution dominating early cyber policy dialogues about strategy and doctrine.

Air Force doctrine for cyberspace operations describes the attribution problem in the following terms:

> Perhaps the most challenging aspect of attribution of actions in cyberspace is connecting a cyberspace actor or action to an actual, real-world agent (be it individual or state actor) with sufficient confidence and verifiability to inform decision- and policymakers... The nature of cyberspace, government policies, and international laws and treaties make it very difficult to determine the origin of a cyberspace attack. The ability to hide the source of an attack makes it difficult to connect an attack with an attacker within the cyberspace domain. The design of the Internet lends itself to anonymity.... Nations can do little to combat the anonymity their adversaries exploit in cyberspace.... Nevertheless, nations have the advantage of law and the ability to modify the technological environment by regulation.[16]

The Air Force appears to be following the traditional attribution framework emphasizing perpetrator identification. The result is that cyber operators are being asked to inform decision and policy makers with accurate and precise evidence.[17] While these requirements might be appropriate in a law enforcement context, such standards are misapplied in military and strategic contexts. The statement of USAF doctrine relating to law and policy modifying the technological environment is more appropriate. However, laws and regulations take time and resources to develop, as in the decades-long processes that led to the UN Convention on the Law of the Sea (1982).

Attribution

Technologically, attribution works better than the dire picture some might suggest. Several attacks coming from within China over the past five years have been publicly traced to operators with Chinese characteristics.[18] Furthermore, several high-profile cyber crime cases, such as the FBI's multinational effort in Operation Takedown, illustrate the need for international law enforcement cooperation to bring criminal justice into cyberspace.[19] Such cases offer evidence that individual perpetrators can be brought to justice when there is solid international cooperation. Countries and nonstate actors not cooperating in cyber investigations claim that because of anonymity on the Internet they cannot trace cyber attackers, while efforts of likeminded nations, the United States and United Kingdom, have resulted in the dismantling of a global network of "anonymous" hackers. Admittedly, attribution in cyberspace is complicated, but it is not impossible, as is often portrayed.

Thus, nations should be held culpable for the malicious actions and other cyber threats originating in, transiting through, or owned by their registered corporate entities. This cannot be done without clear and accepted norms of responsible state behavior in cyberspace. Only by creating such norms and regulations can deterrence succeed.

The process of establishing these norms has begun in forums associated with the United Nations and its International Telecommunications Union (ITU), but the United States is trying to lead the development of global cybersecurity initiatives within other forums. Instead, the majority of nations, including American allies and partners, prefer to follow the lead of Russia and China in support of ITU frameworks. To prevent marginalization, the United States should increase participation in the ITU and get behind the international efforts on behalf of cybersecurity. American sponsorship of the global norms coming out of the ITU would immediately increase cooperation between states to create a more secure cyber ecosystem and allay fears of a hegemonic United States.

Broad Solutions

In 2011, the White House released the *International Strategy for Cyberspace* emphasizing development, diplomacy, and defense in the US government's cyberspace vision. The strategy highlights a commitment to development through working to "play an active role in providing the knowledge and capacity to build and secure new and existing digital systems."[20] This element is important in helping reduce the numbers of safe havens in cyberspace.

Through diplomacy, the United States will strive "to create incentives for, and build consensus around, an international environment in which states—recognizing the intrinsic value of an open, interoperable, secure, and reliable cyberspace—work together and act as responsible stakeholders."[21] The Department of State and FBI both have roles in developing relationships with foreign governments so that when a cyber attack originates or transits through their territory, the mechanisms to respond and act responsibly are in place. These partnerships are considered essential to ensure the necessary mechanisms for cooperation are in place to identify and prosecute cyber criminals and terrorists. Diplomacy also offers a channel through which the United States can voice its concerns to foreign governments implicated in malicious acts in cyberspace. If governments are not forthcoming, more coercive diplomatic measures can be employed to stem malicious cyber activities.

Finally, when all else fails, the DoD has a duty to "respond to hostile acts in cyberspace as we would to any other threat to our country."[22] The DoD's role is also diplomatic in that it is to build partnerships with foreign militaries and as a last resort, defend the nation. Within DoD the US Air Force, in particular, has an important role to play in military-to-military relations since the USAF sustains a leading edge in cyber. By actively working with friends and allies, building norms of behavior across a growing community of nations, those nations that desire to violate the norms that develop, run the risk of a large-scale diplomatic, economic, and military backlash. This may serve as a deterrent.

The United States accepts the paradigm of state responsibility. However, the substance of "development, diplomacy, and defense" is unclear. The success of the *International Strategy for Cyberspace* depends on the United States shifting from trying to lead the world toward sponsoring the existing global culture of cybersecurity—organized through the ITU. This will support US global engagements to secure cyberspace while leading by example. Along these lines, specific recommendations for US cyberspace development, diplomacy, and defense are presented below.

Multi-Stage, Multi-Jurisdictional Attacks

Understanding network behavior requires examining relations among network events. The technological issues related to Transmission Control Protocol/Internet Protocol (TCP/IP) are only part of the attribution problem. With attribution typically thought of as an investigator's ability to trace attacks back to either an attacker or the attacker's machine's location, being able to do so allows an appropriate response to the attack via law enforcement or military action.[23] If attackers knew that their actions could be accurately traced, they could be deterred. Solving the technical attribution challenge by implementing new methodologies and techniques is widely seen as the way forward when responding to cyber attacks. This can be seen in the pressure to deploy the upgraded IPv6.[24]

Although strengthening network protocols is desirable, respected cyber experts David Clark and Susan Landau suggest that "better attribution techniques will neither solve nor prevent" the complex multi-stage, multi-jurisdictional nature of computer exploitations occurring today.[25] It is not the purpose here to delve into the intricacies of methods and techniques to technically attribute attacks. It is noteworthy, however, that the multi-stage and cross-jurisdictional characteristics of cyber attacks determine the complexity of determining the attack's source. These factors highlight that gaps in international cooperation actually lie at the core of the attribution dilemma.

Spoofing Machines to Mask Geography

Very few people are capable of designing Stuxnet-like cyber weapons. However, the capabilities to mount less sophisticated exploits of vulnerabilities, such as spoofing a machine's location, have a much lower cost of entry. This is due to the inherent weakness of the protocols on which networks, including the Internet, transport data. The availability of tools providing anonymizing services are also inexpensive.

Because computer networks are dependent on the use of internationally standardized communications protocols, known as TCP/IP, to send and receive data packets and information, this allows for the flow of data packets and information across computer networks.[26] Designed and deployed for military and research purposes in the late 1960s, IP was not intended to function as the backbone of the global project that became the Internet.

Approved in 1982 as the standard protocol for military computer network communications, the protocol was designed to allow for data packets to be sent across a computer network in the most efficient way the network deemed possible at a given time. The reasoning was that in the aftermath of a nuclear war a nonhierarchical network structure that could reroute data packets in an uncorrupted manner from point A to B via other pathways was required. The ability to track and trace user behavior in a high-threat computing environment was not built into communications protocols because they were intended for use within a trusted military environment.[27]

Yet, it is on this foundational protocol that other networks began to build, eventually morphing into the National Science Foundation Network and the Internet.[28] According to Internet expert Tom Leighton, the Domain Name System (DNS), ports, and IP address systems are plagued by flaws that "imperil more than individuals and commercial institutions. Secure installations in the government and military can be compromised" as well.[29] Consequently, the current flaws in the network architecture of the Internet are a result of relying on protocols that were built 35 years ago when the Internet was not a global entity but a closed research network.

Manipulating TCP/IP to spoof identities has become very common in cyberspace. In the past, a significant understanding of networking was required to spoof an IP address. Over the past 15 years tools that anonymize Internet activities proliferated. "Onion Routing" of networks allows for the masking of a data packet's point of origin. Activists may enter the Internet from unsecured wireless or "WiFi" networks and cyber-cafes or dial into Internet service providers (ISPs) all over the planet to hide their identity from the prying eyes of government censors. Malicious actors can propagate zombies to serve as proxies for cyber attacks. Actors might spoof IP addresses to inject malicious data into critical infrastructures, commit fraud, or bypass authorities.[30]

These kinds of spoofing attacks are the crux of the attribution challenge. Masking one's location on the Internet destroys trust in identity and security in cyberspace. An individual may manipulate various layers of the TCP/IP protocol to create a false appearance of a user, a device, or even a Web site. With the global nature of the Internet, it is possible for a malicious actor to exploit software vulnerabilities in such a way that the actor's computer appears to be another. This technique allows skilled attackers to thwart cyber crime investigations. Dorothy Denning aptly writes that to "trace an intruder, the investigator must get the cooperation of every system administrator and network service provider on the path."[31] While accurate, it would not be an impossible challenge with the appropriate global cyber policies in place.

Although the ability to spoof a location is a critical element of cyber crime, cyber espionage, and cyber sabotage, the Department of State (DOS) is developing tools that utilize these same vulnerabilities in IP and network design to promote freedom of speech in closed regimes. Such efforts complicate the attribution of cyber attacks since people are trained to anonymize their Internet activities. Prospects for international cooperation are diminished because some closed regimes view the breaching of censor systems as cyber warfare and might not be forthcoming with information during cyber attack investigations.

The Onion Router (TOR) is one example of such software. It is a distributed anonymous network of proxy servers connected by virtual encrypted tunnels that allows for anonymous communications. A computer linked to a TOR network transmitting data sends the data through a series of randomly selected proxy servers that strip away one layer of encryption along with the IP identification information. The IP information is replaced and the data are sent off to another proxy server to repeat the same process before connecting to another server for final distribution of the information. The effect is that observers of the network traffic on any of the proxy servers will neither be able to discern the true location of point A nor be able to tell what the destination of the data is, unless the observer can see the final transmission point.

An observer at point B will not know where the data is really coming from as only the location of the last proxy server from which the data arrived at point B can be detected. In this way a network address is masked—there is no direct link between the data packet's point of origin and final destination. However, an observer operating the TOR server node prior to the final connection might be able to detect digital artifacts within the network traffic providing clues to the user's identity and location.[32] While TOR certainly complicates attribution efforts, weaknesses exist that can be exploited to identify machines or persons on the Internet.

Wrongful Acts in Cyberspace

Global norms, institutions, and patterns of cooperation among state and private-sector stakeholders can serve as a foundation for solving the attribution problem in cyberspace. Norms of state responsibility in cyberspace must be institutionalized at the international level, and they must be enforced by relevant US government departments, including defense, state, justice, and commerce, and by other appropriate federal, national, state, and tribal agencies. Such a framework is essential to the creation of a successful cyberspace deterrence strategy.

In August 2001 the International Law Commission adopted the *Draft Articles on the Responsibility of States for Internationally Wrongful Acts* which established the principle of state responsibility in international law. It can be extended to cyber if the nature of a cyber attack is such that malicious data packets are traced back to national territory. Chapter 2, Article 4, states "the conduct of any State organ shall be considered an act of that State under international law, whether the organ exercises legislative, executive, judicial or any other function, whatever position it holds in the organization of the State, and whatever its character as an organ of the central Government or of a territorial unit of the State."[33] State responsibility might be extended to cyber attacks from national territory as an accepted principle of due diligence under the global culture of cybersecurity. That is, state responsibility could be inferred in an act of omission (as opposed to an act of commission).

Furthermore, Article 5 states "the conduct of a person or entity which is not an organ of the State under article 4 but which is empowered by the law of the State to exercise elements of the governmental authority shall be considered an act of the State under international law, provided the person or entity is acting in that capacity in the particular instance."[34]

How can a state be held responsible for activities in cyberspace? Some arguments focus on tests for the degree of control the state might have over nonstate actors within their territory.[35] Past precedent within the United Nations suggests that nonstate actors function as de facto agents of the state if the state harbors them. After the events of September 11, 2001, NATO attacked al-Qaeda and the Taliban. Few thought the Taliban controlled al-Qaeda, but they did not prevent their use of Afghan territory. The international community accepted intervention against a state for the actions of nonstate actors in part because the UN Security Council passed Resolution 1267 in 1999, placing sanctions on both al-Qaeda and the Afghan-Taliban. As recent analysis of nonstate actor success and failure suggests, groups lacking a safe haven and some level of state sponsorship are unsuccessful. Thus developing the norms suggested—which will largely eliminate safe havens and state sponsorship—is likely to serve as an effective deterrent.[36]

Sponsorship of "illegal" acts and actual control over nonstate actors within national territory are important. For example, if a state provides hacker tools online and encourages hackers to use those tools, the state is culpable for the hackers' actions. However, the level of official involvement is most often difficult to discern, much less prove. This is why the responsibility to respond, as stated in UN resolutions, is an important norm to sponsor and enforce. In the Estonia cyber attack of 2007, patriotic hackers in Russia were launching attacks against Estonia. However, since the Russian government was not openly encouraging the hackers, Russia could not be held responsible under the law of state responsibility. At the same time, it was not responding to requests for assistance, contrary to its support of the tenets of a global culture of cybersecurity in the UN and the ITU.

A Framework for Development, Diplomacy, and Defense

Cyber statecraft specialist Jason Healey has developed a taxonomy of actions for state responsibility.[37] It provides a useful framework for categorizing state actions regarding cyber attacks. It is a starting point for developing a broader response framework for actions or inactions in responding to cyber incidents. It is important to note that state-prohibited cyber attacks are those for which a state has laws against and for which it has sufficient enforcement mechanisms in place but they still occur. In such cases, the state is in violation of its responsibility to prevent its territory from being used against other states but is eligible for US aid in combating cyber crime. Refusing aid would place the state in a category for response.

The range of response options is one in which sanctions are either authorized bilaterally or pursued multilaterally. If there is some state involvement, US countermeasures could be justified. Effective control standard, a central component of any American action, requires proof of state involvement without any reasonable doubt.[38] The problem with this standard is that it relies on a world where perfect attribution exists. This world does not exist. On the other hand, the overall control standard that would allow a victim state to hold governments liable for damages caused by citizens acting on behalf of a competent government organ does exist. However, governments must be made aware of their obligation and the implications of failure to comply with their responsibility under international law.

Development, Diplomacy, and Defense Responses

In this section, a framework is introduced based on sponsoring global norms.[39] The development, diplomacy, and defense structure articulated within the White House's recent *International Cyber Strategy* is a positive step toward American sponsorship of global norms. As has been noted, embarking on a path that diverges from the accepted global culture of cybersecurity established within the ITU will result in noncooperation from many states and may lead to a perception that the United States is imperialistic in cyberspace.[40] Indeed, this is already the case.

Closed forums such as the Organization for Economic Cooperation and Development (OECD), which is being pursued as a vehicle to forward US Internet policy, will not serve the purpose of global cooperation to secure the cyber commons except among already likeminded states. A way forward would be for likeminded states to use the OECD and other regional councils to develop common positions that they can articulate and negotiate at the ITU. In this way, the United States could begin to manage the behaviors of states within their borders with broad support and cooperation with the international community at large. Thus, development, diplomacy, and defense could all be within the context of US sponsorship of global policy initiatives.

Development   Not all countries have an equal cyber investigations capacity. Some need assistance to help stem the flow of malicious activities through their borders, such as the ITU's toolkit for cyber crime legislation.[41] This is one way to provide technical assistance and education with a country, especially to government and law enforcement officials.

The White House's *International Strategy for Cyberspace* states that the United States:

> [W]ill expand and regularize initiatives focused on cybersecurity capacity building—with enhanced focus on awareness-raising, legal and technical training, and support for policy development. Such programs must address more than technology issues; we will work with states to recognize the breadth of the cybersecurity challenge, assist them in developing their own strategies, and build capacity across the whole range of sectors—from network security and the establishment of Computer Emergency Readiness Teams (CERTs), to international law enforcement and defense collaboration, to productive relationships with the domestic and international private sector and civil society.[42]

This echoes several of the elements of the global culture of cybersecurity, as well as the work being done within the ITU's IMPACT. With US sponsorship these endeavors could be undertaken within existing multilateral institutions. The existing institutional frameworks, such as those being developed at IMPACT, could be used to avoid duplicating efforts within frameworks accepted by other countries. This would avoid the risk of the United States appearing imperialistic.

Diplomacy To better offer technical assistance and development, partnerships with countries need to be established on the basis of trust and confidence. The White House strategy notes that "as countries develop a stake in cyberspace issues, we intend our dialogues to mature from capacity-building to active economic, technical, law enforcement, defense and diplomatic collaboration on issues of mutual concern."[43] The strategy also clearly articulates that the White House will take steps to "facilitate relationships among countries developing cybersecurity capacity—using both regional forums and technical bodies possessing specialized expertise—and will continue to promote the sharing of best practices, lessons learned, and international technical exchanges."[44] While these are positive words, the practice of forum picking should be abandoned. Despite the shortcomings of the ITU, the United States must lead within this institution to assure that others follow.

The DoD and the Air Force with its global mission also have roles to play in diplomacy. The 2011 *National Military Strategy* maintained that the DoD is essential in fostering regional and international cooperation in response to transnational threats. For example, cooperative security could be further developed by funneling transnational threats through combatant commanders who can leverage their resources "tailor[ed] to their region and coordinate[d] across regional seams."[45]

The Air Force conducts an array of diplomatic missions established in the *Air Force Security Cooperation Strategy* and performs many additional irregular and ad hoc diplomatic missions.[46] Given its cyber technical expertise, the Air Force would be optimally positioned to assist nations in their development—with foreign officer cybersecurity training within its Air University—and in building international partnerships for exchanging technical information on cyber attacks. Since the Air Force was the first to stand up its Cyber Command, Air Force experience would be useful in assisting friends and allies in standing up their own versions.

Stronger diplomatic initiatives would also be initiated for states that chose to continue down the path of ignoring, encouraging, shaping, and/or coordinating cyber attacks. The American policy community could also explore a framework for invoking Chapter VII of the UN Charter to authorize sanctions against countries that fail to abide by global norms of behavior in cyberspace. Proposals for new legal mechanisms on combating cyber crime and global cyber attacks have also been suggested.[47] However, these will be time-consuming legal obstacles similar to the UN Convention on the Law of the Sea and International Court of Justice processes; the same controversy surrounding the latter would likely exist with the formation of such institutions.

Both soft and coercive diplomacy thus serve to strengthen the role of capacity-building initiatives. They also provide institutional frameworks for cooperation among likeminded countries wishing to benefit from a trustworthy cyber environment. By eliminating the plausible deniability of states for the actions of groups within their territory, states would be denied the benefit of the doubt and would be held responsible for their actions, with consequences following their inaction or belligerence.

Defense   Inevitably, the United States will face adversaries who order, execute, and integrate attacks and may cooperate with rogue entities. The role of defense within the cyber domain is to "be prepared to demonstrate the will and commit the resources needed to oppose any nation's actions that jeopardize access to and use of the global commons and cyberspace, or that threaten the security of our allies."[48] Holding states responsible for their actions within this domain would not present a challenge since a state's government forces could be directly executing a cyber attack. Defensive options for cyber could include:

1. Throttling Internet traffic
2. Blocking Internet traffic
3. Offensive computer operations in hot pursuit
4. Kinetic attacks in response to cyber events of national significance

It is important to note that responses 1 and 2 are not easy given that the private sector controls the infrastructure that the DoD uses in such a response. Additionally, the argument can be made that such measures are contrary to the free flow of information across the global networks. A proper policy framework could dictate the terms under which a state was inhibiting the free flow of information globally through its failure to restrain cyber attacks within its sovereign territory. A discussion is thus required to articulate exactly what degree of negligence or what kind of attacks will constitute certain types of responses.

Sanctions, blocking, throttling, and other actions are all options short of war. Conflict in cyberspace that escalates into kinetic attacks could occur if the effects of cyber attack are consequential enough—attacks against critical infrastructures that create effects of national significance. In *Cyber War*, Richard Clarke offers many such hypothetical scenarios. However, this would be a policy decision and not an automatic response. A state may not even care to mask its involvement in the attack, thereby obviating the attribution challenge altogether.[49]

Linking It All Together

It is often argued that "attribution of a cyber attack to a state is a— if not *the*—key element in building a functioning legal regime to mitigate these attacks (emphasis in the original)."[50] Others suggest that standards for technical evidence—admissible in US or international courts—are far from development and perhaps unnecessary.[51] Drafting treaties for cyberspace that include enunciating state cyberspace accountability and obligations to assist have been suggested.[52] Such would be a desired outcome. Multi-stage and multi-jurisdictional attacks launched by cyber superpowers are on the rise, and negotiating such agreements will take years if not decades. An alternative approach is to shift away from technical attribution and move toward creating the policy tools that will allow for the United States to hold states responsible for actions that occur in their sovereign cyberspace. In many respects, this is a two-pronged approach to creating a more effective deterrence framework for cyberspace. The reality is that without the United States taking the lead, credible cyber deterrence is unlikely.

National cyber policies and statements by senior officials have all suggested an emphasis in cybersecurity on the creation of global norms of cyber behavior without specifying what the norms should look like. For the past decade, the UN and the Cyber Centre of Excellence (COE) have laid the groundwork for international norms with cooperation from private parties within multilateral processes. Examples include the World Summit on the Information Society and the Internet Governance Forum. The United States has been active in venues such as the OECD in developing behavioral norms, but less active in the ITU/UN forums. Although the institutionalization of global norms is progressing, the United States is absent in promoting and enforcing the ITU/UN norms of cyber behavior.

Legislative Language for "Victims of Trafficking of Malicious Code"

What is required for US government sponsorship is legislation to mandate international engagement on cyber crime. Current draft legislation, such as the *Cybersecurity Act of 2012*, is indicative of movement in Congress toward legislative action. Sections of the bill include provisions for the coordination of international cyber issues with the US government, and consideration of cyber crime in foreign policy and foreign assistance programs.[53] Overall, what is needed is a framework for engagement in multilateral and bilateral diplomacy to develop frameworks for international cooperation and development to enhance foreign nation capabilities to combat cyber threats.

Legislation

One difference between the *Trafficked Victims Protection Act* (TVPA) model and a potential adaptation of it for cyber attacks is that the DoD should be mandated to serve as the data clearinghouse pertaining to state behavior of cyber attacks. Current draft legislation places the overarching international engagement strategy within the Department of State. However, unlike in human trafficking, where the sources of information are non-governmental organizations (NGOs) with whom the DoS maintains close affiliations via its diplomatic work, the DoD has the technical capacity and relationships with private entities to provide both accurate annual reports wherein countries would be ranked as well as capacity-building mechanisms. The US Air Force in particular is best suited to provide its best practices and lessons learned to nations requiring development assistance.

Further steps are required—with Congress drafting legislation similar to TVPA—to create the framework for guiding the government's efforts to name and shame countries in cyberspace. Minimum standards would need to be created for the elimination of cyber crime applicable to the government for a country of origin, transit, or destination of a malicious code used to execute severe cyber attacks. The following elements should be included as minimum standards that would be indicative of a government making serious and sustained efforts to eliminate cyber crime:

- Review and update legal authorities that may be outdated or obsolete and develop necessary legislation for investigation and prosecution of cyber crime, including extradition measures.
- Determine key stakeholders from national and local governments, industry, civil society, and academia with a role in cybersecurity to develop networks and processes of international cooperation to enhance incident response and contingency planning.
- Assure prosecutors, judges, and legislators have an adequate level of understanding of cyber issues.
- Create a government point of contact that monitors data patterns for evidence of malicious cyber activities.
- Create a 24/7 international cyber crime contact (CERT/ Computer Security Incident Response Team [CSIRT]) to cooperate with international counterparts for investigating transnational malicious cyber events in those instances in which infrastructure is situated in or perpetrators reside in national territory but victims reside elsewhere.
- For the knowing commission of any cyber attack involving officials who are members of the government of a country, said country should prescribe punishment commensurate with that for grave crimes, such as criminal behavior or armed attacks.
- For the knowing commission of any cyber attack, the government of the country should prescribe punishment that is sufficiently stringent to deter and that adequately reflects the reality of the offense.

In addition to the above factors, the following factors should be considered as an indication of serious and sustained efforts to eliminate cyber crime and cyber attacks from a country:

- Vigorous investigation and prosecution of acts of cyber crime that take place wholly or partly within the territory of the country, including, as appropriate, requiring incarceration of individuals convicted of such attacks. A government that does not provide data regarding investigations, prosecutions, convictions, and sentences after requests from the US government, consistent with the capacity of such government to obtain such data, shall be presumed not to have vigorously investigated, prosecuted, or sentenced such acts.

- Prevention and education: Whether the government of the country has adopted measures to prevent cyber crime, such as measures to inform and educate the public, including potential victims, about the causes and consequences of cyber crime.
- Whether the government of the country cooperates with other governments in the investigation and prosecution of cyber crime.
- Whether the government of the country extradites persons charged with malicious cyber acts on substantially the same terms and extent as persons charged with serious crimes or, to the extent such extradition would be inconsistent with the laws of such country or with international agreements to which the country is a party, whether the government is taking all appropriate measures to modify or replace such laws and treaties so as to permit such extradition.
- Whether the government monitors data patterns for evidence of malicious cyber activities and whether law enforcement agencies of the country respond to any such evidence in a manner that is consistent with vigorous investigation and prosecution.
- Whether the government of the country vigorously investigates, prosecutes, convicts, and sentences public officials who participate in or facilitate cyber attacks, including nationals of the country who are deployed abroad.
- After reasonable requests from the Department of State for data regarding such investigations, prosecutions, convictions, and sentences, a government that does not provide such data consistent with its resources shall be presumed not to have vigorously investigated, prosecuted, convicted, or sentenced such acts.
- Whether the victims of malicious cyber incidents in the country are noncitizens of such countries is insignificant.

Solving the cyber problem and developing a credible deterrence strategy rely on having a framework passed through Congress that allows the United States to bring its elements of power to bear as mechanisms for enforcement of global norms. As recent strategic documents suggest, strengthening international partnerships to secure the cyber domain requires an understanding of what gaps exist in the capabilities of international partners within the technical, legal, and organizational domains.[54] Identifying these gaps and their causes will provide the US policy community with the knowledge required to support partners to strengthen their national cybersecurity, thereby contributing to a cyber environment less hospitable to attempted misuse.

Leading by Example: US-Based Entities Responsibility

In addition to holding countries responsible, the US government needs to understand that it has its own role to play in securing the global commons. Undoubtedly, industry will push back against regulatory efforts. But, with the potential effect of destructive activities, both economically and militarily, it is time that goodwill and industrial volunteerism are scrapped for a regulatory framework that provides incentives for or punishment of industry in order to encourage compliance with minimum standards. Any regulatory framework must be crafted on the basis of policies informed by technical realities to assure a positive impact. Doing so will give the United States more legitimacy as a leader in the fight to hold other states responsible while also having a positive impact on the public good.

US-Based Internet Intermediaries

Germany, Japan, and other countries have developed partnerships that involve industries voluntarily setting up processes for ISPs to notify subscribers whose computers are suspected of being infected by malware. Security experts caution that imposing policy objectives on Internet intermediaries could impact competition by favoring large, established firms. They also indicate that additional security risks could be generated because intermediaries would have to build surveillance and control systems that may invite abuse.[55]

However, much like the auto industry fought against the introduction of safety belts in the mid-twentieth century, industry will also see that a peaceful and prosperous cyberspace is only possible through government regulations. For starters, ISPs should also be held responsible under a regulatory framework for malicious activities that occur within their systems. The largest number of network attacks originates from the United States. US-based entities own a large percentage of the Internet backbone, in addition to more localized access points onto the global network. However, they appear reluctant to invest in initiatives that could significantly curb malicious activities originating on US networks. Comcast's Web notification system "is being used to provide near-immediate notifications to customers, such as to warn them that their traffic exhibits patterns that are indicative of malware or virus infection."[56] Such systems are good indicators that industry is moving forward on cybersecurity; however, there needs to be a more proactive effort on their part to assure that malicious software does not infest their customers' computers.

Where Do We Go from Here?

The only way forward for a formal international agreement is to hold states accountable for malicious activities either originating from or transiting their territories. In order to achieve this objective, the United States should sponsor existing international frameworks and institutions to hold states responsible for such negative cyber actions.

Attribution of a cyber attack requires a rapid response to the event and is often difficult to determine with absolute certainty. Experts have suggested that the high standard of evidence for criminal prosecution is not required from a purely legal standpoint.[57] Instead, the technical community increasingly does not view attribution as a technical problem. It is state and nonstate actors who exploit the lack of international law and cooperation by routing their multi-stage attacks through multiple jurisdictions to camouflage their activities and identities.[58] The White House strategy recognizes this and, in its clearest advocacy of one norm of state responsibility, states that such cooperation "is a responsibility and duty that every nation, and its people, all share."[59] This statement implies that states may be held responsible for actions their citizens take within cyberspace. What is required is for the United States to begin documenting the capabilities of states to enact and enforce laws against cyber crime and their cooperation in international cyber crime investigations.

The United States has recently begun to pursue an international cyber policy aimed at promoting international cooperation within political and military contexts. While attribution is often considered to be a complex technical problem that presents many challenges in responding to cyber attack, the focus is too often on the technical components from which cyberspace has emerged. Aiding technical attribution is what Herb Lin describes as "All source attribution...a process that integrates information from all sources, not just technical sources at the scene of the attack, to arrive at a judgement (rather than a definitive proof) concerning the identity of the attack."[60] While this framing is within the law enforcement context of identifying which individual is responsible for an attack, it may be extended to the national security context to judge from which state an attack is originating or transiting through. From there, it becomes that state's responsibility to identify and prosecute the perpetrators, cooperate in investigations, or take measures to reduce the risk of their Internet infrastructure being used as a pivot point for malicious actors to send their code through. Should a state decide not to take such measures, then its government can be held responsible for any damages that occur. The level of responsibility and response could then be guided by a policy toolkit modeled on the anti-trafficking agenda described above. With the large number of victims of cyber crime worldwide, the United States could deal directly with individual governments on the issue—and be met with little criticism.

Recent cyber policy documents detail the strengthening of international partnerships for securing the cyber domain. They require an understanding of the existing gaps in the capabilities of allies and partners within the technical, legal, and organizational domains.[61] To improve the US government's effectiveness in achieving the objectives described in the preceding pages, the Air Force should utilize its cyber capabilities to provide the wider interagency community with an empirically based approach to developing credible cyber deterrence. This will require the Air Force to identify existing gaps, determine their causes, and provide the policy community with the knowledge required to support allies and partners in strengthening their national cybersecurity. The result will invigorate international cooperation and create a cyber environment that is less hospitable to malicious actors—deterring their acts. Admittedly, even if credible, deterrence will not always work. The continued threat of war demonstrates that deterrence periodically fails. However, increasing the number of instances in which it works, through the means described above, will assist in making cyberspace a safer and more secure domain.

Endnotes

1. Joseph Nye, Nuclear Lessons for Cyber Security? *Strategic Studies Quarterly* Vol. 4, No. 4 (Winter 2011), 21.
2. David D. Clark and Susan Landau, The Problem Isn't Attribution: It's Multi-Stage Attacks, in *ReArch 2010: Proceedings of the Re-Architecting the Internet Workshop* (New York: Association for Computing Machinery, 2010), 1, http://conferences.sigcomm.org/co-next/2010/Workshops/REARCH/ReArch_papers/11-Clark.pdf.
3. Technical attribution refers to "the ability to associate an attack with a responsible party through technical means based on information made available by the cyber operation itself—that is, technical attribution is based on clues available at the scene (or scenes) of the operation." Herbert Lin, Escalation Dynamics and Conflict Termination in Cyberspace, *Strategic Studies Quarterly* Vol. 6, No. 3 (Fall 2012), 46–70.
4. Thomas C. Schelling, *Arms and Influence* (New Haven, CT: Yale University Press), 1–35.
5. See Dimitri Alperovitch, *Revealed: Operation Shady RAT* (McAfee White Paper version 1.1 2011), http://www.mcafee.com/us/resources/white-papers/wp-operation-shady-rat.pdf.
6. Articulated global norms of behavior include UN General Assembly (UNGA). Developments in the field of information and telecommunications in the context of international security, A/RES/56/19, preliminary para.7, January 7, 2002, UN General Assembly, Combating the Criminal Misuse of Information Technologies A/RES/Resolution 56/121 (2002), UN General Assembly, Creation of a global culture of cybersecurity, A/RES/57/239, preliminary para. 5, January 31, 2003, http://www.itu.int/ITU-D/cyb/cybersecurity/docs/UN_resolution_57 _239.pdf. For more on norms development and the norms life cycle see Martha Finnemore and Kathryn Sikkink, International Norm Dynamics and Political Change, *International Organization* 52 (Autumn, 1998): 887–917, Simon Reich with Panayotis Yannakogeorgos, *Global Norms, American Sponsorship and the Emerging Pattern of World Politics* (New York: Palgrave 2010).

7. Solange Ghernouti-Hélie, A National Strategy for an Effective Cybersecurity Approach and Culture, presentation at the International Conference on Availability, Reliability, and Security (Krakow, Poland, February 15–18, 2010), http://www.computer.org/portal/web/csdl/doi/10.1109/ARES.2010.119.

8. Robert Gates, *Quadrennial Defense Review Report* (Washington, DC: Department of Defense, 2010), 37–39. See also Barack Obama, *National Security Strategy* (Washington, DC: White House, 2010), 28.

9. Jason Healey, The Spectrum of National Responsibility for Cyber Attacks, *Brown Journal of World Affairs* Vol. 18, No. 1 (2011), 57–70. Sean Kanuck, Sovereign Discourse on Cyber Conflict under International Law, *Texas Law Review* Vol. 88 (2010), 1571–1597. Panayotis Yannakogeorgos and L. Mattice, Strategically Using Global Norms to Resolve the Cyber Attribution Challenge, Essential Questions for Cyber Policy (Montgomery, AL: Air University Press, 2011).

10. Michele Zanini and Sean Edwards, The Networking of Terror in the Information Age, in John Arquilla and David Ronfeldt, Eds., *Networks and Netwars* (Santa Monica, CA: RAND, 2001), 29–60.

11. Neal Ungerleider, The Chinese Way of Hacking. *Fast Company* (July 13, 2011), http://www.fastcompany.com/1766812/chinese-way-hacking.

12. James A. Reddy, People's Republic of Hacking, *Wall Street Journal* (February 20, 2010), A1.

13. This can be attributed to Chinese interpretations of cyber crime. Their definition includes content and, thus, using Facebook to mount jasmine revolutions would be considered a crime in China, whereas the United States considers such actions as social networking enabling the development of democracy (in most cases).

14. US-China Economic and Security Review Commission, Occupying the Information High Ground: Chinese Capabilities for Computer Network Operations and Cyber Espionage, http://www.uscc.gov/RFP/2012/USCC%20Report_Chinese_CapabilitiesforComputer_NetworkOperationsandCyberEspionage.pdf.

15. Michael Levi, *On Nuclear Terrorism* (Cambridge, MA: Harvard University Press, 2007), 127.

16. Air Force Doctrine Document (AFDD) 3-12, *Cyberspace Operations*, 2010, 10.

17. Howard F. Lipson, *Tracking and Tracing Cyber-Attacks: Technical Challenges and Global Policy Issues*, Special report no. CMU/SEI-2002-SR-009 (Pittsburgh, PA: Carnegie Mellon University, Software Engineering Institute, 2002), 3–5.

18. See Dimitri Alperovitch, *Revealed: Operation Shady RAT*, McAfee White Paper version 1.1 2011, http://www.mcafee.com/us/resources/white-papers/wp-operation-shady-rat.pdf.

19. Federal Bureau of Investigation, Manhattan U.S. Attorney and FBI Assistant Director in Charge Announce Additional Arrests as Part of International Cyber Crime Takedown, (July 11, 2012), http://www.fbi.gov/newyork/press-releases/2012/

manhattan-u.s.-attorney-and-fbi-assistant-director-in-charge-announce-additional-arrests-as-part-of-international-cyber-crime-take-down/.

20. White House, *International Strategy for Cyberspace, Prosperity, Security, and Openness in a Networked World,* (May 2011), 14, http://www.whitehouse.gov/sites/default/files/rss_viewer/international_strategy_for_cyberspace.pdf.

21. Ibid., 11.

22. Ibid., 14.

23. Martin C. Libicki, *Cyberdeterrence and Cyberwar* (Santa Monica, CA: RAND Corporation, 2009), 41–52, 99–100. David D. Clark and Susan Landau, Untangling Attribution, in *Proceedings of a Workshop on Deterring Cyberattacks: Informing Strategies and Developing Options for U.S. Policy* (Washington, DC: National Research Council, The National Academies Press, 2010), 25, http://www.nap.edu/catalog/12997.html.

24. A note of caution with the hope latched onto IPv6. While it works well on a small scale, it will still contain vulnerabilities that may not be known until deployed on a large scale. New security vulnerabilities will be discovered and exploited, and the learning curve will be just as steep as for the deployment of IPv4.

25. David D. Clark and Susan Landau, Untangling Attribution, *Harvard National Security Journal* Vol. 2 (Summer 2011), 531–533.

26. TCP/IP is standardized by the International Organization of Standards (ISO) for the Open Systems Interconnection (OSI) model as the basis of Internet and other networking.

27. See Howard F. Lipson, *Tracking and Tracing Cyber-Attacks: Technical Challenges and Global Policy Issues,* Special report no. CMU/SEI-2002-SR-009 (Pittsburgh, PA: Software Engineering Institute, Carnegie Mellon University, 2002).

28. Mitch Waldorp, DARPA and the Internet Revolution, *DARPA* (2008), 79–85. See also Tom Leighton, The Net's Real Security Problem, *Scientific American* (September 2006), 44.

29. Ibid., 44.

30. As part of its Internet freedom agenda, the US State Department, in cooperation with Internet companies, is distributing tools for and running seminars on how to mask identity in cyberspace. While the goal is the free flow of information, these tools and tactics can be used to attack US-based information systems as well. This does not contribute to a safe cyber ecosystem.

31. Dorothy E. Denning, Cyberspace Attacks and Countermeasures, in *Internet Besieged: Countering Cyberspace Scofflaws,* Dorothy E. Denning and Peter J. Denning, Eds. (New York: ACM Press, 1998), 35.

32. Kim Zetter, Rogue Nodes Turn TOR Anonymizer into Eavesdropper's Paradise, *Wired* (September 10, 2007), http://www.wired.com/politics/security/news/2007/09/embassy_hacks?currentPage=1.

33. UN General Assembly, Articles on Responsibility of States for Internationally Wrongful Acts, in *Yearbook of the International Law Commission*, Resolution 56/83, 2001, vol. 2 (pt. 2), chap. 2, art. 4. Adopted by the commission at its 53d sess., 2001, and submitted to the General Assembly as part of the commission's report covering the work of that session.

34. Ibid., chap. 2, art. 5.

35. S.J. Shackelford, State Responsibility for Cyber Attacks: Competing Standards for a Growing Problem, http://irps.ucsd.edu/assets/001/501281.pdf.

36. Adam Lowther, *Americans and Asymmetric Conflict* (Westport, CT: Praeger, 2007), 40–50.

37. Jason Healey, *Beyond Attribution: A Vocabulary for National Responsibility for Cyber Attacks* (Vienna, VA: Cyber Conflict Studies Association, 2010), 4.

38. Scott J. Shackelford, State Responsibility for Cyber Attacks: Competing Standards for a Growing Problem, 120.

39. It should be noted that the stages of covert activity could also be classified in the category of "short of war." However, covert action requires a presidential finding. The processes and political risks involved in the planning and execution of covert activity are beyond the scope of this chapter.

40. See Simon Reich, *Global Norms, American Sponsorship and the Emerging Patterns of World Politics* (New York: Palgrave-McMillan, 2010).

41. International Telecommunications Union, *ITU Toolkit for Cybercrime Legislation*, Geneva: International Telecommunications Union, 2010.

42. Barack Obama, *International Strategy for Cyberspace* (Washington, DC: White House, 2011), 15.

43. Ibid.

44. Ibid.

45. Joint Chiefs of Staff, *National Military Strategy* (Washington, DC: Department of Defense, 2011), 14.

46. Gen John A. Shaud, *Air Force Strategy Study 2020–2030* (Maxwell AFB, AL: Air University Press, 2010), 15.

47. Stein Schjolberg, *An International Criminal Court or Tribunal for Cyberspace (ICTC)* (Washington, DC: *East West Institute Cybercrime Legal Working Group*, 2011).

48. Joint Chiefs of Staff, *National Military Strategy*, 14.

49. See Martin Libicki, *Cyberdeterrence and Cyberwar* (Santa Monica, CA: Rand Publishing, 2009).

50. Shackelford, 201.

51. David D. Clark and Susan Landau, Untangling Attribution, 4.

52. Richard A. Clarke and Robert K. Knake, *Cyber War: The Next Threat to National Security and What to Do About It* (New York: HarperCollins, 2010), 251–253. See also Jason Healey, The Spectrum of National Responsibility for Cyberattacks, *Brown Journal of World Affairs* Vol. 18 (Fall/Winter 2011), 57–69.

53. See House, *Draft Bill to Enhance the Security and Resiliency of the Cyber and Communications Infrastructure of the United States*, 112th Congress, 2012.

54. Robert Gates, *Quadrennial Defense Review Report*, 37–39. See also Barack Obama, *National Security Strategy*, 28.
55. Organization for Economic Co-operation and Development (OECD), *The Role Of Internet Intermediaries in Advancing Public Policy Objectives* (Paris: OECD, 2011).
56. C. Chung, A. Kasyanov, J. Livingood, N. Mody, and B. Van Lieu, Comcast's Web Notification System Design, *Request for Comments 6108* (February 2011), http://tools.ietf.org/html/rfc6108.
57. David D. Clark and Susan Landau, Untangling Attribution, 4. Criminal investigations where cyber evidence would not be permissible in court provides law enforcement authorities other leads, such as money trails, that eventually allow for the apprehension and prosecution of a suspect.
58. Ibid., 39.
59. Barack Obama, *International Strategy for Cyberspace*, 8.
60. Herb Lin, Escalation Dynamics and Conflict Termination in Cyberspace, *Strategic Studies Quarterly* (Fall 2012) Vol. 6, No. 3, 46–70.
61. Robert Gates, *2010 Quadrennial Defense Review Report*, 37–39. See also Barack Obama, *National Security Strategy*, 28.

PART II
TECHNOLOGY

7

CHALLENGES IN MONITORING CYBERARMS COMPLIANCE

NEIL C. ROWE

SIMSON L. GARFINKEL

ROBERT BEVERLY

PANAYOTIS A. YANNAKOGEORGOS[*]

Contents

Introduction	81
Approach	83
Models for Cyberweapons Use	84
Technical Obstacles	86
Analysis of Drives to Find Cyberweapons	86
Network Monitoring for Cyberweapons	88
Encouraging More Responsible Cyberweapons	91
Support for International Cyberarms Cooperation in the United States	93
Conclusion	96
Bibliography	97

Introduction

Cyberweapons are digital objects that can be used to achieve military objectives by disabling key functions of computer systems and networks. They can be malicious software installed secretly through concealed downloads or deliberate plants by human agents, or they can

---

[*] The views expressed are those of the authors and do not represent those of any part of the US government.

be malicious data or maliciously delivered data as in denial-of-service attacks. Cyberweapons are a growing component in military arsenals (Libicki, 2007). Increasingly countries are instituting "cyberattack corps" with capabilities to launch attacks in cyberspace on other countries as an instrument of war, either alone or combined with attacks by conventional military forces (Clarke and Knake, 2010). Cyberattacks appeal to many military commanders. They seem to require fewer resources to mount since their delivery can be accomplished in small payloads such as malicious devices or packets that can be primarily delivered through existing infrastructure such as the Internet. They also seem "cleaner" than conventional weapons in that their damage is primarily to data and data can be repaired, although they are difficult to control and usually entail actions close to perfidy, something outlawed by the laws of war (Rowe, 2010). Cyberweapons can be developed with modest technological infrastructure, even by underdeveloped countries (Gady, 2010), by taking advantages of international resources. So there is a threat of cyberattacks from "rogue states" such as North Korea and terrorist groups that hold extreme points of view, as well as from countries with well-developed cyberweapons capabilities such as China.

Many information-security tools we use today to control threats and vulnerabilities with criminal cyberattacks (Brenner, 2010) help against the cyberweapon threat. Good software engineering practices in design and construction of software, access controls on systems and data, and system and network monitoring for suspicious activity all help. But they are insufficient to stop cyberattacks today because there are ways, albeit challenging, to subvert each of them, and the increasing complexity of cybersystems provides increasing opportunities for finding flaws in software. State-sponsored cyberattacks should be especially hard to prevent because states can exploit significant resources and can use them to develop highly sophisticated attacks. States will likely employ a variety of methods simultaneously to achieve a high probability of success, and will test them considerably more carefully than the hit-or-miss approach of most criminal attacks today. Such challenging state-sponsored cyberattacks will be difficult or impossible to defend against with current information-security defensive techniques.

Approach

What can be done against such threats then? We believe that countries must negotiate international agreements similar to those for nuclear, chemical, and biological weapons. Such agreements (treaties, conventions, protocols, and memoranda of understanding) (Croft, 1996) can stipulate the ways in which cyberweapons can be used, as for instance stipulating that countries use cyberweapons only in a counterattack to a cyberattack. Agreements can also stipulate policing of citizens such as "hacker" groups within a country, so that a nation cannot shift blame for cyberattacks and cyberweapons onto them. A few such agreements are in place today for cybercrime, but the growing threat suggests that it is time to plan out what such agreements will entail and how they should be enforced. As an example, the EastWest Institute in the United States recently proposed a cyberwar "Geneva Convention" (Rooney, 2011). Deterrence, a key aspect of nuclear weapons control, is not possible with cyberweapons because revealing capabilities significantly impedes their effectiveness.

Johnson (2002) was skeptical of the ability to implement cyberarms control, citing the difficulty of monitoring compliance. But his arguments are less valid today. Cyberweapons are no longer a "cottage industry" but require significant infrastructure for finding exploits, finding targets, gaining access, managing the attacks, and concealing the attacks. This necessary infrastructure leaves traces even when concealed. The cyberweapon infrastructure needs to be increasingly complex because target software, systems, and networks are increasingly hardened and complex, and because vulnerabilities are being found and fixed faster than ever. Advances in network monitoring make it possible to detect coordinated attacks and remote control of one machine by another as in botnets, since botnets need aggregate effects to be useful to attackers, and aggregate effects can be detected with statistics. Digital forensics has advanced significantly since 2002, making it possible to find many useful things about digital artifacts. Anonymity and encryption techniques that attackers depend upon are easy to see and are good clues to something suspicious. Some techniques central for criminal cyberattacks today such as code obfuscation have little legitimate use and are good indicators of cyberattack development and hence, in the right context, cyberweapons.

Thus many international agreements on cyberweapons could be feasibly monitored despite the challenges. The situation is similar to that with chemical weapons for which there are, for example, many methods for making mustard gas that can use easily available chemicals with legitimate uses. Although proving that a facility is used for chemical or biological weapons production is difficult, the type of equipment at a facility can provide a good probability that it has been used to manufacture such weapons, as U.N. inspectors realized in Iraq in the 1990s when they discovered evidence of airlocks in alleged food-production facilities. International conventions banning chemical and biological weapons have been effective despite the difficulties of verifying production and stockpiling of such weapons (Price, 1997). We think that similar examinations, and therefore conventions, should be possible in the cyberdomain. For instance, even if developers of cyberweapons delete or hide evidence on their disks, there are often ways to reconstruct it such as finding data deleted but not yet overwritten, data assembly from fragments (Garfinkel, 2006), and examination of magnetic residues.

Cyberinspection technology can have other uses, too. It helps law enforcement, military organizations, and intelligence communities within a country in examining captured computer systems belonging to suspected criminals or terrorists for cyberweapons.

We realize that policy is too often driven by crises, so it may take a serious cyberattack to interest a country in negotiating cyberarms limitations. Such a cyberattack is technically feasible (Clarke and Knake, 2010) and could happen at any time. Model agreements can be developed in advance of a crisis. In the meantime, progress can be made by international organizations in negotiating broad cyberarms agreements as well as more specific agreements that can be used against rogue states and organizations.

Models for Cyberweapons Use

Two recent cases provide possible models for future cyberwarfare. One is the cyberattacks on Georgia in August 2008 (discussed in Rowe, 2011). Attacks were launched to coincide with a military invasion of Georgia by Russia (the "South Ossetia War") and appeared to be well planned and timed. These were primarily denial-of-service attacks against predominantly Georgian government Web sites, including some Web-site defacement (USCCU, 2009). Some of the attacking machines were known malware hosts, some were new sites created specifically for the attack, some were botnets of otherwise innocent computers, and some were machines of people recruited to attack from social-networking sites. None of these were government or military sites.

The targets of the attack were government and business organizations in Georgia that were viewed as key in withstanding the conventional military attack by Russia that followed shortly thereafter. They included government agencies associated with communications as well as news-media organizations, apparently with the goal of making it difficult for Georgians to determine what was happening. Later attacks broadened the scope to financial and educational institutions, as well as businesses associated with particular kinds of infrastructure. These cyberattacks were clearly targeted at civilians and were targeted precisely. Reconstruction of the attacks was possible from a variety of international resources since Internet traffic is routed through many countries. While the attribution of the perpetrators of the attacks does not meet standards of international law, the circumstantial evidence is strong for the involvement of sources in Russia. This conclusion was reached by the US Cyber Consequences Unit by piecing together Internet traffic records (USCCU, 2009).

The other important recent case is the so-called "Stuxnet" worm and corresponding exploits targeting industrial-control systems (Markoff, 2010). These used traditional malware methods for modifying programs. Since Stuxnet targeted systems with no financial incentive, it was most likely developed by an information-warfare group of a nation-state. After the attack, forensic investigators discovered many distinctive properties of the attack software. For example, it used previously unknown attacks and a variety of concealment methods, and it appears to have targeted a specific industrial control system associated with uranium enrichment. These features were unusual in cyberattacks. Stuxnet was discovered because it spread far beyond its intended target although its damage was highly targeted. This dissemination was necessary to propagate it to its targets and was a clue to the international community that something was happening. So even though Stuxnet was a highly sophisticated cyberattack, it was recognized quickly by the international community.

Technical Obstacles

We discuss three key technical challenges to achieving international cyberarms control: (1) locating cyberarms on computers, (2) noticing cyberarms use, and (3) developing more responsible kinds of cyberweapons. Cyberarms also raise important challenges to the laws of warfare that we do not have space to discuss here, including distinguishing a cyberweapon from other malicious software, assigning legal responsibility for a cyberattack, and setting norms for proportional and discriminatory counterattacks (Wingfield, 2009).

Analysis of Drives to Find Cyberweapons

The United States analyzed a number of captured computers and devices in its recent military operations in Iraq and Afghanistan. This was useful in identifying insurgent networks and their interconnections. Similarly, a good deal can be learned about a country's or terrorist group's cyberweapons from the computers used to develop or deploy them. Alternatively, a country may agree to forego cyberweapons as part of a negotiated settlement of a conflict and may agree to submit to periodic inspections to confirm this (United Nations, 1991).

Detection of cyberweapons might seem difficult. But there are precedents in the detection of nuclear, chemical, and biological weapons (O'Neill, 2010). Cyberweapons development generally requires unusual computer usage in secret facilities since most cyberweapons require secrecy to be effective, which rules out most software development facilities. Clues to cyberweapons can also be found inside computers. Certain types of software technology such as code obfuscation and spamming tools are good clues to malicious intent. Code for known attacks (for providing reuse opportunities) and stolen proprietary code such as Windows source code (for testing attacks) are other good clues. Technologies such as systematic code testers, "fuzzing" utilities, and code for remote control of other computers provide supporting evidence of cyberweapons development though they have some legitimate uses. Data alone can be a clue, such as detailed reconnaissance information on adversary computer networks. Diversity of software techniques is a clue to cyberweapons development, because the unreliability of cyberweapons encourages the use of multiple methods. Once suspected cyberweapons are found, they can be studied systematically to confirm their nature using malware analysis (Malin, Casey, and Aquilina, 2008).

A cyberweapons inspection would have to be performed on-site and with automated tools, as a party to a cybermonitoring regime would not allow a potential adversary to remove materials from a secret facility. Cyberweapon monitors would likely be required to use bootable read-only storage that would contain programs to analyze the contents of a computer system and look for evidence of cyber-weapon development. Inspection would require a scheme for obtaining temporary use of the necessary passwords and keys for the systems inspected, which could be aided by "key escrow" methods. Inspection regimes should also require "write-blockers" to assure that the monitors did not themselves plant cyberweapons on the systems being monitored. Other useful ideas from monitoring of nuclear capabilities (O'Neill, 2010) include agreed inspector entry into the inspected country within a time limit, allowed banning of certain inspectors, designation of off-limits areas, and limits on what kind of evidence can be collected.

A good prototype of what can be done in analysis of drives is our work on the Real Data Corpus, our collection of drive images (computer disks, mobile device storage, and storage devices) collected from around the world. Currently this collection includes 1467 images. Recent work has characterized disks and drives as a whole, including understanding what is distinctive about the files in each of several dimensions such as file size, number of image files, number of deleted files, and number of files frequently edited (Rowe and Garfinkel, 2011). Clusters of files that have no counterpart for others in a corpus are particularly interesting and can be the focus of more detailed forensic analysis. For quicker analysis, random pieces of files can be selected, and this can be surprisingly good at identifying many types of data (Garfinkel et al., 2010). Deception markers in particular can be sought since illegal cyberweapons development would need to be concealed. Deception could be in the form of oddly named, renamed, or encrypted files, and could be enhanced by other techniques such as changing the system clock or manipulating a log file.

In a histogram of the mean suspiciousness metric on files of 325 Windows disk drives in our corpus (Rowe and Garfinkel, 2011), the suspiciousness metric included the use of double file extensions, long file extensions, rarity of the file extension, and presence of large numbers of nonalphabetic characters in the file path. These are clues to concealment because double file extensions and nonalphabetic characters suggest concealment of purpose, and long and rare file extensions suggest anomalous usage of a computer. Several drives were unusually suspicious, beyond what would be expected in the Poisson distribution of most values, and most of these were in fact suspicious. This analysis only took a few seconds per drive and could save inspectors time in hunting for cyberweapons.

Another way to simplify inspections is to cluster the files of a drive into meaningful groups such as images, spreadsheets, and programs, and calculate statistics on groups. This way an inspector could first focus on group differences and not be overwhelmed by large numbers of files. An investigator should examine files in small superclusters of executable files to have a better chance of finding malicious software.

Network Monitoring for Cyberweapons

Many tools can discriminate legitimate from abusive network traffic. Such inferential intrusion detection has limitations due to the difficulty of defining malicious traffic in a sufficiently general way without incurring a large number of false positives (Sommer and Paxson, 2010; Trost, 2010). But the attack landscape is different for politically and economically motivated state-sponsored cyberattacks:

1. *Targets*: State-sponsored attacks will be targeted to particular regions and political agendas, in contrast to criminal attacks which usually target victims indiscriminately.
2. *Sophistication*: Cyberarms will be the product of well-funded nations with significant resources. Thus they will use new and sophisticated techniques rather than those of the common attacks we see on the Internet. That means that we can ignore most malicious traffic we see when searching for cyberweapons usage. While some initial stages of cyberweapons activity will be hard to detect—this is why we need international agreements about them—to be useful weapons, cyberweapons must

eventually produce a significant effect, and that effect should be easy to see. The Georgia attacks, for instance, were obvious.

3. *Attribution*: As with conventional warfare, the warring parties will likely follow specified (nondigital) protocols. Protocols will likely dictate that combatants reveal who they are at least in general terms so that the attacks will achieve the desired political effect.

These features provide three kinds of clues to cyberweapons use that we can detect by network monitoring. This does not mean detecting the setup of an attack, merely the active or "attack" phase, because these attacks will be sophisticated and stealthy in their setups. Detection of active attacks does require a sufficiently broad deployment of network-traffic vantage points, secured both physically and virtually from tampering, run by an international organization such as the International Telecommunications Union (ITU). One approach to deploying them is to have the vantage points be entirely passive and communicate over separate infrastructure via encrypted and authenticated channels. Centralized collection of data would be efficient for an international organization. Ideally, a vantage point should exist at the ingress to each important network of a country, capable of full-rate traffic processing. If this is difficult, random sampling of traffic can be done. The monitoring infrastructure could be realized via government mandate as it is in many countries today including the United States.

Cyberweapon usage is likely to be quite focused. A cyberweapon might attack a particular country, a type of service (e.g., electrical grid or water systems), or systems used by a certain political, ethnic, or religious persuasion. Both the Georgia and Stuxnet attacks employed focused targeting (insufficiently focused according to critics). However, we should also be able to see cyberweapons testing in Internet traffic. That is because potential vulnerabilities and attack vectors will not correlate well with desirable targets, and there must be significant testing, something generally unnecessary for criminal cyberattacks. Also, cyberweapons by their nature are complex pieces of software that include components for penetrating remote systems, controlling the remote systems, and propagating to other systems. Understanding the behavior of a cyberweapon in isolation, or in simulated environments is difficult—the more secret the testing, the less like the real world it will be, and the less accurate it will be at predicting real-world performance. We can see this demonstrated in the poor initial performance of complex new conventional weapons systems such as aircraft. We expect that countries wishing to employ cyberweapons will first unobtrusively try them against real targets to understand their real-world efficacy. An example is the attacks on Estonia in 2007 prior to the attacks on Georgia in 2008. This initial testing provides a clue to forthcoming cyberweapons use.

Thus, detecting pre-hostility events at the network level is possible. It can be aided by metrics for detecting national, political, social, or cultural bias in the targets of malicious network traffic. Standard statistical techniques can suggest that the victims represent a particular political perspective or country's interest more than a random sample would (Rowe and Goh, 2007). For instance, a significance test on a linear metric encoding political or social agendas can provide a first approximation, while the Kullback-Leibler divergence can characterize the extent of difference between expected and observed traffic distributions. How do we identify the political or social agenda to search for? This requires help from experts on international relations. Nations have longstanding grievances with other nations, and particular issues are more sensitive in some nations than others. We can enumerate many of them and identify associated Internet sites.

This comparison monitoring needs to recognize that cyberattacks are bursty, however, and rates should only be compared during bursts (and there may be no comparable bursts at some targets due to the randomness of targeting).

Other broad properties of the observable network traffic can provide precursors to attack such as the number of packets, the number of bytes transferred, the size of an average "flow" (set of related packets), the frequency of flows, and so on (Munz and Carle, 2007). Measurement of relatively crude properties works well in tracking and analyzing attacks supported by amateurs such as the Chinese hacker groups that are harnessed to attack Western organizations at times of political or social grievances against them (Hvinstendahl, 2010). Feature selection methods in finding discriminating network traffic features (Beverly and Sollins, 2008) can provide a more rigorous basis for choosing more sophisticated properties. We also can look for particular sequences of events indicative of a systematic attack, say a broadcast of many footprinting packets followed by more specific footprinting, something not seen much in criminal cyberattacks.

An additional tool useful in detecting cyberweapons development is a decoy, a site deliberately designed to encourage attacks. A decoy can be designed to be more useful than a normal site by narrowing its content to just that necessary to invoke a response. For instance, for the Georgia attacks it would have been useful to monitor decoys giving government announcements. Decoys need to be situated in plausible Internet sites, however, so that a government decoy is on a government computer system. We need to then design "differential honeypots" that compare attacks on a decoy with those on a similar non-decoy system. A decoy can also be equipped with more detailed monitoring of its usage that would not be possible for most sites, and should use honeypot technology to implement attack resilience and intelligence-gathering capabilities that are not easily disabled. Decoys do not generally raise ethical concerns because they are passive, but guidelines should be followed in their use (Rowe, 2010) since decoys are also used by phishers.

Data fusion on World Wide Web usage can complement our network monitoring. If a country's government shows a sudden increase in visits to hacker Web sites, it may also suggest cyberweapons development since such activity is knowledge intensive.

Finally, the aforementioned forensics techniques can enhance network monitoring. For instance, Beverly, Garfinkel, and Cardwell (2011) showed the presence of residual network packets on nonvolatile storage may be correlated with observed traffic and attacks.

Encouraging More Responsible Cyberweapons

International agreements can also stipulate acceptable types of cyberweapons. Two important aspects of this are attributability and reversibility of attacks. For attribution, a responsible country will find it in its interests to make attacks clear in origin to better enable desired political and social effects of an attack, which are often more important than the actual military value. The ability of the USCCU to trace the Georgia cyberattacks back to people in Russia says that Russia was sending a political message to Georgia. Contrarily, it could be useful to a country to be able to prove it was *not* the source of a cyber-attack for which it is being blamed. Attribution can be done by using digital signatures attached to attack code or data, identifying who is responsible for an attack and why. They could be concealed steganographically (Wayner, 2002) to avoid giving advance warning to the victim that the victim is being attacked, but allowing it to be demonstrated later to the international community. For attacks without code like denial of service, a signature can be encoded in the low-order bits of the times of the attacks.

Nations should also be encouraged to use attack methods that are more easily repairable, following the same logic behind the design of more easily removable landmines. Rowe (2011) proposed four techniques that can be used to make cyberattacks that are easier to reverse by the attacker than by the victim even when the victim tries to restore from backup (Dorf and Johnson, 2007). The four methods are (1) "locking up" the operating system of the victim's computers by encryption of key software by the attacker, where the victim does not have the key to decrypt it; (2) obfuscation of a victim's system by the attacker by data manipulations that are hard to decipher yet algorithmic and reversible (such as turning document "document" into "tnemucod" by reversing its bits); (3) intercepting and withholding by the attacker of key information that is important to the victim, while saving it in backup; and (4) deception by the attacker of the victim to make them think their systems are not operational when they actually are. In the first two cases, reversal can be achieved by software operations by the attacker; in the third case, the attacker can restore missing data; and in the fourth case, the attacker can reveal the deception. Note that reversal can be done at a distance so the attacker does not necessarily require visiting the victim's territory.

How do we encourage attackers to use reversible attacks? There are several possible incentives. One would be if the attacker will eventually need to pay reparations, as the United Nations could stipulate as part of a negotiated settlement of a conflict (Torpey, 2006). Even in an invasion or regime change, it is likely that the impacts of cyberweapons will need to be mitigated—indeed, the perceived possibility of mitigation will likely drive the adoption of cyberweapons. Another incentive comes from international outcry at using unethical methods and the resulting ostracism of the offending state, as with the use of biological weapons. Another incentive is if a victim can respond in like kind, wherein use of a reversible attack could encourage an adversary to do the same to avoid appearing to escalate the conflict (Gardam, 2004). Also, nonreversible attacks may in the future be interpreted as violating the laws of warfare in regard to unjustified force when reversible methods are easily available. Responses of the international community to analogous such violations with traditional arms include sanctions, boycotts, fines, and legal proceedings (Berman, 2002).

Support for International Cyberarms Cooperation in the United States

Many of the ideas mentioned here benefit from international cooperation, but obtaining such cooperation has been difficult. We focus here on the role of the United States. Until recently, the United States would not discuss international cooperation in matters of military cybersecurity (Yannakogeorgos, 2010, 2011). This policy began to shift in early 2010. It is now recognized that although a cyberarms control treaty is most desirable, negotiating it will take decades since it requires agreement on global norms of behavior built from multilateral institutions of diplomacy.

Embryonic global norms found in international agreements dealing with cybercrime can serve as models for cyberarms control. The Council of Europe Convention on Cybercrime, adopted in November 2001, seeks to align domestic substantive and procedural laws for evidence gathering and prosecution, and to increase international collaboration and improve investigative capabilities for coordinating European Union efforts on cybercrimes. Adopted and ratified by the United States in 2007, it is considered a model law for the rest of the world. The UN General Assembly and the World Summit on the Information Society Declaration of Principles endorsed a global culture of cybersecurity that is promoted, developed, and implemented in cooperation with all stakeholders and international expert bodies. The ITU and UN General Assembly have also passed several resolutions addressing the criminal misuse of information. The efforts of the ITU have culminated in the International Multilateral Partnership against Cyber Threats (IMPACT), although the United States does not currently support it. IMPACT is a Global Response Centre based in Cyberjaya, Malaysia. It was set up in 2009 to serve as the international community's main cyberthreat resource by proactively tracking and defending against cyberthreats. The center's alert and response capabilities include an Early Warning System that enables IMPACT members to identify and head off potential and imminent attacks before they can inflict damage on national networks.

A major obstacle to any international agreement is the concept that states the need to acknowledge responsibility for malicious cyber actions within their borders. Several recent studies of cyberespionage, and some corporate investigations, have traced recent attacks on the US's commercial infrastructures to China (Areddy, 2010). Denying its official involvement, the government of China bemoaned its fate as the greatest victim of cybercrime. (The Chinese definition of cybercrime includes content, and thus using social networks to mount revolutions would be considered a crime in China, whereas the United States considers such actions as part of democracy.) The individuals responsible were not caught, and China received only a slap on the wrist via a State Department "note verbal" and the launching of the Department of State's Internet Freedom Agenda in 2010. Recent policing of internal hacker groups in China has not improved. Increasing the consequence of a state for cyberattacks originating within their territory is an appropriate course of action for the United States.

Catalyzed in part by events involving the Google corporation in China, and discussions with the Russian delegation in January 2010, senior leaders began to talk publicly about global norms of behavior in cyberspace, including military cyberspace (Lynn, 2010). Formal shifts in policy began in 2011, with the *National Military Strategy* identifying the cyber threat as being "expanded and exacerbated by lack of international norms, difficulties of attribution, low barriers to entry, and the relative ease of developing potent capabilities" (USDOD, February 2011). Subsequently the Department of Defense Strategy for Operating in Cyberspace stated that DOD "will work with interagency and international partners to encourage responsible behavior and oppose those who would seek to disrupt networks and systems, dissuade and deter malicious actors, and reserve the right to defend these vital national assets as necessary and appropriate" (USDOD, July 2011). These are steps in the right direction toward a US international cyber policy that holds states responsible, and represents high-level acknowledgement that in addition to being a law enforcement, diplomacy, and development issue, cyber is also a military issue. However, the US government appears to be playing a game of forum picking with "like-minded states," rather than supporting international initiatives already underway at the ITU. There is no mention of elements related to cybersecurity within the World Summit for the Information Society *Tunis Agreement* and *Geneva Action Plans*, work of the High Level Experts Group of the Global Cybersecurity Agenda, and the ITU's IMPACT program. Further refinement of US cyber policy is required to enhance future positions within international cyberarms control discussions.

So the US international cyber strategy currently encourages the development of global norms, while fighting the institutionalization of cyber issues within preexisting frameworks that have been under development for the past decade. This is done to avoid diplomatic hurdles within them on the grounds that there are challenges posed to US norms of openness "by some governments and international institutions intent on imposing pre-Internet-era telecommunications regulatory schemes to provide them control over the flow of information (and money) they enjoyed in the old days of the monopoly phone company" (Kornbluh and Weitzner, 2011). The alternative of setting up parallel dialogues for norms discussion could be unworkably complex. By extension, the US aspiration to lead the world in setting global norms could fail as others fail to follow. The result could be that the United States could lose an opportunity to focus its diplomatic resources on the parallel structures that the Europeans, Russians, and Chinese have forged over the past decade with the United Nations and its specialized agency, the ITU. Like-minded states are important allies within diplomatic forums. Creating an alliance of cyber security with state and private-sector partners that could push the norms discussion within the ITU would serve US interests well in what will likely become heated diplomatic debates. However, those states that are resisting this talk of state responsibility within cyberspace will still need to be compelled in one way or another to cooperate in investigating cyberattacks. The United States should begin documenting and issuing reports on the overall capacity of each nation's efforts to both create and enforce legal mechanisms within their countries to assure their people can be prosecuted, and also to measure to what extent said state is cooperating in investigations. On this basis, international arms control agreements will be guided by norms and customs of behavior that have been qualified by years of documentation.

Criminal prosecution of a nation's hacker groups by its government could be an important detail in the stipulations of agreements. For instance, when Philippine hackers in 2000 launched a virus that attacked computers worldwide and the Philippine government was initially unhelpful, improvements under international pressure were subsequently made by it, both legally and managerially, to enable a better response in the future. Other possible agreements could follow those of traditional arms control, as for instance a commitment to use cyberweapons only in self-defense, or agreed export controls on cyberweapons technology. We do need to make legal distinctions between cybercrime, cyberconflict, cyberespionage, and cyberterror, as this is necessary when creating a regulatory regime for cyberweapons (Wingfield, 2009). One model that could be studied is the Wassenaar Arrangement for export controls, which could be extended to information technology products.

Other specific technical details can be negotiated as part of cyberarms agreements. An example would be a mandate for countries to use IPv6 instead of IPv4 to enable better attribution of events on the Internet; rogue states could be told that they cannot connect to the Internet unless they use IPv6. Other mandates could stipulate architectures in which attribution of traffic is easier such as minimum requirements on persistence of cached records. Others could prohibit less-controllable attacks such as worms and mutating viruses to achieve better discrimination of military from civilian targets in cyberattacks (Shulman, 1999).

Conclusion

Cyberarms agreements have been said to be impossible. But technology is changing that. We can seize and analyze drives on which cyberweapons were developed; we can detect attacks and the necessary testing of cyberweapons; we can create incentives for self-attributing and reversible cyberattacks; and we can develop and ratify new kinds of international agreements. While we cannot stop cyberweapons development, we may be able to control its more dangerous aspects much as we control chemical, biological, and nuclear weapons, and limit it to responsible states. It is time to consider seriously the possibility of cyberarms control.

Bibliography

Areddy, J. (2010, February 20). *Wall Street Journal*, A1.

Baron, K. (2011, July 14). US cyber defenses "way too predictable" says Cartwright. *Stars and Stripes Central*. Retrieved July 15, 2011, from www.strips.com/blogs/stripes-central/stripes-central-1.8040.

Berman P. (2002). The globalization of jurisdiction. *University of Pennsylvania Law Review, 151* (2), 311–545.

Beverly, R., & Sollins, K. (2008). An Internet Protocol address clustering algorithm. In *Third Workshop on Tackling Computer Systems Problems with Machine Learning Techniques*. Berkeley, CA: Usenix.

Beverly, R., Garfinkel, S., & Cardwell, G. (2011). Forensic carving of network packets and associated data structures. In *Digital Forensics Workshop*.

Brenner, S. (2010). *Cybercrime: Criminal Threats from Cyberspace*. Santa Barbara, CA: Praeger.

Clarke, R., & Knake, R. (2010). *Cyberwar: The Next Threat to National Security and What to Do about It*. New York: HarperCollins.

Croft, S. (1996). *Strategies of Arms Control: A History and Typology*. Manchester, UK: Manchester University Press.

Dorf, J., & Johnson, M. (2007). Restoration component of business continuity planning. In Tipton, H., and Krause, M. (Eds.), *Information Security Management Handbook*, 6th edition (pp. 1645–1654). Boca Raton, FL: CRC Press.

Erbschloe, R. (2001). *Information Warfare: How to Survive Cyber Attacks*. Berkeley, CA: Osborne/McGraw-Hill.

Gady, F.-S. (2010, March 24). Africa's Cyber WMD. *Foreign Policy*.

Gardam, J. (2004). *Necessity, Proportionality, and the Use of Force by States*. Cambridge, UK: Cambridge University Press.

Garfinkel, S. (2006, September). Forensic feature extraction and cross-drive analysis. *Digital Investigation, 3*, Supplement 1, 71–81.

Garfinkel, S., Roussev, V., Nelson, A., & White, D. (2010). *Using Purpose-Built Functions and Block Hashes to Enable Small Block and Sub-file Forensics*. Ithaca, NY: Digital Forensics Research Conference.

Ghernouti-Helie, S. (2010). *A National Strategy for an Effective Cybersecurity Approach and Culture*. New York: IEEE Press.

Johnson, P. (2002). Is it time for a treaty on information warfare? In Schmitt, M., and O'Donnell, B., *Computer Network Attack and International Law (International Law Studies Volume 76)* (pp. 439–455). Newport, RI: Naval War College.

Hvistendahl, M. (2010, March 3). China's hacker army. *Foreign Policy*.

Kornbluh, K., & Weitzner, D. (2011, July 14). 21st century statecraft: Foreign policy of the Internet. *The Washington Post*.

Libicki, M. (2007). *Conquest in Cyberspace: National Security and Information Warfare.* New York: Cambridge University Press.

Lynn, W. (2010, September/October). Defending a new domain: The Pentagon's cyberstrategy. *Foreign Affairs.*

Malin, C., Casey, E., and Aquilina, J. (2008). *Malware Forensics: Investigating and Analyzing Malicious Code.* Waltham, MA: Syngress.

Markoff, J. (2010, September 26). A silent attack, but not a subtle one. *New York Times,* A6.

Mel, H., & Baker, D. (2000). *Cryptography Decrypted,* 5th edition. Boston, MA: Addison-Wesley Professional.

Munz, G., & Carle, G. (2007, May). Real-time analysis of flow data for network attack detection. In *10th IFIP/IEEE International Symposium on Integrated Network Management* (pp. 100–108). New York: IEEE.

O'Neill, P. (2010). *Verification in an Age of Insecurity: The Future of Arms Control Compliance.* New York: Oxford.

Price, R. (1997). *The Chemical Weapons Taboo.* Ithaca, NY: Cornell University Press.

Rooney, B. (2011, February 4). Calls for Geneva Convention in cyberspace. *Wall Street Journal.*

Rowe, N. (2010). The ethics of cyberweapons in warfare. *Journal of Technoethics, (1)*1, 20–31 [JTE].

Rowe, N. (2011). Towards reversible cyberattacks. In J. Ryan (Ed.), *Leading Issues in Information Warfare and Security Research, Volume I* (pp. 145–158). Near Reading, UK: Academic Publishing International.

Rowe, N., & Garfinkel, S. (2011) Finding anomalous and suspicious files from directory metadata on a large corpus. *Third International ICST Conference on Digital Forensics and Cyber Crime,* Dublin, Ireland.

Rowe, N., & Goh, H. (2007, June). Thwarting cyber-attack reconnaissance with inconsistency and deception. In *Eighth IEEE Information Assurance Workshop* (pp. 151–158). New York: IEEE.

Shulman, M. (1999). Discrimination in the laws of information warfare. *Columbia Journal of Transnational Law, 37,* 939–968.

Sommer, R., & Paxon, V. (2010). Outside the closed world: On using machine learning for network intrusion detection. In *IEEE Symposium on Security and Privacy.* New York: IEEE.

Torpey, J. (2006). *Making Whole What Has Been Smashed: On Reparations Politics.* Cambridge, MA: Harvard University Press.

Trost, R. (2010). *Practical Intrusion Analysis.* Upper Saddle River, NJ: Addison-Wesley.

United Nations. (1991). *Final Document: Third Review Conference of the Parties to the Convention on the Prohibition of the Development, Production, and Stockpiling of Bacteriological (Biological) and Toxin Weapons and on Their Destruction.* BWC/DONF.II/23, Geneva, Switzerland.

USCCU (United States Cyber Consequences Unit). (2009, August). US-CCU special report: Overview by the US-CCU of the cyber campaign against Georgia in August of 2008. Retrieved November 3, 2010, from www.usccu.org.

USDOD (United States Department of Defense). (2011, February). National military strategy. Retrieved September 11, 2011, from https://hsdl.org./hslog/?q-node/5994.

USDOD (United States Department of Defense). (2011, July). Strategy for operating in cyberspace. Retrieved September 11, 2011, from www.defense.gov/news/d20110714cyber.pdf.

USGAO (United States Government Accountability Office). (2010, March 5). Cybersecurity: Progress made but challenges remain in defining and coordinating the comprehensive national initiative. Washington, DC: Government Accountability Office.

Wayner, P. (2002). *Disappearing Cryptography: Information Hiding: Steganography and Watermarking*. San Francisco, CA: Morgan Kaufmann.

Wingfield, T. (2009). International law and information operations. In Kramer, F., Starr, S., and Wentz, L. (Eds.), *Cyberpower and National Security* (pp. 525–542). Washington, DC: National Defense University Press.

Yannakogeorgos, P. (2010, October). Cyberspace, the new frontier—and the same old multilateralism. In Reich, S., *Global Norms, American Sponsorship and the Emerging Patterns of World Politics*. Houndsmills, UK: Palgrave.

Yannakogeorgos, P. (2011). Promises and pitfalls of the US national strategy to secure cyberspace. Carlisle, PA: Army War College.

8

DIGITAL POLICY MANAGEMENT

A Foundation for Tomorrow

NATIONAL SECURITY AGENCY (NSA), ENTERPRISE SERVICES DIVISION, IDENTITY AND ACCESS MANAGEMENT BRANCH

Contents

Introduction	101
Digital Policy Management of Today	102
Operations of Tomorrow	103
Operations of Tomorrow Require Changes Today	103
Supporting the Delivery of the Enterprise for Tomorrow	104
Open Development Philosophy	105
Defining the Functionality	105
Adapting Capabilities for Government Use	106
How to Get Involved	106

Introduction

During the last decade we have grown ever more dependent on information technology. In fact many facets of our daily life, including personal and corporate communications, healthcare data, energy systems, and commerce utilize common and private Information Technology (IT) infrastructures.

The danger of operating on the Internet, closed defense classified environments, or other open cyber enterprise environments is that they are susceptible to threats. Some threats may result in the loss of personal private information, large ex-filtrations of information, the use of cyber attacks as nation-state war-fighting tactics, and Wiki Leaks (insider attacks).

This is coupled with the recognition that in this Information Age, our national security is highly dependent on our ability to create, access, and share information securely in these environments. To that end we needed a standard by which we can communicate the level of security and available functions to protect the valuable information within such systems. The foundation of the enterprise cyber operations relies on consistent and fully encompassing digital policies that are defined by humans and digested by computers.

Digital Policy Management of Today

Administration of policy is manual and decentralized. Policies originate from many sources and can be interpreted in different ways, leading to less effective and potentially conflicting implementations. Policy managers may not be confident that the policy they specified is really the policy implemented in their systems. Lack of synchronization in the deployment of policies may lead to inconsistencies between systems in different domains. The inability for policy managers to monitor the effects of policies creates uncertainty that the policies are actually enforcing controls accurately or are producing the desired effect. Local system administrators may update policies in their local systems to meet local operational requirements. Managers may never know about these changes that may conflict with other enterprise-level policies. Policies have evolved over time, and it is not uncommon for new policies to conflict with those active policies issued earlier. Many existing policies associated with Information Assurance (IA) were established before the widespread use of computer systems and the advent of global enterprise operations. IA devices enforce policies, whether hard coded into the hardware design or software implementation. In short there is a lack of policy coordination across and through the enterprise. For example, firewalls control port or protocol access, gateways enable access to external enterprise connections, access management structures to authorize and enforce access to information and mission systems are all independently configured and administered, and alignment is more by coincidence than by design.

Operations of Tomorrow

As we move toward cloud computing and mobile devices, the amount of devices that comprise an enterprise is exponentially growing. With any type of growth, this comes with its benefits and challenges. Users expect to leverage their commercial workstation or laptop as well as their commodity mobile devices wherever and whenever required to support mission execution. Users want to take advantage of all the content and applications provided by the free market to reduce the need to carry both work and personal devices. In addition to having multi-persona devices that would allow for a merger of both work and personal usage on devices, users want to integrate the commercially available services and capabilities into business execution infrastructures so that they can use applications familiar to them and remain "connected" both at home and at work. This includes social networking, online information repositories (e.g. wikis), collaboration utilities, and other open source software and services. Users want to minimize the duplication of effort associated with physically and logically separating information due to classification or Community of Interest (COI)-based associations. Alternatively the operations, management, and maintenance functions want to gain a perspective of the entire enterprise so to adjust as necessary in real time.

Operations of Tomorrow Require Changes Today

All of this capability comes with its challenges. Smaller, faster, more capable, and less expensive devices allow for more of them to be brought into the enterprise. Additionally, more vendors increase competition while reducing per unit cost. Having more devices requires more administration, and having more vendors requires more work to maintain consistency. Cheaper storage and faster network speeds are pushing information and services into the cloud. These environments are powerful and valuable but require a different security and protection scheme. On a more technical level, services and devices are deployed across multiple tiered hierarchies that allow and require both top-down and bottom-up management and reconciliation to operate as a seamless enterprise.

Digital policy management enables the enterprise to overcome these challenges. It allows for a common way to review and evaluate the current operational structure, but also allows for a way to adjust all aspects uniformly and consistently at net speed. Digital policies are an implementation where operating paradigms and access rules are created and maintained in executable formats that can be processed, downloaded to, and enforced by IA devices. Digital Policy Management (DPM) enables authorized operators to generate, adjudicate, validate, disseminate, and monitor policies. To address the problems of multiple sources of policies and conflicting policies, the policy manager can define digital policies at a central location creating a policy hierarchy.

Lawyers, decision makers, mission managers, Congress, and executive and legislative leadership establish and govern what and how the enterprise will operate. It divides and delegates roles and responsibilities to appropriate organizations. This articulation and delegation typically originates in spoken English and is translated into legal documents. On the other end of the spectrum, computing services require clear and concise statements to function accurately. The merger of these two spectrums is paramount to moving into the net-centric operating environment of the future. It requires policy sets, doctrine, guidelines, governance and other standardized inputs to be interpreted and implemented into discrete unambiguous forms that do not introduce conflicts or contradictions into enterprise operations.

Supporting the Delivery of the Enterprise for Tomorrow

The National Security Agency (NSA)-sponsored DPM team is focused on working with the community to define and develop digital policy and digital policy management capabilities and services in an open and vendor neutral standard process. As capabilities become available, the executive agents, responsible agencies, and/or the service components with a vested interest in those capabilities will consider them for usage as appropriate. The goal of the DPM team is to advance the definition, security, applicability, scope, functionality, technology, standards, and adoption of digital policy throughout the US government.

Open Development Philosophy

From a mission space, the US government does not operate as a single non-federated corporate structure. It trains, fights, supports, procures, and shares services with many mission partners, both commercially and governmentally, with various levels of trust. Federating both legal decisions and policies must be exportable, digestible, and verifiable across the entire US government cyber enterprise. Furthermore, they must extend to external partners as well as foreign, domestic, and commercial.

The movement toward commercial technologies brings in new challenges that require attention. Since the US government is only a small fraction of the target audience for technology and services, other strategies are needed to bring the commercial product vendors to the required capabilities to support government and military operations. DPM has selected to embrace and sponsor activities that lead to open standards and specifications in technical, functionality, ontological, usage, and deployment areas. The team has established regular Technical Exchange Meetings (TEMs) to collaborate and define use cases, functionality and architecture; discuss hard problems; and develop input for standards needed to support this effort.

Defining the Functionality

As part of the DPM TEMs, the team is constantly identifying and developing use cases to serve as the operational driver for the uses of digital policy. As part of that development a discrete list of functionality was developed. This functionality will serve as the basis of analysis for current and future technology needs as well as the intersection with other capabilities and US government programs to demonstrate the touch points between policy inputs, mission execution points, and situational awareness.

Adapting Capabilities for Government Use

In addition to the open design and definition processes already discussed, the DPM team is working with US government partners to develop and demonstrate capabilities within existing programs and operational arenas. These ideas leverage the development and work products being generated as part of the open development activities but are customized and adapted for specific environments. It is envisioned that down range these capabilities will be built into the greater enterprise and not require direct support or procurement from a specific user environment.

How to Get Involved

The DPM TEMs are held twice per year and are open to US federal government organizations and agencies. This includes government-sponsored contractors and academia participants as well. The group is working on expanding participation to vendors and international parties to ensure that what is being delivered will accommodate a global federated enterprise, with commercial solutions at the heart of the capabilities. Currently all content is being stored on Intelink (unclassified wiki site: https://intellipedia.intelink.gov/wiki/Digital_Policy_Management) with links to a SharePoint Site (https://intelshare.intelink.gov/sites/dpm/default.aspx). For more information and to receive information regarding upcoming TEMs contact the DPM team via email at dpm@nsa.gov. The DPM team is looking for participation and support.

9

ON MISSION ASSURANCE

KAMAL JABBOUR

SARAH MUCCIO

Contents

Introduction 107
Assuring Legacy Missions 109
Assurance-in-Depth 115
Cyber Test and Evaluation 117
Mission Assurance in Public Clouds 122
Time-Domain Mission Assurance 123
Conclusion 124
Endnotes 124

Introduction

Department of Defense (DoD) Directive 3020.40 defines Mission Assurance (MA) as "a process to ensure that assigned tasks or duties can be performed in accordance with the intended purpose or plan. It is a summation of the activities and measures taken to ensure that required capabilities and all supporting infrastructures are available to the DoD to carry out the National Military Strategy."[1] In accordance with this directive, a principal responsibility of a commander is to ensure mission execution in a timely manner. The reliance of a Mission Essential Function (MEF) on cyberspace makes cyberspace a center of gravity an adversary may exploit and, in doing so, enable that adversary to engage directly the MEF without the employment of conventional forces or weapons.

Several global trends make the task of mission assurance all the more daunting. These include an increased dependence on cyberspace and the proliferation of information-centric missions, the outsourcing of many hardware and software production activities, the reliance on commercial information infrastructure of many critical national security functions, the lack of systematic cyber test and evaluation across the weapons acquisition life cycle, and the absence of an educated workforce to address these challenges.

Information sharing and information centricity enabled the US military to shorten significantly the kill-chain from sensor to shooter, compressed the Observe-Orient-Decide-Act (OODA) loop for many time-sensitive missions, and provided a force multiplier for kinetic weapon systems. With this leap in capabilities came an increased vulnerability from the dependence on information. The increased education and sophistication of our adversaries have turned our unilateral advantage into an asymmetrical vulnerability and permitted a modest technology investment to hold at risk complex weapon systems.

The flattening of the industrial world and the offshore relocation of many hardware and software production facilities introduced a corresponding vulnerability in our critical missions. A significant proportion of integrated circuits at the heart of our weapons are built and tested overseas, introducing potential vulnerability of low-quality products or worse, maliciously embedded vulnerabilities that an adversary may exploit at inopportune times and circumstances. Similarly, software development is happening increasingly overseas, including operating system and application software used in defense systems.

In addition to congressional mandates to reduce weapon costs by incorporating Commercial Off-The-Shelf (COTS) components into national security missions and office automation systems alike, the DoD turned to commercial providers for much information processing and communication. COTS computers, servers, and routers made their way into bombs, tanks, ships, and aircraft, and critical information travels increasingly over commercial communication trunks and commercial satellites. To compound the uncertainty of using COTS systems and commercial infrastructure, any mapping of critical mission dependence on the underlying infrastructure—let alone in a dynamic and timely manner—poses scientific and technical challenges that remain elusive.

Spanning the spectrum from basic research to final operational capability, the acquisition life cycle lies at the heart of weapons development and stretches over a timeline of a few years to several decades.

The development of weapons in the current arsenal did not take into consideration a contested cyber environment and failed to incorporate cyber vulnerability Test and Evaluation (T&E) across the acquisition life cycle. As a consequence, existing processes mistook cyber defense for cyber T&E and missed numerous opportunities to identify and mitigate cyber vulnerabilities in critical missions.

The absence of an educated cyber workforce denied us the opportunity to mitigate these problems early on, and permitted fundamental vulnerabilities to occur and perpetuate. Training without education proved insufficient to assure mathematically complex, information-centric systems. In a world where our peers educate first their cyber warriors on the science of information assurance, then train them on the art of cyber warfare, our cyber workforce development continues to shun specialized education in favor of generalized training—a too-little-too-late process with an established record of inadequacy for national security missions.[2]

In this chapter, we discuss the challenges of assuring national security systems against cyber threats. We present a systematic approach to mapping mission dependence on cyber systems. We introduce the information life cycle as a tool to locate cyber vulnerabilities, and explore the fractal nature of mission assurance. Finally, we discuss time-dependent mission assurance, where the requirements for mission assurance are specified for a finite duration, rather than indefinitely.

Assuring Legacy Missions

The National Institute of Standards and Technology (NIST) defines risk to information systems as "a function of the likelihood of a given threat-source exercising a particular potential vulnerability, and the resulting impact of that adverse event" and a threat as "the potential for a particular threat-source to successfully exercise a particular vulnerability."[3] Threat and vulnerability are dependent variables in the NIST definition; thus a threat requires the existence of a vulnerability to exploit.

Mission assurance against cyber threats requires identifying vulnerabilities in the underlying cyber infrastructure of the MEFs that constitute a mission. A systematic process of assuring a mission requires the following steps[4]:

1. *Prioritization*: Enumerating the functions that make up a mission, and listing these functions in order of priority. Prioritization addresses the *consequences* component of risk (vulnerability, threat, consequences). Certain functions are more critical than others to mission success.

2. *Mission mapping*: Mapping the dependence on cyberspace of each MEF. The criticality of a MEF dictates the fidelity of the mapping. We may map a low-priority MEF at the function level and yet decompose a higher-priority MEF into systems, subsystems, components, and devices for a higher-fidelity mapping. In a highly dynamic infrastructure topology, automatic and timely mission mapping provides great opportunity for the infusion of new science and technology.

3. *Vulnerability assessment*: Identifying exploitable vulnerabilities in the hardware and software across the information life cycle of information generation, processing, storage, transmission, consumption, and destruction. An intelligence assessment of adversary cyber capabilities supplements vulnerability assessment with an estimate of technology, talent, time, and treasure to exploit identified vulnerabilities.

4. *Mitigation*: Developing and implementing technology to mitigate vulnerabilities and disrupt potential threats. A mathematical modeling of MEF specifications allows a formal verification of the security properties of its implementation and permits systematic mission mapping, vulnerability assessment, and mitigation.

5. *Red teaming*: The evolution of the cyber threat landscape dictates conducting this MA process at all stages of weapon-system development. In the notional timeline of the Integrated Defense Acquisition, Technology and Logistics Life Cycle Management System, we recommend conducting MA analysis at the Material Solution Analysis Phase (Milestone A), Technology Development Phase (Milestone B), Engineering and Manufacturing Development Phase (Milestone C), Production and Deployment Phase (Initial

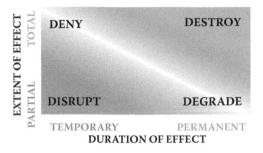

Figure 9.1 D4 effects in relation to extent and duration.

Operating Condition), and Operations and Support Phase (Full Operating Condition).[5] An integrated team of weapon domain experts and cyber experts can provide effective red teaming of the processes at every phase of weapon development across the acquisition life cycle.

Offensive cyber operations provide a lexicon to assess the criticality of a MEF to a parent mission. Figure 9.1 shows the D4 effects of disrupt, deny, degrade, and destroy on a two-dimensional grid of the *extent* versus the *duration* of an effect. The MEF prioritization task requires at least a qualitative, but preferably a quantitative, assessment of the mission impact of a D4 effect on a constituent function. This first step of prioritization requires an exhaustive tabulation of the mission impact of a disruption, degradation, denial, or destruction of each MEF, and a resulting prioritization of the MEFs based on the consequence of a compromise.

For example, let us consider a sensor that resides on the front end of the information life cycle, namely information generation. A temporary-and-partial effect against a sensor may DISRUPT information generation by delaying the flow of raw data, introducing consequently more latency into the decision process. A permanent-and-partial effect may DEGRADE the quality of information by reducing its temporal or spatial resolution, making it less useful and introducing ambiguity into the decision process. A temporary-and-total effect may DENY information generation by disabling the sensor or shutting down its external interface. Finally, a permanent-and-total effect seeks to DESTROY information generation by destroying either the sensor or its external interface.

The mission mapping step of the MA process poses unique challenges and warrants further discussion. Several realities complicate the mapping process, including:

1. The DoD owns only a fraction of the information infrastructure on which national security missions depend. Outside of tank, ship, plane, and base boundaries, mission-critical information rides on private cables, fibers, and satellites on lease to the DoD, and travels through bridges, switches, and routers over which the DoD exerts no operational control.

2. A bottom-up mapping strategy that allocates known DoD resources to supported missions provides a partial picture at best, as it fails to account for most of the critical supporting information infrastructure outside of DoD control.

3. Architecture frameworks that enumerate mission dependence on cyber exist for only a few critical missions, and even those tend to be static and do not maintain faithfully all the changes, updates, and upgrades to the architecture or the underlying infrastructure.

4. Virtual circuits that connect MEFs across the global commons may reroute dynamically to optimize performance and increase robustness.

5. Legacy communication protocols and software development practices do not take into consideration the requirement for mission mapping, nor do they lend themselves to automatic mission mapping.

Vulnerability assessment requires a systematic and exhaustive enumeration of all information handlers within a mission. The MEF prioritization in step 1 guides an educated determination of the fidelity and granularity of decomposition of the mission. Generically, we decompose a mission into MEFs, a MEF into interconnected systems of sub-systems, a sub-system into components, and a component into devices. The lowest atomic level of decomposition consists of a process, or a stored program executing on a processor with memory and input-output (I/O) interfaces. We use generically the term *element* to refer to any information-handling piece of the mission at any decomposition level.

Overlaying the information life cycle atop the functional decomposition of a mission provides the necessary means to assess mission vulnerability to cyber threats. Through a process-coloring methodology, we label each element based on its roles in the information life cycle:

1. Information generation
2. Information processing
3. Information storage
4. Information transmission
5. Information consumption
6. Information destruction

This process-coloring allows vulnerability visualization and subsequent exposure of an element to cyber threats. While an element with internal-only connections may be vulnerable to supply chain threats, an element that communicates with the outside world becomes additionally vulnerable to external cyber threats.

Besides process-coloring along the information life cycle, mission vulnerability assessment requires an enumeration of embedded hardware and software protocols and standards together with their known vulnerabilities. The proliferation of COTS in weapon systems brought along a corresponding proliferation of mission vulnerabilities at all phases of the acquisition life cycle from design to implementation. A systematic enumeration of all protocols, standards, tools, and products within a mission provides a starting point for vulnerability assessment.

The intelligence community plays a key role on the complementary side of vulnerability assessment, namely threat assessment. A potential vulnerability poses no risk to a mission until a threat exhibits the capability to exploit the vulnerability. We measure the threat capability necessary to exploit a specific vulnerability in terms of the T4 of technology, talent, time, and treasure. For example, conducting a successful hardware supply-chain attack requires substantially more T4 than a script attack exploiting a known operating system vulnerability.

While the intelligence community can generate targeted intelligence on current and projected adversary T4 capabilities against specific missions, the task of risk management rests ultimately with the mission commander. Rather than a binary decision of secure versus non-secure, mission risk management consists essentially of an economic trade-off decision along four variables, two of them blue and two red:

1. The cost to blue of additional security to assure a mission
2. The cost to blue of mission failure
3. The increased cost to red to compromise an assured mission
4. The benefit to red of a successful compromise

The four-pronged breakdown of cost-benefit analysis of mission assurance boils down to the economic goals of:

1. Spending little on mission assurance
2. While minimizing the cost of failure
3. All the while increasing the cost to an adversary
4. While lowering their return-on-investment

This formula has a side benefit of providing a way forward for cyber deterrence without attribution. Increasing disproportionately the cost to an adversary while reducing the profits serves to deter a certain class of attackers where attribution is impractical or impossible.

Vulnerability mitigation offers both the largest challenge and largest payoff for mission assurance. Legacy weapon systems consist commonly of millions of lines of code, un-maintainable and un-patchable, developed in obsolete programming languages and unsupported operating systems, running on outdated hardware. Identifying vulnerabilities becomes less challenging than mitigating them. Such difficulties notwithstanding, the information life cycle offers a viable approach to mitigating vulnerabilities in legacy systems.

A logical analysis of information flow in a legacy system shows that those components with external information transmission functions are the most likely vectors of attack against internal system vulnerabilities. This realization suggests that developing COTS wrappers to mediate information flows between a vulnerable system and the outside world may reduce the information risk of the system. At one extreme, a wrapper may seek to cut off all external communication, isolate the system, and insulate it from external threats. The practical necessity of information exchange with the outside world dictates flexibility in wrapper design and implementation. We consider system wrapping a more practical and more effective approach to vulnerability mitigation than endless code patching.

We advocate the use of red teams at all stages of the acquisition lifecycle, from requirements generation through final Operational Test and Evaluation (OT&E), including mission assurance through vulnerability mitigation. A balanced red team composed of mission domain experts and information assurance professionals can ensure the acquisition of weapon systems under realistic operating and threat conditions, as well as the assurance of legacy systems on the sustainment end of the lifecycle.

Assurance-in-Depth

An effective cyber defense-in-depth strategy must seek to avoid and prevent mission compromise. However, when a compromise occurs, a second layer of defense must detect the compromise and react in a timely manner to protect the mission. In the event of detect-react failure, a third layer must ensure mission resilience and survival, even with possible degradation. Finally, a fourth layer must provide for orderly and timely recovery following mission failure.

Figure 9.2 represents defense-in-depth as a single-queue Markov chain with λ transition probabilities corresponding to risk as a product of threat and vulnerability at each queue state, and μ service probabilities of successful return to a higher state of assurance.

The four layers of defense-in-depth correspond directly to the four possible states of a mission:

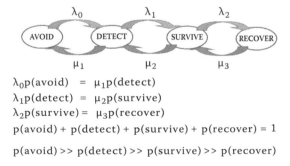

$$\lambda_0 p(\text{avoid}) = \mu_1 p(\text{detect})$$
$$\lambda_1 p(\text{detect}) = \mu_2 p(\text{survive})$$
$$\lambda_2 p(\text{survive}) = \mu_3 p(\text{recover})$$
$$p(\text{avoid}) + p(\text{detect}) + p(\text{survive}) + p(\text{recover}) = 1$$

$$p(\text{avoid}) \gg p(\text{detect}) \gg p(\text{survive}) \gg p(\text{recover})$$

Figure 9.2 Defense-in-depth as a Markov chain.

1. *Pristine mission*: Assurance-in-depth seeks to prevent mission compromise by avoiding threats through vulnerability mitigation. The ideal goal of mission assurance is to maintain a mission in pristine condition.
2. *Exploited mission*: When prevention fails and an adversary exploits a mission by gaining a foothold without inflicting D4 effects.
3. *Attacked mission*: When timely detect-and-react action fails to defeat an exploitation, which then turns into an attack that disrupts or degrades the mission. The goal of mission survival is to ensure mission completion under cyber attack, despite disruptions, even with graceful degradation.
4. *Failed mission*: When all preceding assurance-in-depth layers fail and a cyber attack denies or destroys mission completion. At this point, the goal of mission resilience is to enable orderly and timely recovery to a known state that permits assured mission resumption.

While the primary goal of mission assurance remains that of mitigating vulnerabilities and disrupting threats in order to maintain a pristine mission, the secondary goals aim to shape the mission environment to permit timely detection, ensure survival, and facilitate recovery.

Shaping the environment for timely detection of exploits must occur at the tactical, operational, and strategic levels of a mission. At the tactical level, selective insertion of Government Off-The-Shelf (GOTS) components into an essentially COTS system hinders system exploitation, increases the noise of the exploit, and permits timely detection. Operational agility through process distribution and migration plays a significant role in threat disruption, and subsequently timely detection. At the strategic level, the adoption of distinct Courses of Action (COA) to accomplish the same task allows for a looser detect-react OODA loop through heterogeneity and diversity.

The benefits of environment shaping extend beyond timely detection into mission survival. The activities that disrupt threats by making them noisier and more detectable tend to improve mission survival through agility and diversity. To this effect, a departure from a homogeneity culture in hardware and software in favor of deliberate heterogeneity and diversity improves mission survival against targeted attacks. A mission incorporating a mix of Windows and

Linux operating systems, running on a mix of Intel and AMD processors, utilizing IPv6 and IPv4 protocols atop Token Ring and Fiber Distributed Data Interface (FDDI) Media Access Controls (MAC), with deliberately inserted Field Programmable Gate Array (FPGA)-based interfaces implementing minimal protocol subsets, and the selective use of formally-verified hypervisors and separation kernels, are bound to increase disproportionately the cost of a successful exploit and reduce its effects, and consequently improve mission survival.

Resilience refers to the ability to recover from misfortune, or in our case from mission failure. The benefits of environment shaping extend readily into the fourth layer of assurance-in-depth, namely orderly recovery, by pre-positioning mission elements for instant insertion and restoration of compromised elements to a known pristine state. Artificial diversity, a hallmark of mission survival, contributes to resilience by permitting the orderly recovery of selected high-priority mission elements. Since not all systems are likely to be affected equally during a cyber attack that denies or destroys a mission, agility in process reassignment may speed up recovery by repurposing usable systems to ensure rapid restoration of critical processes.

Cyber Test and Evaluation

Cradle-to-grave mission assurance requires conducting Test and Evaluation (T&E) in a realistic threat environment, including cyber threats that represent current and projected adversary capabilities. Developmental Test and Evaluation (DT&E) during pre-systems acquisition and OT&E during acquisition and sustainment play vital roles in mission assurance.

DoD Directives 5000.01 and 5000.02 provide the principles and policies governing T&E and identify the flow of T&E activities within the acquisition life cycle (Figure 9.3). According to Defense Acquisition University,[6] DT&E seeks to identify technical capabilities and limitations, stresses the system to ensure robust design, and assesses performance under a number of environmental parameters such as adverse weather, while OT&E seeks to evaluate the operational effectiveness and suitability of a system operating under realistic combat conditions. Both DT&E and OT&E must take the cyber

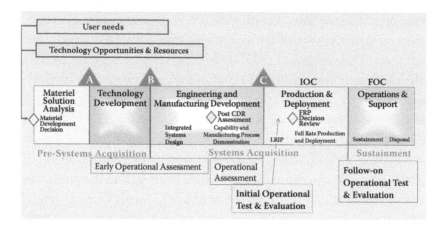

Figure 9.3   Acquisition life cycle chart.

environment into consideration as both an environmental parameter and as a hostile combat condition.

Figure 9.4 shows our OODA-loop construct for conducting T&E in a realistic cyber environment.[7] John Boyd claimed to have integrated the Incompleteness Theorem of Kurt Gödel, the Uncertainty Principle of Werner Heisenberg, and the Second Law of Thermodynamics into the development of the OODA loop.[8] The OODA loop provides a recursive model that appears to be scalable as well as responsive to the cyber T&E environment where we cannot see the totality of the

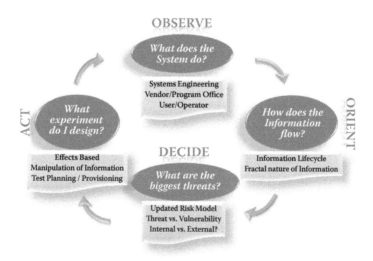

Figure 9.4   OODA loop construct for cyber T&E.

problem at one time, we operate in increasing ambiguity and chaos, and we must adapt decision making at each level of resolution:

1. *Observe*: What does the system do and in what type of environment does it operate?
2. *Orient*: How does information flow through the system, and where are the vulnerabilities?
3. *Decide*: What are the most serious threats to the mission, so that we can test against them?
4. *Act*: How do you plan and execute an experimental test?

We incorporated this methodology into the Cyber T&E component of the Systems Course at the USAF Test Pilot School, emphasizing DT&E of flight systems in a contested cyber environment. For this specific purpose, we expanded on each step in the OODA loop as follows:

1. *Observe*: Analyze the "system of systems" from a hierarchical perspective, starting with big-picture capabilities-based requirements down to little-picture technology requirements, to answer the question "What does the system do, and how does it do it?" The big-picture view of a system seeks to identify the mission that the system fulfills and the capability gap it was intended to fill, the information it provides, the environment within which it operates, and the user community it serves.

   Specific questions that help answer the big-picture question include

   • What functions does the system contribute to fulfill the mission?
   • Is there an architecture that describes the mission as a system of systems, or a topology that outlines the information flow through the system and between its components?
   • What hardware and software technologies did the designers use to build the system, and how well did these technologies integrate functionality and security?
   • How do subsystems share information, and what raw data do the subsystems collect and distribute to the other subsystems?
   • What information do the various sensors, inputs, and nodes deliver to the system, and what processed information does the system deliver to the user?

- What algorithms does the system use to process raw data into actionable information?

Since we do not expect test pilots or flight test engineers to know a priori the answers to the above questions, they must call on domain experts for these answers. Such resources include

- System program offices
- System and technology domain experts
- Contractor technical representatives

2. *Orient*: Decompose the system along the information life cycle, and label the information handling processes in each system component. Since functional decomposition along the information life cycle applies equally to data (raw unprocessed information) and information (contextually processed data), we use interchangeably these two terms.

- Information generation—data from various sensors
- Information processing—data processed into information and/or fused with other information to generate meta-information
- Information storage—data at rest until needed
- Information transmission—data moved to node/users as required, wired or wireless
- Information consumption—end user or end system
- Information destruction—archival of long-term data, removal of transient data

3. *Decide*: You can never have enough time or money to test everything, so you must tackle the challenge of reducing the number of test conditions.

- Use a risk-based decision process to select the most critical test conditions. D4-based vulnerability-threat-consequence risk assessment drives the decision on what to test. This is standard practice in both classical systems engineering and flight test processes.
- Map the information flow and information life cycle down to the component level of systems and subsystems. In other terms, generate an information wiring diagram or data flow diagram.

- Identify the fractal qualities of the system under test. Similar patterns of information flow appear at multiple mapping levels, from high-level mission system information, down to component data flows.
- Break down the information flow, latencies, and protocols to the lowest levels, and examine attack vectors to the information flow at all levels. Attack vectors must match those vulnerabilities with realistic threat capabilities.
- Assess the risk to the system of systems. The overall risk is the product of the vulnerability, the threat that can exploit that vulnerability, and the consequences of the threat exercising successfully the vulnerability.

4. *Act*: Once you understand physical system interconnections and the information life cycle as it pertains to the system under test, as well as the vulnerabilities in individual protocols, hardware, operating system, and applications software, you can design a test against a specific subsystem function using a specific vulnerability as an axis of attack:

- Design a test for the highest overall risk as a product of vulnerability, threat, and consequence.
- Base test requirements on the system and information being targeted, and the scope and duration of the D4 effects of each vulnerability and corresponding threat vector.
- Follow standard test methodology of establishing a stimulus—the test condition—and observing the effect.
- Design a scalable test concept, since systems-of-systems may be huge—millions of components and millions of lines of code. Start with simple test conditions against individual sub-systems and then proceed to more complex, multiple-variable factors.
- Ensure that the test setup and results are representative of the configuration that will be used operationally.
- Collaborate with cyber red teams to design the cyber penetration tests at the operational level. As you attempt to answer the fundamental questions of "what can an adversary with root access do to the system," defer to the red teams the corollary question of "how can an adversary obtain root access on a system?"

- Make reasonable assumptions to bound the scope of the test and to establish a context for the test and the results.
- Document your assumptions, and plan to revisit them as part of a risk analysis of the test results—be prepared to answer the critical question of how far off the results would be if certain assumptions did not hold.
- Pursuant to the risk analysis of the assumptions, brainstorm "what if" scenarios that could significantly change the results of the test.
- Identify the logistics of the test, the required resources, instrumentation, expertise, test facilities, time, and cost.

Mission Assurance in Public Clouds

As missions migrate from dedicated information systems and spill into public clouds, a new reality challenges the end goal of mission assurance. Public clouds present three new absolutes that we must deal with:

1. We do not own the computers on which our processes reside.
2. We did not write the software on which our processes run.
3. We do not control the neighborhood in which our processes execute.

Supply chain vulnerabilities take on a new dimension when we do not own the hardware, and we have little-to-no say in its specifications. It is a fact that someone else has root access to the server that hosts our data and our programs. In addition, we have no control over the quality or pedigree of the hypervisor and operating system software that interface our data and programs onto the host hardware. Finally, it is probable that other applications and services co-exist in the same hosting facility, even on the same computer, as our mission data and programs.

The basic tenets of information assurance—confidentiality, integrity, and availability—take on a new meaning in a public cloud environment. While encryption can ensure for the most part the confidentiality and integrity of information, availability is often at the mercy of the cloud provider. A machine turned off is simply not available, nor is the information it hosts, regardless of the level of encryption.

Obfuscation, duplication, and distribution provide a significant improvement in information availability in a public cloud. The competition among providers of cloud services and the commensurate drop in cost make it attractive to host the same information on hundreds, even thousands, of servers around the world, increasing its availability for contingency operations.

While traditional private-key and public-key encryption provide adequate security for information storage and transmission in public clouds, the technology for secure program execution in a public cloud remains immature. Homomorphic encryption promises to permit someday arbitrary operations on encrypted data, yet its intensive computing requirements make it impractical at this time.[9] Partially homomorphic operations may be viable in specific applications, and research is necessary to identify classes of national security missions that may benefit from this technology.

Time-Domain Mission Assurance

The DoD definition of mission assurance as "a process to ensure that assigned tasks or duties can be performed in accordance with the intended purpose or plan" makes no explicit reference to a time frame in the "intended purpose" over which the "assigned tasks and duties" must be assured. In future acquisitions where we specify mathematically the requirements of a mission, then verify formally that the implementation satisfies the security properties of the original specification, we may have the ability to assure indefinitely a given mission. However, as we deal with legacy systems with varying levels of assurance, introducing a time dimension reduces an otherwise daunting challenge into a more manageable task.

Many critical missions have finite life expectancy. For example, precision airdrop, space launch, and theater missile defense have missions that last seconds to minutes, requiring mission assurance over a very narrow time frame. In contrast, operational plans for emergency disaster relief may require assurance for periods of days to weeks.

Introducing a time dimension to mission assurance invites a paradigm change in which just-in-time execution may become the norm. One implementation of Time-Domain Mission Assurance involves just-in-time creation of a piece of cyberspace just for that mission, ensuring its mathematical incompatibility with prevalent threats. Throw-away processor instruction sets, programming languages, and protocols increase significantly the cost to an adversary seeking to compromise a mission that exists for a very short period of time.

Adding a time dimension to the mission assurance process impacts all four phases of MEF prioritization, mapping, vulnerability identification, and vulnerability mitigation. A MEF that is high-priority in the long term may fall into a lower priority in the opening seconds or minutes of mission execution. Similarly, a gaping vulnerability if left unattended on the long term may pose an acceptable risk over a much narrower time interval.

Conclusion

In this chapter we have discussed the assurance of national security missions against cyber threats. We have reviewed the challenges facing defense missions, and introduced a methodology to assure legacy missions in a contested information environment. We have introduced the information life cycle as a mechanism to identify system vulnerabilities, and discussed assurance-in-depth. We have presented new technology for cyber test and evaluation, discussed mission assurance in public clouds, and concluded with the introduction of a time dimension to mission assurance.

Endnotes

1. Department of Defense (DoD) Directive 3020.40, *DoD Policy and Responsibilities for Critical Infrastructure*, July 2010, available at: http://www.dtic.mil/whs/directives/corres/pdf/302040p.pdf.
2. Kamal Jabbour, ST, The Time Has Come for the Bachelor of Science in Cyber Engineering, *High Frontier Journal*, vol. 6, no. 4, August 2010, pp. 20–23, available at http://www.afspc.af.mil/shared/media/document/AFD-101019-079.pdf.
3. Gary Stoneburner, Alice Goguen, and Alexis Feringa, *Risk Management Guide for Information Technology Systems*, National Institute of Standards and Technology, NIST Special Publication 800–30, July 2002, available at: http://csrc.nist.gov/publications/nistpubs/800-30/sp800-30.pdf.

4. Kamal Jabbour and Sarah Muccio, The Science of Mission Assurance, *Journal of Strategic Security*, vol. IV, no. 2, 2011, pp. 61–74, available at http://scholarcommons.usf.edu/cgi/viewcontent.cgi?article=1106&context=jss.
5. *Integrated Defense Acquisition, Technology and Logistics Life Cycle Management System*, Defense Acquisition University, December 2008.
6. Defense Acquisition University, *Test and Evaluation Overview*, Lesson 18, 2006.
7. Kamal Jabbour, ST, and Randolph Kelly, *Cyber Test and Evaluation*, Systems Course, US Air Force Test Pilot School, October 2012.
8. John R. Boyd, *Destruction and Creation*, US Army Command and General Staff College, 1976.
9. Craig Gentry, A Fully Homomorphic Encryption Scheme, PhD Dissertation, Department of Computer Science, Stanford University, September 2009.

10

STUXNET

A Case Study in Cyber Warfare

ERIC P. OLIVER

Contents

A New Reality	128
Offense	132
Stuxnet and National Security Strategy	133
Prevention, Preemption, and US National Security Strategy	133
Truth 1: Cyber Attack Is Consistent with Our National Security Strategy if Done as Part of a Collective Action	133
Truth 2: Cyber Attack on Strategic Targets Can Reduce Casualties	133
Truth 3: Cyber Attack Can Achieve Significant, Long-Lasting Effects	134
Truth 4: Cyber Attacks Are Not Silver Bullets	135
Truth 5: Cyber Weapons Can Be Reverse Engineered to Strike Unintended Targets.	136
Defense	137
Truth 6: Cyber Weapons Can Defeat Even Well-Architected Cyber Systems	142
Truth 7: Traditional IT Defense Skills Remain Important in ICS Environments	145
Truth 8: Specialized ICS Environment Knowledge Is Required to Defend ICS	145
Truth 9: System Operators Are a Critical Part of the ICS Defensive Team	147
Implication 1: ICS Defenders Must Regularly Train Together	149
Implication 2: Defenders Must Be Equipped to Detect Deceptions	149
Implication 3: Embedded Control Devices Should Require Physical Access for All Firmware Updates	151

Conclusions   153

Endnotes   155

A New Reality

On January 15, 2011, *The New York Times* published an article alleging that Americans and Israelis collaborated to develop, test, and deliver Stuxnet.[1] By wasting time and ink writing a speculative "whodunit," the *Times* missed the opportunity to enter the more important debate on the topics of preemption and the value of offensive cyber weapons.

For almost 40 years, people have discussed the possibility of software-based attacks on critical infrastructures—energy, transportation, critical manufacturing, banking and finance, chemical processing, communications, and similar vital areas. Until 2010, most knowledgeable people agreed such attacks were possible if one could successfully attack the industrial control systems (ICSs) these infrastructures rely upon. However, there was a wide diversity of opinions regarding the likelihood of such an attack actually occurring or succeeding. The disagreements were generally rooted in differing assessments of opportunity and motivation. Unfortunately (or fortunately depending on how you look at it), there were no real-world cases to study in order to illuminate the debate. Stuxnet changed that.

Stuxnet served as an existence proof for the theory that malicious software (malware) can have strategically important, physically destructive effects on ICSs employed by modern states. Stuxnet is the name given to a masterfully crafted piece of malware first discovered in June 2010 by a computer security company in Belarus. It targeted and apparently successfully sabotaged uranium enrichment systems in Iran.[2] The significance of Stuxnet and its implications are great enough that the Congressional Research Service describes Stuxnet as a "Harbinger of an Emerging Warfare Capability."[3] Udo Helmbrecht, the executive director of the European Network and Information Security Agency (ENISA) called Stuxnet a "paradigm shift,"[4] and Sean McGurk, the head of the Cybersecurity Center at the Department of Homeland Security (DHS), described it as a "game-changer."[5]

In this chapter, Stuxnet is used as a case study to examine the question, "How should the United States (and the Air Force in particular) adapt to this new operational environment in which ICS attacks are a well-understood reality and not just an academic possibility?" It will do so by examining truths and myths revealed by analyzing the details surrounding Stuxnet in particular, and ICS in general, and then drawing some implications from those truths and myths. However, before digging into those questions, it is important to first understand a bit of detail about Stuxnet and the ICS it targeted for destruction.

Stuxnet displayed a level of technical sophistication and integration never before seen in malware. As the Symantec Security Response team wrote after 7 months of analysis, "Stuxnet is one of the most complex threats we have analyzed."[6] It exploited several Windows vulnerabilities, at least four of which were described as "zero-day exploits." Zero-day exploits are attacks targeting security vulnerabilities in which the software's developer learns about the vulnerability at the same time the public does; the developer has "zero days" to fix the flaw before it is exploited.

The presence of four zero-day exploits in a single piece of malware is stunning. If a piece of malware contains a single zero-day exploit, it is an extraordinary event. Zero-days in the Windows Operating System (O/S) are very difficult to find, and they sell in the hacker underground for as much as $100,000.[7] Not only did the developers have the resources and/or skills required to acquire and utilize these exploits, the Stuxnet developers required expertise in a wide variety of other concepts and technologies as well. Not only did the developers have the resources and/or skills required to acquire and utilize these exploits, the Stuxnet developers required expertise in an extraordinarily wide variety of other concepts and technologies as well.

The targeted uranium enrichment systems in Iran were controlled by an ICS developed by the German company Siemens. To successfully attack the Siemens ICS, Stuxnet initiated its malware delivery process using infected thumb drives. When an infected thumb drive was inserted in a computer running Windows and browsed using Microsoft Explorer or any other file manager that could display icons, the thumb drive would infect the machine and immediately make the infection invisible to the user. If that had been all Stuxnet did, it would have been practically indistinguishable from the almost 55,000 other malware samples that appear daily.[8]

However, Stuxnet was unique. It was not a tool for financial cyber-crime since it was not designed to make money. Nor was it strictly for computer network exploitation (CNE) or Cyber Operational Preparation of the Environment (C-OPE); it wasn't designed to simply maintain access and harvest information. Finally, it wasn't designed solely to inconvenience users by disrupting information systems. Instead, Stuxnet was designed to reprogram components of an ICS known as programmable logic controllers (PLCs). By reprogramming PLCs, Stuxnet was able to use them to direct physical devices (centrifuges) into self-destruction. By destroying the centrifuges, Stuxnet disrupted the physical process (uranium enrichment) that relied upon those devices.[9] Stuxnet was not simply targeting PLCs in an ICS; it was attacking what the ICS controlled. In short, Stuxnet was a destructive cyber attack on an industrial process.

The term "cyber attack" is widely used in the press and even formal publications; however, there is a no universally agreed-upon definition of the term and debates continue to rage daily. This paper will adopt the current definition found in the Joint Terminology for Cyberspace Operations memorandum released by the Vice Chairman of the Joint Chiefs of Staff. It defines cyber attack as:

> A hostile act using computer or related networks or systems, and intended to disrupt and/or destroy an adversary's critical cyber systems, assets, or functions. The intended effects of cyber attack are not necessarily limited to the targeted computer systems or data themselves—for instance, attacks on computer systems which are intended to degrade or destroy infrastructure or C2 capability. A cyber attack may use intermediate delivery vehicles including peripheral devices, electronic transmitters, embedded code, or human operators. The activation or effect of a cyber attack may be widely separated temporally and geographically from the delivery.[10]

This definition is not perfect; however, it does have utility. One of its weaknesses is its use of the ambiguous term "cyber systems." Stuxnet illuminates the ambiguity in the term. As stated earlier, the overwhelming body of evidence indicates that PLCs used in a uranium enrichment facility at Natanz, Iran were the target.[11] PLCs are not the traditional information technology (IT) systems predominantly associated with the "cyber operations" career field in at least one part of the Department of Defense (DoD)—the Air Force (AF). However, despite the fact that PLCs are not "traditional" IT systems, it would be difficult to argue that Stuxnet was not a cyber attack based upon that distinction when using the definition above.

Another weakness is that it does not clearly state that cyber attack can have kinetic effects. The definition says a cyber attack can destroy cyber systems or assets. It also says these attacks may affect more than the targeted computer system and the data it utilizes. However, as Stuxnet demonstrated, using a cyber attack to target an ICS can result in physical destruction of equipment and/or can cause the underlying process to go out of control. Extrapolating from the Stuxnet example, it is easy to imagine scenarios in which ICSs are attacked and complete facility destruction with mass casualties are the results.

Few experts expect Stuxnet to be the last sophisticated attack on control systems. As Ralph Langner, a recognized expert on Stuxnet in particular and ICS in general, wrote,

> Even though Stuxnet as such is not a generic attack on control systems, several parts of the attack in fact are generic, and these generic parts are easy to copy. With these generic attack techniques at his or her disposal, a follow-up attacker may not only implement a similar targeted and surgical strike, but may choose to create widespread, random havoc, using any vendor's controller.[12]

Given Stuxnet's visibility, we can expect a surge in published ICS exploits as many more investigators begin looking for them. In fact, it has already begun. On March 21, 2011, Luigi Auriemma, a security researcher who professed to have no background in control systems, published 35 new zero-day exploits affecting four different vendors' products.[13]

In a particular noteworthy episode, Dillon Beresford, a security researcher, canceled a talk he was scheduled to give in May of 2011 at TakeDownCon. The talk was supposed to be about a supervisory control and data acquisition (SCADA) exploit proof-of-concept against Siemens' systems—the target of the Stuxnet worm. He canceled the talk after consulting with representatives from Siemens and the DHS over security concerns. Beresford stated he developed the exploit "in my bedroom, on my laptop" in 2 1/2 months. DHS officials asked the researcher to delay the presentation until patches for the vulnerabilities were fully developed—a process Siemens said would take a "few weeks."[14] Unfortunately, the reality is that ICS operators do not, and cannot (for reasons to be explained later in this chapter), apply patches to their systems as soon as they are available. Therefore, if the researcher publishes his finding soon after the patches are released by Siemens, there will still be an extended period of vulnerability where critical infrastructures will be operating systems with known vulnerabilities.

Clearly, the landscape has changed. To survive and thrive in this new environment where malware can target critical infrastructures for destruction, it is imperative to consider how best to adapt. As a nation, the United States can sit back and wait for future events to shape its response, or it can actively study the environment revealed by Stuxnet and seek ways to adapt to it.

Offense

Stuxnet was an offensive weapon. The old adage is "The best defense is a good offense," but is that true when employing cyber weapons? If the United States wishes to employ offensive cyber attack capabilities (cyber weapons) like Stuxnet in the future, it should first consider a few questions. How effective can cyber weapons be? What are the risks of employing such weapons? Are such weapons consistent with our National Security Strategy? These and similar questions are the ones this chapter will explore.

However, before delving into the questions surrounding cyber weapons, it is important to first define the terms "weapon" and "cyber weapon." Although the terms are often used loosely in many forums, this paper will adopt narrow definitions. A weapon is defined to be "something used to alter the behavior of a target by directly or indirectly inflicting suffering, bodily harm, or physical damage." Following from that definition, a cyber weapon is defined to be "malware[15] used to alter the behavior of a target by directly or indirectly inflicting suffering, bodily harm, or physical damage." This narrow definition does not cover the full range of potential effects one may achieve with malware, but it does provide a basis for identifying cyber weapons as a distinct form of malware. A cyber weapon's direct or indirect "weapon effect" must include suffering, bodily harm, or physical damage. Just as a hammer can be a tool or a weapon depending on how it is employed, malware can be a cyber tool useful for a variety of purposes (criminal, espionage, deception, etc.), or it can be a cyber weapon. Stuxnet was a cyber weapon.

Stuxnet and National Security Strategy

Prevention, Preemption, and US National Security Strategy

Truth 1: Cyber Attack Is Consistent with Our National Security Strategy if Done as Part of a Collective Action   For the sake of exploring the general question of preemptive action, let's not debate Iran's intentions at Natanz. If one accepts the assertion that this uranium enrichment facility is producing raw materials for weapons, our National Security Strategy makes it a legitimate target for disruption.[16] In that case, what options are available short of using "force," which appears to be synonymous with "war" in the current national security strategy? Economic and political actions have been employed for years, but Iran has continued to develop the facility. As a result of the continued development, it is widely reported that Israel wanted to bomb the facility two years ago. That would have crossed the "war threshold" the United States is seeking to avoid, so the country did not support the action. So what to do?

Perhaps the United States could employ a cyber weapon. If one analyzes the details of Stuxnet, it is fairly easy to build a compelling, albeit circumstantial, case that it was developed to precisely target Natanz. The desired effect appears to have been to hinder uranium enrichment by disrupting the centrifuges operating there. This novel approach meets both strategic goals of avoiding "war" and preventing Iran from building nuclear weapons.

America has the ability to take unilateral action and doing so is not prohibited by our current National Security Strategy; however, acting in collaboration with other nations is more consistent with our current National Security Strategy.[17]

Truth 2: Cyber Attack on Strategic Targets Can Reduce Casualties   Targeting an Iranian nuclear weapon production process is essentially the same strategic targeting strategy employed by the United States in

World War II. One strategic objective in that conflict was to disrupt Nazi weapons production by bombing ball-bearing factories in Schweinfurt—the source of approximately 50% of all ball-bearing output.[18] The allies bombed the city 22 times. It took 2285 aircraft delivering a total of 7933 tons of bombs (592,598 individual bombs), which destroyed half of the houses and four-fifths of the industrial buildings with 1079 civilian casualties reported. The first two raids alone cost the Americans 980 men and 98 aircraft.[19]

In the case of Stuxnet, there are no reports of deaths associated with delivering the weapon, and physical destruction appears to have been limited to the intended target. It would seem that a cyber weapon is a better means of striking a strategic target if minimizing casualties and destruction is a goal.

Truth 3: Cyber Attack Can Achieve Significant, Long-Lasting Effects   In the case of the Schweinfurt raids, the reward was an approximate 34% decrease in production,[20] followed by a dispersal that led to at least an 85% recovery of capacity a year later.[21] In summary, the strategic bombing survey authors concluded:

> From examination of the records and personalities in the ball-bearing industry, the user industries and the testimony of war production officials, there is no evidence that the attacks on the ball-bearing industry had any measurable effect on essential war production.[22]

When compared to the costs of the raids, this doesn't seem to be a very good value proposition.

Stuxnet on the other hand appears to have hindered Iran's uranium production facilities for almost two years at the time of this writing and can reasonably be expected to have long-term, ongoing effects as well.

There were at least three distinctly different waves of Stuxnet launched in Iran. The first wave was launched from four different locations in June and July of 2009. The next launch occurred in March 2010 and appears to have come from one of the original launch sites. The final re-attack was launched from two of the original sites and one new site. These launches occurred between April and May 2010. All three waves of attack used different variants of Stuxnet, and they all would have had different weapon effects based upon improvements and modifications included in the newer variants.[23] This highlights the reality that cyber attack can be more like a siege than a single strike with ephemeral effects, but what were the siege's effects?

A report published by the Institute for Science and International Security (ISIS) in February 2011 identifies several specific impacts of Stuxnet[24]:

- It destroyed about 1,000 out of 9,000 centrifuges housed in Natanz at the time of the attacks.
- Of the 9,000 housed there, only about 4,000 were enriching at the time of the attack, and Stuxnet "delayed Iran from expanding the number of enriching centrifuges, in essence keeping large sections of the plant idle for many months."
- It created a shortage of raw materials for building more centrifuges. "With 9,000 centrifuges already deployed at Natanz, and an estimated 1,000 centrifuges broken during routine operation, adding in the 1,000 centrifuges destroyed by Stuxnet brings the total to 11,000 centrifuges deployed over the lifetime of the FEP." The report assessed Iran had only enough raw materials to build 12,000 to 15,000 centrifuges total.
- It caused Iran to worry about the overall quality of their enrichment program: "Without knowing the cause was malware, Iran would have struggled to understand this failure and likely would have lost valuable time worrying about more failures."
- It created a heightened sense of vulnerability to outside attack since "it demonstrated that foreign intelligence agencies had learned a considerable amount of information about their secret operations."
- It made Iran "feel less secure about the goods its smuggling networks acquire abroad for its nuclear programs," forcing it to "resort to relying more heavily on reverse engineering and domestic production of a greater variety of advanced industrial goods," despite the fact it "has limited advanced industrial capabilities and has encountered difficulties in successfully reverse engineering equipment and technology."

Truth 4: Cyber Attacks Are Not Silver Bullets Although Stuxnet had significant effects, it is also important to note that it does not appear to

have stopped the continued buildup of low enriched uranium; production actually increased in the fall of 2009 and early 2010. There
was a small decrease in the rate of production in mid-2010, but by the
fall, production appeared to have reached new record levels.[25]

Almost certainly, the Iranians would have been able to ramp up
production much more quickly if not for Stuxnet; data from the
IAEA safeguards report, as cited by ISIS, indicate this is true. These
data show the number of centrifuges installed and under vacuum
decreased after November 2009, and they also show that the number
of centrifuges being fed uranium hexafluoride for enrichment dropped
in August 2009. A year later (the latest data available), the Iranians
didn't appear to have solved either of these problems.[26] Nevertheless,
this fact remains: the Iranians were able to almost continuously
increase production throughout the three waves of attack.

*Truth 5: Cyber Weapons Can Be Reverse Engineered to Strike Unintended
Targets*   Regardless of any other value propositions, Stuxnet raises
one very important consideration for employing cyber weapons.
Unlike a traditional weapon, Stuxnet did not destroy itself as it
achieved its intended effect. Once it was discovered, the world began
reverse engineering it. Stuxnet's attack code, now readily available
on the Internet, provides a blueprint and a jumpstart for developing
Stuxnet 2.0, which could be directed at the United States. At the end
of 2004 (the latest data available), the United States had an estimated
$1.3 trillion worth of privately owned critical infrastructure in our
electric generation, transmission, and distribution systems.[27] That,
along with all other critical infrastructures controlled by an ICS (e.g.,
transportation, critical manufacturing, chemical processing, and the
like), is now presumably at risk. Simply put, proliferation of a cyber
weapon appears to be uncontrollable. If a cyber weapon is discovered and publicly analyzed, all potential attackers' skill level is raised.
Consequently, the entire world's risk level is raised until the newly
identified vulnerabilities can be addressed—a process that can take
years in the case of ICSs.

*The Benefits of Unleashing a Cyber Weapon—Even if They Are Enormous—
May Be Dominated by the Risk of a "Return Fire"*   The reality is that anyone
releasing a cyber weapon needs to have a fool-proof means of ensuring

it cannot be reverse engineered and sent back like a boomerang to attack its creators or innocent third parties. It does not matter who releases a new cyber weapon into the wild. The initial attacker may have the benefit of surprise, but that surprise may come at great cost; third parties may quickly become involved, and they may use the weapon—as well as its accompanying tactics, techniques, and procedures—to rebuild it as their own weapon system and become attackers in their own right. Third parties may also become involved as additional, unintended targets.

Unfortunately, there does not appear to be any foolproof means of preventing a "boomerang attack" today unless targeted technology simply does not exist outside the targeted country. Even then, the tactics, techniques, and procedures revealed through analysis of a cyber weapon may have general applicability. They could be adapted to support development and employment of new cyber weapons aimed at new targets.

Until countermeasures are in place, the reality that a cyber weapon may fall into non-friendly hands must infuse future debates as our nation "carefully weigh[s] the costs and risks of action against the costs and risks of inaction" with cyber attack.

Defense

In sports, it is often said that a good defense will never win a game, but a bad defense can lose it. The same is true of cyber warfare. Cyber defense will not win conflicts, but a lack of adequate cyber defense can assure defeat.

Even if the United States is judicious in its employment of cyber weapons, and the world limits them with international treaties, rogue individuals and organizations are likely to continue to develop them for use; the risk/reward calculus is too great to deter all potential aggressors. Since the danger of cyber weapon proliferation is great, impact of a cyber weapon can be great, and international agreements will likely be ineffective against determined adversaries. The United States must invest in the defense.

As a nation, the United States spends untold fortunes[28] defending against improvised explosive devices (IEDs) that have limited direct impacts. We should be even more concerned and spending equally vigorously to defeat cyber weapons that can have strategic-level direct effects on critical infrastructure and ICS. Therefore, we must prepare defenses capable of minimizing the benefits a cyber weapon would provide to rogue actors.

Stuxnet highlights many challenges defenders must confront and overcome.

Martin Libicki Was Incorrect   In his widely read and influential book, *Cyberdeterrence and Cyberwar*, Martin Libicki writes that "organizations are only vulnerable to the extent they want to be" and "cyberwar operations neither directly harm individuals nor destroy equipment."[29] As soon as he published those statements, they sparked a vigorous debate about their accuracy. Stuxnet demonstrated that these assertions are at best overstated, and arguably completely false.

Undoubtedly, the Iranians were more vulnerable than they *wanted* to be—all indications are that they wanted to enrich uranium without interference. However, their vulnerability was not a result of negligence on the part of the uranium enrichment system developers or operators. It was a result, in large measure, of the unique characteristics of ICSs and the cyber weapons that were used, as well as a lack of understanding of the aggressor's capability (i.e., the Iranians didn't truly understand the threat).

ICSs Are Different from Traditional IT Systems from a "Defendability" Perspective   ICSs are fundamentally different from traditional IT systems in that they cannot be quickly or cheaply secured. As the DHS writes in its "Recommended Practices: ICS" security publication,

> From a mitigation perspective, simply deploying IT security technologies into a control system may not be a viable solution. Although modern industrial control systems often use the same underlying protocols that are used in IT and business networks, the very nature of control systems functionality (combined with operational and availability requirements) may make even proven security technologies inappropriate. Some sectors, such as energy, transportation, and chemical, have time sensitive requirements, so the latency and "throughput" issues associated with security strategies may introduce unacceptable delays and degrade or prevent acceptable system performance.[30]

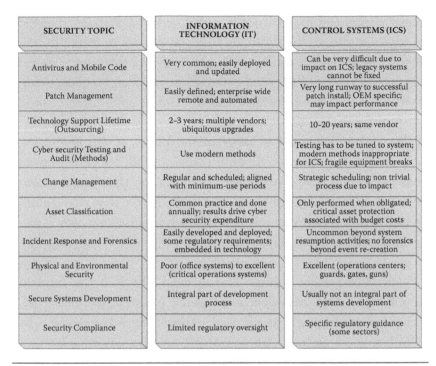

SECURITY TOPIC	INFORMATION TECHNOLOGY (IT)	CONTROL SYSTEMS (ICS)
Antivirus and Mobile Code	Very common; easily deployed and updated	Can be very difficult due to impact on ICS; legacy systems cannot be fixed
Patch Management	Easily defined; enterprise wide remote and automated	Very long runway to successful patch install; OEM specific; may impact performance
Technology Support Lifetime (Outsourcing)	2–3 years; multiple vendors; ubiquitous upgrades	10–20 years; same vendor
Cyber security Testing and Audit (Methods)	Use modern methods	Testing has to be tuned to system; modern methods inappropriate for ICS; fragile equipment breaks
Change Management	Regular and scheduled; aligned with minimum-use periods	Strategic scheduling; non trivial process due to impact
Asset Classification	Common practice and done annually; results drive cyber security expenditure	Only performed when obligated; critical asset protection associated with budget costs
Incident Response and Forensics	Easily developed and deployed; some regulatory requirements; embedded in technology	Uncommon beyond system resumption activities; no forensics beyond event re-creation
Physical and Environmental Security	Poor (office systems) to excellent (critical operations systems)	Excellent (operations centers; guards, gates, guns)
Secure Systems Development	Integral part of development process	Usually not an integral part of systems development
Security Compliance	Limited regulatory oversight	Specific regulatory guidance (some sectors)

Figure 10.1 Security in ICS and traditional IT. (From DHS-CSSP, 2009.)

The low-level protocols that underlie modern ICS systems are increasingly the same protocols used in IT networks because the transport infrastructure is increasingly shared between IT and ICS. Therefore, ICS benefits from security enhancements on those underlying protocols. However, the higher-level protocols an ICS uses are unique and often proprietary. Securing those protocols requires a dedicated effort by researchers and cooperation with ICS developers or protocol standards developers.

Figure 10.1 illustrates several other key differences. Of the various security topics found in this figure, five items have the greatest negative impact on ICS cyber security and presumably strongly impacted the Iranians' ability to defend themselves from Stuxnet.

Antivirus and Mobile Code   Stuxnet specifically targeted at least three different technologies. It targeted the Windows O/S, it targeted ICS-related applications that ran on Windows, and it targeted PLCs that were part of the ICS. Although Iran may have had protections against viruses and mobile code installed on its IT systems, they did not have any antivirus software installed on devices in their PLCs or attached devices. The reason is simple: antivirus software does not exist for the Siemens PLCs and Fararo Paya or Vacon Frequency converter drives that drove the centrifuges.

It is also worth noting that if the Iranians had antivirus software on the workstations used to program the PLCs, it was ineffective. Those workstations were successfully compromised, but perhaps more importantly, they were compromised in such a way that if the Iranians used them to try and purge Stuxnet from the PLCs, they would automatically reinstall Stuxnet on the PLCs while simultaneously masking the fact that they had done so.

Patch Management/Change Management   Even if the Iranians had a flawless patch management program, it would have been ineffective against Stuxnet, which used multiple zero-day exploits. By definition, there are no patches available for zero-day exploits; they must be rapidly developed and made available to system users *after* attacks have already been discovered (which may also be after an attacker's strategic objective has been achieved).

However, even when faced with less severe threats, patch management is difficult in an ICS environment. First, the vendors have to make a patch available; this can take days to months—or longer—to accomplish. Then, obtaining patches from all the vendors involved and getting them installed on an ICS is typically a lengthy process.

Natanz was typical of many ICS environments where system availability is of utmost importance. That need drives a requirement for careful regression testing and complicates scheduling downtime for installing the patches. The result is long delays in eliminating vulnerabilities.

Another factor delaying the installation of patches (and presumably antivirus/mobile code protections, assuming they become available) is the fact that most ICS environments are purpose-built and maintained by an outside contractor. Operators of these systems do not want to take independent action to secure their environment; doing so can invalidate the warranty on their system, which can cost millions of dollars.

Technology Support Lifetime   Natanz, like most ICS environments, was a long-term investment. It was built (and continues to be built) with hardware and software that is expected to run for years uninterrupted. It was purpose-built, and its developers were almost certainly not expecting to upgrade components, add or subtract components, or in any other way fundamentally alter the design and/or function of the system for many years. Being a relatively static target, it was easier to attack than a traditional IT environment would be. In contrast to ICS environments, IT environments are general-purpose environments, where system hardware and software are routinely changed out, configurations constantly change, nodes continuously appear and disappear, and an attacker can more easily lose existing accesses or access to exploitable vulnerabilities. A four-year-old computer is probably on an IT organization's planned replacement list. A four-year-old PLC is typically in the early stages of its life.[31]

Cyber Security Testing and Audit   Although there is no direct evidence publicly available, it seems reasonable to assume Iran did not attempt active cyber security testing of its facilities at Natanz. There are a couple of reasons this is likely the case. First, the availability of skilled ICS penetration testers is limited worldwide. Stuxnet created a surge in demand, but prior to widespread awareness of Stuxnet, there were relatively few people engaged in this arena when compared to traditional IT security. Second, the Natanz operators, like many ICS operators, probably assumed they were secured by their air-gapped architecture.[32] Their failure was ultimately a failure of imagination.

Another more pragmatic reason the Iranians may not have conducted cyber security testing is this: ICSs typically require very fast response times between the controllers and their associated sensors and actuators. Attempting penetration tests on an ICS can place additional traffic on, and induce unacceptable latency on, the communication pathways carrying that traffic. Many ICS applications cannot withstand even the most basic scans without faulting. The ability to break an ICS by inducing latency is a critical aspect of the "fragility" that the DHS cited as a reason for *not* testing and auditing ICS cyber security.

Physical and Environmental Security   The DHS publication asserts that physical and environmental security is excellent in an ICS.

That is almost certainly the case for the Natanz facility. However, this is not true in all ICS environments. In fact, physical and environmental controls for isolated sensors and actuators in large-scale, geographically dispersed ICSs (often referred to as supervisory control and data acquisition, or SCADA, systems) can be poor or even non-existent.

Prime examples are SCADA systems controlling pipelines or railroads. Remote terminal units (RTUs) or intelligent end devices (IEDs) are often used to pass sensor data from remote sites back to a central control system and to pass actuation orders from the central system out to remote sites. These RTUs/IEDs are almost always unmanned, often miles from civilization, and often not alarmed. This situation creates significant vulnerability to the entire system.

Typical SCADA architectures in place today assume any communication between RTUs/IEDs and the central control system are trustworthy. Unfortunately, this assumption is made without the aid of any deception-detection mechanisms. By compromising a remotely located device, an attacker can inject arbitrary sensor inputs or arbitrarily actuate devices—effectively defeating control/feedback loops that are the very reason SCADA systems exist. The end result is deliberate, malicious manipulation of an entire system which is possible due to poor physical security of remote devices.

Truth 6: Cyber Weapons Can Defeat Even Well-Architected Cyber Systems   A comparison between the ICS defense-in-depth recommendations put out by the DHS's Industrial Control System Computer Emergency Response Team (ICS-CERT)[33] and the reported architecture of the Natanz enrichment facility reveals the Iranians did many things right.

The DHS's recommended architecture divides a typical industrial control into five distinct zones and inserts firewalls, de-militarized zones (DMZs), intrusion-detection systems (IDSs), and security-incident and event management (SIEM) systems as shown in Figure 10.2.

It appears the Natanz architecture was even better than the DHS's recommendations. The Iranians apparently had no continuous external physical connections into the data and control zones—they were air-gapped from the Internet and corporate environment just like the safety systems were. Nevertheless, Stuxnet—which was released

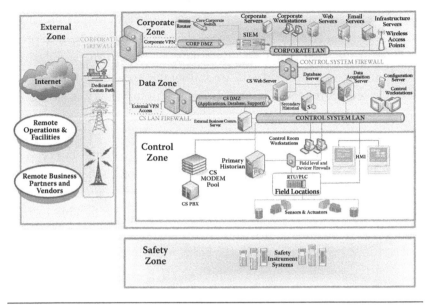

Figure 10.2 Architecture zones and defenses in depth for ICS. (From DHS-CSSP 2009, 24.)

at five Iranian companies with no public association with Natanz, and without any "publicly traceable history of being associated with Natanz"[34]—ultimately made its way into Natanz.

In the end, the Iranians proved the principle put forth in DHS's publication, "Manipulation of the industrial control systems information resources can be devastating if [the control system local area network (LAN)] is compromised. In many sectors, the malicious attack on the control systems will have real-world, physical results."

The bottom line is this: Stuxnet proved Martin Libicki was wrong. Cyber operations can and did directly harm people or destroy equipment. However, in fairness to Libicki, his statement "organizations are only vulnerable to the extent they want to be" can be construed as true, but only as far as similar statements, such as "the US is only as vulnerable to air attack as we want to be," are true.

Similar to the way the nation responded to patch its vulnerability after the air attacks of September 11, 2001, the nation can continually respond to patch vulnerabilities in cyber systems as they are discovered. But that is no assurance of adequate defense.

Just as the nation hasn't done (and can't do) everything possible (e.g., stop commercial air travel over the United States) to protect itself for future air attacks, the nation hasn't done (and can't do) everything possible (e.g., shut down power production, chemical manufacturing, and other critical ICS until patches are developed and applied) to protect itself from cyber attack. If it is only a matter of time and desire, would anyone in the world still be vulnerable to aerial attack more than 100 years after the advent of powered flight? Libicki's assertion may be true, but it grossly oversimplifies reality.

As Sun Tzu said thousands of years ago: "The art of war teaches us to rely not on the likelihood of the enemy's not coming, but on our own readiness to receive him; not on the chance of his not attacking, but rather on the fact that we have made our position unassailable."[35] Unfortunately, "unassailability" does not appear to be feasible in the arena of cyber warfare, so we must be prepared to defend vigorously, then continue to operate through the losses we will most assuredly take.

Force Packaging for Defense   In air operations, "force packaging" is an important concept. Effectively attacking an adversary from the air is a team effort requiring people and platforms capable of (among other things) electronic warfare/jamming; suppression of enemy air defenses; air surveillance; counter-air operations; command and control; air refueling; and intelligence, surveillance, and reconnaissance. Similarly, effectively attacking an adversary's cyber systems requires a broad array of capabilities.

In addition to a very broad range of more traditional computer network attack (hacking) skills, Stuxnet required people who understood mechanical engineering (to determine likely breaking points of centrifuges), PLC programming (to create the PLC rootkit), electrical engineering (to understand the impacts of manipulating frequency converters), human-machine interface (HMI) systems, and engineering workstations (to understand how to conceal attack symptoms from system developers, operators, and maintainers). Only by packaging all these skills together were the creators of Stuxnet able to successfully mount the attack.

If it took a broad array of skills to successfully prosecute the attack, what sorts of skills are required to defend against such an attack? Fortunately, DHS sponsors a program at Idaho National Laboratory that sheds some light on the question.

The DHS Control System Security Program includes a hands-on, advanced, technical-level training course known as the Control

Systems Cyber Security Advanced Training and Workshop. This week-long program provides intensive, hands-on training on protecting and securing control systems from cyber attacks. It includes a very realistic Red-Team/Blue-Team exercise conducted within an actual control-systems environment. The exercise provides a competition as the red team tries to attack the control system and the blue team works to defend against the cyber attacks.

Based upon the author's observation and/or participation in five of these events, it appears the skills required to successfully defend are similar to the skills required to attack. The most successful blue teams displayed teamwork and collaboration, but they also had a well-rounded "force package" of skills for defense. To address the need for ICS defense, the United States (and the USAF in particular) should build force packages for defense. The following paragraphs will describe the composition of effective defensive force packages.

Truth 7: Traditional IT Defense Skills Remain Important in ICS Environments The most successful defensive teams included people who had deep understanding of traditional IT defense skills. They understood employment of firewalls, proxies, IDSs, and other defensive tools to the point where they were actively building their own defensive systems or at least building customized defensive system rule-sets based upon a deep understanding of the ICS environments they were defending. They understood how to properly implement the secure architecture found in Figure 10.2. They understood how to search for and eliminate unnecessary means of access, optimally reshaping the attack surface they exposed to the aggressors while maintaining critical operations. They also understood how to employ SIEMs to find the needles in the haystacks. Finally, they understood how to patch vulnerabilities. In short, they were experienced and well-rounded in traditional IT security.

Truth 8: Specialized ICS Environment Knowledge Is Required to Defend ICS In an ICS environment, traditional IT defense skills were not enough, and were sometimes counterproductive. First, the most successful blue teams understood which portions of the system were most critical to their mission, and they focused their main efforts on protecting those portions of their system. However, they did so while ensuring those critical components continued to operate and perform their intended functions.

As an example, consider the HMI systems. As shown in Figure 10.2, an HMI is located in the most sensitive part of an ICS, the control zone. HMIs provide ICS operators with the ability to monitor and control the process the ICS is running. If HMIs stop functioning properly, operators can lose insight into the state of the process and may even lose the ability to control it.

In the DHS's Control System Security training environment, the O/S on the machines hosting the HMI systems had well-known exploitable software vulnerabilities. However, patching them was not an option because the HMI software was not compatible with the patched versions of the O/S. Traditional IT security professionals, lacking adequate knowledge of HMI systems, were inclined to patch them as soon as they discovered vulnerabilities. In cases where they did so, they prevented operators from being able to remotely monitor and control their ICS. The risk to the system could not be eliminated by patching the vulnerabilities; it had to be creatively managed in other ways.

Management of the risk required collaboration and cooperation between the ICS experts and the IT security experts. The IT security experts knew how to monitor traffic between devices and disrupt undesirable traffic. The ICS experts knew the HMI systems should only have a very few well-defined other systems ever connecting to them.

Given the relatively static nature of those connections, the successful defenders teamed up their ICS engineers and their IT security professionals. The ICS engineers used their knowledge of HMIs and the underlying process they were controlling to rapidly identify legitimate connections. Armed with that information, IT security professionals were then able to use traditional IT defense tools to rapidly and continuously identify and disrupt illegitimate connections. It required extensive teamwork between the traditional IT security professionals and the ICS designers and operators to initially identify the baseline of expected legitimate connections. Then, it required a well-executed change management process to continually maintain the baseline of known legitimate connections. However, the reward was that teams that did this work were able to ensure operations continued while illegitimate traffic was rapidly identified and addressed.

Without an understanding of the purpose of an HMI, it would be easy for a traditional IT security professional to treat it as "just another system," rather than the critical component it is. Similar arguments can be made for PLCs, RTUs, IEDs, engineering workstations, historians, and other unique, critical components of an ICS. The bottom line is that highly specialized ICS environment knowledge is required to defend an ICS, and defense is a continuous, collaborative process, not a one-time project.

Truth 9: System Operators Are a Critical Part of the ICS Defensive Team   As stated earlier, the most successful blue teams understood what portions of their system were most critical to their mission, but it suggests the question, "How did they determine which were most critical?" The answer is simple: they understood the system as a whole, and they understood the operational impacts of losing control of any device in the ICS. Furthermore, they understood how to work around individual parts in the event they lost control of them.

As an example, let's consider the artificially simple case of a chemical manufacturing facility controlled by a single PLC. A generalized diagram of any closed-loop control system is shown in Figure 10.3. In our hypothetical example, the individual pumps, valves, mixers, sensors, etc., are all connected to a single PLC, which receives inputs from the sensors, makes computations based upon those inputs, and outputs control signals back to the system. The PLC arguably is the most critical part of this system since it ensures the chemical manufacturing process stays under control. If it is reprogrammed by an attacker, the operational impacts, which will be at the discretion of the attacker, could be catastrophic. Notice, this is a fully automated process—there are no humans involved aside from the potential attacker. As stated,

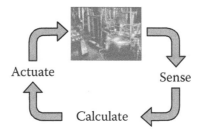

Actuate

Sense

Calculate

Figure 10.3   Generalized closed-loop control system.

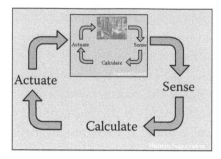

Figure 10.4 Human supervision of an automated control system.

this is somewhat contrived; practically all automated control systems do have human involvement. At the very least, they typically have manual overrides that can be implemented by human operators.

Figure 10.4 shows a generalized diagram of a human supervising an automated control system. Notice that the human can be considered simply another closed-loop control system sensing the status of the automated control system, calculating a response, and initiating action. Because a human is monitoring performance of the automated control system, that human must be able to identify various failure modes, know how the system will act in those modes, and be prepared to react appropriately.

In a very real and practical sense, the human monitoring and responding to failures of our hypothetical ICS is a defender; he or she assures the mission of the system. Operators are the ones who know how to manually override the PLC or various other pieces of equipment should they become unreliable. Furthermore, they and the ICS engineers who designed the system are in the best position to identify equipment that is not performing properly (e.g., valves that are open when they should not be, temperatures that are slightly out of tolerance, motors that are running at abnormal speeds, etc.). They are in the best position to identify improper performance because they understand the underlying process, and they understand how it must be regulated to ensure nominal operation. For these reasons, their specialized knowledge absolutely *must* be included in the process of defending the ICS and assuring mission accomplishment.

In summation, perhaps the DHS said it best. In the introduction to their excellent publication, *Recommended Practice: Developing an*

Industrial Control Systems Cybersecurity Incident Response Capability,[36] they wrote:

> This recommended practice was written for the team charged with creating a computer cyber incident response capability focused on protecting the ICS environment from cyber attack. This includes *operations and plant managers, process engineers, security professionals, network administrators, legal, physical security, and other IT professionals* [emphasis added].

Implication 1: ICS Defenders Must Regularly Train Together

Defense of industrial control systems requires a force package, and just as air operations' force packages must regularly come together and practice for effective combat, cyber operators' force packages must also regularly come together and practice for effective combat. Building and maintaining cyber-defense force packages must be as natural as building and maintaining fire departments. Just like fire departments, they will not usually be actively working on their defensive mission—they will typically be training and monitoring—but they are a cost of doing business. Cyber defense force packages must be immediately available and effective when and where the need arises; they cannot be a pickup game cobbled together after a crisis has arisen.

Implication 2: Defenders Must Be Equipped to Detect Deceptions

In the case of Stuxnet, the attack combined a "denial of control" attack with a "denial of view" attack. By reprogramming the PLCs, the attackers effectively co-opted the legitimate process operators' ability to automatically control their system. Furthermore, by attacking the HMI machines and engineering workstations, the attackers were able to deny the operators' ability to sense the out-of-control condition. In essence, the attackers deceived the Iranian system operators into believing everything was operating nominally. By taking these steps, the attackers had covertly seized control of the uranium enrichment process.

To successfully regain control of their process, the Iranians had to first discover the deception and then develop methods to eliminate the cover Stuxnet was employing. As Barton Whaley, one of the foremost experts on military deception, points out, *all* deceptions are discoverable because *all* deceptions differ from the truth in *at least* one way.[37] The challenge is to identify the discrepant information that will reveal the deception.

Stuxnet made it clear that identifying discrepant information to reveal deceptions in an ICS environment is a requirement for assured operations (or "cyber surety" to use one of the AF's terms). In the case of Stuxnet, the discrepant information could have been something as simple as acoustic information; the system operators may have been able to hear a change in pitch as the spinning centrifuges accelerated and decelerated. Once again, this illustrates the point that system operators are a critical part of the defensive team; however, perhaps there are technical means that would be useful for detecting deceptions.

A corollary to Whaley's theorem could be "illegitimate ICS communication traffic always differs from legitimate traffic in at least one way; the key to identifying illegitimate traffic is to identify the difference." Once again, this supports the argument that defenders must understand the underlying processes and the baseline of communications required for nominal control of those processes. As an example, if a PLC is designed to communicate with only three endpoints, an HMI, IEDs, and a historian, any other traffic should immediately be considered illegitimate until proven otherwise.

That is a good start, but can all communications from expected endpoints be trusted? Unfortunately, most existing ICS communication protocols do not typically protect against compromised endpoints; they assume the endpoint is trustworthy and accept its input. Therefore, supplementary measures must be implemented.

Stuxnet was able to mask its malicious activities by first recording nominal data as it was transmitted from the frequency converters to the HMI during normal operation of the centrifuges. The malware then replayed the nominal data back to the HMI while the centrifuge sabotage routines were running (Falliere, Murchu, and Chien, 2010). Thus, instead of seeing the anomalous operating frequency data and being alarmed, the monitoring systems (including the system operators) believed the frequency converters were operating normally.

Although there do not appear to be any published techniques for identifying replayed data that are unique to an ICS environment, traditional information assurance practices, such as the use of nonces,[38] could be implemented to address such problems. Unfortunately, implementation of these practices would suffer from the same challenges (discussed earlier) as any other patching/upgrading effort on an ICS. ICS vendors would first have to implement these techniques in their protocols. Then, system owners would have to field the new protocols. The process will take years from start to finish, assuming the vendors are all motivated to get it started.

A potentially faster way to approach the problem is to analyze existing data stream for signs of tampering. To minimize potential for disruption of an ICS, the data stream could be simply tapped for analysis. The original data would flow through the system uninterrupted, and the tapped copy would be analyzed for anomalies. Today, there are robust statistical methods for analyzing noise features to detect still and video image tampering.[39] It seems reasonable that similar techniques could be applied to data streams to detect tampering. This is an area of research the DoD should invest in, given the criticality of ICS data streams vis-à-vis mission assurance.

Implication 3: Embedded Control Devices Should Require Physical Access for All Firmware Updates

As tough as it was to detect Stuxnet, it could have been hidden much deeper than it was. Stuxnet compromised PLCs that controlled frequency converters which controlled centrifuges. The sabotage routines for all of the centrifuges were resident in software on the PLCs. It was not an easy task to identify the infected PLCs, but it would have been monstrously harder to detect and defeat Stuxnet if the attack had occurred at the firmware level.

The world is reacting to Stuxnet. System developers and operators are looking at ways to add defenses at the PC or PLC level. Tools such as antivirus-scanners, firewalls, patch management, password policies, external-storage-usage policies, code-integrity checkers, etc., are all being developed and fielded in the ICS environment. These are all positive developments; however, these are all focused at the software level. What if Stuxnet had remotely upgraded (i.e., "flashed") the firmware on the frequency converters? Firmware upgrades using existing ICS protocols[40] are possible. Had Stuxnet done this, no malware would have had to exist on the PLCs, and no anomalous communications would have had to pass across the network. Therefore, none of the tools mentioned above would have been able to detect the infection or prevent Stuxnet's effects.

Since there is typically no way to look at a device's firmware, it would have been very difficult to figure out what was going wrong, even if the system operators detected anomalous centrifuge operation. If the frequency converters' vendors supplied the tools and the technical expertise required to troubleshoot the firmware, it would still have been a very tedious process, involving pulling each one of the hundreds of frequency converters offline to analyze them individually.

In the past, physical access was required to upgrade firmware on embedded devices. Unfortunately, that is no longer true, and it will become less true as Industrial Ethernet[41] technology makes remote upgrades even easier. This is a case where the efficiency gains may introduce unacceptable risks of covert firmware attacks.

Interestingly, the problem of remote attacks on firmware is not a problem that has been solved in the traditional IT security community either. The firmware can be remotely flashed in every PC sold in America today. One possible solution to that challenge is technically trivial: PC manufacturers could implement a physical jumper that is shipped from the factory in a "non-upgradeable" position. In the rare event a computer needed its firmware upgraded, a person would physically access the computer and set the jumper to the "upgradeable" position, complete the upgrade, then reset the jumper to its safe "non-upgradeable" position. The challenge is that PC manufacturers would have to add this minor modification to their system designs. Absent any demand for the change, they are unlikely to make the investment; therefore, the DoD should make the demand. The DoD, like most consumers, practically never has a need to upgrade firmware on their machines; however, they do have great need to protect their mission-enabling technology from remote tampering at the firmware level.

An identical technical approach could be used to protect firmware in ICS systems, but the same challenges exist with motivating vendors to implement the change. Legislation would help in this regard if it declared that devices with remotely upgradeable firmware must include jumpers to disable remote upgrade capability when used in US critical infrastructures. Furthermore, it could declare that such hardware must ship from the factory with the jumper set to disable upgrades. Then, in the event a critical infrastructure is compromised through remote manipulation of firmware, liability for damages would be on the ICS system operator if the jumper has been changed. By implementing these laws, the manufacturers would be forced to give system operators a means of protecting themselves, and system operators would have a choice about how much liability risk they wanted to assume in exchange for efficiency. Today, system operators have no choice; as new devices are fielded, they are assuming the vulnerabilities inherent in all devices that allow remote firmware upgrades by default.

Implementing physical protections that require physical access will certainly not defeat the most determined attacker, but it will increase the level of effort and risk of detections they will have to assume in order to succeed.

Conclusions

Stuxnet stands as a singular example of a cyber weapon. It shocked governments and critical infrastructure owners and operators around the world. It would be comforting if one could retain intellectual honesty and yet believe it was a true black-swan event—unlikely to be emulated or seen again for years to come. Unfortunately, one cannot; Stuxnet 2.0 will appear. It may target a different ICS and achieve different effects, but make no mistake: it will certainly come.

In this brave new world where it is possible to create destruction with nothing more than electron manipulations and clever thinking, the United States should use the opportunity afforded by Stuxnet to learn from it and adapt. Stuxnet demonstrated the clear potential for, and potential advantages of, employing cyber weapons to achieve strategic effects. Therefore, the United States would be wise to take advantage of that potential and develop it. However, the nation should be very cautious in employing such weapons or aiding others in their employment; a cyber weapon that is modified and "returned to sender" could have disastrous consequences for the United States.

To maximize global restraint against using cyber weapons to achieve their most disastrous potential effects, the United States should work to establish international agreements limiting them. This should be done within the existing framework of international laws concerning *jus ad bellum* and *jus in bello*. Furthermore, the United States should advocate for international agreements that establish an affirmative obligation for governments to cooperate in any attribution investigations where:

- There is credible evidence a cyber weapon originated from, or transited through, their territory, and
- The effect of the cyber weapon violated the aforementioned laws concerning *jus ad bellum* and *jus in bello*.

Unfortunately, neither offensive capability nor international agreements are likely to deter all potential aggressors from employing cyber weapons against the United States, particularly if they can create disastrous effects on the United States for little cost. Therefore, the United States should take several concrete steps to improve its defensibility against such aggressors.

- ICS defense must be treated as a force package, bringing together system operators with traditional IT defenders to ensure mission-critical processes supported by ICS are assured.
- ICS defenders must be equipped to detect deceptions. This may require additional investment in research, but Stuxnet clearly demonstrated the risks assumed when a HMI is providing an abstracted, untrustworthy view of an ICS-controlled process. Operators must be able to detect deliberate manipulations of the ICS that result in deceptive presentations of reality.
- The United States should require physical access in order to upgrade firmware in ICS devices controlling critical infrastructures. The requirement should be flexible so companies can choose to allow remote upgrades, but there should be liability implications for companies that take this security risk and are compromised. Readjusting the risks/rewards calculus for these decisions can improve security in critical infrastructures and help avoid unacceptable impacts of cyber weapons.

None of the lessons Stuxnet had to offer will be easily implemented, but that does not mean they are not worth doing. The environment has changed. It has become more dangerous. Let's change our thinking about cyber weapons now, before we regret a missed opportunity.

Endnotes

1. William J. Broad, John Markoff, and David E. Sanger, Israeli Test on Worm Called Crucial in Iran Nuclear Delay, The New York Times, sec. World, Middle East, January 15, 2011, http://www.nytimes.com/2011/01/16/world/middleeast/16stuxnet.html (accessed March 2, 2011).

2. The word "apparently" is used to acknowledge the possibility of deception on the part of the Iranians. However, there are no publicly available reports indicating deception. In fact, the February 15, 2011, update of the ISIS report, *Did Stuxnet Take Out 1,000 Centrifuges at the Natanz Enrichment Plant?*, uses International Atomic Energy Agency (IAEA) surveillance reports and results of malware analysis to make a compelling case that Stuxnet actually did destroy ~1000 centrifuges at Natanz, Iran.

3. Paul Kerr, John Rollins, and Catherine Theohary, The Stuxnet Computer Worm: Harbinger of an Emerging Warfare Capability (Washington, DC: Congressional Research Service, [2010]), http://www.fas.org/sgp/crs/natsec/ R41524.pdf (accessed January 7, 2011).

4. Elinor Mills, EU Calls Stuxnet "Paradigm Shift" as US Responds More Mildly, CNET News, http://news.cnet.com/8301-27080_3-20019124-245.html (accessed January 13, 2011).

5. Pam Benson, Computer Virus Stuxnet a "Game Changer," DHS Official Tells Senate, http://articles.cnn.com/2010-11-17/tech/stuxnet.virus_1_stuxnet-nuclear-power-plants-target?_s=PM:TECH (accessed January 13, 2011).

6. Nicholas Falliere, Liam Murchu, and Eric Chien, W32.Stuxnet Dossier (Cupertino, CA: Symantec, 2011), http://www.symantec.com/content/en/us/enterprise/media/security_response/whitepapers/w32_stuxnet_dossier.pdf.

7. Michael J. Gross, A Declaration of Cyber-War, Vanity Fair, http://www.vanityfair.com/culture/features/2011/04/stuxnet-201104? printable=true (accessed March 3, 2011).

8. Pedro Bueno and others, McAfee Threats Report: Fourth Quarter 2010 (McAfee Labs, 2010), http://www.mcafee.com/us/resources/reports/rp-quarterly-threat-q4-2010.pdf (accessed February 14, 2011).

9. Falliere, Murchu, and Chien, W32.Stuxnet Dossier; Aleksander Matrosov, and others, Stuxnet Under the Microscope (Bratislavia, Slovakia: ESET, 2011), http://www.eset.com/us/documentation/white-papers; Ralph Langner, How to Hijack a Controller—Why Stuxnet Isn't just about Siemens' PLCs, ControlGlobal.com, http://www.controlglobal.com/articles/2011/IndustrialControllers1101.html?page=print (accessed January 17, 2011); Mark Clayton, Stuxnet: Ahmadinejad Admits Cyberweapon Hit Iran Nuclear Program, Christian Science Monitor, http://www.csmonitor.com/layout/set/print/content/view/print/346249 (accessed March 1, 2011); David Albright, Paul Brannan, and Christina Walrond, Did Stuxnet Take

Out 1,000 Centrifuges at the Natanz Enrichment Plant? (Washington, DC: Institute for Science and International Security, 2010), http://www.isis-online.org/isis-reports/detail/did-stuxnet-take-out-1000-centrifuges-at-the-natanz-enrichment-plant/ (accessed March 1, 2011); David Albright, Paul Brannan, and Christina Walrond, Stuxnet Malware and Natanz: Update of ISIS December 22, 2010 Report (Washington, DC: Institute for Science and International Security, 2011), http://www.isis-online.org/isis-reports/detail/stuxnet-malware-and-natanz-update-of-isis-december-22-2010-reportsupa-href1/; http://www.isis-online.org/uploads/isis-reports/documents/stuxnet_update_15Feb2011.pdf (accessed March 1, 2011).

10. Vice Chairman Joint Chiefs of Staff, Memorandum: Joint Terminology for Cyberspace Operations, November 2010, http://www.nsci-va.org/CyberReferenceLib/2010-11-Joint%20Terminology%20for%20Cyberspace%20Operations.pdf (accessed February 28, 2011).

11. Falliere, Murchu, and Chien, W32.Stuxnet Dossier; Matrosov, and others, Stuxnet Under the Microscope; Langner, How to Hijack a Controller—Why Stuxnet Isn't just about Siemens' PLCs; Clayton, Stuxnet: Ahmadinejad Admits Cyberweapon Hit Iran Nuclear Program; Albright, Brannan, and Walrond, Did Stuxnet Take Out 1,000 Centrifuges at the Natanz Enrichment Plant?; Albright, Brannan, and Walrond, Stuxnet Malware and Natanz: Update of ISIS December 22, 2010 Report.

12. Langner, How to Hijack a Controller—Why Stuxnet Isn't just about Siemens' PLCs.

13. Luigi Auriemma, Bugtraq: Vulnerabilities in some SCADA Server Softwares, Bugtraq, http://seclists.org/bugtraq/2011/Mar/187 (accessed March 25, 2011).

14. Shaun Waterman, Homemade Cyberweapon Worries Federal Officials, The Washington Times, http://www.washingtontimes.com/news/2011/may/24/homemade-cyberweapon-worries-feds/ (accessed May 31, 2011).

15. The term "malware" here is used loosely. A cyber weapon can take the form of software, firmware, or even hardware-based code. The form is not important; its effect is what defines a piece of malware as a "cyber weapon."

16. The 2006 *National Security Strategy of the United States* set a precedent for preemption. It stated "the first duty of the United States Government [is] to protect the American people and American interests. [This] duty obligates the government to anticipate and counter threats, using all elements of national power, before the threats can do grave damage . . ." With respect to nuclear weapons, the policy was very clear. It read "Countering proliferation of WMD requires a comprehensive strategy . . . to deny these weapons of terror . . . before they are unleashed." The current National Security Strategy does not specifically include phrases like "before they can do grave damage" and "before they are unleashed," but it does not disavow preemption, and it is very clear

in stating our intentions with regard to Iran and nuclear weapons: "The United States will . . . work to prevent Iran from developing a nuclear weapon."

17. "[W]e must focus American engagement on strengthening international institutions and galvanizing the collective action that can serve common interests such as . . . stopping the spread of nuclear weapons and securing nuclear materials . . . ." To adversarial governments, we offer a clear choice: abide by international norms and achieve the political and economic benefits that come with greater integration with the international community, or refuse to accept this pathway, and bear the consequences of that decision. Our engagement will underpin a just and sustainable international order—just, because it advances mutual interests, protects the rights of all, and holds accountable those who refuse to meet their responsibilities; sustainable because it is based on broadly shared norms and fosters collective action to address common challenges.

18. United States Strategic Bombing Survey, The United States Strategic Bombing Survey: Summary Report (European War) (Washington, DC: US Government Printing Office, 1945), 5.

19. Ibid., 5.

20. Thomas M. Coffey, Decision Over Schweinfurt: The US 8th Air Force Battle for Daylight Bombing (New York: D. Mckay, 1977), 373; United States Strategic Bombing Survey, The United States Strategic Bombing Survey: Summary Report (European War), 6.

21. Donald L. Miller, Masters of the Air: America's Bomber Boys Who Fought the Air War Against Nazi Germany (New York: Simon & Schuster, 2006), 671, http://www.loc.gov/catdir/enhancements/fy0664/2006050461-d.html (publisher description); http://www.loc.gov/catdir/enhancements/fy0668/2006050461-t.html (table of contents); http://www.loc.gov/catdir/enhancements/fy0703/2006050461-s.html (sample text); http://www.loc.gov/catdir/enhancements/fy1013/2006050461-b.html (contributor biographical information); United States Strategic Bombing Survey, The United States Strategic Bombing Survey: Summary Report (European War), 6.

22. Ibid., 6.

23. Falliere, Murchu, and Chien, W32.Stuxnet Dossier, 7–11.

24. Albright, Brannan, and Walrond, Stuxnet Malware and Natanz: Update of ISIS December 22, 2010 Report, 4–5.

25. Albright, Brannan, and Walrond, Did Stuxnet Take Out 1,000 Centrifuges at the Natanz Enrichment Plant?; Albright, Brannan, and Walrond, Stuxnet Malware and Natanz: Update of ISIS December 22, 2010 Report.

26. Ibid., 8.

27. Asieh Mansour and Hope Nadji, Opportunities in Private Infrastructure Investments in the US (San Fransisco: RREEF Real Estate Research, 2006), http://www.irei.com/uploads/marketresearch/67/marketResearchFile/Opp_Priv_Infr_Inv.pdf (accessed July 12, 2011).

28. During FY 2007 through FY 2010, Congress provided more than $13 billion for the Joint IED Defeat Fund, primarily through supplemental appropriations. JIEDDO PA Michael Coderre, JIEDDO Fiscal Year 2011 Budget, JIEDDO, https://www.jieddo.dod.mil/article.aspx?ID=854 (accessed May 25, 2011). The Joint IED Defeat Office was budgeted for $3.465 billion in FY 2011. JIEDDO 2010 Annual Report (JIEDDO, 2010), https://www.jieddo.dod.mil/content/docs/JIEDDO_2010_Annual _Report_U.pdf (accessed May 25, 2011). Although these are large expenditures, these appropriations do not cover the costs of all operations to defeat IEDs, hence the characterization as "untold fortunes."

29. Martin C. Libicki and Project Air Force, Cyberdeterrence and Cyberwar (Santa Monica, CA: Rand, 2009), xiv.

30. DHS-CSSP, Recommended Practice: Improving Industrial Control Systems Cybersecurity with Defense-in-Depth Strategies (Department of Homeland Security, Control Systems Security Program, 2009), http://www.us-cert.gov/control_systems/practices/documents/Defense_in_Depth_Oct09.pdf (accessed March 3, 2011).

31. Mean Time between Failure for a Rockwell Automation PLC-5 is >45 years. Anecdotal evidence is the average PLC remains in use for about 12 years.

32. Air-gapped architectures are not inviolate. The fact that the space station has been repeatedly infected with malware via removable media should clearly illustrate this fact. See Gregg Keizer, Malware Infects Space Station Laptop, Computerworld, http://www.computerworld.com/s/article/325193/Malware_Infects_Space_Station_Laptop (accessed June 22, 2011). This was only one of 1048 cases in Fiscal Years 2007 and 2008 where an intruder successfully gained unauthorized access or malware was installed on NASA systems. See US Government Accountability Office, NASA Needs to Remedy Vulnerabilities in Key Networks (GAO, 2009), http://www.gao.gov/new.items/d104.pdf (accessed June 22, 2011).

33. DHS-CSSP, Recommended Practice: Improving Industrial Control Systems Cybersecurity with Defense-in-Depth Strategies.

34. Albright, Brannan, and Walrond, Stuxnet Malware and Natanz: Update of ISIS December 22, 2010 Report, 2.

35. Sun Tzu, The Art of War, trans. Lionel Giles (Cosimo, New York, 2010), 50.

36. Published in October 2009, it can be found at http://www.us-cert.gov/control_systems/practices/documents/final-RP_ics_cybersecurity_incident_response_100609.pdf.

37. Barton Whaley, Personal conversation between the author and Barton Whaley, May 2, 2007.

38. In security engineering, "nonce" is an abbreviation of number used once. It is a random or pseudo-random number issued in an authentication protocol to ensure that old communications cannot be reused in replay attacks.

39. See Hongmei Gou, A. Swaminathan, and Min Wu, Noise Features for Image Tampering Detection and Steganalysis (2007), and G. Chetty, M. Biswas, and R. Singh, Digital Video Tamper Detection Based on Multimodal Fusion of Residue Features (2010) for good examples.
40. Fieldbus is one example of a protocol that supports remote upgrading of firmware. Fieldbus is a collection of common ICS protocols supported by a variety of chip manufacturers and device vendors.
41. Industrial Ethernet is another ICS communication protocol. Its installed base is increasing because of the standardization benefits. It used standard Ethernet hardware.

11

THE INTERNET AND DISSENT IN AUTHORITARIAN STATES

JAMES D. FIELDER

Contents

Introduction	161
A Synthesis Model of Dissent	164
The Internet and Dissent	167
Theory of Internet-Mediated Dissent	169
Data and Methods	172
Dependent Variable	172
Key Independent and Control Variables	174
Results	175
Conclusions	181
Endnotes	184
References	188

Introduction

In 1996, Internet access in Myanmar (Burma) was available only through a single, state-run Internet service provider. That year, Myanmar's State Law and Order Restoration Council (since renamed the State Peace and Development Council) passed the Computer Science Development Law, which imposed up to 15-year prison sentences and $5,000 fines for anyone who owned a modem or fax machine that was not registered with the government.[1] Despite these limitations, activists inside and outside of Myanmar were still able to use the Internet to spread anti-regime information over encrypted communications channels; in particular, activists posted videos of the December 1996 student demonstrations to the Internet within days of recording—a significant feat considering the limited access, restrictive rules, and less-sophisticated Internet technologies at the time.[2] Relative to other forms of broadcasting available in the mid- to late-1990s, Internet-based communications offered dissent movements far greater benefit in terms of cost, speed, and ease of use.

In Internet time, however, 1996 was an eternity ago. Since then, the Internet has advanced from dial-up modems and Web 1.0 applications such as the first web browser (Netscape Navigator) and email to broadband access and Web 2.0 applications such as Facebook, YouTube, and Twitter. To paraphrase Reporters Sans Frontières, a single video shared in the collaborative Web 2.0 age can expose government abuses to the entire world.[3] Indeed, the theoretical sentiment that the Internet offers social movements greater tools for organization and communication remains just as strong now as in 1999, if not more so.[4]

Older electronic communication mediums have been used to organize, mobilize, and advertise social movements, such as leveraging global television networks in Eastern Europe protests (1980s), fax machines in China's Tiananmen Square uprising in 1989, and amateur video during the Los Angeles Rodney King riots of 1992.[5] The Internet, in turn, enables organizations and individuals to breach barriers of geographical distance, cost, censorship, and even personal accountability.[6] The Internet allows users across the network to exchange information and ideas through text, link exchanges, multimedia file sharing, and real-time voice and video streaming. Such rapid and open communication helps shape perceptions and allows social movements to circumvent the state and directly address national and international audiences.[7] Moreover, due to the Internet's collaborative and decentralized nature, ordinary citizens and the politically marginalized are no longer limited to top-down, "one-to-many" mainstream media outlets.[8] For example, "The Great Firewall of China" failed in 2001 when Internet users in Jiangxi province mounted an online campaign criticizing the government over a schoolhouse explosion. Despite censorship efforts, the campaign brought the issue to national-level importance and induced the government to make a public apology and reparations.[9]

More recently, following perceived voting irregularities in the June 2009 Iranian presidential election, supporters for challenger Mir-Hossein Mousavi poured into the streets in violent protests reminiscent of the 1979 revolution. Unlike the 1979 revolution, however, the June 2009 protests were broadcast online in real time through social media networks. Although quick to shut down the national telephone system, Iran's authoritarian regime was slow in blocking Internet-based outlets, and Iranian protesters flooded the web with a continuous stream of Twitter links, Flickr photos, and Facebook updates over landline and wireless networks. Ultimately, organizers mobilized hundreds of thousands of people to a rally in central Tehran in defiance of an Interior Ministry ban on such actions.[10] Iran opposition leaders further argued that Internet applications allow them to spread messages farther and organize larger rallies.[11] Although the regime cracked down on Internet outlets, the system remains porous: only a complete—and unrealistic—shutdown of the entire Iranian communications network can halt Internet communication.

The key argument of this chapter is that the Internet increases the likelihood of dissent inside authoritarian states through three factors: distance, decentralization, and interaction. First, the Internet fosters dissent mobilization by allowing protesters to communicate relatively cheaply and instantaneously over great distances. While other communication mediums such as the radio and telephone also reduce distance costs, the second factor, decentralization, allows dissenters to evade state controls and reduces the state's ability to restrict information flows. Third, the Internet's interactive nature allows users to become both consumers and producers of information. Interactivity also fosters trust between individual users and online communities which can evolve into offline action. To frame these three factors with a popular military catchphrase, the Internet functions as a "force multiplier" for social movements inside authoritarian states.

From a normative policy standpoint, recent turmoil in the Middle East region—collectively referred to as the Arab Spring—illustrates the efficacy of the Internet as a mobilizing structure. However, protest events in Iran, Libya, and Syria rapid escalated from verbally contentious to physically violent interaction between protesters and regimes. The violence became part of the mobilizing discourse as text reports, images, video, and other multimedia reports spread across the Internet to wider audiences. Understanding the causal mechanisms of Internet-mediated dissent will help policymakers more quickly gauge and react to regional and systemic developments.

A Synthesis Model of Dissent

In the mid-1990s, McAdam, McCarthy, and Zald (1996) proposed a synthesis of previous theories into a model that links three broad sets of factors for analyzing a social movement's *repertoires of contention*, or available means of protest: mobilizing structures, political opportunity structures, and collective action (or, cultural) frames.[12] The first factor, mobilizing structures, consists of formal organizations and everyday social interactions, including organizational leadership and connective structures that link the group and foster coordination.

Second, political opportunity structures are the static or dynamic opportunity structures available to social movements (affected by constraints), including events that lower the costs of collective action, reveal potential movement allies, demonstrate how and where elites and authorities are most vulnerable, and trigger social networks and collective identities into action around common themes and symbols. Additionally, more individuals and groups are encouraged to join as initial participants achieve gains against their target.[13]

Third, collective action frames are cultural factors that provide ideological inspiration and motivation for group identity, claims, and action.[14] Collective action frames develop through the processes of injustice, agency, and identity, with injustice being the grievance that inspires social change, agency the development of share consciousness that collective action can alter injustice conditions, and identity the process of defining the movement. In sum, the synthesis model (Figure 11.1) explains protest by identifying the flow of dissent from the catalyst that motivates protests to the moment where movements and regimes interact over given issues, with occasionally violent outcomes.

The first step (1), social change, represents mechanisms that motivate protest movements. The mechanism can be a sudden change in opportunities and constraints (or threats). In the Iranian example cited at the beginning of this chapter, mass sense of injustice following President Ahmadinejad's reelection was the social change mechanism and resulting protest. As another example, on December 17, 2011, Tunisian merchant Mohamed Bouazizi immolated himself in despair over lack of opportunity and public embarrassment at the hands of Tunisian security forces. Bouazizi's act enflamed long-simmering anti-regime grievances which resulted in mass protests and the eventual collapse of the

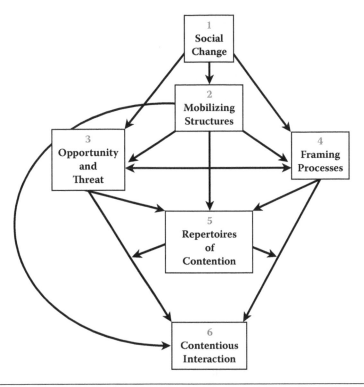

Figure 11.1 Synthesis model of contentious politics. (From McAdam, Doug, Sidney Tarrow, and Charles Tilly. *Dynamics of Contention*. Cambridge: Cambridge University Press, 2001, 17. With permission.)

Ben-Ali regime.[15] Indeed, Internet access may be a protest catalyst in that the medium provides informational access.

The second step, mobilizing structures (2), are the everyday social interactions that either foster or discourage mass protest. This step includes influences from civil society, social presence, the public sphere, and social ties. Hardin (1995) posits that it is such social ties that encourage individuals to act in concert. McCarthy and Zald (1977) also contend that available Information and Communication Technologies (ICTs) influence how movements communicate to gather and expend resources.[16] A relevant pre-Internet example is Egypt's Muslim Brotherhood during the 1950s and 1960s, who tapped into local social networks through face-to-face communication. By interacting on a personal level, the movement not only spread information through local channels but also encouraged individuals to join or provide other tacit support.[17]

In turn, opportunity and threat (3) represent the environmental constraints that influence social movement development, particularly in regard to the structure of the state.[18] The literature offers two relevant hypotheses on the effects of opportunity and threat on protest activity. The first suggests the closed political systems are more likely to encourage protest outside of conventional channels. According to this theory, protests are more likely in societies with fewer participation options or in highly coercive states.[19] Contrasting studies claim that political systems with a mixture of open and closed structures are most conducive to protest.[20] The second hypothesis specifically considers coercive restrictions. Gurr (1970) argues that the state's repressive capacities, as measured by the size of the police or military forces, negatively influence protest activity.[21]

The fourth step, framing processes (4), represent collective identities, shared goals, and how group members jointly define and interpret social change. Such norms not only provide group stability, but are also the lens through which frames are interpreted and the clay from which new cultural elements are created. This step is alternatively referred to as *cultural* framing, in that how individuals and groups react to social change is conditioned by cultural norms.[22] Framing processes are also enhanced or constrained by opportunity structures (e.g., regime type), and information crossing through mobilizing structures can alter cultural perceptions. In particular, framing processes further influence social consensus if they not only resonate with existing beliefs, but also clearly offer solutions for social change and identify where to cast blame.[23] For example, Thornton (2002) notes that the *falun gong* movement in China initially evaded government censure since it was seen as a relatively benign religious group.[24] However, the group gained notoriety for a series of anti-regime protests; actions which, in turn, resonated with and attracted more like-minded individuals. The group's rapid growth in both membership and protest activity eventually alarmed Beijing, resulting in a massive crackdown against the group in 1999.

Interaction between mobilizing structures, opportunities and threats, and framing processes leads to the fifth step: repertoires of contention (5). These are the available means for social movement participants to articulate collective claims. The sixth and final step, contentious interaction (6), is simply the interaction between protesters and the regime.[25] Protest movements across the Middle East since 2009 offer stark examples between successful protest movements and regime coercion. On one hand, protests in Tunisia, Egypt, and Libya escalated in favor of anti-regime movements and ultimately resulted in the collapse of the respective regimes. In contrast, Iran quickly quelled the 2009 protests, and some observers contend that the ongoing contentious interaction in Syria may escalate to civil war.[26]

The Internet and Dissent

Modern social movements depend on literacy, classless associations, and information flows: communication creates informed social movements, which in turn create opportunity structures by diffusing collective action and creating political space.[27] The spread of previous communication mediums such as newspapers, pamphlets, and books diffused information across class lines and linked urban centers with rural peripheries, and such diffusion also significantly reduced the time between publishing and reception. Mass communication shifted formerly highly localized and specific repertoires of collective action to new repertoires that were cosmopolitan, modular, and autonomous in nature, creating the conditions for broad, organized, cross-cleavage, and persistent social movements.[28]

The traditional dissent and repression literature does not speak directly to how the Internet may influence dissent against authoritarian states. However, if effective communication fosters opportunity structures, one can reasonably assess that the Internet is a premier tool for fostering social movements. Communication and law scholars have theorized that the Internet reduces protest costs and increases protest space by acting as a decentralized, rapid, and relatively inexpensive "architecture of participation [that] challenge or alter dominant, expected or accepted ways of doing society, culture and politics."[29]

But, what is the Internet? The Internet is an electronic network of one-to-one, one-to-many, many-to-many, many-to-one, local, national, and global information and communication technologies with relatively open standards and protocols and comparatively low barriers to entry.[30] The Internet's technological characteristics were also founded on the norms of its designers and initial user community, which made it difficult to censor. The technology was originally the tool of a small group of engineers and academics that were wary of bureaucracy, trusted each other, and worked well through consensus.[31] In light of this culture, they made specific technical design choices that rendered the network resistant to centralized control.

Internet functionality is based on the *Transmission Control Protocol/Internet Protocol* (TCP/IP) and *packet switching*. First, TCP/IP breaks data transmissions into small packets for fast transfer (the *TCP* segment) and then seamlessly reassembles data at the receiving end (the *IP* segment). As long as an ICT system can "speak" TCP/IP, it can join the network at any access point.[32] Second, packet switching sends data packets through the most efficient routes; thus a simple email is divided into small pieces that each travel through hundreds of global servers to reach the recipient. In addition to speed and packet reliability, basic anonymity is a crucial benefit of both TCP/IP and packet switching: that is, only the system is authenticated through its unique numerical IP address (e.g., 166.18.250.1), not the user. Although there is no interstate body governing the Internet, international regimes such as the Internet Corporation for Assigned Names and Numbers (ICANN) regulate naming and numbering conventions, hardware and software protocols, and the transfer of domain names between private parties.[33]

The Internet, then, serves as a mechanism for linking groups and fostering communication across great distances while at the same time reducing participation costs. The Internet typically functions on existing communication infrastructure (twisted-pair telephone wire is sufficient for dial-up and Digital Subscriber Line modem access), through which any TCP/IP-capable system can communicate with other systems. This not only allows users to communicate with others almost instantaneously, but also provides user access to vast stores of information. Unlike previous one-to-many or one-to-one ICTs (such as television and the telephone), the Internet allows individuals to broadcast not only one-to-many and one-to-one, but also many-to-many. These varied formats encourage like-minded individuals to interact on various topical and interest-based sites.

Users are also encouraged to share information and engage in discussion: for example, modern Web 2.0 applications allow many users to collaborate simultaneously on projects such as electronic maps and shared news archives. Moreover, the Internet lets the user become the "one" communicating to the "many," which reduces dependence on professional informational gatekeepers such as newspapers and radio stations. Indeed, while Internet access in many developing and non-democratic countries is limited by censorship, cost, and other factors, a potential outcome of Internet diffusion—even under strict government controls—may be a gradual liberalization of an otherwise restricted public sphere due to increased information access.

Theory of Internet-Mediated Dissent

This chapter's theoretical model is embedded in the mobilization structure and opportunity/threat structure stages of McAdam, McCarthy, and Zald's synthesis model. The theory expects that Internet access allows dissidents to use the Internet as a mobilizing structure, in that the Internet offers social movements a relatively inexpensive, anonymous, and agile means of mobilizing individuals and resources across long distances. With the understanding that mobilizing structures consist of interpersonal social networks and associate communications, the Internet serves as a mechanism for linking groups and fostering communication across greater distances more rapidly and cheaply than other communication channels. For example, Web 2.0 tools such as YouTube and Twitter allowed Arab Spring protesters to cheaply and instantaneously spread information and organize activities.

The theory further posits that Internet access creates conditions for social mobilization which, if well organized, are difficult for regimes to counter. Despite attempts at social control, as a state's Internet user base grows, so do the odds that users will challenge social boundaries and use the Internet to mobilize dissent. Thus, Internet diffusion as quantitatively measured through the number of Internet users may be correlated with increased dissent against authoritarian regimes. The Internet model is overlaid onto the classic model in Figure 11.2.

Events leading up to and during the January 25, 2011, protests in Egypt serve as a relevant illustration for this model. While anti-regime discontent had been fomenting in Egypt for years, demands for social change (1) markedly increased between 2003 and 2006 following a serious of elections and political referendums.[34] In June 2009, Facebook released an Arabic version of the eponymous Internet

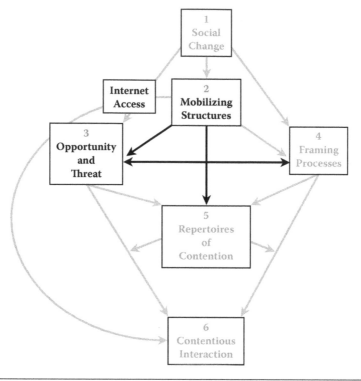

Figure 11.2 Model of Internet-mediated dissent.

application. Facebook is a social networking application that allows users to construct profiles consisting of personal histories and contact information, and "post" textual, image, and video updates. Users then "friend" other users, who are typically individuals they know: family, friends, and acquaintances. Internet users readily adopted Facebook, as it allowed them to easily maintain interpersonal contacts over long distances. Facebook also allows users to build pages centered on given topics, which other users with similar interests can then follow. In April 2011, the *April 6 Youth Movement* (which was founded to support a labor strike) built a Facebook page entitled "We are all Khaled Said," which was in homage to a young man who had been beaten to death in Alexandria by Egyptian police. The page soon attracted 80,000 users and became a hub for sharing dissent information.[35]

Then, in January 2011, the Ben Ali regime in Tunisia came to a rapid collapse following almost a month of continuous anti-regime protests. This shifted the perceived opportunity structure in Egypt, convincing members of the *April 6 Youth Movement* group to organize their own protest on January 25, 2011, outside of the Ministry of the Interior, with January 25 coinciding with Egypt's National Police Day.[36] Word of the protest spread rapidly through Facebook and was further magnified after *April 6 Youth Movement* member Asmaa Mahfouz recorded a personal call to action and posted the video to YouTube, a popular video sharing application.[37] Thus, Facebook and YouTube (along with other applications such as Twitter) acted as mobilizing structures (2) and increased available opportunities (3) for the January 25 movement. Tufecki and Wilson (2012) conclude that far fewer Egyptians would have attended the initial January 25 protest without social media.[38] They argue that in authoritarian regimes, high participation on the first day is often necessary to initiate larger protests that ultimately result in movement success. Their results suggest that politicized social media use was associated with increased likelihood of first-day participation.

In turn, the Mubarak regime was caught with its Internet pants down, and thus was initially unable to apply threat and reduce the Internet's political opportunity (3). Cairo had not established serious technical censorship programs previously and thus was initially limited in electronic response options. Barring the ability to filter network traffic, the regime decided to take the entire country offline on January 27, 2011—the first time in Internet history that a state purposely went offline to halt information flows.[39] However, this can even have the opposite effect of mobilizing individuals who were otherwise apolitical but depended on the Internet as an information conduit. Despite taking the Internet offline, however, technically savvy protesters were able to find alternative Internet access routes to organize and mobilize increasingly larger protests, which ultimately resulted in President Hosni Mubarak stepping down from power on February 11, 2011. While this is not to say that the Internet was the sole causal factor in bringing down the regime, this illustrative case highlights how the Internet is a particularly powerful mobilizing structure, particularly in a state without significant Internet control measures. To test this theory, this chapter hypothesizes that anti-regime protest incidents increase as Internet use increases inside nondemocratic states.

Data and Methods

This chapter used a cross-sectional time series analysis spanning 1999 to 2010 to measure the relationship between Internet growth and protest. The time frame was selected since World Bank Internet data are available through 2010 but are increasingly sporadic prior to 1999. Furthermore, while the Internet was available prior to 1999, graphic web browsers were not widely available until the release of Netscape Navigator in 1994 and Microsoft Internet Explorer in 1995. Web browsers dramatically improved Internet functionality for average users.[40]

A second goal in this study is to analyze patterns of dissent within non-democracies. Data from Polity IV are used to select for non-democracies as the observations to study. Polity IV uses a 21-point ordinal scale to measure democratic and autocratic "patterns of authority" through qualities of executive recruitment, constraints on executive authority, and political competition.[41] States' scores from −10 (absolute autocracy) through +5 (anocracy) are included, with the final set consisting of 88 countries (listed in Table 11.1) and 863 country/year pairs.

Dependent Variable

For the dependent variable *protest*, this study uses the variable *anti-government demonstrations* (labeled in the original dataset as *domestic8*) from the Cross-National Time-Series Archive (CNTS). These events are, "any peaceful public gathering of at least 100 people for the primary purpose of displaying or voicing their opposition to government policies or authority, excluding demonstrations of a distinctly anti-foreign nature."[42] Such anti-government events are seen as characteristic protest events and have been used in previous studies that analyze protest as the outcome variable.[43] The data are not perfect, however; other scholars have critiqued CNTS for hand coding anti-regime demonstrations through open-source news analysis. In particular, there are concerns that events from non-democratic states go unreported, or that journalistic biases exaggerate other events.[44] However, the author concurs with Allen (2008) that CNTS provides the best breadth of reporting despite coding concerns. The number of anti-government demonstrations per

Table 11.1   List of Countries

Afghanistan	Gambia	Papua New Guinea
Albania	Georgia	Peru
Algeria	Ghana	Qatar
Angola	Guinea	Russia
Armenia	Guinea-Bissau	Rwanda
Azerbaijan	Haiti	Saudi Arabia
Bahrain	Iran	Senegal
Bangladesh	Iraq	Singapore
Belarus	Jordan	Solomon Islands
Bhutan	Kazakhstan	Somalia
Burkina Faso	Kenya	Sri Lanka
Burundi	Korea North	Sudan
Cambodia	Kuwait	Swaziland
Cameroon	Kyrgyzstan	Syria
Central African Republic	Laos	Tajikistan
Chad	Lesotho	Tanzania
China	Liberia	Thailand
Comoros	Libya	Togo
Congo Brazzaville	Madagascar	Tunisia
Congo Kinshasa	Malawi	Turkmenistan
Cote d'Ivoire	Malaysia	UAE
Cuba	Mauritania	Uganda
Djibouti	Morocco	Uzbekistan
Ecuador	Mozambique	Venezuela
Egypt	Myanmar	Vietnam
Equatorial Guinea	Nepal	Yemen
Eritrea	Niger	Zambia
Ethiopia	Nigeria	Zimbabwe
Fiji	Oman	
Gabon	Pakistan	

year ranges from 0 to 15, with 0 incidents (644 country/year pairs) and 1 incident (79 country/year pairs) the most common counts.[45]

Key Independent and Control Variables

The key independent variable is *Internet access*, which is measured through World Bank data on *number of Internet users per 100 people*, including private access at home or public access at cafes, work, school, and other venues.[46] While World Bank also has country data on the total number of Internet users, this study assesses that the measuring per 100 people better captures the proportion of users in each state and prevents incorrectly magnifying results for larger, more populated states.

Previous studies have operationalized human rights violations and personal integrity abuse, economic growth, education, and population size as factors leading to dissent. To measure repression through human rights violations and personal integrity abuse, this study employs the Political Terror Scale.[47] The score is an ordinal measure ranging from 1 (countries under secure rule of law) to 5 (limitless regime terror applied to the entire population). Previous research programs have found that repression tested through the Political Terror Scale has expected negative effects on protest inside non-democratic states.[48]

Next, resource mobilization theory posits that economic growth increases the availability of monetary and temporal resources that protesters can expend as mobilization resources.[49] In turn, lack of economic opportunity can also increase the likelihood of dissent.[50] To control for economic development, World Bank data are used on both gross domestic product (GDP) per capita in US dollars and annual GDP growth. Studies have also suggested that increased education positively influences the likelihood of protest by increasing political knowledge, self-expression values, and an individual sense of political efficacy.[51] To control for education, this study uses the CNTS variable *total school enrollment* from primary through university studies per capita (labeled *school11* in the dataset). School enrollment was selected over literacy rates since literacy varies little over time and does not capture breadth of knowledge beyond functional reading and writing skills. Literacy data are also missing for many countries in both CNTS and World Bank. To control for population, World Bank data total population data are used and converted to a logarithm for ease of interpretation.

Finally, another factor assessed to effect dissent is coercive capacity, or resources available to agents that carry out negative sanctions. Previous models suggest that social movements will more likely be dissuaded if a regime's coercive agents have access to substantial resources.[52] Coercive capacity is measured at the World Bank with the variable military expenditures as percent of GDP, which Davenport (1996) also examines. This is not a perfect measure, however, as not all states include police, paramilitary, auxiliary, or other civil forces in their defense budgets. To mitigate this, the Political Terror Scale also partially captures intrastate use of coercive force.

As a control against endogeneity, the data are set as an annual time series and then with each independent variable lagged by one year. Specifically, this controls for simultaneous effects from using the most current annual data to predict the respective annual outcome. A lagged dependent variable *protest* was also created to test whether or not the occurrence of protest in the previous year affected the likelihood of protest the following year.

The data were then tested with negative binomial regression, given that protest is a count variable and consists largely of zero protest incidents. Count variables are "dependent variables that take on nonnegative integer values for each of n observations" and are thus presumed to not be normally distributed.[53] Using ordinary least squares (OLS) regression to analyze a count variable, then, is inappropriate since count variables violate linearity, and normal distribution assumptions of OLS can result in incorrect statistical findings.

Results

The results of the negative binomial regression statistically support the hypothesis in the expected direction: holding all other variables constant, a one-unit increase in Internet access increases protest by 0.034 ($p < 0.062$). The results for the full model are detailed in Table 11.2. However, a negative binomial regression coefficient is not interpreted in the same fashion as an OLS regression. Thus, incidence-rate ratios (IRRs) are included in order to clarify the substantive impact of the independent variables in protest. IRRs represent the relative change

Table 11.2 Effect of Internet Use on Protest, Negative Binomial Regression Model

	PROTEST β(SE)	INCIDENCE RATE RATIO%
Protest (lagged)	.158	
	(.132)	
Internet Users per 100 People	0.034*	3
	(0.020)	
Political Terror Scale	0.370**	44
	(0.177)	
GDP per capita	−0.00005	
	(0.00005)	
GDP growth	−0.067**	−6
	(0.033)	
Total school enrollment	6.08	
	(2.62)	
Total population, logged	0.594***	81
	(0.168)	
Military spending as a percentage of GDP	−0.150**	−14
	(0.077)	
Intercept	−13.52	
	(2.91)	
n	505	
Log alpha	1.02	
Alpha	2.78	
Wald chi-square	117.96	
Prob > Chi-square	0.00001	

Sources: Correlates of War (Sarkees et al. 2010); Cross-National Time-Series Data Archive (Banks 2011); Polity IV (Marshall et al. 2009); Political Terror Scale (Gibney et al. 2008); World Bank (I4CD 2012).

Notes: The dependent variable *protest* is a count measure of anti-regime demonstrations per year ranging from 0 to 15. Two-tailed tests with robust standard are calculated by country code clustering.

$*p \leq 0.1$, $**p \leq 0.05$, $***p \leq 0.01$.

in the incidence rate for a one-unit change in a particular variable (Allen, 2008).[54] Put differently, using the IRR, a one-unit increase in Internet users per 100 people increases the incidence rate of protest by 3 percent.

The following example illustrates the substance of the findings. Mass demonstrations erupted in Rangoon, Myanmar, on August 19, 2007, in protest against a sudden increase in fuel prices. Protests escalated throughout August and September, led by a cross-section of society ranging from students to Buddhist monks.[55] Throughout the protests, individuals turned to the Internet to find information, post their own "citizen journalist" data, and use the Internet as an organizational tool.

As of 2007, Myanmar had only 101,867 Internet users out of a total population of 46,915,816 people.[56] However, the Internet had become an increasingly important information and communication tool for many citizens, in particular well-educated, affluent, and urban users. Even after the Myanmar regime started their brutal crackdown on September 26, protesters continued to post information despite the increase in threat. Ultimately, the regime had to cut all Internet and cell phone service throughout the country in an attempt to quell Internet-mobilized dissent.[57] The OpenNet Initiative (2007) concluded that "a relatively small group of Burmese citizens achieved a disproportionate impact on the global awareness and understanding of this current crisis, despite operating in a very limited online space where information is severely controlled."[58] In short, these findings indicate that the Internet acts as a power mobilization structure even in physically coercive and restricted information environments.

A second model that included a squared term of Internet users per 100 people uncovered a curvilinear effect of Internet use on protest (Table 11.3). In the first model, the effect of Internet use on protest is depressed due to the linear slope. Including the squared term not only more accurately captures the substantive effect of Internet use on protest, but this also depicts the point at which the likelihood of protest begins to decrease. The second model indicates that for every one-unit increase in Internet users per 100 people, the incidence rate of protest increases 23 percent ($p < 0.0001$).

Xu and Long's (2005) predicted values software tool was then used to predict the rate of protest at different Internet users per 100 values.[59] For the prediction values, a detailed summary of Internet users per 100 people and predicted rates of protest were calculated for the following percentiles: 1, 5, 10, 25, 50, 75, and 95.[60] The predicted results are illustrated in Figure 11.3. The predicted rate of protest remains below 1 from states with 0 to 7 Internet users per 100 people (7 users being the 75th percentile). However, the rate of protest increases from 0.08 to 1.25 between 7 and 21 users per 100 people (the 90th percentile), and then increases dramatically from 1.25 to 7.62 between 21

Table 11.3 Effect of Internet Use on Protest, with Internet Users per 100 Squared Term

	PROTEST β(SE)	INCIDENCE RATE RATIO %
Protest (lagged)	0.168	
	0.111	
Internet users per 100 people	0.209***	23
	(0.021)	
Internet users per 100 people (squared)	−0.006***	0.7
	(0.001)	
Political terror scale	0.379**	46
	(0.173)	
GDP per capita	−0.00003	
	(0.00005)	
GDP growth	−0.078**	7
	(0.031)	
Total school enrollment	3.03	
	(2.14)	
Total population, logged	0.519***	68
	(0.145)	
Military spending as a percentage of GDP	−0.177**	−16
	(0.075)	
Intercept	−12.05	
	(2.47)	
n	505	
Log alpha	0.836	
Alpha	2.30	
Wald chi-square	179.65	
Prob > chi-square	0.00001	

Sources: Correlates of War (Sarkees et al. 2010); Cross-National Time-Series Data Archive (Banks 2011); Polity IV (Marshall et al. 2009); Political Terror Scale (Gibney et al. 2008); World Bank (I4CD 2012).

Notes: The dependent variable *protest* is a count measure of anti-regime demonstrations per year ranging from 0 to 15. Two-tailed tests with robust standard errors calculated by country code clustering.

*$p \leq 0.1$, **$p \leq 0.05$, ***$p \leq 0.01$.

and 30 users per 100 people (the 95th percentile). The predicted values suggest that although very low levels of Internet use have negligible influence on protest, Internet use only must reach 10 to 20 users per 100 people for protests incidents to increase substantively.

This finding is further supported by the traditional threshold model, which suggests that the costs of movement mobilization decline once

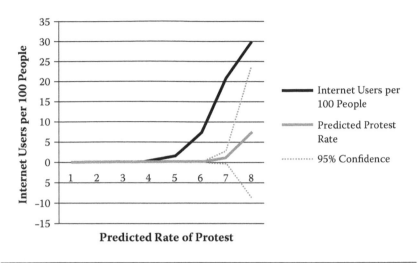

Figure 11.3 Linear predicted effect of Internet use on protest.

an unspecified threshold of participants is crossed.[61] These results also follow Kulikova and Perlmutter's (2007) and Howard's (2010) contentions that the Internet's effectiveness as a mobilization medium is apparent at relatively low adoption rates.[62] The model, however, also suggests that the likelihood of protest declines as user rates increase. The negative sign on the squared term indicates that the curve opens downward. The IRR is not a meaningful measure for a squared term, though, making it difficult to discern the effect through numbers alone. Thus, a predicted probability graph is used (Figure 11.4) to illustrate the curvilinear effect.

While the previous predictions identify a dramatic increase in protest rates between 20 and 30 users per 100 people, Figure 11.4 highlights a peak at 30 users per 100 people, after which the likelihood of protest begins to taper off. This may be a function of GDP growth and thus increased life satisfaction. A simple tabulation chart analysis indicates that no protests occurred in any state with more than 29.4 Internet users per 100 people: specifically, Bahrain, Kuwait, Malaysia, Morocco, Oman, Qatar, Saudi Arabia, Singapore, Tunisia, The United Arab Emirates, and Venezuela. Note, however, that the steep drop in protest rates is likely overly exaggerated in the graph, as there are only 20 state/years where Internet use exceeds 40 users per 100 people.

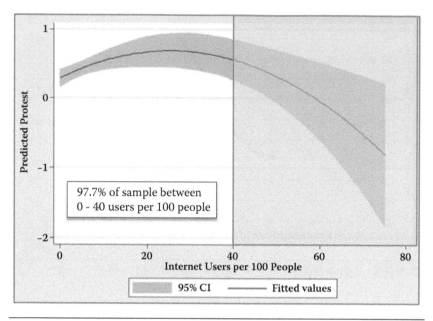

Figure 11.4 Curvilinear predicted effect of Internet use on protest.

The control variables also present interesting findings. While GDP per capita is not statistically significant, a one-unit increase in GDP growth decreases the likelihood of anti-regime demonstrations by 7 percent. This may be explained by increased quality of life associated with increasing income, which decreases the likelihood of anti-regime protest. The rate of protest also increases 68 percent for each unit increase in the total population. This aligns with previous findings that suggest increasing populations place additional burdens on the state and make it more difficult for regimes to meet societal demands. Next, while it is admittedly a crude measure of coercive capacity, protests also decrease as military spending/GDP ratios increase, with each unit increase decreasing the rate of protest by 16 percent. This finding suggests that the state's coercive capacity has a chilling effect on anti-regime protests. Surprisingly, incidents of protest increase as political terror increases, with a 45 percent increase in rate of protest for each unit increase of the Political Terror Scale. This diverges from previous works that find political terror decreases protest. One explanation is that grievance toward political terror is the social change trigger that fosters mobilization. Lastly, education as measured through school enrollment is not statistically significant.

A review of the states' characteristics further identifies factors that illustrate the curvilinear effect. Five of the countries are Organization of Petroleum Exporting Countries (OPEC) members. Eight had GDPs greater than $10,000 in 2010; and of those eight, four had GDPs greater than $20,000. Seven of the eleven states were scored as pure autocracies in 2010 (Polity IV score –10 to –6). Five of the states spend greater than 4 percent of GDP on defense: indeed, 88 percent of all protests between 2006 and 2010 occur in states that commit less than 4 percent of GDP to defense. This analysis lends further support to previous findings that suggest economic growth and coercion both suppress dissent, albeit for different reasons. On one hand, higher GDP per capita and GDP growth provide citizens greater economic opportunity and thus reduce economic-driven grievances. On the other hand, higher defense spending suggests greater coercive capacity and associated means of quelling dissent through force. Tunisia, however, is an outlier on this list in that the regime swiftly collapsed in January 2011, due potentially in part to Internet mobilization.

Conclusions

The case examples and quantitative analysis suggest that increased Internet access increases the likelihood of protest in non-democratic states, making the Internet a formidable protest mobilizing structure. The findings also reinforce the contention that Internet-mediated dissent challenges authoritarian regimes through distance, decentralization, and interaction. First, the Internet allows individuals to communicate almost instantaneously and relatively cheaply across great distances (although cost remains a factor in some areas). Not only can individuals keep in contact with close friends and family, but they can also interact with any like-minded individual using a TCP/IP enabled device. Second, TCP/IP's decentralized structure helps maintain user anonymity while at the same time allowing information to flow freely over multiple conduits. However, states such as China and Myanmar have tried different methods to identify users, with varying degrees of success. Finally, the "many-to-many" broadcast method fosters interaction by allowing users to be both consumers and producers of content. Perlmutter (2004) presents the term "interactor" as a descriptive for many-to-many interpersonal communication in the Internet age.[63]

Furthermore, three control variables remained consistently strong across almost all the empirical tests. Both economic growth and coercive capacity decreased the likelihood of protest, while state population levels increased the likelihood of protest. These controls may help explain the tapering effect above 30 users per 100 people. On the one hand, increased Internet use may suggest greater economic opportunity and reduced grievance; while on the other hand, increased Internet use may also indicate greater state wealth and thus a means to expand coercive capacity.

While some technological theorists remain cautious at evangelizing the Internet as the ultimate mobilizing tool, others contend that Internet access has the capacity to overwhelm state coercion.[64] Consider events in the Middle East since 2009. The Iranian presidential elections of 2009 depicted the first "Twitter Revolution," with dissenters fully embracing Internet technologies to plan, organize, and execute events. Information spread beyond the Iranian firewall and attracted international audiences. What was particularly provocative from a policy standpoint during the Iranian protests was the State Department calling the CEO of Twitter directly to ask that the company postpone going offline for system maintenance so that the Twitter service remained available to the Iranian protest movement.[65] In short, a government directly appealed to a private corporation to ensure that the corporation's service remained available in order to subvert an opposing government.

But while the Iranian regime successfully quelled the protest, the regimes of Tunisia, Egypt, Yemen, and Libya were not so fortunate. As in Iran, protesters in each state embraced the Internet as a mobilizing structure. But in each case the movements succeeded in removing the respective regimes from power. This is not to say that Internet access was the only causal factor. However, the use of Google Maps to plot troop movements rivals sophisticated order of battle tracking employed by professional militaries. In the early 1990s, this kind of reporting was highly classified and collected with specialized equipment: fast forward to 2013, and intelligence previously available to professionals is now freely available on the Internet. From a policy standpoint, the implications of this type of public collection and reporting are extraordinary.

These illustrative examples, however, also indicate that states are willing to impose Internet restrictions in order to restrict political opportunity, with violent results in some cases. Even successes such as Egypt's Internet-mediated movement have been tempered by bloodshed: the protests erupted on January 25, and by January 29, 100 people had been killed and 2000 wounded.[66] The potential for bloodshed is an apt segue into policy ramifications. As Bimber (1998) and Garrett (2006) suggest, the Internet accelerates and intensifies the social mobilization and state response cycle.[67] The Arab Spring's rapid diffusion across the Middle East illustrates this, as does China's quick imposition of related keyword blocks to prevent similar protest outbreaks.

On the one hand, the Internet is an inexpensive alternative for engaging with and supporting dissent movements: asking Twitter to keep their servers running had fewer foreign policy costs than intervening in Iran directly. As the Internet supplanted the newspaper, radio, and television previously as a mobilization tools, Internet engagement fills the same role as the radio-based Voice of America but with far more interactivity. On the other hand, Internet engagement is a double-edged sword, with the risk of Internet engagement rapidly transitioning to armed confrontation.

Internet mobilization was a common thread throughout the Arab Spring revolts, symbolically culminating in *Time* Magazine naming "The Protester" as the 2011 person of the year. The artist's rendition of the young, masked dissident capped a year that spoke to the end of authoritarianism at the hands of new social movements. Yet, what started with a single man immolating himself in Tunisia in protest has also since metastasized into not only three fallen regimes, but also thousands dead, thousands more wounded, and US military involvement in Libya through the auspices of NATO. The policy risk, then, is that Internet mobilization can quickly spiral from a cheap, hands-off alternative to physical involvement and conflict diffusion outside the target area.

Endnotes

1. Tiffany Danitz and Warren Strobel. The Internet's Impact on Activism: The Case of Burma. Washington, DC: Virtual Diplomacy Series, US Institute of Peace, 1999, 259; John Naughton. Contested Space: The Internet and Global Civil Society. In *Global Civil Society 2001*, edited by Helmut Anheier, Marlies Glasius, and Mary Kaldor, 147–168. London: Centre for the Study of Global Governance, London School of Economics, 2001, 160.
2. Danitz and Strobel, The Internet's Impact on Activism, 259.
3. Enemies of the Internet: Countries under Surveillance. Paris, France: Reporters Sans Frontières (RSF), 2010, 2.
4. Andrew Chadwick. *Internet Politics: States, Citizens, and New Communications Technologies.* Oxford: Oxford University Press, 2006, 115; R. Kelly Garrett. Protest in an Information Society: A Review of Literature on Social Movements and New ICTs. *Information, Communication & Society* 9, no. 2 (2006): 204–207; Leah A. Lievrouw. *Alternative and Activist New Media.* Cambridge: Polity Press, 2011, 12–13.
5. Chadwick, *Internet Politics*, Chapter 6.
6. Suzanne Brunsting and Tom Postmes. Social Movement Participation in the Digital Age: Predicting Offline and Online Collective Action. *Small Group Research* 33, no. 5 (2002): 526; Karen Mossberger, Caroline J. Tolbert, and Ramona S. McNeal. *Digital Citizenship: The Internet, Society, and Participation.* Cambridge, MA: MIT Press, 2008, 67.
7. Michael Dartnell. Weapons of Mass Instruction: Web Activism and the Transformation of Global Security. *Millennium-Journal of International Studies* 32, no. 3 (2003): 492.
8. Chadwick, *Internet Politics*, 6.
9. Shanthi Kalathil and Taylor C. Boas. *Open Networks, Closed Regimes: The Impact of the Internet on Government Rule.* Washington, DC: The Carnegie Endowment for International Peace, 2003, 26.
10. Patrick W. Quirk. Iran's Twitter Revolution. *Foreign Policy In Focus*, June 17, 2009, para. 11.
11. Philip N. Howard. *The Digital Origins of Dictatorship and Democracy.* New York: Oxford University Press, 2010, 5.
12. Doug McAdam, John D. McCarthy, and Mayer N. Zald. *Comparative Perspectives on Social Movements: Political Opportunities, Mobilizing Structures, and Cultural Framings.* Cambridge: Cambridge University Press, 1996. Illustrated in Doug McAdam, Sidney Tarrow, and Charles Tilly. *Dynamics of Contention.* Cambridge: Cambridge University Press, 2001, 17.
13. Sidney Tarrow. *Power in Movement: Social Movements and Contentious Politics.* Cambridge: Cambridge University Press, 1998, 24.
14. Tarrow, *Power in Movement*, 21; Christian Davenport. Introduction. In *Repression and Mobilization*, edited by Hank Johnston and Carol Mueller Christian Davenport, vii–xli. Minneapolis, MN: University of Minnesota Press, 2005, xv.

15. Kareem Fahim. Slap to a Man's Pride Set Off Tumult in Tunisia. *The New York Times*, January 21, 2011.
16. Russell Hardin. *One for All: The Logic of Group Conflict*. Princeton, NJ: Princeton University Press, 1995; John D. McCarthy and Mayer N. Zald. Resource Mobilization and Social Movements: A Partial Theory. *American Journal of Sociology* 82, no. 6 (1977): 1212–1241.
17. Ted Robert Gurr. *Why Men Rebel*. Princeton, NJ: Princeton University Press, 1970, 225.
18. Tarrow, *Power in Movement*, 80, 83.
19. Russell J. Dalton and Alix van Sickle. The Resource, Structural, and Cultural Bases of Protest. *Working paper, UC Irvine: Center for the Study of Democracy* (2005), 7.
20. Peter K. Eisinger. The Conditions of Protest in American Cities. *American Political Science Review* 67, no. 1 (1973): 11–28; David S. Meyer. Protest and Political Opportunities. *Annual Review of Sociology* 30 (2004): 125–145.
21. Gurr, *Why Men Rebel*, 83.
22. Tarrow, *Power in Movement*, 21; Doug McAdam, Sidney Tarrow, and Charles Tilly. *Dynamics of Contention*. Cambridge: Cambridge University Press, 2001, 14; Ronald Inglehart and Christian Welzel. Political Culture and Democracy: Analyzing Cross-Level Linkages. *Comparative Politics* 36, no. 1 (2003): 64.
23. Patricia M, Thornton. Framing Dissent in Contemporary China: Irony, Ambiguity and Metonymy. *The China Quarterly* 171 (2002): 661–681, 663; Dalton and van Sickle, Cultural Bases of Protest, 9.
24. Thornton, Framing Dissent in Contemporary China, 672.
25. Tarrow, *Power in Movement*, 19.
26. Anne Barnard and Rick Gladstone. Steps up Drive against Insurgents, Invading Enclaves in Northern City. *The New York Times*, March 14, 2012, A15.
27. Tarrow, *Power in Movement*, 72.
28. Ibid. 31; Dieter Rucht. 2007. The Spread of Protest Politics, in Russell Dalton and Hans-Dieter Klingemann, eds., *The Oxford Handbook of Political Behavior*. Oxford: Oxford University Press, 716.
29. Chris Atton. *An Alternative Internet*. New York: Columbia University Press, 2004, 19.
30. Chadwick, *Internet Politics*, 7. Also, see Merrill Morris and Christine Ogan. The Internet as Mass Medium. *Journal of Computer-Mediated Communication* 1, no. 4 (1996).
31. Taylor C. Boas. Weaving the Authoritarian Web: The Control of Internet Use in Nondemocratic Regimes. In *How Revolutionary Was the Digital Revolution? National Responses, Market Transitions, and Global Technology*, edited by John Zysman and Abraham Newman, 361–378. Stanford, CA: Stanford University Press, 2006, 7.
32. Naughton, Contested Space, 148; Behrouz Forouzan. *TCP/IP Protocol Suite*. 4th ed. New York: McGraw-Hill, 2009.
33. Chadwick, *Internet Politics*, 31.

34. Marc Lynch. After Egypt: The Limits and Promise of Online Challenges to the Authoritarian Arab State. *Perspectives on Politics* 9, no. 2 (2011): 303.
35. Alexandra Dunn. Unplugging a nation: State media strategy during Egypt's January 25 uprising. *The Fletcher Forum of World Affairs* 35 (2011): 19; Zeynep Tufecki and Christopher Wilson. Social Media and the Decision to Participate in Political Protest: Observations from Tahrir Square. *Journal of Communication* 62, no. 2 (2012): 365.
36. Muslim Brotherhood to Participate in 25 January Protest. *Egypt Independent* (January 23, 2011); Ekaterina Stepanova. The Role of Information Communication Technologies in the "Arab Spring": Impications Beyond the Region. PONARS Eurasia Policy Memo No. 159, May 2011, 1–2.
37. Mona el-Naggar. Equal Rights Takes to the Barricades. *The New York Times,* February 1, 2011.
38. Tufecki and Wilson, Social Media, 13–14.
39. Dunn, Unplugging a Nation, 19.
40. Janet Abbate. *Inventing the Internet.* Cambridge, MA: MIT Press, 1999; Chadwick, *Internet Politics,* Chap. 3.
41. Monty Marshall, Ted Gurr, and Keith Jaggers. Polity IV Project: Political Regime Characteristics and Transitions, 1800–2010. edited by Center for Systemic Peace. Arlington, VA: George Mason University, 2011; The Polity IV scale ranges from −10 (pure autocracy) to 10 (pure democracy).
42. Arthur S. Banks. Cross-National Time-Series Data Archive. Jerusalem, Israel: Databanks International, 2011, 11.
43. See Susan Hannah Allen. The Domestic Political Costs of Economic Sanctions. *Journal of Conflict Resolution* 52, no. 6 (2008): 916–944.
44. Peter Hocke. Determining the Selection Bias in Local and National Newspaper Reports on Protest Events. In *Acts of Dissent: New Developments in the Study of Protest,* edited by Ruud Koopmans and Friedhelm Niedhardt Dieter Rucht, 131–163. Berlin: Edition Sigma Rainer Bohn Verlag, 1998; Patrick P. Meier. The Impact of the Information Revolution on Protest Frequency in Repressive Contexts. Paper presented at the 50th International Studies Association (ISA) Convention New York, February 15–18, 2007, 9.
45. Allen, Domestic Political Costs, 927.
46. (I4CD), Information and Communications for Development. World Bank Data Query, edited by World Bank Group, Washington, DC, 2011.
47. Mark L. Gibney, Linda Cornett, and Reed Wood. Political Terror Scale 1976–2008, 2008.
48. Patrick M. Regan and Daniel Norton. Greed, Grievance, and Mobilization in Civil Wars. *The Journal of Conflict Resolution* 49, no. 3 (2005): 328; Dalton and van Sickle, Cultural Bases of Protest, 12; Christian Davenport, David A. Armstrong, and Mark I. Lichbach. From Mountains to Movements: Dissent, Repression, and Escalation to Civil War. Paper presented at the International Studies Association, San Diego, CA, 2006, 13.

49. Dalton and van Sickle, Cultural Bases of Protest, 6–7; Ruud Koopmans. Perspectives on Political Participation. In *The Oxford Handbook of Political Behavior*, edited by Russell Dalton and Hans-Dieter Klingemann, 693–707. Oxford: Oxford University Press, 2007, 696.
50. Howard, *Digital Origins*, 185; Ronald Inglehart and Christian Welzel. Changing Mass Priorities: The Link between Modernization and Democracy. *Perspectives on Politics* 8, no. 2 (2010): 557.
51. Ronald Inglehart. *Culture Shift*. Princeton, NJ: Princeton University Press, 1990; Pippa Norris. "Political Protest in Fragile States." Paper presented at the International Political Science Association World Congress, Fukuoka, Japan, July 13, 2006, 13; Howard, *Digital Origins*, 185.
52. Douglas Hibbs. *Mass Political Violence*. New York: Wiley, 1973; Steven G. Walker and Ivy S. Lang. The Garrison State Syndrome in the Third World: A Research Note. *Journal of Political and Military Sociology* 16, no. 1 (1988): 105–116; Christian Davenport. The Weight of the Past: Exploring Lagged Determinants of Political Repression. *Political Research Quarterly* 49, no. 2 (1996): 377–403.
53. Gary King. Variance Specification in Event Count Models: From Restrictive Assumptions to a Generalized Estimator. *American Journal of Political Science* 33 (1989): 762; J. Scott Long and Jeremy Freese. *Regression Models for Categorical Dependent Variables Using Stata*. 2nd ed. College Station, TX: Stata Press, 2006.
54. Allen, Domestic Political Costs, 934; Incidence rates can also be converted to percent change through the following formula: $(e^b - 1)*100\%$.
55. Burma Monks Issue Defiant Message. *BBC News* (September 21, 2007).
56. I4CD, World Bank Data Query.
57. U.N. Envoy Ends Mission to Myanmar. *Associated Press*, October 2, 2007.
58. Pulling the Plug: A Technical Review of the Internet Shutdown in Burma. Cambridge, MA: OpenNet Initiative, 2007, 3.
59. Jun Xu and J. Scott Long. Confidence Intervals for Predicted Outcomes in Regression Models for Categorical Outcomes. *The Stata Journal* 5, no. 4 (2005): 537–559.
60. I did not assess the 99th percentile because it consists of only eight state/year pairs out of 863. Moreover, the predicted rate of protest for state/years in the 99th percentile was extreme: 3480%. Given the low number of state/years, I assess the 99th percentile predicted rate as highly exaggerated.
61. Karen Rasler. Concessions, Repression, and Political Protest in the Iranian Revolution. *American Sociological Review* 61, no. 1 (1996): 135, 143.
62. Svetlana V. Kulikova and David D. Perlmutter. Blogging Down the Dictator? The Kyrgyz Revolution and Samizdat Websites. *International Communication Gazette* 69, no. 1 (2007): 31; Howard, *Digital Origins*, 11.
63. David D. Perlmutter. The Internet: Big Pictures and Interactors. In *Image Ethics in the Digital Age*, edited by John Stuart Katz, Larry Gross, and Jay Ruby, 1–26. Minneapolis: University of Minnesota Press, 2004, 1.
64. Evgeny Morozov. *The Net Delusion: The Dark Side of Internet Freedom*. New York: PublicAffairs, 2011; Howard, *Digital Origins*.

65. Howard, *Digital Origins*, 7.
66. Alison Williams and John Boyle. Death Toll in Egypt's Protests Tops 100—Sources. *Reuters* (January 29, 2011).
67. Bruce Bimber. The Internet and Political Transformation: Populism, Community, and Accelerated Pluralism. *Polity* 31, no. 1 (1998): 136; Garrett, Protest in an Information Society, 207.

References

Abbate, Janet. *Inventing the Internet*. Cambridge, MA: MIT Press, 1999.

Allen, Susan Hannah. The Domestic Political Costs of Economic Sanctions. *Journal of Conflict Resolution* 52, no. 6 (2008): 916–944.

Atton, Chris. *An Alternative Internet*. New York: Columbia University Press, 2004.

Banks, Arthur S. *Cross-National Time-Series Data Archive*. Jerusalem, Israel: Databanks International, 2011.

Barnard, Anne, and Rick Gladstone. Steps Up Drive against Insurgents, Invading Enclaves in Northern City. *The New York Times*, March 14, 2012, A15.

Bimber, Bruce. The Internet and Political Transformation: Populism, Community, and Accelerated Pluralism. *Polity* 31, no. 1 (1998): 133–160.

Boas, Taylor C. Weaving the Authoritarian Web: The Control of Internet Use in Nondemocratic Regimes. In *How Revolutionary Was the Digital Revolution? National Responses, Market Transitions, and Global Technology*, edited by John Zysman and Abraham Newman, 361–378. Stanford, CA: Stanford University Press, 2006.

Brunsting, Suzanne, and Tom Postmes. Social Movement Participation in the Digital Age: Predicting Offline and Online Collective Action. *Small Group Research* 33, no. 5 (2002): 525–554.

Burma Monks Issue Defiant Message. *BBC News* (September 21, 2007). Accessed December 5, 2012. http://news.bbc.co.uk/2/hi/asia-pacific/7005974.stm.

Chadwick, Andrew. *Internet Politics: States, Citizens, and New Communications Technologies*. Oxford: Oxford University Press, 2006.

Dalton, Russell J., and Alix van Sickle. The Resource, Structural, and Cultural Bases of Protest. *Working paper, UC Irvine: Center for the Study of Democracy* (2005).

Danitz, Tiffany and Warren Strobel. The Internet's Impact on Activism: The Case of Burma. Washington, DC: Virtual Diplomacy Series, US Institute of Peace, 1999.

Dartnell, Michael. Weapons of Mass Instruction: Web Activism and the Transformation of Global Security. *Millennium-Journal of International Studies* 32, no. 3 (2003): 477–499.

Davenport, Christian. The Weight of the Past: Exploring Lagged Determinants of Political Repression. *Political Research Quarterly* 49, no. 2 (1996): 377–403.

Davenport, Christian. Introduction. In *Repression and Mobilization*, edited by Hank Johnston and Carol Mueller Christian Davenport, vii–xli. Minneapolis, MN: University of Minnesota Press, 2005.

Davenport, Christian, David A. Armstrong, and Mark I. Lichbach. From Mountains to Movements: Dissent, Repression, and Escalation to Civil War. Paper presented at the International Studies Association, San Diego, CA, 2006.

Dunn, Alexandra. Unplugging a Nation: State Media Strategy during Egypt's January 25 Uprising. *The Fletcher Forum of World Affairs* 35 (2011): 15–24.

Eisinger, Peter K. The Conditions of Protest in American Cities. *American Political Science Review* 67, no. 1 (1973): 11–28.

el-Naggar, Mona. Equal Rights Takes to the Barricades. *The New York Times* (February 1, 2011). Accessed December 16, 2012. http://www.nytimes. com/2011/02/02/world/middleeast/02iht-letter02.html.

Enemies of the Internet: Countries under Surveillance. Paris, France: Reporters Sans Frontières (RSF), 2010.

Fahim, Kareem. Slap to a Man's Pride Set Off Tumult in Tunisia. *The New York Times*, January 21, 2011. Accessed November 5, 2012. http://www. nytimes.com/2011/01/22/world/africa/22sidi.html.

Forouzan, Behrouz. *TCP/IP Protocol Suite*. 4th ed. New York: McGraw-Hill, 2009.

Garrett, R. Kelly. Protest in an Information Society: A Review of Literature on Social Movements and New ICTs. *Information, Communication & Society* 9, no. 2 (2006): 202–224.

Gibney, Mark, L., Linda Cornett, and Reed Wood. Political Terror Scale 1976– 2008. edited by http://www.politicalterrorscale.org/, 2008. Last Updated December 18, 2012.

Gurr, Ted Robert. *Why Men Rebel*. Princeton, NJ: Princeton University Press, 1970.

Hardin, Russell. *One for All: The Logic of Group Conflict*. Princeton, NJ: Princeton University Press, 1995.

Hibbs, Douglas. *Mass Political Violence*. New York: Wiley, 1973.

Hocke, Peter. Determining the Selection Bias in Local and National Newspaper Reports on Protest Events. In *Acts of Dissent: New Developments in the Study of Protest*, edited by Ruud Koopmans and Friedhelm Niedhardt Dieter Rucht, 131–163. Berlin: Edition Sigma Rainer Bohn Verlag, 1998.

Howard, Philip N. *The Digital Origins of Dictatorship and Democracy*. New York: Oxford University Press, 2010.

Information and Communications for Development (I4CD). World Bank Data Query. Edited by World Bank Group. Washington, DC, 2011.

Inglehart, Ronald. *Culture Shift*. Princeton, NJ: Princeton University Press, 1990.

Inglehart, Ronald, and Christian Welzel. Political Culture and Democracy: Analyzing Cross-Level Linkages. *Comparative Politics* 36, no. 1 (2003): 61–79.

Inglehart, Ronald, and Christian Welzel. Changing Mass Priorities: The Link between Modernization and Democracy. *Perspectives on Politics* 8, no. 02 (2010): 551–567.

Kalathil, Shanthi and Taylor C. Boas. *Open Networks, Closed Regimes: The Impact of the Internet on Government Rule.* Washington, DC: The Carnegie Endowment for International Peace, 2003.

King, Gary. Variance Specification in Event Count Models: From Restrictive Assumptions to a Generalized Estimator. *American Journal of Political Science* 33 (1989): 762–784.

Koopmans, Ruud. Perspectives on Political Participation. In *The Oxford Handbook of Political Behavior*, edited by Russell Dalton and Hans-Dieter Klingemann, 693–707. Oxford: Oxford University Press, 2007.

Kulikova, Svetlana V., and David D. Perlmutter. Blogging Down the Dictator? The Kyrgyz Revolution and Samizdat Websites. *International Communication Gazette* 69, no. 1 (2007): 29–50.

Lievrouw, Leah A. *Alternative and Activist New Media.* Cambridge: Polity Press, 2011.

Long, J. Scott, and Jeremy Freese. *Regression Models for Categorical Dependent Variables Using Stata.* 2nd ed. College Station, TX: Stata Press, 2006.

Lynch, Marc. After Egypt: The Limits and Promise of Online Challenges to the Authoritarian Arab State. *Perspectives on Politics* 9, no. 2 (2011), 301–310.

Marshall, Monty, Ted Gurr, and Keith Jaggers. Polity IV Project: Political Regime Characteristics and Transitions, 1800–2010. Edited by Center for Systemic Peace. Arlington, VA: George Mason University, 2011.

McAdam, Doug, John D. McCarthy, and Mayer N. Zald. *Comparative Perspectives on Social Movements: Political Opportunities, Mobilizing Structures, and Cultural Framings.* Cambridge UK: Cambridge University Press, 1996.

McAdam, Doug, Sidney Tarrow, and Charles Tilly. *Dynamics of Contention.* Cambridge: Cambridge University Press, 2001.

McCarthy, John D., and Mayer N. Zald. Resource Mobilization and Social Movements: A Partial Theory. *American Journal of Sociology* 82, no. 6 (1977): 1212–1241.

Meier, Patrick P. The Impact of the Information Revolution on Protest Frequency in Repressive Contexts. Paper presented at the 50th International Studies Association (ISA) Convention, New York, February 15–18, 2007.

Meyer, David S. Protest and Political Opportunities. *Annual Review of Sociology* 30 (2004): 125–145.

Morris, Merrill, and Christine Ogan. The Internet as Mass Medium. *Journal of Computer-Mediated Communication* 1, no. 4 (1996).

Morozov, Evgeny. *The Net Delusion: The Dark Side of Internet Freedom.* New York: PublicAffairs, 2011.

Mossberger, Karen, Caroline J. Tolbert, and Ramona S. McNeal. *Digital Citizenship: The Internet, Society, and Participation.* Cambridge, MA: MIT Press, 2008.

Muslim Brotherhood to Participate in 25 January Protest. *Egypt Independent* (January 23, 2011). Accessed December 3, 2012. http://www.egyptindependent.com/node/303296.

Naughton, John. Contested Space: The Internet and Global Civil Society. In *Global Civil Society 2001*, edited by Marlies Glasius and Mary Kaldor Helmut Anheier, 147–168. London: Centre for the Study of Global Governance, London School of Economics, 2001.

Norris, Pippa. Political Protest in Fragile States. Paper presented at the International Political Science Association World Congress, Fukuoka, Japan, July 13, 2006.

OpenNet Initiative. Pulling the Plug: A Technical Review of the Internet Shutdown in Burma. Cambridge, MA, 2007. Accessed December 30, 2012. http://opennet.net/research/bulletins/013.

Perlmutter, David P. The Internet: Big Pictures and Interactors. In *Image Ethics in the Digital Age*, edited by John Stuart Katz, Larry Gross, and Jay Ruby. Minneapolis: University of Minnesota Press, 2004, 1–26.

Quirk, Patrick W. Iran's Twitter Revolution. *Foreign Policy In Focus*, June 17, 2009. Accessed December 3, 2012. http://www.fpif.org/articles/irans_twitter_revolution.

Regan, Patrick M., and Daniel Norton. Greed, Grievance, and Mobilization in Civil Wars. *The Journal of Conflict Resolution* 49, no. 3 (2005): 319–336.

Rasler, Karen. Concessions, Repression, and Political Protest in the Iranian Revolution. *American Sociological Review* 61, no. 1 (1996): 132–152.

Rucht, Dieter. The Spread of Protest Politics, in Russell Dalton and Hans-Dieter Klingemann, eds., *The Oxford Handbook of Political Behavior*. Oxford: Oxford University Press, 2007, 708–723.

Stepanova, Ekaterina. The Role of Information Communication Technologies in The "Arab Spring": Implications Beyond the Region. PONARS Eurasia Policy Memo No. 159, May 2011.

Tarrow, Sidney. *Power in Movement: Social Movements and Contentious Politics*. Cambridge: Cambridge University Press, 1998.

Thornton, Patricia M. Framing Dissent in Contemporary China: Irony, Ambiguity and Metonymy. *The China Quarterly* 171 (2002): 661–681.

Tufecki, Zeynep, and Christopher Wilson. Social Media and the Decision to Participate in Political Protest: Observations from Tahrir Square. *Journal of Communication* 62, no. 2 (2012): 363–379.

U.N. Envoy Ends Mission to Myanmar. *Associated Press*, October 2, 2007.

Walker, Steven G., and Ivy S. Lang. The Garrison State Syndrome in the Third World: A Research Note. *Journal of Political and Military Sociology* 16, no. 1 (1988): 105–116.

Williams, Alison, and John Boyle. Death Toll in Egypt's Protests Tops 100—Sources. *Reuters* (January 29, 2011). Accessed December 19, 2012. http://www.reuters.com/article/2011/01/29/us-egypt-dead-idUSTRE 70S3ZM20110129.

Xu, Jun, and J. Scott Long. Confidence Intervals for Predicted Outcomes in Regression Models for Categorical Outcomes. *The Stata Journal* 5, no. 4 (2005): 537–559.

PART III
ETHICS, LAW, AND POLICY

12

CAN THERE BE AN ETHICAL CYBER WAR?*

GEORGE R. LUCAS, JR.

Contents

Endnotes   204

This may seem at first a strange question. One might reasonably wonder whether it even makes sense to talk about ethics, morality, or possible legal constraints on our behavior in the development and use of cyber weapons, or engaging in cyber warfare, when adversary nations, organized crime, and terrorists are relentlessly engaged in attacking the United States. The vulnerabilities, the threats posed, and the genuine harm already done are all very real. Would not a consideration of ethics or legal governance at this point merely serve to hamper us with constraints on our ability to respond to these vulnerabilities, and advantage adversaries who give such matters no credence?

Nevertheless, we and our potential adversaries would derive considerable advantage by giving some thought to governance in both morality and the law, in that it encourages all concerned to reflect more cogently upon strategic goals that might be served by cyber conflict. An ethical analysis of cyber conflict simply invites all parties to it to think clearly about what we are doing, what we are willing (and perhaps unwilling) to do, and why. It is therefore appropriate and important to talk about what we in the United States can and should do in response to what appear to be a relentless barrage of espionage and cyber attacks directed against military, commercial,

---

* A subsequent expanded version of this original presentation was delivered as the 11th Annual Stutt Lecture on Ethics at the US Naval Academy (March 26, 2012), forthcoming in *The Routledge Handbook of Ethics and War* (2013).

and vital infrastructure targets in our nation by persons or entities unknown. We must also consider whether there are limits (of an ethical sort) on what we are willing to do, and finally about whether, just as in conventional or counterinsurgency conflict, it is really true that acknowledging and abiding by such limits automatically puts us at a disadvantage in our conflict with adversaries and criminals.

So let's talk first about threats and vulnerabilities. Authors Richard A. Clark, Joel Brenner, and Mark Bowden (among many others) have all done a service by raising public awareness of the significance of cyber conflict, pointing out the extensive risks and vulnerabilities, and by inviting us to think more carefully about how to manage that risk.[1] At the same time, it is important not to move all the way from abject lack of concern (a fair description, for example, of the US Naval Service's attitude toward cyber conflict barely two or three years ago) to an exaggerated or hysterical assessment of our vulnerabilities. Threat inflation is of no more use to us in thinking through these difficult questions than ignorance and avoidance.[2]

Conceptual confusion and linguistic equivocation (in which different parties to a dispute employ similar-sounding language in often divergent and misleading ways) are enormous obstacles to the clear analysis of military technologies and threats, and nowhere is this more apparent than in the arena of cyber conflict. For example, Clarke and Brenner both offer chilling scenarios of a potential cyber "Pearl Harbor on steroids," with dams bursting and flooding, trains derailing, planes falling from the sky, poison gases escaping from chemical storage plants in large cities, and the like.[3] But most of the subsequent discussion of actual cyber conflict documents criminal activity, vandalism, theft, and acts of espionage. There is a heated debate in the literature about whether well-publicized cyber events in Estonia and Georgia and Iran (that we will turn to momentarily) even constituted cyberattacks at all, since (as the critics complain) no lives were lost and no permanent harm was done.[4] All of these debates frame difficult and as yet unanswered questions, such as:

- What constitutes the use of force in the cyber realm?
- When, if ever, does such force rise to the level of an armed attack of the sort envisioned in the UN Charter (e.g., Articles

2.4, 39, and 51), constituting a legitimate cause for war in self-defense?

- More generally, what is the nature of the harm or damage done through such attacks, when it is not explicitly kinetic or physical harm?
- When does the harm (on whatever account) done through relentless intrusion and invasion and theft of vital information and potential sabotage of vital infrastructure rise to a level that justifies retaliation, either in kind or by means of kinetic reprisal?
- And finally, when formulating strategies for cyber security and defense, what is the relation between privacy—and any right an individual citizen may reasonably claim to such privacy—and anonymity? Are these really equivalent?

These are all questions about which we are still largely unclear, in part because the domain of cyberspace appears to be so novel and unique,[5] and our history of backing into it until just a few years ago was so casual and largely unreflective.[6] Just as with earlier questions about professional ethics, law, and private military contracting, or the advent of military robotics, these issues pertaining to cyber warfare have arisen not through judicious pursuit of carefully formulated strategic policies, but largely through the unreflective evolution of behaviors and through the gradual emergence of new possibilities and unanticipated prospects over the course of time.

These, of course, are questions that have begun to be addressed in our emerging cyber security strategy, of which there are now two versions: the Department of Defense (DoD) and the Department of State/White House.[7] The rhetoric of both is quite distinct and different, but both manage in their own way (in American humorist James Thurber's phrase) "to amuse with their pretensions." The latter, the State Department document, was largely drafted by a doctoral student at Oxford University's Ethics and the Law of Armed Conflict (ELOAC) program. It is visionary and aspirational, acknowledging the cyber security threats and vulnerabilities, to be sure, but focusing largely on the prospects for global peace and international prosperity that an open, transparent, universally accessible global Internet promises to yield.

I stopped in Oxford to lecture on this topic on November 21, 2011, on my way home from teaching these subjects for new 2nd Lieutenants at the French Military Academy in Saint-Cyr. I confessed that I admired the vision but thought the students' underlying policy recommendations were perhaps too sanguine, and too naïve concerning the security threats. By contrast, a DoD document, released in Spring 2011, displays the protective paternalism one might expect from responsible military, intelligence, and security forces. The document is full of threat assessment, cognizant of the bewildering array of vulnerabilities, and bristling with proposals for defensive and counter-offensive measures in response—the cyber equivalent of barbed wire, steel, and land mines. One DoD official summed it up for the *Wall Street Journal*, "if you shut down our power grid, maybe we will put a missile down one of your smokestacks!"[8]

This is the tough talk of deterrence that might give pause to reasonable, self-interested adversaries. I'm less certain that criminals and terrorists will be dissuaded by it. In any case, it poses some hard questions: first, of course, *whose* smokestacks, given the difficult problem of attribution. Perhaps just as important: *how many* missiles, down *how many* smokestacks? What cyber damage or harm would we need to sustain in order to provoke such a response? And the trick is, we would need to have an answer to inform policy. But, as Martin Libicki at the RAND Corporation points out, we would not want to advertise it, since adversaries invariably try to press the limits.[9] For the desired deterrent effect, it is better to keep them guessing and worrying: we need to remain deliberately vague about where those limits lie—just the sort of "double-deek" deception we used to practice with the Soviets during the Cold War.

Finally, are "smokestacks" and power grids the proper sorts of targets? Perhaps responding in kind to such an infrastructure attack would be appropriate, but would we want to make such attacks on civilian infrastructure part of an offensive strategy? Would we be willing, for example, to take out the Three Gorges Dam and subject millions of ordinary farmers and citizens to drowning, starvation, and immiseration to counter an armed confrontation or military standoff in the Straits of Taiwan, or worse, over competing claims of regional states over mineral rights in the South China Sea, in which we have no direct interest?

How are we to go about formulating policy in response to such questions and scenarios? Such questions drive us back to foundational resources for dealing with crisis response, resources and traditions that attempt to guide us in balancing important guiding principles and values against the lives and welfare of large numbers of people who might be affected by such events. This is never an easy balancing act, but we do have resources and experience in applying them to questions like these. We find these resources in the cardinal principles of international law that reflect centuries of philosophical evaluation of such moral dilemmas, known as the "just war tradition." That tradition and the body of international law derived from it counsel us in two respects: (1) *when* we are entitled to use force or engage in an armed attack against adversaries who have harmed, or threaten to harm us; and (2) *how* we are to go about doing so.[10]

In answer to the first set of questions, the use of force is justified in this tradition only reluctantly, on behalf of a grave or serious matter of state, and only after all reasonable attempts by duly constituted or legitimate authorities to resolve the conflict have failed. When the resort to force is found necessary, moreover, the conventional responses to the second set of questions declare that force must be employed only to the degree required to achieve legitimate military objectives and should be directed only against representatives of the military forces of the adversary, and never deliberately against third parties or noncombatants. These guiding principles of just war doctrine are likewise the cardinal principles of the international law of armed conflict, known broadly by their philosophical names (more than by their specific legal expression) as *proportionality* (the economy of force), *military necessity*, the principle of *noncombatant immunity* and discrimination (or distinction in the law), and prohibitions against weapons or uses of force that inflict cruel and unnecessary suffering.

Those cardinal principles or strictures of LOAC reflect a grudging moral consensus over centuries of state practice between rivals and adversaries to attempt to limit the collateral damage of war (as we were reminded in the Kosovo air campaign a decade ago). We don't deliberately target civilians or civilian infrastructure, and we take reasonable care to limit the degree of force deployed in pursuit of a legitimate military objective in order to avoid disproportionate collateral damage. In my own teaching and writing I have attempted to show how such legal constraints emerge from the proper practice of the profession of arms, constituting its most sacred and fundamental values and professional principles.[11] They are thus not imposed externally as "handcuffs" on military personnel, placing us at a competitive disadvantage against ruthless and unprincipled adversaries. Rather, such norms and constraints on permissible action arise as a reflection of professional identity, and the underlying purpose of the military profession itself as a vital form of public service. The question we face presently is how, and perhaps even whether, such longstanding principles and traditions can offer any useful guidance in the cyber realm, or rightly constrain our efforts to respond to and resolve cyber conflict.

Consider, for example, that by far the greatest areas of vulnerability are not hardened, encrypted, and securely firewalled military and security targets (although these are still surprisingly and disturbingly vulnerable). Rather, as in nuclear conflict, the areas of greatest vulnerability are civilian populations, civilian objects, and vital public infrastructure. Accordingly, most cyber weapons, and many scenarios for cyber warfare, have been focused upon such targets in apparent violation of the most fundamental principles of international humanitarian law and the just war tradition.[12] Critics of both, however, have offered these facts as demonstration that these approaches are antiquated, outmoded, and useless, and ought not to be invoked in the analysis and evaluation of cyber conflict, especially when the harm done appears to involve little or no loss of life or destruction of property.[13]

I dissent from that view, largely because the insights stemming from conventional or traditional just war doctrine and lying at the philosophical and judicial core of present international law constitute the only resources we have to bring to bear upon such questions. We must at least attempt (as human beings invariably are driven to do whenever faced with a set of novel circumstances) to extrapolate from the known to the unknown, by means of analogy, comparison, and interpretation. At least we must make the attempt, and explore the intuitive soundness of the results, before abandoning such resources altogether.

When attempting this interpretive extrapolation, moreover, we confront immediately an interesting cultural feature of cyber conflict: it is "information warfare" and so reflects the tolerated and traditional practices of the professional communities most deeply engaged in intelligence, surveillance, and reconnaissance (ISR): the clandestine services and intelligence communities, which are not coextensive with those of traditional combat forces. In international espionage, for example, the name of the game is usually thought to be dirty tricks and deception: to steal more information from them than they do from us, and in the ensuing conflict to "do unto them before they do unto you." What has happened, inadvertently, is that cyber conflict has blurred the heretofore sharp, traditional boundaries between espionage, covert action, and ongoing low-intensity inter-state conflict and competition on one hand, and full-scale kinetic conflict on the other.[14] How have those boundaries moved? How have those rules and conventions changed, if at all? Are we speaking metaphorically or literally when we describe cyber attacks and cyber warfare? (We don't normally, for example, label a massive breach of security by enemy espionage agents as an armed attack, or classify our response as constituting warfare.)

In any area of new or relatively unfamiliar terrain, the usual advice is to proceed with caution, speak and think carefully, and observe as closely as possible the sorts of behaviors that are actually taking place and are found to test the limits of minimally acceptable conduct. In international law, this is known as the search for emerging norms of state behavior. Here, I have argued in my writings and presentations on cyber conflict, that we have begun to have enough experience with this relatively new domain to know, both as individuals and as nations, what we would like to see transpire there, and what kinds of behaviors we would like to condemn and discourage.[15] That international norms have begun to crystalize in the conduct of cyber conflict may be demonstrated by considering four instances of such conflict with which the general public is now reasonably familiar: Russia versus Estonia (2007), Russia versus Georgia (2008), Israel versus Syria (2007), and Stuxnet (2010).[16]

Of course, no one has taken credit for Stuxnet, although allegations have flown since its discovery in 2009–2010. The usual default is to credit those who smile the most broadly, cough gently, and decline to comment for the record. Likewise the Russians and Israelis either deny or refuse to discuss responsibility for the other altercations.

Here I have come to believe that the so-called attribution problem is neither all that big nor all that unprecedented.[17] Cyber forensics has taken enormous strides in the detection of crime and the origins of state conflict. When in doubt, apply not Asimov's laws, but Agatha Christie's principle: ignore the background distractions and focus upon who stands to benefit most from the deed. Nine times out of ten, you've got your perpetrator, and 90 percent certainty is probably close enough for government work. A government may respond (as Russia did in the Estonian case) that it can't be held responsible for the actions of "patriots, criminals, or outraged vigilantes" within its borders, but that defense is nonsense. It didn't work for the Taliban in disclaiming responsibility for what Al Qaeda did "beyond its control" but within its sovereign borders, and it probably shouldn't work here either.

Our response should be the same in cyber as in conventional conflict: either you stop the illegal actors, arrest them, or throw them out, and take responsibility for what goes on within your borders, or we will regard you as complicit in these acts. That declaration moves us from the realm of international criminal law alone, to that of inter-state conflict and LOAC.[18] That, coupled with effective cyber forensics and the "Agatha Christie principle," probably is enough to counter cyber subterfuge and take care of the attribution problem. Besides, denials, disclaimers of responsibility, and non-attribution are nothing new in warfare. The Italians denied their small flotilla of submarines was responsible for sinking or damaging British supply ships near Gibraltar early in World War II. When the British threatened to bomb the Italian peninsula into the Stone Age unless the attacks ceased, however, they mysteriously ceased!

So let's move to cyber weapons, tactics, and targeting. Estonia represents a wholesale and indiscriminate assault on civilians and civilian (and government non-military) infrastructure almost exclusively. There were no military targets, and more important, no reasonable military objectives served by the attacks. Moving a war memorial from one place of honor to another within one's sovereign borders may be cause for annoyance or even diplomatic protest, but hardly for war, and certainly not for an indiscriminate and disproportionate assault on noncombatants.

Stuxnet resides at the opposite extreme. The targets were purely military. No one was killed, no civilians or civilian infrastructure were deliberately targeted. The damage done and harm suffered were surely proportionate to the threat of harm posed by the target itself, and most importantly, every conceivable effort short of attack was undertaken to persuade the adversary to cease and desist. Notice how what in ethics and law are called new norms of inter-state conduct are already emerging from these instances.

The middle ground is occupied by the Georgian and Syrian cases. Here the Russians showed both discrimination and restraint, employing cyber tactics to destroy or disrupt the adversarial governments and military's command and control preceding a conventional attack, limited in turn to forcing a resolution of the specific issue in dispute (the status of breakaway province of Ossetia, and status of Russian citizens living there). This is a perfectly acceptable wartime tactic.[19] We may choose to side with our NATO allies in Georgia in that dispute, but it is a legitimate inter-state conflict, a difference of opinion with reasonable claims on both sides. Clausewitz might scold us that this is what wars are designed to solve. The same holds true in the case of the alleged Israeli bombing of the Syrian nuclear facility, apparently under construction (with technical assistance from North Korea) at Dayr al Zawr. A cyber attack dismantled Syrian radar, permitting a conventional bombing raid on an illicit nuclear weapons facility, undertaken at night when deaths and collateral damage might be reasonably minimized, and presumably after diplomatic initiatives to cease and desist had failed.

Notice that in these cases, I am deliberately trying not to interpose my judgment of the merits of each side's dispute: only how they came to resort to war, and how they conducted their conflict with cyber weapons and tactics. Here, I think, we can identify the following norms of acceptable behavior. A cyber attack is morally justified and should be legally sanctioned whenever the following conditions are met:

1. The underlying issue in conflict is sufficiently grave to serve as a *casus belli*.

2. Only the adversary's military assets are targeted, and the harm inflicted (kinetic or cyber) is proportionate and reasonable in light of the threat posed by the targeted assets.

3. Specifically civilian lives and infrastructure are not the objects of attack, and every effort is made to avoid or minimize damage to same.

4. Every effort has been made short of war to resolve the dispute in question.

This is a substantive set of conclusions to draw from these examples, and it constitutes a good beginning for the ethics of cyber warfare. It sorts the examples into both acceptable and unacceptable modes of conduct and seems to explain our different responses to each, independent of which side we politically favor in the dispute, and so offers a reasonable guide for future action.[20] Interestingly, as the case of Stuxnet suggests, these norms seem to permit even a *preemptive* or *preventive* cyber strike, as well as guide our thinking about retaliation for an unacceptable strike on our own assets. That is, the guidelines seem to work for both offense and defense.[21]

In fact, something like this list of criteria emerged as a proposal over a decade ago, in an interesting and path-breaking article on ethics and information warfare by John Arquilla, currently the Chair of the Department of Defense Analysis at the Naval Postgraduate School (Monterey, CA) and buried in an obscure RAND Corporation report issued in the late 1990s.[22] Our team of resident Stockdale Fellows was working on the Stuxnet case I first discovered this article. I contacted John to introduce myself and ask him to speak to a consortium of engineers, scientists, lawyers, and ethicists with whom I collaborate on military operations and national security. I pointed out the coincidence and observed, "John, it sure seems to me as if whoever developed this weapon not only read your article, but followed its ethical guidelines to the letter!" He smiled broadly, coughed gently, and declined to comment for the record.

Endnotes

1. Richard A. Clark and Robert K. Knake, *Cyber War: The Next Threat to National Security, and What to Do About It* (New York: HarperCollins, 2010); Joel Brenner, *America the Vulnerable: Inside the New Threat Matrix of Digital Espionage, Crime, and Warfare* (New York: Penguin Books, 2011); and Mark Bowden, *Worm: The First Digital World War* (New York: Atlantic Monthly Press, 2011).

2. See, for example, the treatments of this topic by highly respected journalists: James Fallows, Cyber Warriors, *The Atlantic Monthly* (March 2010): 58–63; and Seymour M. Hersh, The Online Threat, *The New Yorker* (November 1, 2010), both of whom echo the concerns of Clarke and Knake, cited above (n.1).

3. CDR Todd C. Huntley, USN complains of the problems of misuse of concepts and terminology as a fatal flaw in the analysis of cyber conflict and vulnerabilities: Controlling the Use of Force in Cyber Space: The Application of the Law of Armed Conflict during a Time of Fundamental Change in the Nature of Warfare, *Naval Law Review LX* (2010): 1–40. See especially his characterizations of cyber activity at p. 4.

4. One such skeptic is Thomas Rid (University of London), who argues that all of the highly touted cyber "attacks" to date have constituted little more than conventional state and commercial espionage and criminal activity, none of which rises to the level of a military use of force or an "armed attack." See Cyber War Will Not Take Place, *Journal of Strategic Studies*, 35:1 (October 2011), 5–32. See also his exchange with John Arquilla in *Foreign Policy*: Think Again: Cyberwar, and Arquilla's rebuttal, Cyber War Is Already upon Us (March–April 2012): http://www.foreignpolicy. com/articles/2012/02/27/cyberwar; and http://www.foreignpolicy.com/ articles/2012/02/27/cyberwar_is_already_upon_us, respectively. I have argued in response that the concern for threat inflation and confusion of true warfare with low-intensity conflict (espionage and covert action) is appropriate, but the author's definition of "harm," "use of force," and "armed attack" are simply too restrictive for this domain. See Permissible Preventive Cyber Warfare, in Luciano Floridi and Mariarosaria Taddeo, eds., *Philosophy of Engineering and Technology* (UNESCO Conference on Ethics and Cyber Warfare, University of Hertfordshire, July 2011), forthcoming from Springer Verlag.

5. Randall Dipert calls attention to what he terms the "unique ontology" of cyber objects, events, and weapons as posing the greatest challenge to understanding both this new domain and the application of conventional conceptions of military ethics, just war doctrine, and the Law of Armed Conflict (LOAC) to it. See Randall Dipert, The Ethics of Cyber Warfare, *Journal of Military Ethics* 9, no. 4 (December 2010), 384–410. Michael Schmitt likewise calls attention to this puzzling feature of cyber events and objects as the principal source of difficulty in determining how to interpret and apply *jus in bello* and the black-letter provisions of international law to cyber conflict. See Michael N. Schmitt, Cyber Operations and the Jus in Bello: Key Issues, *US Naval War College International Law Studies*, vol. 87 (2011), 89–110.

6. As detailed, for example, in Herbert S. Lin et al., *Technology, Policy, Law, and Ethics Regarding US Acquisition and Use of Cyberattack Capabilities*. Washington, DC: National Research Council/American Academy of Sciences, 2009.

7. International Strategy for Cyberspace: Prosperity, Security and Openness in a Networked World (Washington, DC: Office of the President, May 1, 2011). http://www.whitehouse.gov/sites/default/files/rss_viewer/international_strategy_for_cyberspace.pdf.

   Department of Defense Strategy for Operating in Cyberspace (Washington, DC: Department of Defense, July 1, 2011). http://www.defense.gov/news/d20110714cyber.pdf.

8. Military official quoted in Siobahn Gorman and Julian E. Barnes, Cyber Combat: Act of War, *The Wall Street Journal* (May 30, 2011): http://online.wsj.com/article/SB10001424052702304563104576355562313578 2718.html.

9. See Libicki's essay in this Proceedings. See also his earlier, path-breaking work in this field, *Cyberdeterrence and Cyberwar* (Santa Monica, CA: Rand Corporation, 2009); *Conquest in Cyberspace: National Security and Information Warfare* (New York: Cambridge University Press, 2007).

10. There are numerous sources for these just war criteria, and for the distinction between *jus ad bellum* and *jus in bello*. See, for example, George R. Lucas, Jr., and W.R. Rubel, eds., *Ethics and the Military Profession: The Moral Foundations of Leadership*, 3rd edition (New York: Pearson, 2010).

11. That somewhat novel approach to just war doctrine as a manifestation of professional ethics in a military context infuses the textbook presentation cited above. See also G.R. Lucas, "This Is Not Your Father's War": Confronting the Moral Challenges of "Unconventional" War, *Journal of National Security Law and Policy*, 3, no. 2 (2009), 331–342; "Forgetful Warriors"—Neglected Lessons on Leadership from Plato's Republic, *The Ashgate Research Companion to Modern Warfare*, eds. George Kassimeris and John Buckley (London: Ashgate Press, 2010); and the treatment of military ethics as professional ethics in *Anthropologists in Arms: The Ethics of Military Anthropology* (Lanham, MD: AltaMira Press, 2009).

12. This complaint has been lodged most forcefully by computer scientist Neil C. Rowe: War Crimes from Cyberweapons, *Journal of Information Warfare*, 6: 3 (2007): 15–25; Ethics of Cyber War Attacks, in Lech J. Janczewski and Andrew M. Colarik (eds.), *Cyber Warfare and Cyber Terrorism* (Hershey, PA: Information Science Reference, 2008): 105–111; The Ethics of Cyberweapons in Warfare, *Journal of Technoethics* 1, no. 1 (2010): 20–31.

13. For example, as in the works by Randall and Rid, cited above.

14. This is so, I have insisted elsewhere, even though a preponderance of the participants, from General Keith Alexander and VADM William McCollough on down, wear (or wore) military uniforms. In espionage, covert action, and "psych ops," there is no restriction on targeting civilians, although this has begun to be questioned in the intelligence community's own discussions of professional ethics: See Jan Goldman, ed., *The Ethics of Spying: A Reader for the Intelligence Professional*, vol. I, II (Lanham, MD: Scarecrow Press, 2005/2009); David Perry, *Partly Cloudy: The Ethics of Espionage, Covert Action, and Interrogation* (Lanham, MD: Scarecrow Press, 2009).

15. See, for example, Permissible Preventive Cyber Warfare, in Luciano Floridi and Mariarosaria Taddeo, eds., *Philosophy of Engineering and Technology* (UNESCO Conference on Ethics and Cyber Warfare, University of Hertfordshire, July 1, 2011), forthcoming from Springer Verlag.

16. There are a plethora of reliable sources for accounts of each. A succinct and dramatic description of all four cyber conflicts is offered by Richard A. Clark and Robert K. Knake in *Cyber War: The Next Threat to National Security, and What to Do About It* (New York: HarperCollins, 2010). An excellent summary of the circumstances leading up to the attack on Estonia and its consequences can be found in Episode 2, Season 1 of the PBS program, *Wired Science*, from shortly after the incident in 2007, entitled, Technology: World War 2.0, at http://xfinitytv.comcast.net/tv/Wired-Science/95583/770190466/Technology%3A-World-War-2.0/videos?skipTo=189&cmpid=FCST_hero_tv. See also Charles Clover, Kremlin-Backed Group behind Estonia Cyber Blitz, *Financial Times* (London: March 11, 2009), and Tim Espiner, Estonia's Cyberattacks: Lessons Learned a Year on, ZD NET UK (May 1, 2008).

   For an analysis of the attack against Georgia, see E. Tikk, K. Kaska, K. Rünnimeri, M. Kert, A.-M. Talihärm, and L. Vihui, Cyber Attacks Against Georgia: Legal Lessons Identified (Tallinn, Estonia: NATO Cooperative Cyber Defence Centre of Excellence, 2008); and the United States Cyber Consequences Unit (US-CCU), Overview by the US-CCU of the Cyber Campaign against Georgia in August of 2008, US-CCU Special Report (August 2009), available at http://www.registan.net/wp-content/uploads/2009/08/US-CCU-Georgia-Cyber-Campaign-Overview.pdf (accessed 14 April 2013).

   In the Syrian case, see Uzi Mahnaimi and Sarah Baster, Israelis Seized Nuclear Material in Syrian Raid, *The Sunday Times* (London: September 23, 2007): http://www.timesonline.co.uk/tol/news/world/middle_east/article2512380.ece. For a summary of the cyber war elements of this strike, see David A. Fulghum, Robert Wall, and Amy Butler, Israel Shows Electronic Prowess, *Aviation Week* (November 25, 2007): http://www.aviationweek.com/aw/generic/story.jsp?id=news/aw112607p2.xml&headline=Israel%20Shows%20Electronic%20Prowess&channel=defense. See also Cyberwarfare Technology: Is Too Much Secrecy Bad? Airforce-technology.com (April 9, 2008): http://www.airforce-technology.com/features/feature1708/.

   Finally, for Stuxnet, see William J. Borad, John Markoff, and David E. Sanger, Israeli Test on Worm Called Crucial in Iran Nuclear Delay, *The New York Times* (January 15, 2011): http://www.nytimes.com/2011/01/16/world/middleeast/16stuxnet.html?_r=1. Michael J. Gross, A Declaration of Cyber-War, in *Vanity Fair*. http://www.vanity-fair.com/culture/features/2011/04/stuxnet-201104. For an equally thorough but more recent account of the entire Stuxnet affair, see also Kim Zetter, How Digital Detectives Deciphered Stuxnet, the Most Menacing Malware in History, *Wired* Magazine (July 11, 2011): http://www.wired.com/threatlevel/2011/07/how-digital-detectives-deciphered-stuxnet/

all/1. This nickname for the worm was coined by Microsoft security experts, an amalgam of two files found in the virus's code. A study of the spread of Stuxnet was undertaken by a number of international computer security firms, including Symantec Corporation. Their report, W32. Stuxnet Dossier, compiled by noted computer security experts Nicholas Falliere, Liam O. Murchu, and Eric Chien, and released in February 2011, showed that the main countries affected during the early days of the infection were Iran, Indonesia, and India: http://www.symantec.com/content/en/us/enterprise/media/security_response/whitepapers/w32_stuxnet_dossier.pdf. Despite its apparent success as a cyber weapon, concerns have been raised about proliferation and cloning of the design by third parties (e.g., terrorists). This concern is voiced explicitly in the online "infographic" documentary, Stuxnet: Anatomy of a Computer Virus, by Patrick Clair (2011): http://vimeo.com/25118844. See also Ralph Langner's cyber security blog: What Stuxnet Is all about, The Last Line of Cyber Defense (January 10, 2011); A Declaration of Bankruptcy for US Critical Infrastructure Protection, The Last Line of Cyber Defense (June 3, 2011).

17. See the contributions on this subject by Dipert and Yannokageorgos in this text. See also the considerable body of work by Michael N. Schmitt on this problem, including: Cyber Operations in International Law: The Use of Force, Collective Security, Self Defense, and Armed Conflicts, in Herbert Lin, et al., *Proceedings of a Workshop on Deterring Cyberattacks* (Washington, DC: The National Academies of Science, Engineering, and Medicine Press, 2010): 151–178.

18. This is a contested point that, for the most part, exceeds the scope of this paper. Scholars and practitioners of international law are far from unanimous on this point. Although in the past, states have successfully resisted imputing to themselves collectively the responsibility for criminal activities within their borders, that customary practice appears to have changed dramatically in the past decade. The International Convention on Cybercrime (Council of Europe, Convention on Cybercrime, Budapest: November 23, 2001): http://conventions.coe.int/Treaty/EN/Treaties/html/185.htm) explicitly charges states with the responsibility for cyber crimes that occur within their sovereign borders, and the UN Security Council has increasingly demanded that member states own up to this responsibility. An authoritative interpretation of the current status of international law on this topic, supporting the position I adopt in this lecture, is offered by Col. David E. Graham, US Army (retired), Cyber Threats and the Law of War, *Journal of National Security Law and Policy*, 4 (2010): 87–102. For his part, Graham argues that a state's duty to prevent cyber attacks generates an indirect or attributed responsibility for such attacks that can be traced to sources or persons acting within the state's borders. He and Schmitt seem to agree (as do Dipert and Yannakogeorgos) that a combination of these factors is sufficient to

attribute responsibility for an attack, and even to initiate a retaliation that may rise to the level of a justified "belligerent reprisal" under conventional international law.

19. Michael Schmitt's analysis of this conflict in Cyber Operations and the Jus in Bello, op. cit., along with a majority of the sources he cites, support this interpretation of the legality of the cyber component of this attack, and also of its general conformity to the restrictions of LOAC.

20. The opposition to formal governance measures is beginning to decrease in the United States as a formal cyber strategy begins to take shape. At the same time, acknowledging that cyber conflict is likely to resemble features of the nuclear era and the cold war, a decided preference is expressed for bi-lateral and multi-lateral forms of "soft law," such as John Arquilla's proposal for a declaration of "no first use" against civilian targets. See William J. Lynn III, Defending a New Domain: The Pentagon's Cyberstrategy, *Foreign Affairs* 89, no. 5 (September/October 2010): http://www.ciaonet.org/journals./fa/v89i5/08.html [restricted site, accessed February 11, 2011]; VADM Mike McConnell, To Win the Cyber-War, Look to the Cold War, *The Washington Post Outlook* (February 28, 2010): B1; Ellen Nakashima, NSA Chief faces questions about new Cyber-command, *The Washington Post* (April 15, 2010): A19.

21. See my article from the UNESCO cyber security symposium (July 1, 2011), Permissible Preventive Cyberwarfare, loc. cit.

22. John Arquilla, Ethics and Information Warfare, in *The Changing Role of Information in Warfare*, eds. Z. Khalilzad, J. White, and A. Marshall (Santa Monica, CA: RAND Corporation, 1999): 379–401. Arquilla literally coined the term "cyber warfare" to currency and is one of its leading analysts. I have cited some of his more recent work, above. See also Conflict, Security, and Computer Ethics, in the *Cambridge Handbook of Information and Computer Ethics*, ed. Luciano Floridi (New York: Cambridge University Press, 2010): 133–149.

13

PERSPECTIVES FOR CYBERSTRATEGISTS ON CYBERLAW FOR CYBERWAR*

CHARLES J. DUNLAP, JR.

Contents

Cybersizing LOAC	213
The "Act of War" Conundrum	214
A State of War?	219
Cybering and the Citizenry	223
Concluding Observations	225
Endnotes	226

The proliferation of martial rhetoric[1] in connection with the release of thousands of pages of sensitive government documents by the Wikileaks organization underlines how easily words that have legal meanings can be indiscriminately applied to cyber events in ways that can confuse decision makers and strategists alike. The Wikileaks phenomena is but the latest in a series of recent cyber-related incidents that range from cyber crises in Estonia and Georgia[2] to reports of the Stuxnet cyber-worm allegedly infecting Iranian computers[3] that contribute to a growing perception that "cyberwar"[4] is inevitable if not already underway.

All of this generates a range of legal questions with popular wisdom being that the law is inadequate or lacking entirely. Lt Gen Keith B. Alexander, the first commander of US Cyber Command, told Congress at his April 2010 confirmation hearings that there was a "mismatch between our technical capabilities to conduct operations and the governing laws and policies."[5] Likewise, Professor Jeffrey Addicott, a highly-respected cyberlaw authority, asserts that

---

* Reprinted from *Strategic Studies Quarterly*, Spring 2011.

"international laws associated with the use of force are woefully inadequate in terms of addressing the threat of cyberwarfare."[6]

This article takes a somewhat different tact concerning the ability of the law of armed conflict (LOAC) to address cyber issues.[7] Specifically, it argues that while there is certainly room for improvement in some areas, the basic tenets of LOAC are sufficient to address the most important issues of cyberwar. Among other things, this article contends that very often the real difficulty with respect to the law and cyberwar is not because of any lack of "law," per se, but rather relates to the technical ability to determine the necessary facts which must be applied to the law to render legal judgments.

That is not to say that applying the facts—such as they may be discernable in cyber situations—to a given legal principle is anything but a difficult task. Yet doing so has a direct analogy to the central conundrum faced by military decision makers fighting in more traditional battlespaces—that is, the need to make quick decisions based on imperfect data. Because of the inherent fog of war,[8] commanders gamely accept a degree of uncertainty in the legal advice they receive, just as they tolerate ambiguity inherent in other inputs. Too often it seems, however, as if cyberstrategists, schooled in the explicit verities of science, expect a level of assurance in legal matters rivaling mathematical equations. All law, but especially LOAC, necessarily involves subjectivity implicit in human reasoning that may be troubling to those of a technical mindset accustomed to the precision that their academic discipline so often grants.

This essay will not provide cyberstrategists with "cookbook" solutions to all the permutations of every legal dilemma cyberwar could produce. Instead it offers some broad legal considerations to facilitate thinking about the role of LOAC in cyberwar, and it suggests cautions for the military cyberstrategists in the future.

Perspectives on the law are expressed here as definitively as possible so as to counter complaints about indecisiveness of legal analysis. The author chose among differing and even conflicting legal interpretations and theories, and readers should understand that positions in this essay may be disputed by other legal experts. Accordingly, cyberstrategists must always seek the advice of legal counsel for guidance in specific situations, especially as law and policy evolves.

Cybersizing LOAC

Discomfort among cyberstrategists about reliance on existing LOAC norms is understandable. After all, most of the international agreements and practices of nation-states that comprise LOAC predate the cyber era. Indeed, many observers believe the need for a new legal regime designed for cyberwar is urgent.[9] Cyber expert Bruce Schneier warns that time is running out to put in place a cyber treaty that could, he advocates, "stipulate a no first use policy, outlaw unaimed weapons, or mandate weapons that self-destruct at the end of hostilities."[10]

However, to paraphrase former Secretary of Defense Donald Rumsfeld, you go to war with the LOAC you have, not the LOAC you may want. While agreements that might expedite cyber law-enforcement efforts are possible, it is not likely that any new international treaty governing cyberwar or cyberweaponry will be forthcoming for the foreseeable future. To begin with, the utility of such treaties is checkered at best. Although most people cheer international treaties that have banned chemical and biological weapons, some experts see them as unintentionally inhibiting the development of non- and low-lethality weaponry.[11] More generally, pundit Charles Krauthammer gives this scorching analysis:

> From the naval treaties of the 1920s to his day, arms control has oscillated between mere symbolism at its best to major harm at its worst, with general uselessness being the norm. The reason is obvious. The problem is never the weapon; it is the nature of the regime controlling the weapon.[12]

The Obama Administration also seems guarded with respect to cyber arms agreements. Writing in the September/October 2010 issue of *Foreign Affairs*, Deputy Secretary of Defense William Lynn observes that "[t]raditional arms control agreements would likely fail to deter cyberattacks because of the challenges of attribution which make the verification of compliance almost impossible."[13]

Even more substantively, nations may perceive the goals of any cyber treaty differently. For example, the Russians have long proposed an international cyber agreement (although couched in terms of one aimed at "information warfare").[14] However, journalist Tom Gjelten warns that "democracies have reason to proceed cautiously in this area, precisely because of differences in the way cyber 'attacks' are being defined in international forums."[15] The Russians and others see "ideological aggression" as a key cyberwar evil, and appear to be seeking an agreement that assists government censorship of the Internet and bans outside countries from supporting the cyber efforts of dissidents.[16]

Gjelten advises that at a 2009 meeting to discuss the Russian proposals, the "US delegation declared that existing international law could theoretically be applied to cyber conflict and that the United States would support the establishment of 'norms of behavior' that like-minded states could agree to follow in cyberspace."[17] American cyberstrategists, however, should be cautious of even that modest initiative. As attractive as it may be to have more clarity as to what the international community considers, for example, as an "act of war" in cyberspace, once an international norm is established, it forever after can be a legal impediment. If, as Gjelten argues, the US has the most advanced cyberwar capability, any new agreement or norm would likely oblige it to "accept deep constraints on its use of cyber weapons and techniques."[18]

The "Act of War" Conundrum

As already suggested, of all the legal issues bedeviling cyberstrategists, the issue as to when a cyber event amounts to an "act of war" seems to capture the most interest.[19] This is not a new query, but one that is critical because its resolution can define the options available to decision-makers. If it is truly "war," then a response under a national security legal regime is possible; if not, then treating the matter as a law enforcement issue is appropriate. This is a distinction with a difference.[20]

A national security legal regime is one where LOAC largely governs, while the law enforcement model essentially employs the jurisprudence of criminal law. The former is inclined to think in terms of eliminating threats through the use of force; the latter uses force only to contain alleged lawbreakers until a judicial forum can determine personal culpability. An action legitimately in the national security law realm may be intolerant of any injury and, when hostile intent is perceived, may authorize a strike to prevent it from occurring. Law enforcement constructs presume the innocence of suspects and endures the losses that forbearance in the name of legal process occasionally imposes.

All things being equal, cyberstrategists should default to the law enforcement modality. This makes practical sense because many experts see cybercrime (as opposed to cyberwar) as the most serious and most common threat in the cyber domain.[21] "Crime," incidentally, could include acts at the behest of a nation-state such as cyber espionage targeting a government or industry. As a general proposition, nondestructive computer methodologies employed for espionage may violate the domestic law of the victim nation-state but are not contrary to international law.[22]

In any event, "act of war" is a political phrase, not a legal term.[23] It might be said that the UN Charter was designed, in essence, to ban "war" from the lexicon of nations.[24] Article 2 (4) of the Charter demands that nations "refrain in their international relations from the threat or use of force against the territorial integrity or political independence of any state."[25] It sanctions only two exceptions to this prohibition on the use of force: (1) when the Security Council authorizes force, and (2) when a nation acts in self-defense. As to self-defense, Article 51 says that nothing in the Charter shall "impair the inherent right of individual or collective self-defense if an armed attack occurs" against a UN member.[26] It is this self-defense provision that often confounds cyberstrategists and their lawyers. Why?

The logic can be confusing. Specifically, Article 2 prohibits all threats and uses of "force," while Article 51 allows the use of force *only* in response to a certain kind of attacking force, specifically, an "armed attack." Retired Air Force colonel turned law professor Michael N. Schmitt notes that "all armed attacks are uses of force [within the meaning of Article 2], but not all uses of force qualify as armed attacks" that are a prerequisite to an *armed* response.[27] Thus, a nation may be the victim of cyber "force" of some sort being applied against it, but cannot respond in kind because the force it suffered did not amount to an "armed attack." However, a victim state may engage in a number of activities short of the use of force, including the unilateral severance of economic and diplomatic relations, civil lawsuits, as well as application to the UN Security Council for further action. In appropriate cases, pursuing criminal prosecution is an option.[28]

Of course, a cyber technique *can* qualify as an "armed attack." Cyber methodologies may qualify as "arms" under certain circumstances,[29] and existing LOAC provisions provide ready analogies for construing their use as an "attack." Specifically, although cyber techniques may not employ kinetics, as a matter of law an attack may take place even without a weapon that employs them. Protocol I to the Geneva Conventions defines attacks to mean "acts of violence against an adversary,"[30] which is properly interpreted to "extend to violent consequences of an attack which does not consist of the use of kinetic force."[31] The leading view, therefore, among legal experts focuses on the consequences and calls for an *effects-based* analysis of a particular cyber incident to determine whether or not it equates to an "armed attack" as understood by Article 51.[32]

Professor Schmitt pioneered this approach, and he offers seven factors to consider in making the judgment as to whether a particular cyber event constitutes "force" at all: severity, immediacy, directness, invasiveness, measurability, presumptive legitimacy, and responsibility.[33] It is beyond the scope of this article to detail the nuances of each of those factors,[34] but it is important to understand that as to whether the cyber activity is severe enough to amount to the legal equivalent of an "armed attack" (as opposed to merely a use of some force), the consequences must extend to more than mere inconvenience; there must be at least temporary damage of some kind.[35] Professor Schmitt points out that the "essence of an 'armed' operation is the causation, or risk thereof, of death or injury to persons or damage to or destruction of property and other tangible objects."[36]

Cyber events that have violent effects are, therefore, typically legally equivalent to "armed attacks." To be clear, not all adverse cyber events qualify; accordingly, before responding in any way that constitutes a use of "force"—to include even actions that do not amount to an "armed attack"—the evidence must show that the effects of the triggering event amount to the equivalent of an "armed attack." If they do not reach that level, the response must be limited to acts like those mentioned above which do not amount to a use of force. Dispassionately assessing the consequences of a cyber incident to determine its similarity to an armed attack can be difficult as initial impressions of the effects can be wildly inflated.

Further convoluting the analysis is the fact that not all damaging cyber events that seemingly equate to an armed attack may be sufficiently egregious to authorize the use of kinetic or cyber force in response. Although not involving cyber matters, an opinion of the UN-sanctioned International Court of Justice (ICJ) provides some insight. In *Nicaragua v. US*, the ICJ seemed to indicate that an "armed attack" within the meaning of Article 51 did not arise in every case of an armed clash.[37] Rather, the ICJ considered the "scale and effects" of the use of force to determine if it met the Article 51 requirement.[38]

As an illustration of inadequate levels of violence, the ICJ cited a "mere frontier incident."[39] Although the court did not elaborate on this example, the context implies that such an incident would involve some low level of violence. Further, while apparently accepting (without using the words) the concept of an effect-based approach, the ICJ nevertheless held that "assistance to rebels in the form of the provision of weapons or logistical or other support" was insufficient provocation for an Article 51 response.[40] Such activities may be uses of force prohibited by Article 2 of the UN Charter, but did not equate to "armed attacks" so as to permit self-defense actions involving the use of force.

Because not every disturbance sourced in a cyber methodology amounts, as a matter of international law, to an "armed attack," the Department of Defense (DoD) definition of "computer network attack" is not necessarily coterminous with what cyberstrategists should consider as sufficient to trigger a response involving the use of force. Specifically, DoD characterizes "attack" as actions "taken through the use of computer networks to disrupt, deny, degrade, or destroy information resident in computers and computer networks, or the computers and networks themselves." Quite obviously, this definition takes no cognizance of "scale and effects" and would, therefore, encompass activities that are the legal equivalent—in the cyber "world"—of the "mere frontier incidents" that the ICJ found did not permit an Article 51 response.

The principle of self-defense is also complicated by the issue of anticipatory or "pre-emptive" self-defense. This is important to cyberstrategists as cyber weaponry can be employed rapidly and, once a cyberstrike is underway, can be difficult to counter or contain. Nevertheless, many nations claim that bona fide self-defense actions can only be taken *after* an armed attack, not before.[41] However, the

United States and some other countries insist that it permits the use of force before suffering actual injury, that is, taking a self-defense action that anticipates and deflects the blow, or otherwise pre-empts an aggressor's ability to take the proverbial "first shot." So long as the response was proportional to the threat posed, the act is lawful.

Classic anticipatory self-defense theory requires evidence that a specific attack is imminent, that is, about to occur. However, Professor Kenneth Andersen argues that since at least 1980:

> [T]he US has taken the position that imminence can be shown by a pattern of activity and threat that show the intentions of actors. This can satisfy imminence whether or not those intentions are about to be acted upon. Even events taking place in the past can suffice if the risk is severe enough, and those events can include meeting, planning, and plotting. It is not necessarily or only about a threatened specific event, but about a group or a threat in some broader way. This is sometimes called "active self defense."[42]

This may be attractive to some cyberstrategists who want a legal basis to take defensive actions that amount to a use of force against suspicious threats. However, disaggregating intent from capability could have unintended consequences. For example, it may behoove cyberstrategists to avoid embracing a legal interpretation that would categorize the nondestructive insertion of a cyber capability into the computer system of another nation as either a use of force or an armed attack. The better view today would be that such activities—without an accompanying intent for imminent action—would not be uses of force, so long as the cyber capability lies dormant.

In interpreting self-defense under Article 51, cyberstrategists should keep in mind that the UN Charter governs relations between nation-states, not individuals. The DoD General Counsel opines that when "individuals carry out malicious [cyber] acts for private purposes, the aggrieved state does not generally have the right to use force in self-defense."[43] To do so ordinarily requires some indicia of effective state control of the cyber actors to impute state responsibility.[44]

Nevertheless, if the aggrieved nation requests action from the state from whose territory the cyber attack was carried out, and it becomes evident that the state is "unwilling or unable to prevent a recurrence," actions in self-defense are justified.[45] This is the rationale to which Harold Koh, Legal Advisor to the State Department, alluded when he spoke about self-defense in the context of "the willingness and ability of those nation-states to suppress the threat the target poses."[46] Of course, the problem of attribution stubbornly permeates every aspect of cyber operations; it is, indeed, the "single greatest challenge to the application of the law of armed conflict to cyber activity."[47] Essentially, however, this is a technical issue, not a legal one. Nonetheless, the identity of the attacker may well determine if a state of war exists.

A State of War?

Even the occurrence of a cyber event that equates to an "armed attack" warranting a lawful self-defense response does not automatically create a state of war (or armed conflict).[48] The presence—or absence—of a state of armed conflict carries significance because during armed conflict, the actions of belligerents are usually governed by LOAC, not the more restrictive rules applicable to law enforcement situations. In determining the existence of a state of war, we look to traditional definitions, the clearest of which is offered by scholar Yoram Dinstein. Professor Dinstein describes it as:

> [A] hostile interaction between two or more States, either in a technical or in a material sense. War in the technical sense is a formal status produced by a declaration of war. War in the material sense is generated by actual use of armed force, which must be comprehensive on the part of at least one party to the conflict.[49]

For cyberstrategists, the words "States" and "armed force" and "comprehensive" are key because they help distinguish what criminals and cybervandals might do, from the persistent and comprehensive cyber attacks equating to armed force that increasingly appear to be only within that capability of the nation-state. As a matter of legal interpretation, nation-states do not wage "war" against criminals; rather, they conduct law enforcement operations against them. As Professor Schmitt notes, "cyber violence of any intensity engaged in by isolated individuals or by unorganized mobs, even if directed against a government," does not create an armed conflict within the meaning of the Geneva Convention.[50]

That said, certain non-state adversaries can make themselves subject to much the same LOAC regime as a conventional state (albeit without some of the privileges to which a nation-state combatant is entitled). Jamie Williamson, Legal Counsel to the International Committee of the Red Cross (ICRC), acknowledges that non-state actors organized into armed groups can constitute "the armed forces of a non-state party."[51] In accord is Mr. Koh's declaration that "as a matter of international law, the United States is in an armed conflict with al-Qaeda" who he characterizes as an "organized terrorist enemy."[52] And the reasoning applies to the cyber setting. Professor Schmitt observes that "only significantly destructive [cyber] attacks taking place over some period of time and conducted by a group that is well-organized" is sufficient to constitute an internationally recognized armed conflict.[53]

When a state of armed conflict exists, the "fundamental targeting issues are no different in cyber operations as compared to those applicable to kinetic targeting."[54] Mr. Koh summarizes the most important of the targeting rules when he cites:

> First, the principle of distinction, which requires that attacks be limited to military objectives and that civilians or civilian objects shall not be the object of the attack; and Second, the principle of proportionality, which prohibits attacks that may be expected to cause incidental loss of civilian life, injury to civilians, damage to civilian objects, or a combination thereof, that would be excessive in relation to the concrete and direct military advantage anticipated.[55]

Regarding the targeting of civilians and civilian objects, it is also true that only weaponry (cyber or kinetic) capable of discrimination (i.e., directed against legitimate targets) can be used.[56] However, cyberstrategists should know that legitimate targets can include civilian objects—especially those having cyber aspects—that have dual military and civilian uses.[57] So long as the principal of proportionality is observed, they normally can be targeted lawfully if they meet the definition of a military objective.[58]

In this area particularly, cyberstrategists need to distinguish prudent targeting from legal mandates. In his confirmation hearings,

General Alexander said that it "is difficult for [him] to conceive of an instance where it would be appropriate to attack a bank or a financial institution, unless perhaps it was being used solely to support enemy military operations."[59] However sensible that may be from a policy perspective, cyberstrategists should understand that no LOAC rule requires a target that otherwise qualifies as a military objective to be used "solely" to support military operations—it can have "dual" uses.

Of course, there is no such thing as a "dual use" civilian, but civilians can be targeted consistent with the principle of distinction under certain limited circumstances. Mr. Williamson of the ICRC accepts that international law permits the targeting of civilians for such time as they "directly participate in hostilities."[60] If they are members of an organized armed group of non-state actors, the period of vulnerability may be extended to parallel that of the uniformed military of nation-states, that is, they would be subject to attack virtually at any time or place during an ongoing conflict.[61] However, he advises that the ICRC "takes a 'functional'—not membership—approach."[62] So defined, the non-state "armed force" consists "only of individuals whose constant function is to take a direct part in hostilities, or, in other words, individuals who have a continuous combat function."[63]

In determining what amounts to a "continuous combat function" in the cyber context, consider the ICRC illustrations. Its examples of "direct participation" by civilians in hostilities include such cyber activities as "[i]nterfering electronically with military computer networks (computer network attacks) and transmitting tactical targeting intelligence for a specific attack."[64] Accordingly, a civilian can be targeted when performing those acts, and one who continuously engages in such conduct can be said to have a "continuous combat function" making that person susceptible to attack for as long as that status persists. To anticipate what other cyber activities one might reasonably determine to constitute direct involvement in hostilities, it may help for cyberstrategists to consider what activities of the enemy they would consider so intrinsic to a particular cyber process that they would need to target those adversaries performing that function.

As Mr. Koh's remarks suggest, LOAC tolerates "incidental" losses of civilians and civilian objects so long as they are "not excessive in relation to the concrete and direct military advantage anticipated." In determining the incidental losses, cyberstrategists are required to consider those that may be reasonably foreseeable to be directly caused by the attack. Assessing second- and third-order "reverberating" effects may be a wise policy consideration,[65] but it does not appear LOAC currently requires such further analysis. Another hurdle for cyberstrategists may be the difficulty in predicting the effect of a given cyber methodology. Absent a suitable cyber modeling capability that estimates civilian losses, it is unclear how a decision maker fulfills the legal requirement to weigh those effects against the military advantage sought.

LOAC does require that targeteers "do everything feasible" to ensure the target is a proper military objective.[66] How sure must a cyberstrategist be? International courts have used the "reasonable commander" standard, that is whether the decision is one that a "reasonably well informed person in the circumstances of the actual perpetrator, making reasonable use of the information available to him or her" would have concluded met the legal standards.[67] As to degree of certainty, Professor Schmitt offers a clear and compelling standard which is "higher than the preponderance of evidence…standard used in certain civil and administrative proceedings and lower than criminal law's 'beyond a reasonable doubt.'"[68]

Parenthetically, this discussion of civilians has other implications for cyberstrategists, that is, who may conduct cyberwar? Generally, only bona fide members of the armed forces can wage war with the protection of the "combatant privilege." This means so long as LOAC is otherwise observed, military personnel are legally permitted to engage in killing and destruction in war without fear of prosecution for doing so. Thus, conducting cyber activities which have the lethality and destructiveness of traditional kinetic weaponry should be reserved to uniformed members of the military. As Richard Clark puts it in his book, *Cyberwar,* "it will have to be…military personnel [who] enter the keystrokes to take down enemy systems."[69]

In a *Washington Post* op-ed, LOAC expert (and retired Marine judge advocate) Gary Solis takes a harsh view of civilians operating lethal systems.[70] Calling CIA drone pilots "America's own unlawful combatants," he accuses them of "employing armed force contrary to the laws and customs of war" and "violating the requirement of distinction, a core concept of armed conflict."[71] Although Professsor Solis is correct in saying that if captured, CIA civilian employees (and/or CIA contractors) are not entitled to prisoner of war status, and that they could be legally convicted in the capturing state's domestic law for the actions, is his insinuation of war crimes overstated?

A 1999 DoD publication provides some insight. Specifically, in discussing "retaining the requirement that combatant information operations during international armed conflicts be conducted only by members of the armed forces," the DoD General Counsel opined that if cyber operations (amounting to a use of armed force) are "conducted by unauthorized persons, their government may be in violation of the law of war, depending on the circumstances, and the individuals concerned are at least theoretically subject to criminal prosecution either by the enemy or by an international war crimes tribunal."[72]

Cybering and the Citizenry

The nature of the cyber domain is such that it necessarily involves consideration of the domestic environment and its citizenry. Somewhat paradoxically given the above discussion about the role of civilians in cyberwar, concerns also arise about the appropriate role of the armed forces in cyber operations, especially in situations short of armed conflict.

The vast majority of cyberspace usage involves the lawful activities of the public. Unfortunately, the military intelligence apparatus has occasionally been improperly turned inward "to collect personal information about Americans who posed no real threat to national security."[73] The technical potential to do so today is very great. For example, every day DoD (via the National Security Agency [NSA]) "intercept[s] and store[s] 1.7 billion e-mails, phone calls and other types of communications."[74] And DoD is continually seeking new cyber capabilities to collect vast amounts of information more broadly and effectively.[75] Of course, these military intelligence capabilities were designed and built mainly to address external threats, but they are being exploited to address domestic security.

Regrettably, incidents of impropriety still occur. In the aftermath of 9/11, NSA was "secretly given authority to spy on Americans as part of the war on terrorism."[76] Specifically, NSA was allowed to eavesdrop on phone calls, monitor emails, and track Internet activity without getting a warrant from the special courts established by FISA.[77]

The Justice Department vigorously defended what it described as a "terrorist surveillance program" by insisting that bypassing FISA procedures was legal and incident to the President's commander-in-chief authority,[78] but the courts found otherwise. In late December 2010, the government was ordered to pay $2.5 million in attorney fees and damages for NSA's illegal activity.[79]

Other unsettling incidents include reports of the unexplained military monitoring of Planned Parenthood and other organizations.[80] Media stories also show the military as having "burrowed into the mushrooming cyber world of blogs" to post content as a new way to "influence public opinion about US operations in Iraq and Afghanistan."[81] More recently, journalist Walter Pincus reports the military as wanting to expand its intelligence role in cyberspace to counter what is called "the use of the Internet by extremists."[82] Admiral James A. Winnfeld, Commander of US Northern Command, says that although his unit's role is to defend their networks, he has a "very ambitious staff, and they would like nothing more than to own all of the cyber response inside North America."[83]

Because it "possesses extraordinary technical expertise and experience, unmatched in the government, in exploring and exploiting computer and telecommunication systems," powerful imperatives are pushing further NSA involvement in domestic cyber activities.[84] In a major new development, a cybersecurity memorandum of agreement was executed between DoD and the Department of Homeland Security (DHS) in October 2010.[85] For the first time, DoD is becoming directly involved in protecting domestic civilian cyber infrastructure.[86] To do so, a NSA "cyber-support element will move into Homeland Security's Cybersecurity and Communications Integration Center."[87] Although DHS personnel are supposed to ensure privacy and civil liberties are protected, Marc Rotenberg of the Electronic Privacy Information Center says he does not think "DHS can oversee the Defense Department."[88]

With powerful cyber systems like Einstein 3 coming online that call for a major NSA role, thoughtful experts like Professsssor Jack Goldsmith of Harvard Law School offer a roadmap for proceeding consonant with civil liberties. Among other things, he would require NSA to obtain "independent approval…from the FISA court or a FISA-type court" prior to employing advanced cybersecurity measures domestically.[89]

Legislation such as *The Protecting Cyberspace as a National Asset Act* now pending also includes some safeguards intended to protect privacy and civil liberties.[90]

Nevertheless, cyberstrategists may want to encourage the development of fully civilian domestic surveillance cyber systems and, concomitantly, discourage involvement of the armed forces in any cyber activity that might seem to conflict with the sensibilities and mores of the American people, even if technically legal. The armed forces are the most authoritarian, least democratic, and most powerful institution in American society. The restraint intrinsic to a domestic law enforcement mindset is not its natural state; its purpose, as the Supreme Court puts it, is to wage war.[91] And as this paper and other sources suggest, relatively few cyber incidents, domestically or globally, meet that legal standard.[92] If nothing else, the fact that armed forces unapologetically restricts the rights and privileges of its own members,[93] should militate towards avoiding its use in civilian settings where the public properly expects those rights and privileges to flourish.

Cyberstrategists need to be especially conscious of emerging public attitudes. As experts question whether the threat of terrorism,[94] and even the threat of cyberwar is overstated,[95] Americans may be becoming uncomfortable with what Fareed Zakaria describes as the "national-security state" that "now touches every aspect of American life, even when seemingly unrelated to terrorism."[96] The recent furor over full-body scans at airports, along with a generalized distrust of government,[97] reflect what could be burgeoning public discontent with intrusive government activity (some of which may already be percolating with respect to military cyber activities).[98] In short, cyberstrategists must be extremely sensitive to involving DoD in domestic cyber activities that might align such animosity with the armed forces, as doing so could undermine the public support and esteem it needs to sustain it and to prevail on tomorrow's battlespaces.

Concluding Observations

Cyber activities do present a number of legal challenges for cyberstrategists, but many problems masquerading as "legal" issues are really undecided policy issues with a number of legal alternatives. Cyberstrategists rightly carry a heavy element of complicated and difficult policymaking because cyber issues are so entwined with the lawful activities of citizens and the legitimate needs of commerce.

Solid legal advice in cyber matters is imperative, and the Pentagon is moving to improve its resources to provide it.[99] As one expert put it, in today's world law is a "center of gravity" because "our enemies carefully attack our military plans as illegal and immoral and our execution of those plans as contrary to the law of war."[100] Closer to home, cyberstrategists may wish to consider the admonition of Professors Michael Reisman and Chris T. Antoniou in their 1994 book, *The Laws of War*. They point out that for democracies like the United States, "even a limited armed conflict requires a substantial base of public support."[101] That support "can erode or even reverse itself rapidly, no matter how worthy the political objective, if people *believe* that the war is being conducted in an unfair, inhumane, or iniquitous way."[102]

In cyberwar, like any other conflict, victory depends much on what people believe. Cyberstrategists would be well-served to ensure what they do in the coming years not only meets the challenges in cyberspace, but also fulfills the American people's expectations of all their warriors, regardless of the domain in which they operate.

Endnotes

1. See, e.g., John Sutter, *Is WikiLeaks Engaged in "Cyberwar"?*, CNN, December 9, 2010, http://articles.cnn.com/2010-12-09/tech/wikileaks.cyber.attacks_1_cyber-war-cyber-weapons-cyber-attacks?_s=PM:TECH.
2. For a discussion of the Estonia and Georgia incidents, see Richard A. Clarke, *Cyber War* (2010), at 11–21.
3. Norman Friedman, *Virus Season*, Proceedings, November 2010, at 88.
4. For purposes of this chapter, "cyberwar" may be defined as conflict waged by means of "cyber operations." The latter are, in turn, defined by the US Department of Defense (DoD) to be "employment of cyber capabilities where the primary purpose is to achieve objectives in or through cyberspace." DoD defines "cyberspace" as "global domain within the information environment consisting of the interdependent network of information technology infrastructures, including the Internet, telecommunications networks, computer systems, and embedded processors and controllers." *See DoD Dictionary of Military and Associated Terms*, as amended through December 15, 2012, at 118, http://www.dtic.mil/doctrine/new_pubs/jp1_02.pdf.

5. Thom Shanker, Cyberwar Nominee Sees Gaps in Law, *The New York Times*, April 14, 2010 (quoting Lt Gen Keith B. Alexander), http://www.nytimes.com/2010/04/15/world/15military.html.

6. Jeffrey F. Addicott, Cyberterrorism: Legal Policy Issues, in *Legal Issues in the Struggle Against Terrorism* (2010), at 550.

7. This chapter considers LOAC to encompass *jus ad bello* (the international law that rationalizes recourse to armed conflict) and *jus in bello* (the international law that governs actions during armed conflict). For a discussion of *jus ad bello* and *jus in bello* in the cyber context, see generally, Commander Todd C. Huntley, JAGC, USN, Controlling the Use of Force in Cyberspace: The Application of the Law of Armed Conflict During a Time of Fundamental Change in the Nature of Warfare, 60 *Naval Law Review*, (2010), at 1, http://www.jag.navy.mil/documents/navylawreview/NLRVolume60.pdf.

8. The strategist Carl von Clausewitz wrote: "The great uncertainty of all data in war is a peculiar difficulty, because all action must, to a certain extent, be planned in a mere twilight, which in addition not infrequently—like the effect of a fog or moonshine—gives to things exaggerated dimensions and unnatural appearance." Carl von Clausewitz, *On War*. Book 2, Chapter 2, Paragraph 24.

9. See, e.g., Time for a Treaty, *Defense News*, October 18, 2010, at 36 (editorial), http://www.defensenews.com/story.php?i=4921341.

10. Bruce Schneier, It Will soon Be too Late to Stop the Cyberwars, *Financial Times*, December 2, 2010, http://www.ft.com/cms/s/0/f863fb4c-fe53-11df-abac-00144feab49a.html#axzz19cNCeszp.

11. See, e.g., John B. Alexander, Optional Lethality, *Harvard International Review*, May 7, 2006, http://hir.harvard.edu/the-future-of-war/optional-lethality.

12. Charles Krauthammer, The Irrelevance of START, *Washington Post*, November 26, 2010, http://www.washingtonpost.com/wp-dyn/content/article/2010/11/25/AR2010112502232.html.

13. William J. Lynn, Defending a New Domain: The Pentagon's Cyberstrategy, *Foreign Affairs*, September/October 2010, http://www.foreignaffairs.com/articles/66552/william-j-lynn-iii/defending-a-new-domain.

14. See Richard W. Aldrich, Information Warfare & the Protection of Critical Infrastructure, in *National Security Law* (2nd ed., 2005), at 1243–1244.

15. Tom Gjelten, Shadow Wars: Debating Cyber "Disarmament," *World Affairs Journal*, November/December 2010, http://www.worldaffairsjournal.org/articles/2010-NovDec/full-Gjelten-ND-2010.html.

16. *Id.*

17. *Id.*

18. *Id.* In 1999 the Office of General Counsel, Department of Defense, concluded that "There seems to be no particularly good reason for the United States to support negotiations for new treaty obligations in most areas of international law that are directly relevant to information operations." *See* Office of General Counsel, *An Assessment of International Legal Issues in Information Operations*, 2nd edition (Washington, DC: US Department

of Defense, November 1999) [hereinafter "GC Memo"] at 49. http://www.cs.georgetown.edu/~denning/infosec/DOD-IO-legal.doc 19. See, e.g., Anna Mulrine, When Is a Cyberattack an Act of War?, *Christian Science Monitor*, October 18, 2010, at 20, http://www.csmonitor.com/USA/Military/2010/1005/Pentagon-The-global-cyberwar-is-just-beginning.

20. Thomas Wingfield sees a third legal regime as applicable to cyber operations: intelligence collection law. See Thomas C. Wingfield, International Law and Information Operations, in *Cyberpower and National Security* (Franklin D. Kramer, et al., eds., 2009), at 541.

21. Elinor Mills, Demilitarizing Cyberspace (Q & A), *Tech Reviews* (blog), December 2010 (interview with Gary McGraw), http://tech-reviews.findtechnews.net/demilitarizing-cybersecurity-qa/.

22. Walter Gary Sharp, Sr., *Cyberspace and the Use of Force* (1999), at 123–132.

23. See, e.g., GC Memo, *supra* note 18, at 11 (act of war is an "obsolete concept" not mentioned in the UN Charter and seldom heard in modern diplomatic discourse.).

24. Charter of the United Nations and Statute of the International Court of Justice, 1945, http://treaties.un.org/doc/Publication/CTC/uncharter.pdf.

25. Art. 2 (4), UN Charter, *supra* note 24, at 3.

26. Art. 51, UN Charter, *supra* note 24 at 10.

27. Michael N. Schmitt, Cyber Operations in International Law: The Use of Force, Collective Security, Self-Defense, and Armed Conflict, in *Proceedings of Workshop on Deterring Cyberattacks* 163 (2010), http://books.nap.edu/openbook.php?record_id=12997&page=R1.

28. See, e.g., Jeffrey F. Addicott, *Terrorism Law: Materials, Cases, and Comment* (2011), at 311–312.

29. Wing Commander Duncan Blake RAAF and Lt Col Joseph S. Imburgia, USAF, "Bloodless Weapons"? The Need to Conduct Legal Reviews of Certain Capabilities and the Implications of Defining Them as Weapons, 66 *Air Force Law Review* 181–183 (2010).

30. Art 49.1, Protocol Additional to the Geneva Conventions of 12 August 1949, and relating to the Protection of Victims of International Armed Conflicts (Protocol I), 8 June 1977, http://www.icrc.org/ihl.nsf/7c4d08 d9b287a42141256739003e636b/f6c8b9fee14a77fdc125641e0052b079. Although the United States is not a party to Protocol I, it accepts that most of it comprises customary international law which binds all nations.

31. William Boothby, *Weapons and the Law of Armed Conflict* (2009), at 238.

32. For a discussion of other approaches, see David E. Graham, Cyber Threats and the Law of War, *Journal of National Security Law*, vol. 4 (2010), at 91 (discussing the "instrument-based approach" and the "strict liability" approach as competing analyses).

33. Schmitt, *supra* note 27 at 155–156.

34. For a discussion of the Schmitt criteria, *see* Wingfield, *supra* note 20, at 527–531.

35. Boothby, *supra* note 31.

36. Schmitt, *supra* note 33.

37. Military and Paramilitary Activities (*Nicar. v. US*), 1986 I.C.J. 14 (June 27), at para 195.
38. *Id.*
39. *Id.*
40. *Id.*
41. See, e.g., Michael Byers, *War Law* (2005), at 72–81.
42. Benjamin Wittes, Kenneth Anderson on *Baumann v. Wittes, Lawfare Blog*, December 1, 2010, http://www.lawfareblog.com/2010/12/kenneth-anderson-on-baumann-v-wittes/.
43. GC Memo, *supra* note 18, at 20.
44. Schmitt, *supra* note 27, at 157.
45. GC Memo, *supra* note 18, at 20.
46. Harold Koh, *The Obama Administration and International Law*, American Society of International Law, March 25, 2010, (speech), http://www.state.gov/s/l/releases/remarks/139119.htm.
47. Huntley, *supra* note 7, at 34.
48. In this context "war" and "armed conflict" are interchangeable.
49. Yoram Dinstein, *War, Aggression and Self-Defence* (4th ed., 2005), at 15.
50. Schmitt, *supra* note 27, at 175.
51. Jamie A. Williamson, Challenges of Twenty-First Century Conflicts: A Look at Direct Participation in Hostilities, 20 *Duke Journal of Comparative & International Law* (2010) at 464, http://www.law.duke.edu/journals/djcil/.
52. Koh, *supra* note 46.
53. Schmitt, *supra* note 27, at 176.
54. Air Force Judge Advocate General's School, *Air Force Operations & the Law* (2009), at 99.
55. Koh, *supra* note 46.
56. See Burris Carnahan, Weapons, in *Crimes of War* (Roy Gutman and David Rieff, eds., 1999), at 380, http://www.crimesofwar.org/thebook/weapons.html.
57. See, generally, James P. Terry, The Lawfulness of Attacking Computer Networks in Armed Conflict and in Self Defense During Periods Short of Armed Conflict: What Are the Targeting Constraints? 69 *Military Law Review*, September 2001, at 70.
58. Military objectives are defined as "those objects which by their nature, location, purpose or use make an effective contribution to military action and whose total or partial destruction, capture or neutralization, in the circumstances ruling at the time, offers a definite military advantage." Art. 49.1, Protocol I, *supra* note 30.
59. Shanker, *supra* note 5 (quoting Alexander).
60. Williamson, *supra* note 51.
61. *Id.*
62. *Id.*
63. *Id.*
64. *Direct Participation in Hostilities: Questions and Answers*, International Committee of the Red Cross, February 6, 2009, http://www.icrc.org/eng/resources/documents/faq/direct-participation-ihl-faq-020609.htm.

65. See, e.g., Commander J.W. Crawford, The Law of Noncombatant Immunity and the Targeting of National Electrical Power Systems, *The Fletcher Forum of World Affairs*, summer/fall 1997, at 101.

66. Art. 57.2(a)(i), Protocol I, *supra* note 30.

67. See Laurie Blank and Amos Guiora, Teaching an Old Dog New Tricks: Operationalizing the Law of Armed Conflict in New Warfare, *Harvard National Security Journal*, May 13, 2010, at 56–57. http://www.harvardnsj. com/wp-content/uploads/2010/05/Vol.-1_Blank-Guiora_Final.pdf (citing *Prosecutor v. Stanislav Galic*) .

68. Schmitt, *supra* note 27, at 168.

69. Clarke, *supra* note 2, at 40.

70. Gary Solis, CIA Drone Attacks Produce America's Own Unlawful Combatants, *Washington Post*, March 12, 2010, http://www.washingtonpost.com/wp-dyn/content/article/2010/03/11/AR2010031103653.html.

71. *Id.*

72. GC Memo, *supra* note 18, at 7.

73. Stephan Dycus et al., The Military's Role in Homeland Security and Disaster Relief, in *National Security Law* (4th ed., 2007), at 960.

74. Dana Priest and William Arkin, A Hidden World, *Washington Post*, July 19, 2010, http://projects.washingtonpost.com/top-secret-america/articles/a-hidden-world-growing-beyond-control/?referrer=emaillink.

75. See, e.g., Steve Lohr, Computers That See You and Watch Over You, *The New York Times*, January 1, 2011, at 1, http://www.nytimes.com/2011/01/02/science/02see.html?hp (discussing the Defense Advanced Research Agency's award of grant for a research program called the Mind's Eye which seeks "machines that can recognize, analyze and communicate what they see.") and Siobhan Gorman, US Plans Cyber Shield for Utilities, Companies, *Wall Street Journal*, July 8, 2010 (discussing an "expansive" NSA program "dubbed 'Perfect Citizen'"), http://online.wsj.com/article/SB10001424052748704545004575352983850463108.html.

76. Department of Defense, *Joint Statement by Secretary Gates and Secretary Napolitano on Enhancing Coordination to Secure America's Cyber Networks*, October 13, 2010, http://www.defense.gov/releases/release.aspx?releaseid=13965.

77. *Id.*

78. US Department of Justice, *The NSA Program to Detect and Prevent Terrorist Attacks: Myth v. Reality*, January 27, 2006, http://www.justice.gov/opa/documents/nsa_myth_v_reality.pdf.

79. Paul Elias, Judge Orders Feds to Pay $2.5 Million in Wiretapping Case, *Washington Post*, December 21, 2010, at http://www.washingtonpost.com/wp-dyn/content/article/2010/12/21/AR2010122105307.html.

80. Kim Zetter, Military Monitored Planned Parenthood, Supremacists, *Wired*, February 25, 2010, http://www.wired.com/threatlevel/2010/02/military-spied-on-plannet-parenthood/.

81. Jason Sherman, US Military Targets Blogs to Shape Opinions on Iraq, Afghanistan Operations, *InsideDefense.com*, March 3, 2006, http://www.military.com/features/0,15240,89811,00.html.

82. Walter Pincus, Military Expands Intelligence Role, *Washington Post*, June 8, 2010, at A15, http://www.washingtonpost.com/wp-dyn/content/article/2010/06/07/AR2010060704696.html.

83. Mark V. Schanz, Air Sovereignty Never Sleeps, *Air Force Magazine*, December 2010, at 56, http://www.airforce-magazine.com/MagazineArchive/Documents/2010/December%202010/1210sovereignty.pdf (quoting Admiral Winnefeld).

84. Jack Goldsmith, *The Cyberthreat, Government Network Operations, and the Fourth Amendment*, Governance Studies at Brookings, December 8, 2010, at 15, http://www.brookings.edu/~/media/Files/rc/papers/2010/1208_4th_amendment_goldsmith/1208_4th_amendment_goldsmith.pdf.

85. Department of Defense, *Joint Statement by Secretary Gates and Secretary Napolitano on Enhancing Coordination to Secure America's Cyber Networks*, October 13, 2010, http://www.defense.gov/releases/release.aspx?releaseid=13965.

86. William Matthews, DoD to Protect Some Civilian Infrastructure, *Defense News*, October 18, 2010, at 6.

87. *Id.*

88. *Id.*

89. Goldsmith, *supra* note 86, at 14.

90. See, e.g., The Protecting Cyberspace as a National Asset Act of 2010, S.3480, http://hsgac.senate.gov/public/index.cfm?FuseAction=Press.MajorityNews&ContentRecord_id=227d9e1e-5056-8059-765f-2239d301fb7f.

91. The "primary business of armies and navies [is] to fight or be ready to fight wars should the occasion arise." *United States ex rel. Toth v. Quarles*, 350 US 11 (1955).

92. See also, Gary McGraw and Ivan Arce, *Software [In]security: Cyber Warmongering and Influence Peddling*, informIT (blog), November 24, 2010, http://www.informit.com/articles/article.aspx?p=1662328#.

93. See, e.g., *Burns v. Wilson*, 1953, 346 US 137 (1953) ("The rights of men in the armed forces must perforce be conditioned to meet certain overriding demands of discipline and duty") and *Goldman v. Weinberger*, 475 US 503 (1986) ("The essence of military service 'is the subordination of the desires and interests of the individual to the needs of the service.'").

94. Risk-management experts John Mueller and Mark G. Stewart conclude from a survey of many studies that the risk of terrorism is "hardly existential" and is, in fact, "so low that spending further to reduce its likelihood or consequences is scarcely justified." *See* John Mueller and Mark G. Stewart, Hardly Existential: Thinking Rationally about Terrorism, *Foreign Affairs*, April 2, 2010, http://www.foreignaffairs.com/articles/66186/john-mueller-and-mark-g-stewart/hardly-existential.

95. See, e.g., Seymour M. Hersh, The Online Threat, *The New Yorker*, November 1, 2010, http://www.newyorker.com/reporting/2010/11/01/101101fa_fact_hersh.

96. Fareed Zakaria, What America Has Lost; It's Clear We Overreacted to 9/11, *Newsweek*, September 13, 2010, at 18, http://www.newsweek.com/2010/09/04/zakaria-why-america-overreacted-to-9-11.html.

97. See, e.g., Mark Silva, Few trust the government, poll finds, *Los Angeles Times*, April 19, 2010, http://articles.latimes.com/2010/apr/19/nation/la-na-distrust19-2010apr19.

98. See Hersh, *supra* note 99.

99. The new DoD Law of War Manual is expected to have a "17 page chapter on information and cyberspace operations." See W. Hays Parks, National Security Law in Practice: The Department of Defense Law of War Manual, November 18, 2010, (speech), http://www.abanet.org/natsecurity/hays_parks_speech11082010.pdf.

100. William George Eckhardt, Lawyering for Uncle Sam When He Draws His Sword, *Chicago Journal of International Law*, vol. 4, (2003), at 431.

101. W. Michael Reisman and Chris T. Antoniou, *The Laws of War* (1994), at xxiv (italics added).

102. *Id.*

14

A New Normal? The Cultivation of Global Norms as Part of a Cybersecurity Strategy

ROGER HURWITZ

Contents

A Call to Discuss Cyber Norms   235
National Positions for International Cyber Norms   237
Norms for Specific Cyber Behaviors   243
Military Operations   246
Military, Political, and Economic Espionage   249
Cybercrime   252
Technological Foundations   255
Public-Private Partnerships   257
Internet Freedom and a Global Information Society   258
Conclusions   259
Endnotes   261

States are facing a growing crisis of cybersecurity. With many state and non-state actors now having significant cyber attack capabilities, states need strategies that will protect their societies, economies, military, and governments from such disruptive or destructive attacks. The challenge is greatest for the technologically advanced countries, like the United States, whose power and welfare most heavily depend on computationally managed processes and global networks. Their strategies will accordingly need multi-faceted scope and global reach. This chapter argues that an important part of such strategies is the development of international cyber norms, or shared expectations among states regarding their behavior and responsibilities in cyberspace.

States' acceptance of a norm can constrain and regulate their behavior in specific situations, and, to the extent that other states are likely to sanction a state's violation of the norm, the constraint will be greater. States will adopt some cyber norms and willingly accept the associated constraints, because they have a common interest in sustaining and developing cyberspace. Many states have acknowledged the contributions of the Internet to their economic and social development, and they are already accustomed to following mutually beneficial rules at the cyber operational level, most prominently, the network protocols. However, not all cyber behaviors will soon fall subject to broadly accepted norms. First, some states will likely reject proscriptions of certain behaviors by means of which they pursue in cyberspace larger competition with other states (e.g., China's use of cyber espionage as part of a "catch-up" strategy in information and communication technology [ICT] undermines the US's valued technological advantage in that sector). There will also be contention over the formulation and extent of some norms, in part for symbolic reasons, but also because particular wording can confer material or political advantage to a contending party. For example, a norm that a state's control of its national cyberspace is a matter of national sovereignty that can trump, as needed, its citizens' rights to information would support China in struggles with the West over Internet freedom. Finally, a state may choose to selectively follow an accepted norm, but other states will be reluctant to sanction its violations for fear of additional conflict.

Given these exceptions, the time taken for the adoption of norms, and the efforts needed to assure compliance, whatever normative regulation might be achieved seems insufficient to meet the cyber threats. Defense strategy for a technologically advanced state will also need a "reasonable deterrent" capability and "technological transformation." "Reasonable deterrence" includes capabilities for near-real-time, reasonably confident attribution of an attack and for in-domain or cross-domain retaliatory capability sufficient to give an adversary pause. "Technological transformation" seeks to reduce the vulnerability of a state's digital networks, so that efforts to exploit them for cybercrime and espionage or to attack them will either fail outright or become too costly to mount. Together the three strategic components comprise a vulnerability-driven, defense-oriented cybersecurity strategy.

However, efforts to establish some cyber norms can still pay off, even if other countries choose a more aggressive strategy, such as a pre-emptory one that identifies and suppresses threat actors. If there are regulatory norms, it will be easier to identify such agents and organize collective actions against them.

Consideration of international cyber norms as part of a triad resonates with the US 2011 "International Strategy for Cyberspace,"[1] which called for the same triad. That document notes the declared interest of almost all states in preserving the openness and interoperability of the Internet, asserts the importance of norms in enhancing stability, and specifies cyber norms, which the United States will promote for adoption. However, it neither identifies the areas for which states would most readily accept norms nor judges how much their acceptance would stabilize cyberspace by increasing predictability and preventing misunderstandings. This chapter tries to supply the answers and some concepts for the utility of cyber norms. Accordingly, the first section discusses the conditions that led major cyber powers to issue a joint call for discussions of norms and the responses to the call. The second section examines these powers' very different views of what needs to be subject to norms or regulations. The third section distinguishes different areas for norms and identifies those for which discussions are most likely to produce widely accepted norms. Viewing these results, the last section evaluates their potential contributions to stability in cyberspace.

A Call to Discuss Cyber Norms

Since early 2010, many governments, including those of the United States, China, and Russia, have signaled a willingness to discuss international norms for cyberspace. A significant breakthrough occurred in January 2010, when the "UN group of governmental experts on information security" drafted a recommendation, subsequently approved by the General Assembly, that states "discuss norms pertaining to State use of ICTs, to reduce collective risk and protect critical national and international infrastructure."[2] In working on this call, both the United States and Russia changed their respective decade-old positions: the United States had wanted to restrict such discussions to cooperation on cybercrime; Russia had aimed for talks regarding the control of offensive uses of cyber. These changes most likely responded to spikes in the number and severity of cyber attacks, continuing doubts about cyber deterrence, recognition of a common interest in reducing the threats, and realization of the need for international cooperation to combat the criminal misuse of information technology, create a global culture of cybersecurity, and promote other essential measures that can reduce risk.

> According to the call, no state is able to address these [cyber] threats alone. Confronting the challenges of the twenty-first century depends on successful cooperation among like-minded partners. Collaboration among states, and between states, the private sector, and civil society, is important and measures to improve information security require broad international cooperation to be effective.[3]

The group of experts expressed concern that the lack of "shared understanding regarding international norms pertaining to state use of ICTs" risked misperceptions and "could affect crisis management in the event of major incidents" (i.e., provoke escalation). On this euphemistically expressed view, shared norms are instrumental: they help solve planning and coordination problems by standardizing the meaning of an action, so both the agent and target of an action know how it will be interpreted and the likely response to it.[4] Put another way, norms reduce the variability, and hence increase the predictability, of the human contexts in which action is taken. Agreements on particular norms, however arbitrary, may therefore be in every agent's individual interests and reachable, especially if dire consequences are predictable absent the norms.

This notion is conceptually distinct from one that grounds norms on "doing the right thing" and judges the validity of a norm, as Kant does, according to its universality. It is also distinct from an idea, based on Rawls, of norm as a course of action or principle everyone would follow (or not reject) if ignorant of one's specific circumstances when one chooses an action. These last two notions are closer to our commonsense ideas of morality. Contrary to realist theories of international relations, they seem relevant to the United States' and other liberal democracies' policies on human rights and some of their thinking on cyber norms. Thus the "International Strategy for Cyberspace" asserts that one basis of cyberspace norms is the principle that states must respect fundamental freedoms of expression and association, online as well as off. The problem here is that the American and other governments that include Internet freedoms on their lists of cyber norms do not recognize they are juggling two or more concepts of norms. As a consequence, they do not have a basis for prioritizing the norms they would like adopted. While the "International Strategy" does acknowledge that some norms it proposes will be accepted only by the "like minded," it cannot identify the conceptual impediments to wider acceptance of these norms, much less how to address them. To be sure, the Russian and Chinese views that cyber norms be based on an inviolate principle of national sovereignty are no greater help in prioritizing norms for discussion and possible adoption.

National Positions for International Cyber Norms

Unsurprisingly, opportunities have been missed for moving on to substantive discussions. For example, the British government sponsored a conference in late 2011 with the announced purpose of laying out "cyber rules of the road."[5] It showcased strong speeches on Internet Freedom, a riposte to an earlier Russian draft for a cyber convention that would have countries cooperate in suppressing online material that any country deemed a threat to its political stability. According to some apologists, the point was to split non-aligned nations from Russia and China. Yet the conference was ill-prepared by the British Foreign Office to deal with technical and institutional issues.[6] Such occasions suggest that the adoption of specific cyber norms will be hard won, and any set of widely accepted norms will be fairly limited in scope. As noted, the US cybersecurity strategy paper acknowledges that scenario: it anticipates that some cyber norms, favored by the United States, will be observed only among coalitions of the "like minded" (i.e., North Atlantic Treaty Organization [NATO] and some Pacific Rim allies). Since the United States is, of course, a participant to norms discussions, this view implies, at this time, that it will not consider compromise on some of its proposed norms in favor of more widely acceptable ones. It is not alone in this respect.

Broadly speaking, Chinese and Russian policymakers seek to extend the principle of national sovereignty to cyberspace by establishing a norm of the state being the final arbiter of matters relating to cyberspace in their territory.[7] Their likely motives are, first, to control the ideational space that cyber networks afford their populations, and, second, to prevent inquiry into their governments' or state proxies' uses of cyber for military campaigns, political espionage, industrial espionage, and crime. Russia, China, other members of the Shanghai Coordinating Organization, and other authoritarian governments consider the Internet a vector for dissident political information and organizing—one not easily suppressed, but easily exploited by external rivals, in particular the United States. Thus, when cyber-fueled protests occurred in Russia winter 2011–2012, their target, Premier and presidential candidate Vladimir Putin branded them the work of "foreign enemies,"[8] conveniently ignoring the grounds for the protests. On this view, outsiders in enabling dissent within a country do not contribute to its public debate; they are conducting "information warfare" to weaken regimes to the point of greater accommodation with them or even collapse. On that view, already in 2008, Russia, China, and other members of the Shanghai Coordination Organization (SCO) agreed to outlaw supporting or hosting the dissemination of socially disruptive information. In September 2011, in seeming response to foreign governments' and Diasporas' support for cyber activism in the Arab world, Russia proposed that countries log the online activities of their residents suspected of such disseminations, in order to facilitate the identification and suppression of such residents upon complaint of a target country. In practice, however, Russian governments have tolerated considerable online political discourse and protests, despite Chechen insurgents having used the Internet for publicity, recruitment, and coordination in their violent struggle against Russia. This relative openness might have several causes: the much greater emphasis placed by the governments on control of radio and television, strategies of government messaging competing with other online messages for trust, and lack of preparation for the sharp increase in broadband users over the past half decade.

China, on the other hand, has assiduously sought to control the online ideational spaces of its citizens by blocking access to many foreign sites, filtering queries, suppressing blogs, imprisoning bloggers, and taking other censorship measures. These are implemented both algorithmically and by hand to keep out material endangering state security, divulging state secrets, subverting state power, and jeopardizing national unification; damaging state honor and interests; instigating ethnic hatred or discrimination and jeopardizing ethnic unity; jeopardizing state religious policy, propagating heretical or superstitious ideas; spreading rumors, disrupting social order and stability; disseminating obscenity, pornography, gambling, violence, brutality, and terror or abetting crime; humiliating or slandering others, trespassing on the lawful rights and interests of others; and other contents forbidden by laws and administrative regulations.[9]

China's efforts and similar ones elsewhere, as in Iran or Belarus, where citizens' access to foreign sites was recently criminalized, have sparked fears of cyberspace fragmentation and "Internet(s) in one country."[10] These practices represent an extreme in measures that a growing number of states—some liberal democracies among them—are taking to regulate their citizens in cyberspace. The milder measures can include banning online anonymity, prohibiting certain content, like child pornography, and requiring authorization of state security services to search users' data. While these steps can be justified as needed to prevent cybercrime, they imply that users' cyberspace is an extension of national territory and ultimately subject to a state's claim of sovereignty. It is interesting to note in this respect, an echo of the principle of "national sovereignty," as introduced in the Treaty of Westphalia (1648)—the "charter" of our current international system—to bar interventions by states to change the status of a religion in another state: *cuius regio, eius religio* (He who rules determines the religion of his realm).

In contrast, the United States and its NATO allies tend in their pronouncements to view cyberspace as a central institution for a global economy, a means for worldwide scientific and cultural exchange, a commons for political debate and development, and a social medium. Given this variety of its functions, there follows a multi-stakeholder model for cyberspace's control and defense, with states being one type of stakeholder, along with non-governmental organizations, service providers, ICT companies, critical infrastructure entities, corporate users, and individual users. Because cyberspace, particularly the Internet, is prey to attacks and exploits by criminals, terrorists, and even states, states, by virtue of their authority and capabilities, have primary responsibility to provide the needed security, without harming the interests of other stakeholders. Norms and treaties (e.g., the Budapest Convention on Cybercrime) are instruments for fulfilling such responsibility, as are the nurturing of a cybersecurity culture and capabilities around the globe.[11] This view of the Internet ignores the demographic and technological changes that are remaking cyberspace and expectations for it: the change from hundreds of millions of users concentrated in North America and Europe connected to the Internet through computers to billions of users, with the bulk in south and east Asia, connected through mobile devices, and the rise of an Internet of things. As a result, practices that might have once seemed in the interests of all are now controversial and contested.[12] As already noted, many regimes view the American opposition to online censorship and its provision of circumvention software as an effort to undermine them.[13] Similarly, the position that technologists be left free of political interference to decide cyber design issues is seen as a ploy to perpetuate US technological domination of cyberspace.

These differences are exacerbated by disagreements over the auspices for promulgation and monitoring of cyber norms as well as the administration of the Internet. American policymakers insist on the development of cyber architectures and protocols by independent groups, like the Internet Engineering Task Force (IETF), because that arrangement will keep the basic technologies of cyberspace free of political interference. China and many developing countries, however, consider such groups, as well as the Internet Corporation for Assigned Names and Numbers (ICANN) which administers the system of online identifiers, as vehicles for the US's continuing technological domination of the Internet. They contend that the shift in Internet demographics should give them a greater voice in running the Internet and consequently want either the International Telecommunications Union (ITU) or a new UN agency to become the key governing institution. The United States believes that China and other authoritarian states would dominate such an arrangement; they would use it to promote architectures that facilitate their control of domestic information flows and signal intelligence against adversaries. In short, the question of governance crystallizes the distrust among states regarding their respective exploitations of the Internet and many behaviors in cyberspace.[14]

Distrust and differences in concepts, interests, and experiences also separate the cyber powers with regard to the military uses of cyberspace, despite their desires to avoid escalatory conflicts and their agreement in principles. Almost all powers have signaled that they will consider cyber attacks at some level as rising to the level of "armed attack," and reserve the right to respond to it by all means, including the use of force, though none have indicated what that level might be or are likely to do so. With the possible exception of China, the major cyber powers also believe the law of armed conflict (LOAC) should apply to cyber attacks within the context of war: use of force limited to accomplishing military objectives, distinction between military and civilian targets, prohibition on excessive use of force, and efforts to minimize ancillary casualties.[15] There have been some bilateral discussions at the government advisory group level (Track 1.5 and Track 2 diplomacy) on how these constraints might apply to concrete situations of cyber conflict.[16] However, as discussed below, the lack of experience and public information on the effects of possible cyber attacks or of physical attacks on cyber infrastructures (e.g., underwater cables) will impede progress toward a broader understanding and agreements as to how LOAC should apply to cyberspace.

Doctrinally, Russia and China regard cyber attacks as part of information warfare that accompanies kinetic military activity and aims to undermine the adversary's capabilities for fighting, by disrupting its military organization and demoralizing its population. China places particular value on using cyber weapons to distract an enemy and to neutralize any advantages it has from technological superiority and intensely computerized C4ISR.[17] Russia has experience with but not necessarily enthusiasm for information warfare: during a bitter political struggle with Estonia in 2007, and its brief 2008 war with Georgia, the adversary states suffered distributed denial-of-service (DDoS) attacks on their telecommunications infrastructure, with consequent discomfort and even panic in their populations. The extent of Russian military involvement in these attacks, however, is not clear, since they were conducted by Russian hactivists and botnets were controlled by criminal gangs based in Russia.[18] China has not directly or indirectly engaged in information warfare, but it has conducted military, political, and industrial espionage, with the United States as prime target, so broadly that some US officials have described these activities as "economic warfare."[19] Some officials also fear that China may have planted malware or "logic bombs" inside American critical infrastructure and military networks to be activated in case of conflict.

The United States has been more aggressive than either of these countries in integrating cyber in its war-fighting capabilities and, probably for that reason, demonstrated less appetite for "arms control"–type talks. In the 1990s and early 2000s, the American military developed a notion of net-centric warfare—the intense networking of geographically dispersed forces for more effective collaboration that has been partly realized through construction of the Global Information Grid. A 2007 experiment at the Idaho National Laboratory suggested the US government's interest in new types of cyber attacks, as well as defending US critical infrastructure from them. This experiment, which some observers consider a precursor to Stuxnet, demonstrated that remote penetration and corrupt instructions to an electrical generator control system could bring the generator to self-destroy. The US Cyber Command—a dedicated military unit, stood up in 2010—presumably has acquired the capability of launching such attacks or equally damaging ones. Its commanding officer and spokespersons have recently noted that the command's primary mission is to integrate defensive and offensive cyber options in the military's six combatant commands.[20] The pattern of development and their remarks suggest that the primary focus of the offensive capabilities would be on thoroughly dismantling an adversary's military and military support networks rather than panicking its population.

Given the differences across states regarding the appropriate norms for facets of behavior in cyberspace, many states will find something objectionable in any comprehensive proposal and will likely reject it *in toto*. This proved the case with the proposal for an international code of conduct for information security submitted to the UN by China, Russia, Tajikistan, and Uzbekistan, and the previously mentioned Russian draft for a convention on information security presented at Ekaterinburg.[21] Each has provisions that all countries can accept (e.g., assisting countries in developing cybersecurity policies, calling for mediation in cyber conflicts). The liberal democracies dismissed them, however, because the first proposal embraced a very state-centric model for Internet governance, as opposed to a multistakeholder one, and the second called on states to curb the serving from their territories information that another state declares to undermine its security. These political interactions deepened the divisions of states into several contending camps or information orders, one grouped around the United States and its European and Pacific allies, another consisting of SCO members, and a third composed of "nonaligned" nations. The last group, as represented by India, Brazil, and South Africa, wants to give states, especially developing ones, a larger voice in policies and governance for the Internet perhaps through a UN-based agency to replace ICANN. However, it does not support the Russian and Chinese position on issues of information rights and censorship.[22]

Norms for Specific Cyber Behaviors

An obvious lesson of the interactions is that states should avoid presenting grand plans for international cybersecurity. Instead they should seek to develop norms in areas where their current practices have been mutually acceptable or where they have expressed strong interests for cooperation. The remainder of this paper concerns specifying norms that might satisfy these criteria. This discussion is informed by a workshop, in October 2011, on international cyber norms, organized by the present writer and Joseph Nye, as cochairs, with a thirteen-person committee. The American and allied government officials, academicians, think tankers, and practitioners who attended the workshop discussed potential norms in six principal issue areas: (1) military operations; (2) political, military, and economic espionage; (3) cybercrime; (4) development of underlying technologies and supply chain management; (5) public-private partnerships; and (6) global information society and Internet freedom.[23] Table 14.1 presents the norms that attracted the most interest, but the table should not be viewed as a consensus, since any consensus finding process was deliberately avoided.[24] Because discussions were under the Chatham House rule, individuals cannot be credited now for proposals and comments that might be repeated here in part or in whole, but all the participants deserve credit for any value found in this report. Any errors are entirely those of this writer.

The tabled norms tend to reflect a Western vision of how cyberspace should be constructed, since workshop participants came only

Table 14.1 Possible Norms Tabled at a Workshop Hosted by Harvard Kennedy School Belfer Center, MIT CSAIL, and University of Toronto, Canada, 2011

MILITARY OPERATIONS IN CYBERSPACE	POLITICAL, MILITARY, AND ECONOMIC ESPIONAGE	CYBERCRIME	TECHNOLOGICAL FOUNDATIONS AND SUPPLY CHAIN	PUBLIC-PRIVATE PARTNERSHIPS/ DEFENSIVE COORDINATION	INTERNET FREEDOM GLOBAL INFORMATION SOCIETY
In principle, apply law of armed conflict (LOAC) to cyber military responses and operations	Banning of large-scale commercial espionage which could be promoted as a universal customary norm to multiple international bodies and incorporated in bilateral relations	Norm to ensure states and other stakeholders educate themselves on cybercrime, including with respect to the hiring of criminal hackers	States should recognize the international implications of their technical decisions and act with respect for one another's networks and the broader Internet	Governments should seek cooperation with the private sector to assure a clean and healthy Internet	Promote Internet freedom as a global norm, but allow for ambiguity to reduce friction regarding the standards of Internet freedom
Confidence-building measures such as cyber hotline, greater differentiation of cyber incidents, establishing mechanisms for crisis management, and de-escalation	Regulate trade in espionage and surveillance services by defense contractors in developed countries to authoritarian countries for use versus political dissidents	Distinction between low- and high-impact criminals and expectations for cooperation in the pursuit of high-impact criminals	States should act within their authorities to help ensure the end-to-end interoperability of an Internet accessible to all	Norm that limits or calls for arrangements that limit (or specifies circumstances for) surveillance and data collection by private companies	

A structural norm (practice) of military involvement in the protection of domestic critical infrastructure from cyber attack

Encryption of computers and cloud servers to inhibit theft of politically sensitive information (a la WikiLeaks)

Data retention and transborder accessibility for high-impact crime

Respect the free flow of information in national network configurations; no arbitrary interference with internationally interconnected infrastructure

Globally accepted norms and standards to assure cyber supply chain, including third-party certification of production centers, third-party assurances of hardware and software, a certification architecture enabling trusted chains of custody for components

Norms to routinely share information, assist in disaster or attack, cooperate in forensics, collaborate in analysis of attacks

Duty to warn and duty to assist; analogies to mandatory notification should be institutionalized at the international level in data sharing procedures among Computer Emergency Response Teams (CERTs) and North Atlantic Treaty Organization (NATO) allies

Letters of marque, issued by states to license private parties to pursue cyber spies

"Naming and shaming" of insecure producers, and barring their sales to government and defense sectors

from the United States and its allies. Yet the decomposition of cyberspace into issue areas enabled participants to evaluate the ripeness of facets of cyber behavior for formalization and the readiness of governments to accept the formulas as norms. Where possible, the proposed norms are distinguished as to whether they articulate principles for cyberspace, including norms for dealing with states of exception, like conflicts, or recommend best practices and operating rules.

Military Operations

Existing international laws specify neither the types of cyber operations that a targeted country could legitimately consider grounds for war (*ius ad bellum*) nor the constraints on cyber operations a country needs to observe in war (*ius in bello*). Governments have avoided specifying redlines whose crossings would provoke their retaliation, including armed response, for fear that would effectively license adversaries to mount less injurious operations. This reluctance is understandable and consistent with deterrence theory, which argues that leaving an adversary to guess whether an attack might provoke retaliation may be enough to deter the attack. However, this leaves the international community without shared expectations as to the limits of peacetime cyber behaviors, on one hand, and responses from countries subject to attacks, on the other. The uncertainty is compounded by the abilities of non-state actors to mount serious cyber attacks on one state from the territory of other states, and by the absence of norms that hold states responsible for preventing such attacks.

The short history of international cyber conflict provides few landmarks for this uncharted area. The 2007 DDoS attack on Estonia did not provoke retaliation from Estonia's NATO allies, although according to some reports Estonia did ask for some response under Article 5, the collective security provision, of the NATO treaty. With that attack in mind, an advisory group, headed by former US Secretary of State Madeleine Albright, recommended in 2010 that NATO's new strategic doctrine specify that transborder cyber attacks on a member state would ordinarily trigger consultations (Article 4) and certain attacks might even warrant a response under Article 5.[25] NATO, however, passed on this recommendation, preferring a policy of deciding the appropriate response on a case-by-case basis. Similarly, the

DDoS attacks on American government sites apparently did not warrant retaliation, even had the government been able to attribute them to a state actor with a reasonable confidence. (Although the North Korean military or security service was suspected to have launched the attacks, they were originally controlled from South Korea, then from US and European sites, with little evidence of a North Korean link.) The Stuxnet attack, which damaged rather than just disrupted Iranian facilities, generated no timely overt response from Iran, not even a complaint against unknown, presumably state, actors for endangering international security. Iran's leaders, of course, had their reasons for not responding: any complaint would draw more scrutiny to their nuclear program targeted by the attack and reveal more vulnerability of their facilities. Other governments were also silent, some perhaps having been complicit in the attack, and many, no doubt, applauding this sabotage of the Iranian nuclear program.

The lack of forceful responses by the victims in these episodes may indicate a common uncertainty about the gravity of cyber attacks and a reluctance to extend, possibly escalate, a conflict over them. States might not be bluffing when they declare a right to respond to cyber attacks by any means, but in practice they seem either to have no clear redlines or, if they do, no attacks, so far, have crossed them. Scholars of international law and other observers have addressed this void with greater certitude, with at least one characterizing the disruption of critical infrastructure in Estonia as rising to the level of "armed attack."[26] Others set the bar higher, at Stuxnet-like attacks with the potential to destroy infrastructure like nuclear reactors and produce lethal results. In their opinion, these now apparent possibilities should prompt states to agree to prohibit certain types of attacks and to provide remedies for them, such as the right of a state under cyber attack to assistance from other states.[27]

This recommendation is not far fetched, especially if, absent generally accepted redlines, national security officials evaluate cyber attacks on a case-by-case basis and weigh responses to them with the traditional criteria for evaluating kinetic attacks, viz., scope, duration, and lethality. Applied to cyberspace, these criteria would distinguish between disruptive and damaging attacks and restrain military responses to the disruptive ones. Talks that affirmed the applicability of these criteria could get broad support from states and reduce the threat of escalation from relatively minor disruptive attacks. Adoption of these criteria would not rule out the use of force in response to damaging attacks, but the talks could help create a bias against it by advocating several norms, with potential for widespread acceptance, that would mitigate the damage and help identify parties responsible for the attacks. These include an e-SOS or "duty to assist" that requires states to offer help to a state whose cyber-based infrastructures were damaged, a related duty of states to inform others of malware threats they have discovered, cooperation in forensics, and a commitment to seek mediation for cyber-related conflicts.

As noted above, cyber powers, with the exception of China, agree that LOAC should apply to cyber conflicts. However, developing rules of engagement based on its principles of proportionality of response, avoidance of civilian targets, and minimization of ancillary casualties may prove difficult. There is little experience of cyber attacks in war-like contexts and insufficient knowledge of their consequences. While, according to the cliché, the damage done by a bomb of a particular size is well known, that for a cyber attack on a military network or critical infrastructure is not. It can depend as much on the configuration of the target's networks as on the intended scope of the attack. Moreover, cyberspace does not easily afford the distinctions upon which rules of engagement for "meat space" rely, viz., military vs. civilian, attack vs. espionage, state vs. non-state agents, intentional vs. accidental. For example, the US military uses civilian networks in over 90% of its communications, and the figures are probably similar for other militaries. Although international dialogue has begun about measures that might sharpen the distinctions (e.g., digital equivalents of insignia, on packets to indicate their military or humanitarian content), many points need to be addressed.[28] Also for such dialogue to reach results that are applicable to future cyber conflicts, states will need to disclose some of their cyber offensive capabilities and plans for using them.

Two other military-related issues can concern strategies that seek to stabilize cyberspace by promoting appropriate norms: the responsibility of states for attacks originating in their territories, perpetrated by non-state actors, and the involvement of the nation's military in the protection of domestic critical infrastructure. Acceptance of a norm that held states responsible for such attacks would be consistent with current international law for kinetic attacks, with UN efforts to foster a worldwide culture of cybersecurity and with efforts to curtail certain states' use of proxies. However, there might be difficulty in reaching agreement on the appropriate norm because of the various current suggestions as to what cyber attacks rise to a hostile act or armed attack. Some commentators who consider the 2007 DDoS attack on Estonia an armed attack emphasize the mental anguish Estonians suffered because of disrupted online services. Since authoritarian governments consider dissident political speech to disturb their countries' social stability, they could plausibly argue that under this definition, other states that allowed dissidents to communicate from their territories could be blamed for permitting "hostile acts" or "armed attacks." Hence, it might be sensible for the United States and its allies to support a distinction between disruption and damage before proposing a norm of a state's responsibility for cyber attacks originating from its territory.

The United States and many of its allies are currently deliberating about the role that their respective militaries should play in defending from cyber attacks critical infrastructures, which serves their civilian populations. Some officials believe the militaries should take a lead role or a co-equal one with any civilian agency, because the militaries are better resourced and, noted above, depend on the infrastructures. Others are uneasy with the idea because of its implications for the civil-military relationship in their states. Traditionally the militaries have been outward directed, with police and other security agencies responsible for internal protection. Also, giving the military a lead role in responding to an attack on the infrastructure could bias the conflict process toward retaliation and escalation, rather than resilience and recovery, because it introduces an offensive option. The current consensus in the United States and among its NATO allies is that the militaries should share in protecting the civilian networks, but let civilian agencies take the lead. However, the allocation of roles will likely be made country by country, as a matter of internal politics, so it is probably pointless to seek a global standard or best practice for the institutional arrangements.

Military, Political, and Economic Espionage

The use of cyber technology for espionage raises questions about the current norms that permit espionage under international law but allow its prosecution under domestic law. This is because:

- The technology allows the theft of secrets and intellectual property on an unprecedented scale.
- The spying at this scale is done remotely (electronically or digitally), leaving the victim with little in-domain recourse other than "naming and shaming" the perpetrator (i.e., no imprisonment or expulsion of captured spies).
- Cyber systems used in espionage and other intelligence, surveillance, and reconnaissance can blur the line between exploit and attack, causing damage and disruption as well as loss.

Given the traditional understanding of political and military espionage as needed for national security planning and preparation, proposals for their restriction would seem to have little chance of gaining traction. Nevertheless, because the scale of the cyber espionage may provoke aggressive responses from its victims, which in turn would destabilize the international system, some informal, unpublicized understandings might be reached on a bilateral basis as to an accepted level of espionage. In any case, the United States and many of its allies will insist that industrial espionage by state actors is condemned by international law, since it is not motivated by a national security concern or part of anticipatory self-defense. The question is whether this espionage should be considered "economic warfare," which threatens international security, or more an unfair trade practice, which can be redressed by economic penalties. The latter view has the advantage of leading to the decomposition of the charges of espionage to individual cases or types of cases, with some dissipation of the grievance. That consequence can be important, since almost all the industrial espionage has been attributed to China and its principal victim, the United States, has progressed from annoyance to extreme irritation with China over its practice.

Can the United States and like-minded states effectively promote and sufficiently enforce a norm banning industrial spying, so that it might eventually be widely accepted and followed? One model proposed for such an effort is the "proliferation security initiative" (PSI) in nations that through bilateral and multilateral agreements have committed not to traffic in weapons of mass destruction and to act to interdict shipments of such materials. Adherence to the PSI grew from a core of eleven nations to nearly one hundred in less than a decade, despite controversy over the legality of interdiction on the high seas and opposition from China and many non-aligned nations, including India and Indonesia. For a comparable initiative on industrial espionage, the United States and other interested countries would need laws enabling them to try in their own courts foreign nationals and companies for economic espionage originating outside their national boundaries. Prosecution of the same suspects by a number of states might both end the suspects' espionage and force the World Trade Organization (WTO) to develop specific rules and remediation for industrial espionage that states could enact (e.g., damage awards against offending companies, tariffs against existing states). One major obstacle for this scenario is, in contrast to the PSI, which spoke to the fears of many nations over weapons of mass destruction, only the United States and a few other states with major intellectual property stores are victimized by the industrial espionage. Consequently, gaining broader support would depend less on exemplary cases against the espionage but more on the expenditure of diplomatic and political capital—similar to the expenditures by advanced countries to get less developed ones to support their proposals for global copyright and patent protection—in changing domestic laws, assessing the extent of damages, and providing evidence for the charges in domestic courts and international forums. Moreover, the prosecutions of alleged spies, even under new enabling legislation, might prove difficult: many companies will shy at explicitly identifying what properties were stolen, while intelligence agencies may be reluctant to provide the evidence they have for fear of disclosing their sources or their own espionage activities. Galvanizing the international community against industrial espionage should be a goal for its victims, but without a compelling model for doing so, it should not be a high-priority goal. Perhaps more can be accomplished in serious bilateral talks between the respective victims and the chief culprit.

The daily reports of successful penetrations of cybersecurity by unknown hackers indicates that enhanced cybersecurity awareness and hygiene, as called for in the UN resolution noted above, will do little to halt cyber espionage of any type. Because the incumbent cyber technologies are vulnerable, states and non-state actors will find ways to get to the targets of their choice. The value to their take, however, could be reduced by adherence to a norm at the operational level of end-to-end encryption or, failing that, encryption enablement of computers and servers that host politically or economically sensitive data. Enabling these practices should be one goal of international cooperation for capacity building in less developed countries.

An issue related to espionage is the surveillance (and censorship) by governments of their own citizens' online activities, often accomplished in less developed countries with technologies acquired from developed ones. For states that are committed to a global human rights agenda, such surveillance threatens the citizens' rights for information, expression, and political association. One response has been proposals of norms among like-minded states that would impose or broaden existing export controls on the technologies. Such an initiative can prove effective quickly, because the technology suppliers are mainly in a small number of liberal democracies, where public opinion in support of such controls can be grown. In some cases, public reports that a company has supplied an obnoxious regime with such technology has already caused the company to claim it has or will stop the supply. At the operational level, however, there needs to be some distinction between "lawful" and "unlawful" use of the technologies so that vendors will cooperate in enforcing the norms, rather than fear significant loss of sales.

Cybercrime

Strategies that promote international cooperation to combat cybercrime are vital for the stabilization and positive development of cyberspace. This is because cybercrime organizations breed new attack techniques, which can then be acquired by states, and the capabilities of these organizations, when augmented with outsourced specialized skills, can exceed those of almost any state acting alone. Yet a strategy that would focus on international cooperation for the apprehension and prosecution of cyber criminals now faces the choice of promoting the expansion of the Budapest Convention on Cybercrime or advocating a new treaty. The United States and other supporters of the convention argue that it sets a standard for international cooperation in investigating and prosecuting cybercrime, notwithstanding its having acquired only thirty-one signatories over a decade. Critics fault the convention for being regional in character, deficient in provisions for handling data, and outdated by the new types of cybercrime, which have accompanied the exponential growth of Internet use, proliferation of mobile devices, and the emergence of an Internet of things (devices).[29] They also note that many states in the East and South will not join the convention because of its North Atlantic origins.

However, a strategy that campaigns for either the old treaty or a new one might not be cost effective in reducing crime. There will be costs in trying to overcome the resistance that many states will have to joining. There are a variety of reasons for this resistance. Russia and some other states will not easily end policies of giving safe harbor to cyber criminals in return for their intelligence gathering and plausibly deniable offensive cyber operations (e.g., DDoS). Some states will be concerned about limits to their national sovereignty, changes in their criminal laws and procedures, or data retention practices that a new treaty or a revised Budapest convention will require.

Undoubtedly there are benefits from a treaty, including standardizing investigatory procedures at an international level, harmonizing some laws across states, and possibly retarding the growth of cybercrime in member states. Apparently a state's membership in the Budapest convention correlates with fewer cyber attacks originating from its territory than from a demographically comparable non-member state.[30] Possibly joining the convention signaled that the state would henceforth be more cybersecurity aware, and the criminals consequently relocated their operations to more permissive places.

Nevertheless, the promotion of norms that reduce either the vulnerability of users or the incentives for criminals might more easily produce similar effects on the levels of cybercrimes. These norms include information sharing and a duty to warn (or inform). The duty to warn or inform becomes increasingly relevant with the growth of situations where individuals, organizations, or governments are unaware that (1) their information systems are at risk, (2) their data have been stolen, or (3) new organizational routines can produce new vulnerabilities. This duty has already been partially formalized at domestic levels by laws mandating notification of security breaches. It has begun institutionalization at the international level in data-sharing procedures among Computer Emergency Response Teams (CERTs) and regional organizations of states (e.g., NATO). Cloud vendors and tier-1 ISPs, whose operations are not confined to any one state, should also be subject to such norms and laws, although there is no appropriate supervisory authority at this time. Because of their alignment with the UN resolution on cybersecurity, such norms can gain widespread acceptance but will probably not become ubiquitous in practice. Some states and organizations will ignore these expectations due to their imposition of processing costs, reputational risks, and disclosures of possible improprieties in data collection. Moreover, some old vulnerabilities will persist and new ones will be created and with them cybercrime. For that reason, a strategy should also deter cybercrime by promoting passive measures that interfere with criminals' getting their payoffs (e.g., blocking the ways that stolen information is monetized).

This approach, which emphasizes prevention over apprehension, does not preclude cooperation between members and members of the Budapest convention in the investigation of cyber crimes. It recommends that rather than seeking a comprehensive framework for such cooperation, arrangements be developed in the context of bilateral relations, such as extensions, where needed, of mutual assistance treaties, or on a more informal, *ad hoc basis*. To that end, states, such as the United States, which are zealous in the pursuit of cybercrime will need to convince states like Russia and China that such cooperation is also in their interest, possibly by seeking cooperation only in cases of major criminality (e.g., terrorism) or regarding online activities that are unambiguously criminal in the respective jurisdictions (e.g., child pornography). Successful instances of cooperation in such cases can provide reusable routines and encouragement for more cooperation. Thus, China's Minister of Public Security said, after an unprecedented operation involving his police and the US FBI closing down a child pornography ring: "Although China and the U.S. have different judicial systems and cultural values, the two sides share a common view in crime-fighting." The Minister then pledged China would continue to strengthen its law enforcement cooperation with foreign countries and vigorously fight transnational illegal activities, especially crimes committed through the Internet.[31]

Technological Foundations

On the American view, conflict over the development, operations, and supply of equipment for the Internet can be minimized if, as a rule, decisions are based only on the technological merits of the various options and all parties aim for an open and safe Internet, without hidden vulnerabilities. The Chinese government and other governments in less developed nations tend to see demands to that end as subterfuge for maintaining US technological domination of the Internet. It therefore appears sensible for the United States and other states that want to keep technological matters in the hands of technologists to seek support for that position from the technical communities in these states. However, several factors may prevent such a strategy from being effective in gaining acceptance for a norm of technological independence. First, the technologists in developing countries have not yet or are just beginning to work with international bodies that have roles in developing cyberspace (e.g., Internet Engineering Task Force [IETF]) or assuring its security (e.g., International Organization for Standardization [ISO]). Second, the technologists in some of these countries might not have the freedom to take positions that conflict with their governments' views. Third, the standards bodies, which the United States trusts, have not yet worked out standards at the international level for cloud and mobile computing and supply chain assurance.[32] So to ask technologists to support the norm is tantamount to asking them to take on faith that such bodies will do the right thing.

A fallback position, then, in the effort to keep development and operations in cyberspace free of political interference at national levels is for the United States and like-minded nations to articulate principles that approximate the list below, without expecting or demanding that other states will immediately accept them:

- States need to recognize the international implications of technical decisions made at the national level, and act with respect for each other's networks.

- States should act within their authorities to help ensure end-to-end interoperability and accessibility to all.
- States should respect the free flow of information in national network configurations, ensuring they do not arbitrarily interfere with internationally interconnected infrastructures.
- States should recognize and act on their responsibility to protect information infrastructures and secure national systems from damage or misuse.

In the meantime steps can be taken to route around countries that do not follow such principles; the consequent loss of transit revenues or complaints about degraded service might then nudge governments in question toward accepting these principles.

A strategic goal with greater priority is winning commitments to norms and standards that assure the integrity of the supply chain, since that is key for trustworthy ICT. It is important that such expectations be shared widely among consumers so that there will be pressure on producers to satisfy them. Foreseeable operational norms or standard practices would involve third-party certification of production centers, third-party assurances of hardware and software, a certification architecture enabling trusted chains of custody for components, "naming and shaming" of insecure producers, and barring their sales to government and defense sectors. There might initially be a need for incentives or government pressure for large corporations on both the supply and consumer sides to enter such a system. Ultimately, however, the spread and strength of these operational norms will depend on education of consumers and market mechanisms: perceptions of better quality, on one hand, and suspicions of possibly compromised ICT, on the other, can drive the growth of a market segment for secure hardware and assured software. The development of such norms is something of a necessity for most states. The alternative is for states to directly control the manufacture of components for military and critical infrastructure, as the United States now does to some extent and China and Germany are planning to do. But that would be too costly for many states, and providing the needed, trusted oversight could be beyond their capabilities.

Public-Private Partnerships

The UN resolution for cybersecurity, various national strategy papers, and even the Russian draft convention for international information security expect the private sector to play a significant role in protecting cyberspace. Consequently, there should be support for a campaign to encourage states to develop organizational frameworks or at least working relations with local and international private companies to accommodate this participation. The acceptance at the operational level of such a norm can create a "win-win" situation: The companies frequently have more capabilities and practice in dealing with threats in cyberspace but often need authorization from states to act more effectively, as demonstrated by the collaborations against Conficker and other recent malware pandemics.

These collaborations of ISPs, vendor, some governments, and researchers reveal the presence of several "invisible norms," or regular practices, based on the willingness of system operators to cooperate in keeping their networks clean. Because of Conficker's extent, the collaboration grew to over one hundred top-level domain operators and Microsoft in daily touch with ICANN and less frequently with governments. These partners implemented an extensive strategy of prevention, through blocking botnet command and control sites, and remediation, through the disinfection of host computers. This collaboration exposed the difficulties of cooperation at the legal/policy level compared with the relative ease of cooperation at technical levels. In some countries, there was a need to work around legal hurdles, for instance, contractual barriers to take down, anti-trust laws, and protection of privacy. Major legal difficulties were avoided because the prevention strategy could be implemented locally, through blocking at the name (for the C&C) resolution level, and did not require any transborder activity. But despite their success, the anti-Conficker Cabal and other anti-malware collaborations had an *ad hoc* character, with ICANN and other stakeholders lacking the authority to institutionalize the mechanism.

The organizational form for the public-private partnerships will vary over states. In some European countries, these partnerships are well developed for many sectors, and domestic laws to support them are in place. In other countries ICT trade groups exist for information sharing, but governments have sometimes lagged in connecting to them. In less developed countries, there are few such partnerships. National and international organizations, with experience in public and private-sector partnering on economic matters (e.g., the Asian-Pacific Economic Cooperation [APEC]) should be encouraged to guide and nurture the growth of partnerships in such places. However, governments and companies might have different visions and desire different tempos in implementing their partnerships. For example, companies like Goldman Sachs or Lockheed Martin, which operate globally, will want to harmonize the rules across countries, while a government, even if it views itself as an enabler, will face local and legacy issues that might keep it from accepting such norms. Also, some companies might anticipate that by meeting the standards set in their cybersecurity partnership, they can deflect regulation by the government partner in the future. A government agency that suspects such a motive might then move cautiously in such a partnership. In view of these possibilities, perhaps the most states can expect of one another—and what can be formulated in a norm—is that they will seek partnerships with the private sector to assure a clean and healthy Internet.

Internet Freedom and a Global Information Society

As noted earlier, Internet freedom or the free, unfettered flow of information, is the most contentious issue regarding daily operations of the Internet and governments' positions on the Internet's administration and future. This is both a human rights and a cyber issue, since the rights to information, expression, and association have underpinned the use and growth of cyberspace. Yet that growth has led to pushbacks from states whose political and cultural traditions are quite different from those of the liberal democracies where cyberspace first developed. While paying lip service to human rights, these states have claimed that national security concerns, such as internal social stability and terrorist threats, require some restrictions on these rights. In some cases these claims are self-serving and protect authoritarian regimes. In others, they can be partly justified by evidence of ethnic violence or insurgency. In any case, in response to the cyber fueled upheavals in the Middle East, states have increased their restrictions on Internet and social media use. More than forty countries are now involved in developing second- and third-generation filtering techniques.

These circumstances will thwart the effort by the United States and like-minded liberal democracies to gain general acceptance of Internet freedom as a cyber norm. The effort can be seen as divisive. It can also be subject to the criticism that the free flow of information is no longer, if it ever was, an essential driver for development of the Internet, especially now that the economic and social uses of the Internet eclipse the political ones. Critics can also attack the American commitment to openness of information as hypocritical: they can note the readiness of the US Congress to mandate blocking access to certain hosts for commercial reasons (copyright protection), much like China and other states block access to sites for political reasons, and the questionable treatment of the American soldier who downloaded classified material to WikiLeaks.

The bleak prospects for a global norm should not stop a group of like-minded states from adopting norms of openness and unfettered information flows. However, a more fruitful long-term discussion would concern the limits to online dissent and disruption, because even the most liberal states have secrets, resources, and operations to protect. The norm that might emerge from such discussions would almost certainly allow for different and situation-specific standards of free information flows and thereby reduce some of the friction regarding Internet freedom.

Conclusions

The establishment of norms of behavior for international cyberspace quintessentially fits what international relations theorist Arnold Wolfers called a "milieu goal." By that he meant situations, patterns, or regularities whose attainment would enable a state to maintain its position in an international system or more easily obtain more tangible assets, which Wolfers called "possession goals."[33] Because states are interconnected and interdependent in cyberspace, on one hand, and threat capabilities have proliferated rapidly, on the other, an optimal milieu pertains when all states accept the same norms and these tend to conflict avoidance and non-interference. For that reason, state officials who believe that the acceptance of norms by states can help secure their state's cyber activities should promote only a small number whose acceptability has already been signaled by key actors. The review of candidate norms identified five meeting these criteria:

- States should distinguish between disruptive and damaging cyber attacks and evaluate a damaging attack on the basis of its scope, duration, and lethality.
- States have a duty to assist other states that have suffered a major cyber attack or disaster, and also have a duty to inform others of new threats in cyberspace.
- States should cooperate in the certification of ICT supply chains.
- States whose territories or citizens are involved in transborder cyber activities that are unambiguously criminal in their states should cooperate in the investigation of these crimes and the apprehension of their perpetrators.
- States should enable the formation of public-private partnerships for cybersecurity, which include both local and international ICT companies operating in their territories.

These potential norms can win widespread support for two reasons. First, with the exception of cooperation in criminal investigations, they are directed toward reducing vulnerability and confrontation rather than in suppressing threat actors. In some sense then, they demand less action from the state actor, but if all states behave according to these norms, there will be significant reduction in threats and conflicts. Second, these norms are more concerned with maintaining cyberspace for all states rather than satisfying particular parties' agendas. Put another way, they are *status quo* oriented. They respond to that vision of the Internet as a network whose value grows with the number of its users and thus to an expanding positive sum or classic cooperative game. There is, of course, a concurrent competitive game being played between states over this same game board, with rewards, such as status and power, that lie beyond it. For that reason, cybersecurity strategies need the additional components of technological transformation and "reasonable deterrence."

Endnotes

1. International Strategy for Cyberspace: Prosperity, Security, and Openness in a Networked World, May 2011, http://www.whitehouse.gov/sites/default/files/rss_viewer/international_strategy_for_cyberspace.pdf.

2. United Nations General Assembly A/65/201; 7/30/2010. Group of Governmental Experts on Developments in the Field of Information and Telecommunications in the Context of International Security, http://unidir.org/pdf/activites/pdf5-act483.pdf (retrieved February 1, 2012).

3. Id.

4. As demonstrated by the collaborations among cyber security practitioners, companies, and government agencies in response to the Conficker worm, effective international cooperation can be realized *ad hoc*; see M. Bowden, *Worm: The First Digital World War* (New York, 2011). The problem is the lack of ways to institutionalize such success and remove impediments to it for the next time.

5. Perhaps an echo of the "information superhighway" image?

6. London Cyber Conference: Don't be vague, listen to Hague, *The Economist*, November 2, 2011, http://www.economist.com/blogs/newsbook/2011/11/london-cyber-conference; P. Apps, Disagreements on cyber risk east-west cold war. Reuters, February 3, 2012, http://www.reuters.com/article/2012/02/03/us-technology-cyber-idUSTRE8121ED20120203.

7. See the Russian draft for a "Convention on International Information Security," presented to the International Meeting of High-Ranking Official Responsible for Security Matters, Ekaterinburg, Sept. 21–22, 2011, isocbg.files.wordpress.com/.../russian-draft-un-cyber-convention-english.doc

8. Bohm, Michael. Putin Chasing Imaginary American Ghosts, *The Moscow Times*. http://www.themoscowtimes.com/opinion/article/putin-chasing-imaginary-american-ghosts/452802.html.

9. Information Office of the State Council of the People's Republic of China, The Internet in China. June 8, 2010. http://www.china.org.cn/government/whitepaper/node_7093508.htm, q.v. "Protecting Internet Security."

10. Extensive literature, particularly Deibert et al., ed., *Access Controlled: The Shaping of Power, Rights and Rule in Cyberspace* (Cambridge, MA: MIT, 2010); *Access Contested: Security, Identity, and Resistance in Asian Cyberspace* (Cambridge, MA: MIT, 2011). On Iranian efforts to create a national Internet, see http://arstechnica.com/tech-policy/news/2012/02/iran-reportedly-blocking-encrypted-internet-traffic.ars (retrieved February 11, 2012).

11. See UN General Assembly Resolution 64/211: Creation of a global culture of cybersecurity and taking stock of national efforts to protect critical information infrastructures, adopted March 17, 2010.

12. R. Deibert and R. Rohozinski, Contesting cyberspace and the coming crisis of authority, in R. Deibert et al., *Access Contested: Security, Identity and Resistance in Asian Cyberspace* (Cambridge, MA: MIT, 2011), 21–41.

13. The US position is more ambiguous with regard to blocking access or filtering links to sites that host pirated intellectual property, as seen in the recent debates over proposed anti-piracy legislation, viz., SOPA and PIPA. These would have required search engines to bar links to such sites, and Internet service providers to block access to such sites. Responding to a petition against these bills, the Obama Administration said it would not support legislation with provisions that could lead to Internet censorship, squelching of innovation, or reduced Internet security, but supported closing down such sites by judicial means.

14. See P. Yannakogeorgos, The new frontier and the same old multilateralism, in S. Reich, *Global Norms, American Sponsorship and the Emerging Patterns of World Politics* (Houndsmill, UK: Palgrave, 2011), 147–177.

15. J. Westby, A call for geo-cyber stability, in H. Touré et al., *The Quest for Cyber Peace*. International Telecommunications Union, 2011, 67. http://www.itu.int/dms_pub/itu-s/opb/gen/S-GEN-WFS.01-1-2011-PDF-E.pdf; the Russian draft for a Convention on International Information Security, presented to the "International meeting of high-ranking officials responsible for security matters," Ekaterinburg, Russia, September 21–22, 2011, proposes, "in any international conflict, the right of the States Parties that are involved in the conflict to choose the means of 'information warfare' is limited by applicable norms of international humanitarian law."

16. These efforts include but are not limited to the Russia-US bilateral on critical infrastructure protection, Working toward rules for governing cyber conflict, EastWest Institute, February 2011.

17. For Chinese and Russian doctrines of information warfare see, respectively, T. Thomas, *Dragon Bytes: Chinese Information—War Theory and Practice* (Ft. Leavenworth, KS: Foreign Military Studies Office, 2004); T. Thomas, The Russian understanding of information operations and information warfare, in D. Alberts and D. Papp, eds., *Information Age Anthology: The Information Age Military* (Washington, DC: DoD, C4ISR Cooperative Research Program, 2001), 777-815; W. Hagestad II, *21st Century Chinese Cyberwarfare* (IT Governance, 2012).

18. Direct involvement of the Russian government or military command in organizing DDoS attacks on Georgia or the earlier ones on Estonia is a matter of debate, but undoubtedly the government knew of them beforehand and condoned them afterward. Another possible use of cyber weapons during a military action is Israel's alleged penetrations of Syrian military networks to neutralize the missile defense around the nuclear reactor that Israel bombed in 2007, see R. Clarke and R. Knake, *Cyberwar* (New York: Ecco, 2010).

19. See Information Warfare Monitor & Shadowserver Foundation, *Shadows in the Cloud: Investigating Cyber Espionage 2.0*, April 6, 2010, http://www.scribd.com/doc/29435784/SHADOWS-IN-THE-CLOUD-Investigating-Cyber-Espionage-2-0; Information Warfare Monitor, *Tracking GhostNet: Investigating a Cyber Espionage Network*, March 29, 2009, http://www.nartv.org/mirror/ghostnet.pdf; US-China Economic and Security Review Commission, *2010 Report to Congress* (Washington,

DC: US Government Printing Office, 2010), 236–247, http://origin. www.uscc.gov/sites/default/files/annual_reports/2010-Report-to-Congress.pdf, p. 236.

20. Z. Fryer-Biggs, U.S. Military Goes on Cyber Offensive, *Defense News*, March 24, 2012, http://www.defensenews.com/article/20120324/ DEFREG02/303240001/U-S-Military-Goes-Cyber-Offensive; J. Miller, DoD Using Cyber Teams Like Aircraft—For Offense and Defense, FederalNewsRadio.com, May 5, 2012, http://www.federalnews-radio.com/?nid=394&sid=2852854.

21. Letter dated September 12, 2011, from the Permanent Representatives of China, the Russian Federation, Tajikistan, and Uzbekistan to the United Nations addressed to the Secretary General, http://cs.brown.edu/courses/ csci1800/sources/2012_UN_Russia_and_China_Code_o_Conduct.pdf

22. IBSA Multistakeholder meeting on global Internet governance, September 1–2, 2011, Recommendations. http://www.culturalivre. org.br/artigos/IBSA_recommendations_Internet_Governance. pdf; see also T. Ramachandran, Plan for new global body to oversee Internet governance evokes mixed response. *The Hindu*, October 23, 2011. http://www.thehindu.com/scitech/internet/article2565390.ece.

23. The Cyber Norms Workshop, Computer Science and Artificial Intelligence Laboratory, Massachusetts Institute of Technology, October 19–21, 2011. For agenda, participants, framing questions, and prelimi-nary report, see http://www.citizenlab.org/cybernorms/. The sponsors included The Belfer Center for Science and International Affairs at the Harvard Kennedy School of Government; The Canada Centre for Global Security Studies and Citizen Lab at the University of Toronto's Munk School of Global Affairs; Explorations in Cyber International Relations (ECIR), a joint Harvard-MIT research project; Microsoft Corporation's Office of Global Security Strategy and Diplomacy (GSSD); MIT's Computer Science and Artificial Intelligence Laboratory (CSAIL); and The John D. and Catherine T. MacArthur Foundation. The opin-ions, findings, conclusions, or recommendations expressed here do not necessarily reflect those of any of these organizations. A second cyber norms workshop in September, 2012, was sponsored by Belfer Center, Canada Centre, Citizen Lab, MacArthur Foundation, and Microsoft. For information and panel summaries, see http://www.citizenlab.org/ cybernorms2012/

24. Table 14.1 is based on C. Kavanagh, Wither "rules of the road" for cyberspace? CyberDialogue2012, March 18–19, 2012, Toronto, Canada. http://www.cyberdialogue.ca/briefs/.

25. R. Wall, NATO urged on missile and cyber-defense. *Aviation Week*. May 18, 2010. http://www.stopnato.net/?p=45463

26. M. Schmitt, Cyber operations and the jus ad bellum revisited. *Villanova Law Review*, 56 (2011), 569–605.

27. For example, D. Hollis, Could deploying Stuxnet be a war crime? *Opinio Juris*, January 25, 2011. http://opiniojuris.org/2011/01/25/could-deploy-ing-stuxnet-be-a-war-crime/. "Conditions cry out for (a) states to devise

specific rules for launching or defending against cyber exploitations and cyber attacks; and (b) adopting an e-SOS as a first principle for mitigating or avoiding the most severe cyber threats. I don't think such rules would necessarily mean states could never deploy a Stuxnet (or that Iran would have an absolute right to issue an e-SOS if they did so). Rather, I think states themselves will have to devise the specific contours of acceptable (and unacceptable) behavior in cyberspace and then defend their own acts on such terms. Without those rules, I worry that the very technology that we have welcomed for its transformative effects on our everyday lives may generate new forms of death and destruction for which the Stuxnet episode is merely an opening act."

28. K. Rauscher and A. Korotkov, Working Towards Rules for Governing Cyber Conflict: Rendering the Geneva and Hague Conventions in Cyberspace. EastWest Institute, January 2011.
29. S. Schjølberg, Wanted: A United Nations cyberspace treaty. In A. Nagorski, ed., *Global Cyber Deterrence: Views from China, the U.S., Russia, India, and Norway*. EastWest Institute, 2010, 11.
30. S. Kim et al., A comparative study of cyberattacks. *Communications of the ACM*, 55:3, March 2012, 66–73.
31. Chinese police chief vows international cooperation in fighting Internet crimes. *Xinhua*, August 30, 2011. http://news.xinhuanet.com/english2010/china/2011-08/30/c_131085036.htm. Unfortunately the FBI, which initiated the investigation, gave the Chinese police very little credit in its press release on the operation. By not appreciating the importance the Chinese attached to the cooperation, it missed an opportunity for building a relationship.
32. J. Mallery, private communication.
33. A. Wolfers, Discord and collaboration: essays on international relations. Baltimore, MD: 1962, cited in J. Nye, *The Future of Power*. New York: 2011, 16.

15

Cyberdefense as Environmental Protection—The Broader Potential Impact of Failed Defensive Counter Cyber Operations

JAN KALLBERG

ROSEMARY A. BURK

Contents

Introduction	265
The Concept of Cyberwar	268
Environmental Effects of Cyberwar	269
Hydroelectric Dams and Reservoirs	270
US Chemical Industry	271
Public Opinion and Sentiment	271
Loss of Legitimacy and Authority	272
Environmental Cyberdefense	273
Endnotes	274

Introduction

Key in the critique of the likelihood of cyber conflict has been the assumption that cyber does not lead to long-term and irrevocable effects; therefore it cannot be fought as a war. This might be true if cyber attacks are constrained to specific functions of a computer system or set of client computers; however, a failed cyberdefense can have wider effects than discussed in earlier debates of potential consequences and risks. The environmental aspect of cyberdefense has not drawn attention as a national security matter. We all, as people, react to threats to our living space and natural environment. Jeopardizing the environment, unintended or intended, has historically led to the immediate injection of fear and strong reactions in the population. Even unanticipated accidents with environmental impact have triggered strong moves in the public sentiment toward fear, panic, anger against government, and challenges to public authority.

One such example is the Three Mile Island (Pennsylvania) accident that created significant public turbulence and fear—an incident that still has a profound impact on how we envision nuclear power. For a covert state actor that seeks to cripple our society, embarrass the political leadership, and project to the world that we cannot defend ourselves, environmental damages are inviting. An attack on the environment feels for the general public more close and scary than a dozen servers malfunctioning in a server park. We are all dependent on clean drinking water and non-toxic air. Cyber attacks on these fundamentals for life could create panic and desperation in the general public, even if the reacting citizens were not directly affected.

Adversarial nations pursue covertly, or later as open hostile acts in a cyber conflict, the ability to create significant damage and disruption as noted by the President of the United States in the report "Sustaining US Global Leadership: Priorities for 21st Century Defense":

> Both state and non-state actors possess the capability and intent to conduct cyber espionage and, potentially, cyber attacks on the United States, with possible severe effects on both our military operations and our homeland.[1]

The US Secretary of Defense Leon Panetta delivered in his speech on October 12, 2012, a clear assessment of the risk for these attacks:

> These attacks mark a significant escalation of the cyber threat and they have renewed concerns about still more destructive scenarios that could unfold. For example, we know that foreign cyber actors are probing America's critical infrastructure networks. They are targeting the computer control systems that operate chemical, electricity and water plants and those that guide transportation throughout this country.
>
> We know of specific instances where intruders have successfully gained access to these control systems. We also know that they are

seeking to create advanced tools to attack these systems and cause panic and destruction and even the loss of life.[2]

Even if the nation's leadership has identified the risk, expressed concern, and started to allocate resources to improve national cyberdefense, the likelihood of a cyberwar is considered by some scholars to be marginal.[3] One of the leading arguments against the likelihood for future cyberwar has been the absence of long-term damage.[3] This argument is based on a marginalization of cyber attacks as intermittent disruptions of client computers built on crude and unsophisticated distributed malign software that creates temporal havoc.[4] These attacks are portrayed to be anecdotal disruptions of minor importance, maybe not even noticed by the target. The perception of damage is limited to the attacked computer networks, not the external environment that relies on these networks. The wider and holistic outlook on cyber, beyond the computer networks, is embedded in the concerns aired by Secretary of Defense Leon Panetta, originating from the assessment made by the President.

In this chapter we present a tangible argument for the long-term damage cyberwar can inflict on a targeted society beyond the actual destruction of a defending computer network. When a computer system, such as an industrial control system, fails, it is a component of a larger system. A failure in the larger system can create long-term environmental consequences. The environmental damage is a consequence of a lost cyberwar and failed national cyberdefense.

The last decade's intense study of cyber security with a focus on networks and network security has left the environmental risk posed by cyber-controlled networks unaddressed.[5] Cyber security tends to be narrowly focused on information assurance and the network conduit. The focus on cyber security has included providing for restoration of information systems by incorporating detection, protective, and reactive capabilities. From information security's early inception in the 1980s to today's secured environments, we have become skilled in our ability to secure and harden information systems. The fluid, even soon-automated, battlefield of cyber operations is a novelty.

An automated attack can discover and exploit a multitude of vulnerabilities, and by doing so can attack a specific utility at many locations at the same time. Instead of focusing on hardening systems, cyberdefense has to go beyond the actual computer system and see what is impacted by the computer system and the effects that can occur.

The Concept of Cyberwar

Cyberwar, as any war, is a conflict between state actors in the pursuit of seeking a policy change in the other party. Therefore, cyberwar has to be seen first from a strategic viewpoint and second from lower levels of abstraction. A central part in all conflict is the fear of consequences—the actual repercussions of opposition to a will that seeks to subdue. The reason why nuclear weapons are feared is because the weapons have validated and visualized devastating effects. Cyber weapons will need to show damage; otherwise the threat or deterrence with cyber weapons evaporates. In earlier studies of cyberwar, the key focus included technical or military temporal capacity disruptions and resilience through the ability to operate in a degraded environment. The potential ability to destroy opposing systems through digital lethality has only recently been introduced.[6] In these scenarios, the factual long-term damage is limited. For an adversary who seeks to impact US policy, current vulnerabilities in our industrial control systems are an inviting opportunity because of the possibility of tangible damage. Industrial control systems are viable targets mainly by several second-tier effects such as societal impact factors—fear, uncertainty, and public pressure on political leadership if environmental damage occurs.

Attacking industrial control systems in pursuit of environmental damage is an act of war. As long as attribution is unsolved and there is no punitive mechanism in place, the prohibitions against such acts in international law are at the attacker's discretion to recognize. If the adversary is skilled, it is more likely the attribution investigation will end with a set of spoofed, innocent actors whose digital identities have been exploited in the attack rather than attribution to the real perpetrator. A strong suspicion would impact interstate relations, but full attribution and traceability are needed to create a case for reprisal and retaliation. Today, there are limited options to enforce accountability for cyber attacks through international law, if any. The threat posed by the adversarial nations' pursuit to hijack industrial control systems in covert cyber operations becomes real when there are no risks for the attacking party. The scenario becomes more complex if a state actor gathers information about cyber vulnerabilities in the networks of a targeted organization or other nation and then outsources the attack to a criminal or terrorist network. This innovative *modus operandi* creates numerous obstacles and considerations for the targeted country. States can pay to get things done. If necessary, a covertly operating state can pay criminal networks cash, drugs, weapons, or any currency to act as a proxy. Terrorist organizations can finance their operations through cyber operational "entrepreneurship" instead of engaging in other forms of financing far riskier for detection such as drug dealing and credit card fraud. The covert warfare in cyberspace resembles in many cases the covert operations in the Cold War. The targeted country, or organization, could assume where the attack is coming from, but attribution is not strong enough for retribution.

Environmental Effects of Cyberwar

If an adversary can create major irreversible environmental damage to the United States through cyber attacks on industrial control systems, or even pre-conflict establish control over numerous systems, it would defuse US policy options. The threat and risk have to be considered, and it would give a minor power a force multiplying effect in a direct conflict with the United States.

The barrage of cyber attacks on the nation's infrastructure in the last decade is a major concern for the federal government.[7] These attacks have been extended to include SCADA (supervisory control and data acquisition) systems, which are a subset of industrial control systems. SCADA systems control the processes in our industry, energy sector, transportation, lights, and signals, and are the backbone in the technical structure of our society. SCADA systems can remain viable for decades, depending on the processes and machinery these systems control. However, SCADA systems often lack capacity or are difficult to upgrade to meet contemporary cyber security challenges. Many of these systems were never intended or designed to be connected to any other computer, let alone linked to a global information network such as the Internet conduit. The range of vulnerabilities has increased dramatically as embedded software in electro-mechanical machinery has become a standard feature. These programmable controllers in industry and utility companies have limited cyber security features. The hardening and increased protection of American SCADA systems is likely to take decades; the majority of SCADA systems are not upgraded once installed or need additional computer hardware to be secured. Defense in depth, where corporations and municipalities are parties as well as the Department of Defense and other federal agencies, offer the best prospect for defending these systems. The most able components in these defensive layers reside within the federal sphere. The question is that if cyberdefense fails, what could happen? The environmental ramifications have not received appropriate attention in comparison to the potential threat.

Hydroelectric Dams and Reservoirs

As an example, a cascading effect of failing dams in a larger watershed would have significant environmental impact. Hydroelectric dams and reservoirs are controlled using different forms of computer networks, either cable or wireless, and the control networks are connected to the Internet. A breach in the cyberdefenses for the electric utility company leads all the way down to the logic controllers that instruct the electric machinery to open the floodgates. Many hydroelectric dams and reservoirs are designed as a chain of dams in a major watershed to create an even flow of water that is utilized to generate energy. A cyber attack on several upstream dams would release water that increases pressure on downstream dams. With rapidly diminishing storage capacity, downstream dams risk being breached by the oncoming water. Eventually, it can turn to a cascading effect through the river system which could result in a catastrophic flood event. The traditional cyber security way to frame the problem is the loss of function and disruption in electricity generation, overlooking the potential environmental effect of an inland tsunami. This is especially troublesome in areas where the population and the industries are dense along a river; for example, Pennsylvania, West Virginia, and other areas with cities built around historic mills. If the cyber attack occurs during a hurricane[8] when the dams are already stressed, any rapid increase in water level that adds to the hurricane can trigger cascading dam collapses. This could lead to a catastrophic loss of lives and property and a corresponding loss of hydroelectric capacity. The environmental effects would be dramatic and long term: freshwater resources would be contaminated, entire ecosystems destroyed, toxic agents released, and there would be massive soil erosion. Populations of fishes could be decimated along with fisheries that rely upon them. The short-term and long-term effects would be substantial, and restoration efforts could be beyond the national financial reach. The environmental damage is then long-term or permanent.

US Chemical Industry

Another example is the sizable US chemical industry. Manufacturing plants and storage facilities store large quantities of industrial chemicals. The US chemical industry produced chemical products to a value of $759 billion in 2011.[9] Over 96% of all manufactured products in the United States rely on chemical input material. The United States produces 15% of the world's chemicals. In the United States, each year 847 million tons of chemicals are transported on railways, highways, and freight ships.[10] The transportation routes are adjacent or passing creeks, rivers, ground water aquifers, urban areas, and agricultural land. These chemical fluids can, once released, create contamination that requires long-term mitigation, restoration, and in some cases land subsidence equal to an EPA superfund site.[11] If Syria, or any other totalitarian adversarial nation, used chemical weapons against Americans the response would have biblical proportions. An attack on the industrial control systems in our chemical industry could have a similar effect with limited risk of severe repercussions for the attacker. Chemicals can infiltrate to groundwater and make the water a health hazard, pollute the air, contaminate soil, and lead to land subsidence for housing, agriculture, and development.

Public Opinion and Sentiment

Environmental damages are tangible and highly visible—flooding, undrinkable water, mudslides, toxic air, and chemical spills directly affect the population and their surrounding environment. A failed computer server park does not drive media attention as a hundred thousand dead fish floating down a river. The environmental impact is visible, connects with people on a visceral level, and generates a notion that the human core of existence is in jeopardy. Environmental damages can trigger radical shifts in the public mind and general sentiment. For a minor state actor, such as an adversarial developing nation, these attacks can be done with marginal budget and resources and still create significant political turbulence and loss of confidence in the target population of a major power. War, as mentioned, seeks to change policy and influence another nation to take steps that it earlier was unwilling to take. The panic that can follow environmental damages is a political force worth recognizing.

Loss of Legitimacy and Authority

Covert successful cyber attacks that lead to environmental impact are troublesome for the government, not only the damage but also the challenge to legitimacy, authority, and confidence in the government and political leadership. The citizens expect the state to protect them. The protection of th citizens is a part of the unwritten social contract between then citizens and the government. The federal government's ability to protect is taken for granted—it is assumed to be in place. If government fails to protect and safeguard the citizens, legitimacy is challenged. Legitimacy concerns not who can lead but who can govern. A failure to protect is a failure to govern the nation, and legitimacy is eroded. Political scientist Dwight Waldo believed that we need faith in government; for government to have a strong legitimacy it has to project, deliver, and promise that life would be better for citizens. In a democracy, voters need a sense that they are represented, government works in their best interests, and government improves life for citizens and voters. In the "Administrative State,"[12] Waldo defined his vision of the "good life" as the best possible life for the population that can be achieved based on time, technology, and resources.[13] Authority is the ability to implement policy.

Environmental hazards that lead to loss of life and dramatic long-term loss of life quality for citizens trigger a demand for the government to act. If the population questions the government's ability to protect and safeguard, the government's legitimacy and authority will suffer. One example is the Three Mile Island accident that had an impact, even decades after the incident, on how citizens perceived the government's nuclear policies and ability to ensure that nuclear power was a safe energy source. Harold R. Denton, the director of the Office of Nuclear Reactor Regulation, was able to calm the public and reduce fear during the Three Mile Island accident.[14] During the duration of the events, Harold R. Denton was President Carter's personal representative at the site.[15] It was essential for President Carter to show and project ability to handle the incident and to restore confidence in the general public for the government's energy policies. Environmental risks tend to appeal not only to the general public's logic but also to emotions—foremost to the notion of uncertainty and fear. A population that fears the future has lost confidence in government.

The difference between the Three Mile Island incident and cyber attacks on our infrastructure creating environmental damage is that the Three Mile Island incident was local, solitary, and could be contained and understood. During the Three Mile Island incident, millions of Americans had a sincere fear for their life and future when faced with the possibility of a nuclear meltdown.

Cyber attacks on our national infrastructure cannot be predicted or contained, and these attacks can be massive if the exploit utilized for the attack is a vulnerability that many systems contain. The fear generated by the Three Mile Island incident could in retrospect have been marginal compared to the fear that could be generated by a large-scale cyber attack on the national infrastructure.

Environmental Cyberdefense

Defending American infrastructure from cyber attacks is not only protecting information, network availability, or the global information grid, it is also safeguarding the lives of citizens and property and protecting ecosystems and the ecosystem services that we rely upon. Attacks on the environment and the quality of life of the citizenry directly affect the confidence the population has in the government's ability to govern.

The national cyberdefense organized by the Department of Defense and other government agencies is on a "green" mission to ensure that cyber attacks do not create devastating environmental damage within the United States and loss of quality of life. For an adversarial nation that seeks to influence our population and inject fear, cyber-created environmental damages have a high payoff, especially if the cyber operations are covert and unlikely to be attributed. Successful cyberdefense mitigates the risk for significant damage to our natural resources such as drinking water and aquatic and adjacent terrestrial ecosystems—protecting biological diversity. The risk posed by the adversarial nations' pursuit to hijack industrial control systems in covert cyber operations cannot be ignored as a national security concern. Cyberdefense is, due to the consequences of failing, not only a military matter but an environmental protection issue.

Endnotes

1. Obama, Barack, and Leon E. Panetta. Sustaining US global leadership: Priorities for 21st century defense. Vol. 1. Washington DC: The White House, 2012.
2. Defending the Nation from Cyber Attack (Business Executives for National Security), as delivered by Secretary of Defense Leon E. Panetta, New York, October 11, 2012.
3. Rid, Thomas. Cyber war will not take place. *Journal of Strategic Studies* 35, no. 1 (2012): 5–32.
4. Rid, Thomas, and Peter McBurney. Cyber-weapons. *The RUSI Journal* 157, no. 1 (2012): 6–13.
5. Turk, Robert J. Idaho National Laboratory. 2005. US-CERT Control Systems Security Center. Cyber Incidents Involving Control Systems. INL/EXT-05-00671. http://www.inl.gov/technicalpublications/documents/3480144.pdf.
6. Kallberg, Jan, and Adam Lowther. The return of Dr. Strangelove. *The Diplomat*, August 20, 2012.
7. Lynn III, William F. Defending a new domain—The Pentagon's cyberstrategy. *Foreign Affairs* 89 (2010): 97.
8. Susman, Tina, Molly Hennessy-Fiske, and John M. Glionna. Isaac leaves hundreds of homes underwater; dam shows stress. *Los Angeles Times*, August 30, 2012. http://articles.latimes.com/2012/aug/30/nation/la-na-isaac-storm-20120831.
9. American Chemistry Council. http://www.americanchemistry.com/Jobs/EconomicStatistics/Industry-Profile/Global-Business-of-Chemistry.
10. American Chemistry Council. Global Business of Chemistry. http://www.americanchemistry.com/chemistry-industry-facts.
11. EPA. Superfund Sites. National Priorities List. http://www.epa.gov/superfund/sites/npl/where.htm.
12. Waldo, Dwight. (1948) 1984. *The Administrative State*. New York: Holmes & Meier.
13. Waldo, Dwight. 1980. *The Enterprise of Public Administration*. Novato: Chandler & Sharp.

14. Pennsylvania Historical & Museum Collection. Manuscript Group 471: Harold and Lucinda Denton Papers. Accident at Three Mile Island. http://www.portal.state.pa.us/portal/server.pt/community/documents_from_1946_-_present/20426/three_mile_island/999081.
15. PBS. People and Events: Harold R. Denton. http://www.pbs.org/wgbh/amex/three/peopleevents/pandeAMEX87.html.

16

Cyber Sovereignty

STEPHEN K. GOURLEY

Contents

What's in a Definition?   278
Sovereignty over Cyber Space   279
International Law Pertaining to Cyber Space   280
National Security Implications   282
Sovereignty in Cyber Space   286
Conclusion   288
Endnotes   289

In 2011, as the popular uprising in Syria began to take hold, all Internet service in that country stopped, cut off by decree of the Syrian government.[1] Soon thereafter, a deputy assistant secretary of state testified before Congress, noting a recent increase in Internet repression. During the hearing, the blocking of social networking sites in Belarus, government requests to Turkish Internet service providers for information filtering, and website editing in Kazakhstan were noted.[2] Many jurisdictions are using Internet addresses with political boundary designators, such as ".fr," ".uk," and ".co.us." In addition, Iran is in the process of creating its own, internal version of the Internet as a method to control public access only to "halal" information, that which conforms to Islamic law.[3] Why would any nation-state believe it has the authority to take action to limit activities in cyber space? Does the United States have a stake in other nations' policies and conduct as they pertain to cyber activities? One might infer cyber space is subject to sovereignty, one way or another. If so, there are implications to the national security of the United States.

The actions by nation-states to control or limit the use of cyber space within their borders lead to confusion between perception and reality. The perception is that cyber space is universal, ethereal, and open to all. To a great extent, it is attractive, functional, and prosperous because the most common experience is one of universal reach and access. The reality is this reach and access occurs through physical and logical network layers, composed of communications systems, various computational machines, and the software implemented over them, each with a unique geographical location. A full understanding of the dichotomy between perception and reality, and the attendant implications, should inform our national security policies regarding cyber activities, including what we consider to be appropriate norms of conduct. The implications to our national security might also drive us to seek agreements internationally, so as to support common norms and laws acceptable to our national interests.

What's in a Definition?

Most definitions of cyber space focus on the physical aspects of the cyber environment, to include information and communication infrastructures (computers, cables, servers, wireless devices, and software) and interconnected digital networks. Some identify it as a domain, akin to land, sea, air, and outer space. Definitions that are principally physical in nature are inadequate, given the common perception of cyber space as being ethereal. A better approach is to separate the physical and ethereal aspects and deal with them appropriately. Accordingly, the physical and network aspects of cyber become the "cyber domain" (or environment), and the wholly contained "ether" as "cyber space" (written as two words). The cyber domain includes all the physical components and networks (e.g., Internet, bluetooth), and any portion of the electro-magnetic spectrum used for communication; in other words, anything that provides the means to transmit, store, or modify digital information. "Cyber" thereby becomes an adjective for "via digital electronic means," leading to "cyber space" as the virtual volume encompassed by the cyber domain and "cyber activities" as actions taken by a human "cyber actor." Cyber activities take place "through" the cyber domain "in" cyber space. This distinction may allow us to differentiate the domain (the media) from the space. It will allow the juxtaposition of the physical and ethereal concepts, and deal with their implications separately and logically. The distinction may also allow us to address the issue of whether the activities really matter more than the domain.

Sovereignty over Cyber Space

Policies stated and actions taken by other nation-states to control information passing through the cyber domain might be interpreted as exercising sovereignty in cyber space. This is commensurate with the realist concept of sovereignty, which holds that sovereignty exists as control over specific territory, defined by boundaries, nominally the borders of a nation-state. In this concept, the state possesses sole jurisdiction and asserts its jurisdiction via two principles: territoriality and effects. The territoriality principle allows it to control transactions occurring within and across its borders, while the effects principle gives it jurisdiction over external activities that cause effects internally. This concept specifies control as the first criterion of statehood. As the cyber domain is an infrastructure with geographical ties, an artificial, man-made construct, each component is subject to the laws and jurisdiction of a sovereign authority. This is in concert with the territoriality principle of the realist concept.

For cyber space, however, the case is not so clear. First, nation-states universally haven't recognized sovereignty in cyber space. Each nation-state's policies and practices are different. Where one might consider cyber space a global commons (United States), another perceives it to be a domain demanding control, lest undue influences reach its populace (China). Second, nation-states currently don't control directly cyber space or the activities occurring in it. This may be a consequence of the inability to attribute adequately actions to actors, as well as the lack of consensus as to what constitutes reasonable response. Poor attribution increases the uncertainty that responses are properly directed and the attendant risk that the response will be unreasonable or disproportional. Finally, many nation-states have not concluded exerting sovereignty is in their national interest, especially democratic nations, where the civilian populations have the expectation that cyber space is free and open. This conundrum would seem to be reflected in current US strategic thought, which never declares US sovereignty but puts forth a policy of an open, interoperable, secure, and reliable cyber domain with the stated objectives to secure many of the benefits that come with sovereignty.

The motivation for the United States is that cyber security, and ultimately national security, is predicated on certain aspects that sovereignty in cyber space grants, even though other aspects of sovereignty may jeopardize our national security. The trick is to find the right balance. Cyber space needs the jurisdictional authority sovereign control allows to bring security and stability to the daily interactions and transactions occurring in it. Activities in cyber space have real-world effects, and these too are subject to sovereignty under the effects principle of the realist concept.

In the absence of agreement regarding sovereignty *in* cyber space, however, it may be sufficient to recognize effective sovereignty *over* cyber space. It is fully contained within, and constricted by, the cyber domain, which is subject to the jurisdictions of the nation-states in which the components reside. While this may seem like putting a very fine point on terminology, it allows us to address the implications of (effective) sovereignty, while awaiting the solutions to the political and technical challenges of establishing full sovereignty (whether as territory of nation-states or as a sovereign dominion in and of itself), which are only matters of will and time. This recognition also rectifies the behavior of various nation-states' attempts to control cyber activities, especially access to information, with the perception of universal reach and access.

International Law Pertaining to Cyber Space

Cyber space in all its dimensions is used by millions of people in many countries. Social networks, shopping, entertainment, personal interaction, and research have all become easy and convenient with the advent of instantaneous, digital communication. Cyber space transcends national borders, oceanic barriers, and cultural divides. Certainly, there must be a body of international law governing cyber relationships between nation-states and regulating international commerce. Unfortunately, there is not.

Here again is the basic confusion between the perception and the reality of the cyber experience. For most applications, international law evolves from the policy and behaviors of nation-states in the domain, occasionally supplemented by signed, international agreements. Treaties may be the most well-known mechanism for concluding agreement between nation-states, but they are not the principal way of establishing international law.[4] Only in the case of outer space did an agreement come first. The Outer Space Treaty, as it is known, culminated very rapid discussions early in the Space Age, driven by the suddenness of the first space launches and the desire to limit nationalism to the planet. The creation of the cyber domain and the use of cyber space evolved more slowly than outer space, so there was no initial and immediate concern one nation may claim it for itself. More importantly, cyber space came into existence with the broad expectation of being open and free. This perception of universal reach and access, potentially coupled with the existence of informal, technical organizations for Internet governance and the desire for a global commons, has led to a lack of urgency for establishing agreements among nation-states.

The relatively short time frame involved precludes a good baseline of behavior and the evolution of acceptable practices, as it did for the international portions of the sea and air domains. That baseline, however, is emerging with the way nation-states allow the system to operate daily. Permitting universal reach and access through the Internet, as most owners of cyber domain components do allow, establishes a routine practice. This custom of free passage sets precedence, as does the countervailing restriction of certain information by some countries. If free passage is not guaranteed because domain owners exercise some level of control over cyber space, a different precedent is set, potentially the exercise of national sovereignty.

Policy and practice include inaction, as well as action. "Sometimes, even state inaction can establish practice...passiveness and inaction can produce a binding effect under what is called the doctrine of acquiescence."[5] The lack of action after cyber "attacks" in Estonia, Georgia, the United States, and Iran over the last five years begins to set precedent on which to base international law. Inaction may be due to the current inability to establish clearly which cyber actor initiated the activity, whether a nation-state or an individual, and under what circumstances. Nonetheless, acquiescence to cyber activities, regardless of whether they are benign, criminal, or state sponsored, begins to define what acceptable behavior in cyber space is. If unreliable attribution stays the hand of jurisprudence, it puts much greater onus on policy and agreements to shape the cyber environment any differently. "In the long run, negotiated and enforceable agreements governing cyberspace may be a better option than waiting for the necessarily languid development of custom in an area that changes at the speed of thought."[6]

As of 2012, despite the real-world experiences that might demand more rigorous reactions and governance, there is insufficient precedent of policy and practice and no agreements to form the basis of international law in cyber space. And yet, clearly the United States has a great stake in the behavior of all nation-states as it establishes the basis for future (international) law. Current world events, a few policy statements, and actions (and inactions) by nation-states are providing the foundation for future international law regarding sovereignty in cyber space. The majority of these precedents are being set indirectly through control and manipulation of the cyber domain. Although there may not be a collective understanding that sovereignty indeed applies to cyber space; suppose it does—what then?

National Security Implications

> International engagement has become even more important...as nations seek to extend sovereign control into cyberspace. Cyberspace is not a commons; other countries have realized this and are acting to protect their own sovereign interests.[7]

Sovereignty in cyber space might not currently exist, but it may evolve with an improved technical capability to attribute actions and control the space from within (versus controlling the space via the domain). Alternatively, cyber space may be established as a domain subject to sovereignty (by nations or by itself) via policy and practice, or simply declared and agreed to be a purely international space, a free and open global commons. Regardless of the means, what might be the US national security repercussions of sovereignty? The US wields four instruments of national power in the furtherance of its national interest: diplomatic, information, military, and economic. Sovereignty, however, creates ambiguities for US national security.

These ambiguities affect each of the instruments in some ways, many subtle in their action.

Nation-states typically will adopt the realist concept of sovereignty regarding cyber space. Initially, the approach will be to control cyber space via control of the domain but will evolve to more direct control as technical capabilities mature. Moreover, although most nation-states will employ the territoriality principle, some will invoke the effects principle, as well, giving them a mechanism to react to cyber activities conducted outside their territory that have an adverse result within their borders. In essence, it is this principle that will be invoked when an actor outside of a nation-state's jurisdiction employs the universal reach and access of cyber space and perpetrates a perceived slight, whether criminal or war-like.

The physicality of the cyber domain leads nation-states to define, enact, and enforce laws and policies, many times differently across borders. A nation's legal system typically manifests the values and mores of its society, and its laws both reflect and color the population's perception of what is acceptable and what is not. Reducing the impact of effective sovereignty internationally starts with a consensus on definitions, best achieved through diplomatic means. This forms the basis for collaboration and cooperation and may be an easy step toward that end. Consensus on the definitions of the cyber domain (environment), cyber space, and cyber activities may lead to an easier agreement on the norms and legality of behavior in cyber space. Norms of behavior form the basis for consistent laws, followed closely by cooperative policing and prosecution (à la Interpol and potentially the International Criminal Court). Easier, however, is not the same as easy. The initiative led by the European Union to define norms of behavior in outer space, although seemingly straightforward, has met with some resistance from budding space powers.[8] This does not bode well for reaching a quick agreement on cyber behavior. Nonetheless, working toward legal commonality provides both a solid basis to eliminate refuge, as well as standardize the status of cyber actors, to include well-defined boundaries between hacker, criminal, and combatant.

Sovereignty most clearly affects information, which may be the United States' most pervasive instrument and the most feared by potential adversaries. American culture has influenced the Iraqi populace, especially the younger folk, to wear hoodies, listen to American rap music, eat hamburgers and pizza, and adopt American hairstyles. "Young Iraqis agree that the American troops have opened their minds to the outside world," strong evidence of the power of information.[9] Iran, on the other hand, in its drive to create a separate Internet for itself, cites the need to "empower Iran and protect its society from cultural invasion and threats," especially the United States.[10] The only way for Iran to limit or restrict access to unwanted information by its populace is to exercise sovereign control. As much as Americans might find it abhorrent and counter to their concept of free speech, the filtering of information in some countries is well within their sovereign rights as a nation. Google reports even the United States has reasonably requested the deletion or withholding of certain information.[11] The United States requested Google banish specific information fifty-four times during July to December 2010, to which Google agreed about forty-eight times. The rationale for banishment included violence, privacy and security, and national security concerns. The United States should expect information filtering and restrictions as they facilitate national policies crafted to protect the national interests of a nation-state. The United States should not expect these national policies to align unswervingly with its own, but work diligently to mitigate the effects of misalignment.

Sovereignty over cyber space affects economics. In today's world market, finance and commerce depend heavily on unimpeded access to and through electronic means of communication. As demonstrated in the run-up to, and culmination of, the 1997 collapse of the Asian Tigers, money flows in and out of markets at the speed of light in cyber space. The availability of capital, critical to the health of economic systems, is facilitated by being able to move funds unimpeded to where they are most needed, and will yield the investor the greatest return on investment. Commerce is also affected. A greater fraction of commerce occurs over the Internet every year; in the United States alone, the increase in online sales year-over-year has been an average of greater than 13% over the last decade.[12] Although restrictions on financial exchange may be within the bounds of sovereignty, the economic effects would be devastating. Limitations on the free flow of financial and commercial transactions and reporting impede free trade, while an open cyber space promotes it, and should be a major objective of US policy.

Another economic implication of sovereignty is the potential for different tax policies on e-commerce. The Internet provides online businesses with better access to broader or widely dispersed markets, making regionally marginal businesses more viable. As an extreme example, wood carvers in Nepal apparently struggled economically, with marketing their biggest challenge. The advent of computers, coupled with the Internet, allowed them to connect with far distant customers, exchange and refine ideas, and then reach agreement on orders from around the world.[13] Yet, purchases occur between two jurisdictions, one for the seller and one for the purchaser. This leads to tax policy questions: Who owes and who is owed? Should taxes be based on the seller's location or the buyer's? Solutions are especially difficult to reach in the case of international commerce, where even the basic precept of taxation is different from one nation to another (e.g., sales tax versus value-added tax).

Lastly, military operations in cyber space must consider sovereignty. Cyber operations come in several flavors. The US Cyber Command defines cyber space operations as "the employment of the full range of cyberspace operations to support combatant command operational requirements and the defense of DoD information networks." The defense of networks within US territory and on US platforms in international domains is well within US territorial sovereignty. The support of combatant command operational requirements, however, may require reaching through the cyber domain to conduct actively defensive or offensive operations. Military operations, conducted through sovereign territory (whether air, land, or sea), typically are not acceptable without the express permission of the nation-state involved. Cyber operations conducted through systems comprising the cyber domain but outside of US jurisdiction may be similarly restricted. As previously discussed, the legal analysis by Brown and Poellet concluded they would not be restricted,[14] but the analysis was based on the assumption that those cyber activities which result in physical outcomes that are non-destructive are similar in nature to espionage, an activity not deemed a violation of sovereignty under international law. This correlation was an assertion by the authors and will be true if and only if nation-states allow it by practice, policy, and agreement. Presently, it is not commensurate with sovereignty over cyber space as currently practiced. Whether it becomes an accepted tenet in international relations is yet to be seen, especially as cyber activities, both active and passive, become more central in focus in the preservation of national sovereignty.

Sovereignty in Cyber Space

Sovereignty *in* cyber space is different than sovereignty *over* cyber space. Sovereignty *in* cyber space has two potential implementations: national sovereignty from border to border or cyber space as a sovereign entity in and of itself. The concept of national sovereignty is well understood. Each nation-state dictates the laws and policies governing the portion of cyber space contained within its borders, a similar circumstance to sovereignty over cyber space.

Cyber space as a separate entity must meet the criteria for sovereignty by surmounting the obstacles posed by the current state of foreign affairs. First, all nation-states must recognize (agree) cyber space is a sovereign entity, not necessarily an impossible situation. This early in the game and given the actions by various nation-states to date, this recognition would have to be by treaty. Second, each nation-state must decide that cyber space as a separate, sovereign entity is in their strategic interests. One example of motivation may be the unwillingness of a nation-state to accrue liability for the actions of a non-state actor within its borders under the territoriality principle. However, actions to date would indicate several nation-states do not see cyber space exempt from their control as a good thing. While there may be good arguments for a sovereign cyber space, none are as compelling to some governments as preventing independent, seditious thoughts stemming from uncontrolled access to information.

Third, each government must manage the expectations of its population regarding cyber space as the implications of a separate, sovereign entity manifest themselves, for example:

- The physical location and nationality of any given actor would not be important; only activity would matter.
- Citizens would be unable to appeal to their local government for any action in cyber space.

- The "Cyber Security Force" would roam free throughout the cyber domain, independent of national borders.
- Posting and downloading information become indistinguishable actions, subject to whatever cyber regulations specify and regardless of any one person's sensibilities.

Last, some governing entity must develop and effectively employ the technical capability to exert sovereignty in cyber space (aka, "Cyber Security Force"). This global world power would have to exercise control over impediments and undesirable activities in cyber space. No current nation-state has the wherewithal today to enforce sovereignty, and most sovereign nations would be reluctant to cede that kind of power to a world organization over a domain critical to national security, least of all the United States.

No sovereignty in cyber space has its own implications. Cyber space as a free and open, global commons not subject to nation-state sovereignty would be a purely international space, akin to the existing, international parts of sea and air, and all of outer space, where the nationalities of the platforms and actors dictate responsibility for actions. Acceptable behavior would be dictated by a growing and evolving custom, rather than the dictates of any one nation-state. International law regarding cyber space would be supplemented by policies and agreements reached via diplomacy. It would be a purely international space with a need for some power to sustain its international status, much as the United States and Great Britain in their time patrolled the high seas to maintain shipping lanes, thereby supporting the concept of international waters. No nation-state or world organization has the means to directly control activities or enforce acceptable behavior (such as universal reach and access). Potentially, indirect methods of control or influence might be employed, but without the legal or technical means for police, judicial, or military action to establish control, there would be no way to preclude nation-states from imposing their will in cyber space. It would be an unruly and more uncertain place to be, traverse (i.e., lower information assurance), or do business, stifling the economic benefits. Should there be an implied or inferred liability by establishing a presence in cyber space through adding to the cyber domain, it would be equivalent to viewing third parties culpable, not neutral, which is critical to avoiding even more draconian implications. Nonetheless, even absent a definitive determination of cyber space as an international domain, free passage might continue to be allowed routinely, much the same way ship, aircraft, and satellites are afforded unhindered use of the international portions of the sea, air, and outer space domains, further setting a standard for behavior and eventually, international law.

As the United States considers how best to posture regarding cyber issues, the implications of the distinctions between sovereignty over cyber space, sovereignty in cyber space, and no cyber sovereignty may become more important.

Conclusion

> [A]mong these (rights) are Life, Liberty and the pursuit of Happiness. – That to secure these rights, Governments are instituted among Men...[15]

Cyber space, widely viewed by many as a free and open global commons, is more logically bounded by sovereignty. It is critical to recognize the real nature of the cyber domain: it is not natural, but man-made and supported, wholly-owned; constructed by humans for human purposes. Cyber activities are carried out by human actors, are directly relatable to human behavior, and have real-world effects. The Founding Fathers of the United States recognized a universal need for some form of governance to regulate human interaction, and cyber activities are no exception. While the realist concept of sovereignty may not be the end-all for establishing governance in cyber space, it correlates the current actions of various nation-states to control what activities are acceptable within it.

Regardless of the form it takes, cyber sovereignty has multiple implications for US national security. Even more importantly, the United States has a direct stake in the policies, actions, and inactions of other nation-states as they set precedent for future international law. These implications and precedents provide greater impetus to achieving agreement on common definitions and norms of conduct. The concept of a free and open cyber space is rooted in American ideals, but free and open is not guaranteed. The relatively universal reach and access through the cyber domain are (tacitly) permitted by the owners of the components, necessitating an increased and more proactive engagement to establish the precedents and agreements needed to make cyber space a safe and secure medium. Nothing in all this reduces the need or the authority for a military to defend its nation, its cyber domain, and the information within cyber space. Defense of the cyber environment and assuring the information within it are the minimum functions required to maintain the readiness of the military, and to further the national interests of the United States.

Endnotes

1. Flock, Elizabeth; "Syria Internet Services Shut Down as Protestors Fill Street;" *The Washington Post*, Blog Post; 3 June 2011; accessed September 12, 2012.
2. Marke, Joseph; "Internet Repression on the Rise Since Arab Spring;" Nextgov.com; July 15, 2011; accessed September 12, 2012.
3. Rhoads, Christopher and Fassihi, Farnaz; "Iran Vows to Unplug Internet;" *The Wall Street Journal*; December 19, 2011.
4. Brown, Gary, Colonel (USAF) and Poellet, Keira, Major (USAF); "The Customary International Law of Cyberspace;" *Strategic Studies Quarterly*; Fall 2012; pp. 126–128.
5. Ibid; p. 129.
6. Ibid; p. 141.
7. Lewis, James A., et al; "Cybersecurity Two Years Later;" Center for Strategic and International Studies; January 2011.
8. Rajagopalan, Rajeswari Pillai; "Asia and a Space Code;" The Diplomat Blogs; January 4, 2012; the-diplomat.com/flashpoints-blog/2012/01/04/asia-and-a-space-code/
9. Juhi, Bushra; "Troops Leaving Iraqi Youths a Gift—Rap Legacy;" The Associated Press; November 23, 2011.
10. See Rhoads and Fassihi, supra note 3.
11. Bergstein, Brian; "Going Offline;" *MIT Technology Review*; November/December 2011; p. 30.
12. inchoo.net/ecommerce/ecommerce-is-growing-but-how-fast/; accessed January 4, 2012.
13. "An American Carves Out a Career in Nepal;" *Fine Woodworking*; October 2003; p. 20.
14. See Brown and Poellet, supra note 4, p. 134.
15. "Declaration of Independence;" Continental Congress; July 4, 1776.

17

AMERICAN CYBERSECURITY TRIAD

Governmentwide Integration, Technological Counterintelligence, and Educational Mobilization

SUNGHYUN KIM

Contents

Introduction   291
Framing of American Cybersecurity Policy into "American
Cybersecurity Triad" from CNCI   292
Governmentwide Integration   293
    Conceptualization   293
    Related CNCI Initiatives and Executions   295
Technological Counterintelligence   298
    Conceptualization   298
    Related CNCI Initiatives and Executions   299
Educational Mobilization   301
    Conceptualization   301
    Related CNCI Initiatives and Executions   302
Conclusion   304
Endnotes   305

Introduction

Cybersecurity is a growing national, as well as international, security concern. However, with the realization that cyberspace has evolved without much priority or emphasis given to security, this chapter aims to look at what defensive measures and practices exist in the United States. To do this, the chapter looks into America's cybersecurity policy, particularly via the Comprehensive National Cybersecurity Initiative (CNCI) that was established by George W. Bush's Administration in 2008, to analyze what executions have been in progress. From this, it is possible to extract three dimensions that help explore the core facets regarding US cybersecurity policy, which is referred to as the "American Cybersecurity Triad."[1] Consequently, these three dimensions are critical in realizing an effective American cybersecurity policy.

Framing of American Cybersecurity Policy into "American Cybersecurity Triad" from CNCI

The CNCI's 12 initiatives focus on the three major goals of establishing a front line of defense against immediate threats, defending against the full spectrum of threats, and shaping the future environment of cybersecurity.[2] First, a front line of defense can be created by enhancing shared situational awareness within the federal, state, local, and tribal governments, as well as private-sector partners. This matches well with the "governmentwide integration" effort of the Cybersecurity Triad. Second, defending against the full spectrum of threats can take place through counterintelligence capabilities and the enhancement of security for key information technologies. This aspect can be represented by the "technological counterintelligence" sphere. Last, the future cybersecurity environment can be strengthened through cyber education, which resembles the "educational mobilization" dimension of the triad. By looking through the CNCI, these three core facets have been discovered to be representative of America's cybersecurity policy.

Findings show that in order to be able to trust cyberspace as well as other cyberspace users around the world, it is crucial for the triad to be realized when applying cybersecurity policy. And all three of these dimensions need to be equally highlighted. Although it can be seen that more CNCI initiatives fall under the governmentwide integration and technological counterintelligence dimensions compared to educational mobilization, this does not necessarily mean that the former two are more important than the latter. The three parts are equally weighed in terms of the amount of significance that each one provides to a wholesome policy. Thus,

a sought out balance is required between all levels of the government, technological developments, and a widespread education system. Table 17.1 presents the classification of the CNCI into the
American Cybersecurity Triad to display the 12 initiatives' representation of the three spheres.

The following are conceptualizations and features extracted from
the CNCI, as well as related executions of the initiatives, to define
each division of the triad frame.

Governmentwide Integration

Conceptualization

The CNCI consists of a number of mutually reinforcing initiatives,
including the goal of an all-encompassing governmentwide integration effort designed to help secure the United States in cyberspace.
Just as "cybersecurity" is a broad term, it carries a distributed function;
it "spans measures that are personal, corporate, federal, and international...[Thus, its function] is not solely a mission of government, the
private sector, or individuals, but is a function shared among them."[3]
As mentioned, the CNCI aims to establish a partnership with federal,
state, local, and tribal governments, as well as the private sector and
even international allies.

In light of the CNCI's goals, the governmentwide integration
dimension of the cybersecurity triad is about the creation of such a
national cybersecurity program. This requires the "fully coordinated
authority and efforts of all federal departments and agencies, state
and local governments, the private sector, and the international community."[4] A lot of the initiatives proposed in the CNCI, in fact, aim to
manage the federal information network as a single entity.[5]

The United States has worked and continues to work on building
on this comprehensive agenda to ensure an organized response that
has been expressed through the term "governmentwide integration."
The word "governmentwide" is used to stress the inclusiveness of
all the levels and layers of government-related relationships, imply-
ing that each level needs to take responsibility for cyber defense in
both individual and integrated ways. "Government-related relationships" means to include the combined efforts of federal, state, local,

Table 17.1 Classification of Comprehensive National Cybersecurity Initiative (CNCI) in "American Cybersecurity Triad"

CNCI	AMERICAN CYBERSECURITY TRIAD
1. Manage the Federal Enterprise Network as a single network enterprise. This includes deploying Trusted Internet Connections by reducing the number of Internet access points to federal agencies.	Technological Counterintelligence
2. Deploy passive sensors across the federal enterprise. This includes using Einstein 1 and 2 intrusion detection systems, which are designed to scan Internet packets for known signatures of malicious code.	Technological Counterintelligence
3. Pursue deployment of intrusion prevention systems across the federal enterprise. This includes using the Einstein 3 system to assess patterns of malicious code in Internet traffic and block packets that are deemed harmful.	Technological Counterintelligence
4. Coordinate and redirect research and development (R&D) efforts. This involves improving progress in developing new technologies by coordinating disparate government R&D efforts.	Governmentwide Integration
5. Connect current cyber operation centers to enhance situational awareness. This involves connecting government cyber warning centers by establishing connectivity between and among the various federal warning centers to promote awareness of threats.	Governmentwide Integration
6. Develop and implement a governmentwide cyber counterintelligence (CI) plan. This includes advancing a single, integrated plan to address physical and electronic threats to US government information systems.	Governmentwide Integration
7. Increase the security of classified networks. This involves protecting the sensitive information that resides on secure government networks against unauthorized disclosure.	Technological Counterintelligence
8. Expand cyber education. This involves promoting training and professional education for cybersecurity experts.	Educational Mobilization
9. Define and develop enduring "leap-ahead" technology, strategies, and programs. This encourages work on developing transformational technologies.	Technological Counterintelligence
10. Define and develop enduring deterrence strategies and programs to reduce vulnerabilities and deter cyber attacks.	Governmentwide Integration
11. Develop a global supply chain risk management plan. This involves reducing the potential threat from counterfeit or compromised technology acquired on the increasingly global and vulnerable market.	Governmentwide Integration
12. Define the federal role of cybersecurity in private-sector domains. This involves establishing new mechanisms to allow government and the private sector to work together in protecting information systems.	Governmentwide Integration

and tribal governments; interagency interactions and private-public partnerships; as well as international cooperation for the enhancement of mutual situational responsiveness of network vulnerabilities and threats. This "governmentwide" effort also extends to the international realm because America's cybersecurity goals occupy not only domestic but also foreign policies—involving how best to establish laws, regulations, and international treaties that can provide a more secure cyberspace worldwide.

Moreover, governmentwide integration is about cybersecurity governance; how policy coordination and operational activities are to be organized across the executive branch. It also involves the entire architecture on how to enable the performance, cost, and security needed in cyberspace through standards, research and development, procurement, and monitoring of the supply chain. Various federal entities "have responsibilities for, and are involved in, international cyberspace governance and security efforts."[6] In particular, the Departments of Commerce (DOC), Defense (DOD), Homeland Security (DHS), Justice (DOJ), and State (DOS), among many others, are working to produce international standards, create cyber-defense policy, and assist overseas investigations as well as law enforcement.[7] Table 17.2 lists and describes the 12 CNCI projects and identifies the lead agencies responsible for each.

Related CNCI Initiatives and Executions

From the 12 CNCI initiatives, 6 of them have been classified to be the responsibility of governmentwide integration. Those include initiatives 4, 5, 6, 10, 11, and 12. The following are findings on some of the main executions of governmentwide integration regarding these initiatives.

On a federal level, cybersecurity was designated as one of the president's key management priorities, helping to establish a performance metric.[8] The White House and federal agencies have taken steps to plan and put forth CNCI initiatives by creating multiple interagency working groups. These interagency groups have been designated to each of the 12 CNCI activities.[9] The government also conducts interagency-cleared legal analyses of priority cybersecurity-related issues, as well as formulates a coherent policy guidance that clari-

Table 17.2 Comprehensive National Cybersecurity Initiative (CNCI) Projects and Lead Agencies

PROJECT	DESCRIPTION	LEAD AGENCY/ AGENCIES
Trusted Internet Connections	Reduce and consolidate external access points with the goal of limiting points of access to the Internet for executive branch civilian agencies.	OMB/DHS
Einstein 2	Deploy passive sensors across executive branch civilian systems that have the ability to scan the content of Internet packets to determine whether they contain malicious code.	DHS
Einstein 3	Pursue deployment of intrusion prevention system that will allow for real-time prevention capabilities that will assess and block harmful code.	DHS/DOD
Research and Development (R&D) Efforts	Coordinate and redirect R&D efforts with a focus on coordinating both classified and unclassified R&D for cybersecurity.	OSTP
Connecting the Centers (includes National Cyber Security Center)	Connect current cyber centers to enhance cyber situational awareness and lead to greater integration and understanding of the cyber threat.	ODNI
Cyber Counterintelligence Plan	Develop governmentwide cyber counterintelligence plan by improving the security of the physical and electromagnetic integrity of US networks.	ODNI/DOJ
Security of Classified Networks	Increase the security of classified networks to reduce the risk of information contained on the government's classified networks being disclosed.	DOD/ODNI
Expand Education	Expand education efforts by constructing a comprehensive federal cyber education and training program, with attention to offensive and defensive skills and capabilities.	DHS/DOD
Leap-Ahead Technology	Define and develop enduring leap-ahead technology, strategies, and programs by investing in high-risk, high-reward research and development and by working with both private-sector and international partners.	OSTP
Deterrence Strategies and Programs	Define and develop enduring deterrence strategies and programs that focus on reducing vulnerabilities and deter interference and attack in cyberspace.	NSC
Global Supply Chain Risk Management	Develop multi-pronged approach for global supply chain risk management while seeking to better manage the federal government's global supply chain.	DHS/DOD

Table 17.2   Comprehensive National Cybersecurity Initiative (CNCI) Projects and Lead Agencies (continued)

PROJECT	DESCRIPTION	LEAD AGENCY/ AGENCIES
Public and Private Partnerships "Project 12"	Define the federal role for extending cybersecurity into critical infrastructure domains and seek to define new mechanisms for the federal government and industry to work together to protect the nation's critical infrastructure.	DHS

Source: GAO, Cybersecurity: Progress Made but Challenges Remain in Defining and Coordinating the Comprehensive National Initiative, GAO-10-338 (2010), 17–18. With permission.

Notes: DHS, Department of Homeland Security; DOD, Department of Defense; DOJ, Department of Justice; NSC, National Security Council; ODNI, Office of the Director of National Intelligence; OMB, Office of Management and Budget; OSTP, Office of Science and Technology Policy.

fies roles, responsibilities, and the application of agency authorities for cybersecurity-related activities.

Moreover, the National Cybersecurity Center was created in March 2008, which furthered the government's progress in addressing cyber threats by coordinating and integrating information across the interagency.[10] There was also the formation of the National Cyber Investigative Joint Task Force (NCIJTF), which was expanded to include representation from the US Secret Service and other federal agencies.[11] In addition, the National Infrastructure Protection Plan (NIPP) has been used to protect and ensure the resiliency of the critical infrastructure and key resources (CIKR), which is essential to national security.[12] The National Cybersecurity and Communications Integration Center (NCCIC)[13] is responsible for the production of a common operating picture for cyber and communications across the federal, state, and local governments, intelligence and law enforcement communities, as well as the private sector.[14]

On a more state, local, or tribal level, a cybersecurity incident response plan has been prepared and a dialog to enhance public-private partnerships has been initiated. The National Cyber Incident Response Plan (NCIRP) was developed and tested during a national cyber exercise called Cyber Storm III.[15] The NCIRP coordinates "the response of multiple federal agencies, state and local governments, and hundreds of private firms, to incidents at all levels…[where] seven Cabinet agencies, eleven states, twelve international partners, and sixty private sector companies all participated."[16]

On an international level, US government positions for an international cybersecurity policy framework have been developed.[17] An important example is the US Computer Emergency Readiness Team (US-CERT),[18] charged with providing response support and defense against cyber attacks for the Federal Civil Executive Branch and information sharing with state and local governments, industry, and international partners.[19] CERTs have been placed all over the world, through the Forum of Incident Response and Security Teams (FIRST) mechanism. Barack Obama's Administration also released the International Strategy for Cyberspace, which attempts to provide a unified foundation for the nation's international engagement on cyberspace issues.[20] These initiatives are noteworthy because they represent "a growing recognition of the mutual interdependence generated by cyberspace."[21] However, "the international agenda for cybersecurity remains one of the least developed parts of US policy."[22]

The Congress, meanwhile, has also taken part in this governmentwide effort by establishing the Cybersecurity Act of 2012.[23] This is the result of months of negotiations with other committees of jurisdiction—the energy, financial services, and chemical industries; national security and privacy and civil liberties groups; and a number of other government agencies.[24] Building on President Bush's CNCI, President Obama's Cyberspace Policy Review identified several near-term actions to support US cybersecurity strategy, which also pushed for a collaborated governmentwide and intergovernmental effort.[25] All of the above-mentioned efforts and executions signify the importance of a cohesive and integrated governmentwide squad, which helps create a more secure cyber world.

Technological Counterintelligence

Conceptualization

The reality of interactive communication and networking has brought on the need for securing the vastness of cyberspace via appropriate technological counterintelligence means. The American government since the CNCI has thus been working on coordinating exhaustive cyber counterintelligence through technological advancements to protect national properties and infrastructure. This involves the collaborated efforts of private and public sectors for development in extensive technologies and computer systems, in order to act quickly in reducing current vulnerabilities, as well as prevent intrusions from taking place.

To defend against the full spectrum of threats, US counterintelligence capabilities are being enhanced and the security of the supply chain for key information technologies is being increased.[26] In this regard, the CNCI pushes to find effective technology solutions that will ensure US security and prosperity. However, the reality is that industry trends, practices, and technologies are always changing; hence, attackers are also finding new ways to bypass security controls and penetrate systems. This is why security practices and technologies must change accordingly so as to be able to protect against new vectors of attack.[27]

Related CNCI Initiatives and Executions

From the 12 CNCI initiatives, 5 of them belong to the responsibility of technological developments for cyber counterintelligence. Those include initiatives 1, 2, 3, 7, and 9. The following are findings on some of the core executions of technological counterintelligence regarding these initiatives.

Various efforts and implementations of the CNCI have been in progress in regard to this dimension of the triad. A primary accomplishment is the Trusted Internet Connections (TIC)[28] mechanism, which is used to consolidate external telecommunication connections and ensure a set of baseline security capabilities for situational awareness and enhanced monitoring.[29] Because things in cyberspace move at Internet speed, there is also the need to move to a system of automated defenses, with real-time detection capabilities and coordinated responses. The DHS works to "move toward agile, interoperable computer systems and networks that can be reliably authenticated and that can recognize and respond to threats in real-time."[30] The Science and Technology Directorate of the DHS is also leading efforts to deploy more secure Internet protocols to protect consumers and industry Internet users, as well as protect Internet infrastructure from attack by creating new tools to detect malicious software on networks.[31]

Improved technology will reduce cyber threats to US national security and strengthen the ability to respond in self-defense.[32]

Building on the CNCI, President Obama's administration has worked on developing a framework for research and development strategies that focus on game-changing technologies. These mechanisms have the potential to enhance the security, reliability, resilience, and trustworthiness of digital infrastructure.[33] President Obama also released the National Strategy for Trusted Identities in Cyberspace (NSTIC).[34] This aims to make online transactions more trustworthy by moving away from passwords and toward secure and reliable credentials; strong authentication has been emphasized because passwords alone provide little security.[35]

As part of its role in the CNCI, the DHS has focused its resources on improving the people, processes, and technology necessary to prevent future attacks and intrusion attempts.[36] One important example is the Einstein Program, which has been expanded to all federal departments and agencies.[37] In close partnership with other agencies and the private sector, the DHS has deployed the National Cybersecurity Protection System, of which the Einstein intrusion detection system is a core component. Einstein helps block malicious actors from accessing federal executive branch civilian agencies, while working closely with those agencies to bolster their own defensive capabilities.[38]

On an extended note, the DHS, along with nine other agencies and the Executive Office of the President (EOP), were also using Einstein 2 as of 2010. Einstein 2 "detects anomalies in network traffic on a particular system and alerts US CERT to those anomalies."[39] Furthermore, the federal government has been developing a successor to Einstein 2: Einstein 3 is to "rely on pre-defined signatures of malicious code that may contain personally identifiable information."[40] Whereas Einstein 2 merely identified and reported malicious code, Einstein 3 is to be able to intercept hostile Internet traffic before it touches government systems.[41]

Other noteworthy efforts for improved technology vis-à-vis CNCI projects have taken place in the private and public sectors. For instance, Governor Bob McDonnell promotes the cyber industry in the Commonwealth of Virginia to relocate business in the field.[42] In addition, Cisco develops and implements a national cybersecurity strategy, supportive of the CNCI, as it recognizes the broad parameters and urgency of the CNCI to require IT triage using prominent technology practices.[43] Fortinet's technology provides leading-edge security in support of the CNCI as well.[44] Last, by providing comprehensive visibility across an organization's entire network, Lancope's StealthWatch System not only supports compliance with the CNCI, TIC, and other federal initiatives, but also significantly improves the security posture of federal agencies.[45] These aforementioned plans and implementations of the CNCI indicate the importance of a sought-out technological counterintelligence mechanism that is essential in American cybersecurity policy.

Educational Mobilization

Conceptualization

Governmentwide and technological solutions are not enough to ensure the safety and security of essential infrastructure assets and the infinite amount of information that it contains. Another important factor for better defending America's information systems is educational mobilization, which involves an agile public, as well as a highly skilled professional cybersecurity workforce.[46] The CNCI implicates this educational goal, as one of its major objectives is to strengthen the future cybersecurity environment by expanding cyber education.

In order to apply new security practices and technologies successfully, cybersecurity professionals and non-professionals alike need to obtain the appropriate knowledge, skills, and experience for cyber defense. However, most organizations find it challenging to handle the rapid changes taking place within the dynamic nature of cyberspace; hence, it is difficult to keep the "cybersecurity citizen"[47] and workforce up to date. Therefore, the CNCI emphasizes the importance of educational mobilization when it comes to the need for a comprehensive policy. This dimension also includes strengthening sector partnerships by bringing together experts from a wide range of professional disciplines that relate to critical infrastructure protection from all levels of the government.[48]

Related CNCI Initiatives and Executions

From the 12 CNCI initiatives, initiative 8 is classified in educational mobilization. Although only one initiative has been classified in this leg of the triad, this does not mean less emphasis goes to it. The following are findings on some of the most important executions regarding this sphere.

The DHS has been promoting cybersecurity awareness and innovation with various partners outside the department. The University of California, Berkeley, has been a real leader on this front, through its pioneering work in computer science, engineering, and mathematics. The TRUST program is also a key example of the kinds of partnerships taking place between academia, industry, and government. An increasing amount of emphasis continues going into an expansive education system required for cybersecurity training. A value being stressed here is that the entire population needs to learn how to use cyberspace effectively and be aware of the uncontrollable amount of risks posed by information technology. The mobilization of cybersecurity education underscores the aim for raising healthy users of reliable, trustworthy, and resilient digital infrastructures.

On this note, the educational role in realizing cybersecurity is twofold; one, in that it shows how to protect oneself from potential susceptibilities, and two, in that it builds onto one's own conscience and morality to become a good "cybersecurity citizen." Not only is the government or professional workforce to be exposed to this education, but the widespread, general public is also to be enlightened about the significance of cyber defense and the ways of protection. This involves encouraging resources, activities, research, and training to shore up cybersecurity efforts in the public and private sectors. By mobilizing education in this field and developing programs and strategies to deter hostile activity in cyberspace, people can be more informed about cyber dangers and more voluntarily willing to help secure the cybersecurity environment.[49]

Further proceeding with the CNCI, President Obama's Cyberspace Policy Review recognized the need for the initiation of a national awareness and education campaign that promotes cybersecurity.[50] Emphasis is put into partnering with academia and industry to expand cyber education for all US government employees, particularly those who specialize in IT, and enhance worksite development and recruitment strategies to ensure a knowledgeable workforce capable of dealing with the evolving nature of cyber threats.[51] Much effort is put into training not just the current federal workforce (a skilled personnel to protect federal information systems), but also creating K12, college, and graduate-level programs as well. Primary and secondary school students are to be taught safe cyber habits from an early age, and colleges and universities are to make cybersecurity a multidisciplinary pursuit so that policymakers can understand technology while technologists can understand policymaking.[52]

In a multiagency effort particularly, the United States launched the National Initiative for Cybersecurity Education (NICE) in March 2010, led by the National Institute of Standards and Technology (NIST) in partnership with the DHS.[53] NIST highlights the importance of science, technology, engineering, and math (STEM) education as most high schools train students to be users of technology but not *creators* or *adaptors* of technology who can bend computation to their own ends.[54] The NICE Strategic Plan was also released in 2011 to help build a digital nation and improve US cybersecurity by stressing cyber education.

President Obama's administration created this with the dual goals of achieving a cyber-capable workforce and a cyber-savvy citizenry by raising awareness for consumers, enhancing cybersecurity education, and improving the structure, preparation, and training of the cybersecurity workforce.[55] Thus, it identifies goals and objectives that extend from the CNCI, which contribute to the realization of a globally competitive cybersecurity workforce as well as cyber-secure residents.[56]

With the public required to have a critical role in cybersecurity, the DHS launched a National Cybersecurity Awareness Campaign called "Stop. Think. Connect."[57] to cultivate the basic habits and skills for keeping cyber networks safe.[58] In light of this, the DHS ensures that all Americans need to realize that responsibility for cybersecurity begins with each individual user, ultimately extending to "every business, school, and other civic and private enterprise."[59]

Some other executions for educational mobilization include the creation of competitions such as the National Science Bowl by the Department of Energy (DOE).[60] Also OnGuardOnline, the Federal Trade Commission's (FTC) online program has been re-launched to help individuals be safe, secure, and responsible online.[61] This is a site that guides parents, educators, and individuals to learn more about cybersecurity.[62] In addition, EDUCAUSE, a nonprofit association, has been created to advance higher education by promoting the intelligent use of IT.[63] After the 2010 National Cyber Security Awareness Month, the DHS launched a year-round national awareness campaign, which has held events around the country ever since.[64]

Another enactment is the *International Multilateral Partnership against Cyber Threats* (IMPACT), which is a public-private venture that focuses on combating cyberterrorism and protecting critical infrastructure networks. IMPACT has a research division, hosts educational workshops, and conducts high-level security briefings with representatives of member states. "These efforts are intended to make IMPACT the foremost cyber threat resource center in the world."[65] Thus, the educational mobilization leg of the triad not only refers to a nationwide need for cyber education, but also includes a global-level exertion. International institutions are working on building both international and local awareness on cyber defense, adopting an advisory or academic responsibility. The above-mentioned executions of the CNCI show the significance of educational mobilization in building a comprehensive American cybersecurity policy.

Conclusion

It is crucial to look into the CNCI to understand the American fight against cyber threats and explore what facets are representatively involved in America's overall cybersecurity policy. This chapter states that cybersecurity precautions are generated through three essential means: the establishment of a comprehensive governmentwide security policy, the implementation of the latest security counterintelligence technologies, and the creation of a strong security awareness or educational program.[66] All three domains are equally important when producing a well-rounded cyber defense mechanism.

Even though there has been widespread criticism of the American government for not being able to pursue a comprehensive and coherent cybersecurity policy, significant progress has been made since the launch of the CNCI. This chapter shows the effectiveness of the CNCI as various concerning activities and actions have been put into

practice since its establishment. In this regard, the CNCI has provided a notable start in US cybersecurity efforts—the comprehensive
document represents crucial guidelines and progress in constructing
a robust cybersecurity fortress in America by offering one of the first
systematic attempts to fight off cyber insecurities. It also continues to
help improve existing cybersecurity processes as well as introduce new
policies to better protect computer networks.

Endnotes

1. The concept is different but the term "Cybersecurity Triad" has been
   borrowed from the work of Harknett and Stever's 2009 article called,
   The Cybersecurity Triad: Government, Private Sector Partners, and the
   Engaged Cybersecurity Citizen. If Harknett and Stever are representing an "agent-based" model, this chapter is representing a "behavior-
   based" model.
2. NSC, *The Comprehensive National Cybersecurity Initiative* (2009), http://
   www.whitehouse.gov/sites/default/files/cybersecurity.pdf [accessed May
   25, 2011].
3. Gus P. Coldebella and Brian M. White, Foundational Questions
   Regarding the Federal Role in Cybersecurity, *Journal of National Security
   Law & Policy* 4 (2010): 236.
4. Walter Gary Sharp, The Past, Present, and Future of Cybersecurity,
   Journal of National Security Law & Policy 4 (2010): 19.
5. Richard J. Harknett and James A. Stever, The New Policy World of
   Cybersecurity, *Public Administration Review* 71-3 (2011): 456.
6. GAO, Cyberspace: United States Faces Challenges in Addressing Global
   Cybersecurity and Governance, GAO-10-606 (2010).
7. Ibid.
8. The performance metrics has been established through the CyberStats
   program. President Obama's administration has worked with the Office
   of Management and Budget (OMB) to update the Federal Information
   Security Management Act (FISMA) metrics by which departments and
   agencies are graded on their cybersecurity. EOP, *Memorandum for Heads of
   Executive Departments and Agencies* (2010), http://www.whitehouse.gov/
   sites/default/files/omb/assets/memoranda_2010/m10-15.pdf [accessed
   February 8, 2012].
9. Examples include the National Cyber Study Group, the Communications
   Security and Cyber Policy Coordinating Committee, and the Joint
   Interagency Cyber Task Force, which serve as the focal point for moni-
   toring and coordinating projects, as well as enabling the participation of
   both intelligence-community and non-intelligence-community agencies.
   GAO, *Cybersecurity: Progress Made but Challenges Remain in Defining and
   Coordinating the Comprehensive National Initiative*, GAO-10-338 (2010).

10. This center brings together federal cybersecurity organizations by virtually connecting and physically collocating personnel and resources to gain a clearer understanding of the overall cybersecurity picture of federal networks. The center has coordinating authority and is accountable for situational awareness across the .mil, .gov, and .ic domains. DHS, Protecting Our Federal Networks against Cyber Attacks (2009), http://ipv6.dhs.gov/files/programs/gc_1234200709381.shtm [accessed March 3, 2012].

11. Ibid.

12. This cyber investigation coordination organization overseen by the FBI serves as a multi-agency national focal point for coordinating, integrating, and sharing pertinent information related to cyber threat investigations. DHS, National Infrastructure Protection Plan: Partnering to Enhance Protection and Resiliency (2009), http://www.dhs.gov/xlibrary/assets/NIPP_Plan.pdf [accessed October 14, 2011].

13. DHS, About the National Cybersecurity and Communications Integration Center (2011), http://www.dhs.gov/xabout/structure/gc_1306334251555.shtm [accessed October 13, 2011].

14. During a cyber incident, the NCCIC serves as the national response center, which is able to bring the full capabilities of the federal government in a coordinated manner with state, local, and private-sector partners. Ibid.

15. DHS, Cyber Storm: Securing Cyber Space (2011), http://www.dhs.gov/files/training/gc_1204738275985.shtm [accessed October 13, 2011].

16. DHS, Securing Cyberspace: Our Shared Responsibility (2011), http://www.dhs.gov/news/2011/04/25/securing-cyberspace-our-shared-responsibility [accessed April 4, 2012].

17. America's international partnerships have also been strengthened to create initiatives that address the full range of activities, policies, and opportunities associated with cybersecurity. NSC, *Cybersecurity* (2012), http://www.whitehouse.gov/administration/eop/nsc/cybersecurity [accessed February 25, 2012].

18. DHS, US-CERT United States Computer Emergency Readiness Team (2012), http://www.us-cert.gov/ [accessed March 15, 2012].

19. DHS, Protecting Our Federal Networks against Cyber Attacks (2009).

20. EOP, *Fact Sheet: The Administration's Cybersecurity Accomplishments* (2011), http://www.whitehouse.gov/the-press-office/2011/05/12/fact-sheet-administrations-cybersecurity-accomplishments [accessed August 5, 2011].

21. Deibert and Rohozinski (2010): 20.

22. Hunker, Jeffrey, US International Policy for Cybersecurity: Five Issues that Won't Go Away, *Journal of National Security Law & Policy* 4 (2010): 197.

23. U.S. Senate Committee on Homeland Security & Governmental Affairs, *Cybersecurity* (2012), http://www.hsgac.senate.gov/issues/cybersecurity [accessed February 4, 2012].

24. EOP, Fact Sheet: The Administration's Cybersecurity Accomplishments (2011).

25. EOP, *Cyberspace Policy Review: Assuring a Trusted and Resilient Information and Communications Infrastructure* (2009), http://www.whitehouse.gov/assets/documents/Cyberspace_Policy_Review_final.pdf [accessed March 5, 2012].

26. NSC, The Comprehensive National Cybersecurity Initiative (2009).

27. Josh Hammerstein and Christopher May, The CERT Approach to Cybersecurity Workforce Development, Software Engineering Institute (2010), www.cert.org/archive/pdf/10tr045.pdf [accessed July 3, 2012].

28. DHS, Trusted Internet Connections (2011), http://www.dhs.gov/trusted-internet-connections-tic [accessed December 11, 2012].

29. Federal agencies need to comply with the TIC initiative, which mandates the consolidation of the federal government's external access points to minimize risk and improve incident response. EOP, *Federal Departments and Agencies Focus Cybersecurity Activity on Three Administration Priorities* (2012), http://www.whitehouse.gov/blog/2012/03/23/federal-departments-and-agencies-focus-cybersecurity-activity-three-administration-p?utm_source = related [accessed March 24, 2012].

30. DHS, Securing Cyberspace: Our Shared Responsibility (2011).

31. Ibid.

32. Sharp (2010): 25.

33. EOP, Fact Sheet: The Administration's Cybersecurity Accomplishments (2011).

34. The DOC stood up on a program office to coordinate the federal government and private sector in implementing this effort. EOP, *National Strategy for Trusted Identities in Cyberspace: Enhancing Online Choice, Efficiency, Security, and Privacy* (2011), http://www.whitehouse.gov/sites/default/files/rss_viewer/NSTICstrategy_041511.pdf [accessed February 8, 2012].

35. Federal smartcard credentials such as PIV (Personnel Identity Verification) and CAC (Common Access Cards) cards provide multi-factor authentication and digital signature and encryption capabilities, authorizing users to access federal information systems with a higher level of assurance. DHS, Securing Cyberspace: Our Shared Responsibility (2011).

36. DHS, Protecting Our Federal Networks against Cyber Attacks (2009).

37. Einstein provides government officials with an early warning system to gain better situational awareness, earlier identification of malicious activity, and a more comprehensive network defense. Ibid.

38. DHS, Securing Cyberspace: Our Shared Responsibility (2011).

39. Gregory T. Nojiem, Cybersecurity and Freedom on the Internet, *Journal of National Security Law & Policy* 4 (2010): 123.

40. Ibid., 124.

41. Ibid.

42. The Commonwealth is home to more than 300 cybersecurity companies, including the largest leaders in IT. These companies offer technologies and services including network infrastructure, authentication, biometrics, modeling and simulation, encryption products, and network security customization. Virginia.gov., Governor McDonnell Announces New

Virginia Cyber Security Marketing Effort, Commonwealth of Virginia (2012), http://www.technology.virginia.gov/News/viewRelease.cfm?id = 1087 [accessed January 29, 2012].

43. Cybersecurity in Government: Determining Your Priorities for the CNCI, Cisco Systems, Inc. (2010), http://www.cisco.com/web/strategy/docs/gov/cybersecurity_wp.pdf [accessed January 20, 2012].

44. Fortinet is a US-based manufacturer of network security appliances and a leader in Unified Security Threat Management. Fortinet and the Comprehensive National Cybersecurity Initiative (CNCI), Fortinet, Inc. (2009), http://www.fortinet.com/doc/whitepaper/Federal_SOL_CNCI_Support_R1_0809.pdf [accessed January 20, 2012].

45. Leveraging StealthWatch for CNCI and TIC Compliance, Lancope, Inc. (2012), http://www.lancope.com/resource-center/market-briefs/leveraging-stealthwatch-cnci-tic-compliance/ [accessed February 4, 2012].

46. NIST, *National Initiative for Cybersecurity Education* (2010), http://csrc.nist.gov/nice/ [accessed February 2, 2012].

47. Harknett and Stever (2009): 2.

48. Grant Gross, US Government Urged to Focus Cybersecurity Efforts on Education, *IDG News Service* (August 15, 2011).

49. NSC, The Comprehensive National Cybersecurity Initiative (2009).

50. NSC, *Cybersecurity* (2012).

51. DHS, Protecting Our Federal Networks against Cyber Attacks (2009).

52. DHS, Securing Cyberspace: Our Shared Responsibility (2011).

53. The goal of NICE is to "create a Cybersecurity Workforce Framework that defines the architecture and specific functional requirements for all job functions within the cybersecurity workforce." Ronald C. Dodge, Costis Toregas, and Lance Hoffman, Cybersecurity Workforce Development Directions (2011).

54. NIST, *National Initiative for Cybersecurity Education Strategic Plan: Building a Digital Nation* (2011), http://csrc.nist.gov/nice/documents/nicestratplan/Draft_NICE-Strategic-Plan_Aug2011.pdf [accessed February 2, 2012].

55. EOP, Fact Sheet: The Administration's Cybersecurity Accomplishments (2011).

56. To enhance the overall cybersecurity posture of the United States, it is imperative to accelerate the availability of educational and training resources that are designed to improve cyber behavior, skills, and knowledge within every segment of the population. NIST, *National Initiative for Cybersecurity Education Strategic Plan: Building a Digital Nation* (2011).

57. DHS, Stop. Think. Connect (2011), http://www.dhs.gov/files/events/stop-think-connect.shtm [accessed March 3, 2012].

58. DHS, Securing Cyberspace: Our Shared Responsibility (2011).

59. Ibid.

60. DOE, DOE National Science Bowl (2011), http://science.energy.gov/wdts/nsb/ [accessed May 5, 2011].

61. The IT Industry's Cybersecurity Principles for Industry and Government, Information Technology Industry Council (2011), http://www.itic. org/dotAsset/191e377f-b458-4e3d-aced-e856a9b3aebe.pdf   [accessed November 19, 2011].
62. EOP, *National Cybersecurity Awareness Month* (2011), http://www. whitehouse.gov/blog/2011/10/03/national-cybersecurity-awareness-month?utm_source = related [accessed March 5, 2012].
63. Ibid.
64. EOP, Fact Sheet: The Administration's Cybersecurity Accomplishments (2011).
65. Jeremy Ferwerda, Nazli Choucri, and Stuart Madnick, Institutional Foundations for Cyber Security: Current Responses and New Challenges, Massachusetts Institute of Technology (September 2010), http://web. mit.edu/smadnick/www/wp/2010-03.pdf [accessed July 3, 2012].
66. Lech Janczewski and Andrew Colarik. 2005. Managerial Guide for Handling Cyber-terrorism and Information Warfare (IGI Global, 2005).

Index

A

"Active self defense," 218
"Act of war" conundrum, 214–219
    anticipatory self-defense theory,
        218
    "armed attack," 216
    confusing logic, 215
    DoD definition of computer
        network attack, 217
    effects-based analysis, 216
    International Court of Justice,
        217
    national security legal regime,
        214
    political phrase, 215
    principle of self-defense, 217
al-Qaeda, 61, 202
Ambiguity, 27–34
    appropriate punishment, 31
    attribution, difficulties in, 31
    Cold War deterrence, 29
    contemplation of proper response,
        33
    counter-threats, 32
    credibility of threats, 31
    deterministic and probabilistic
        responses to incidents, 29
    deterrence policies, 27, 28
    eroded inhibition, 31
    justification for determinism, 30
    legitimacy of policy, questions
        undermining, 32
    moral hazard, 33
    pessimism, 27
    policy of determinism, advantages
        of, 29, 30
    popular sentiment, 28
    provocation-response curve, 28
    red line, 31
    retaliation, 30, 32
    safe zone, 30, 31
    specified retaliation, 32
    sub rosa response, 33
    target system, attacker's
        observation of, 30
AMD processors, 117
American Cybersecurity Triad,
    291–309

educational mobilization,
301–304
conceptualization, 301
cyber-savvy citizenry, 303
Cyberspace Policy Review,
302
related CNCI initiatives and
executions, 302–304
framing of American
cybersecurity policy into
"American Cybersecurity
Triad" from CNCI,
292–293
"educational mobilization"
dimension, 292
"governmentwide integration"
effort, 292
"technological
counterintelligence," 292
governmentwide integration,
293–298
conceptualization, 293–295
critical infrastructure and key
resources, 297
Forum of Incident Response
and Security Teams
mechanism, 298
mutually reinforcing
initiatives, 293
National Cyber Incident
Response Plan, 297
National Cyber Investigative
Joint Task Force, 297
related CNCI initiatives and
executions, 295–298
technological counterintelligence,
298–301
conceptualization, 298–299
personally identifiable
information, 300
related CNCI initiatives and
executions, 299–301

Trusted Internet Connections
mechanism, 299
Anti-government demonstrations,
172
APEC, *see* Asian-Pacific Economic
Cooperation
Arab Spring, 163
Artificial diversity, 117
Asian-Pacific Economic
Cooperation (APEC), 258
Attacked mission, 11
Attacks
denial-of-service, 84
distributed denial-of-service, 7,
241, 246
methodology, uncovering of, 12
Authoritarian states, *see* Dissent
in authoritarian states,
Internet and

B

Basic Formal Ontology (BFO), 39
BFO, *see* Basic Formal Ontology
Biomedical ontology, 40
Botnets, 7
Bottom-up mapping strategy, 112
Budapest Convention on
Cybercrime, 253

C

CCE, *see* Common Configuration
Enumeration
CERTs, *see* Computer Emergency
Readiness Teams
Chatham House rule, 243
CIA drone pilots, 222
CIKR, *see* Critical infrastructure
and key resources
"Citizen journalist" data, 177
CNCI, *see* Comprehensive National
Cybersecurity Initiative

CNE, *see* Computer network
  exploitation
CNTS, *see* Cross-National Time-
  Series Archive
COE, *see* Cyber Centre of
  Excellence
Coercive capacity, 175, 180
COI-based associations, *see*
  Community of Interest-
  based associations
Cold War deterrence, 29
Commercial Off-The-Shelf (COTS)
  components, 108, 113
Common Configuration
  Enumeration (CCE), 45
Common Vulnerability and
  Exposures (CVE) list, 44
Common Weakness Enumeration
  (CWE) list, 44
Community of Interest (COI)-based
  associations, 103
Comprehensive National
  Cybersecurity Initiative
  (CNCI), 292
Computer Emergency Readiness
  Teams (CERTs), 63, 254,
  300
Computer network exploitation
  (CNE), 130
COTS components, *see* Commercial
  Off-The-Shelf components
Critical infrastructure and key
  resources (CIKR), 297
Cross-National Time-Series Archive
  (CNTS), 172
Cultural framing, 166
CVE list, *see* Common Vulnerability
  and Exposures list
CWE list, *see* Common Weakness
  Enumeration list
Cyberarms compliance, challenges
  in monitoring, 81–99
  approach, 83–84

digital forensics, 83
infrastructure, 83
international agreements, 84
models for cyberweapons use,
  84–85
denial-of-service attacks, 84
malware methods, 85
Stuxnet worm, 85
network monitoring for
  cyberweapons, 88–91
attribution, 89
behavior of cyberweapon in
  isolation, 89
decoy, 91
"differential honeypots," 91
false positives, 88
honeypot technology, 91
properties of observable
  network traffic, 90
sophistication, 88–89
targets, 88
state-sponsored cyberattacks, 82
support for international
  cyberarms cooperation in
  the United States, 93–96
embryonic global norms, 93
hacker groups, criminal
  prosecution of, 96
International Multilateral
  Partnership against Cyber
  Threats, 93
legal distinctions, 96
major obstacle to international
  agreement, 94
State Department "note
  verbal," 94
unworkably complex
  alternative, 95
technical obstacles, 86–93
analysis of drives to find
  cyberweapons, 86–88
clue to cyberweapons, 86
clusters of files, 87

cyberweapons inspection, 87
deception markers, 87
encouraging more responsible
    cyberweapons, 91–93
"fuzzing" utilities, 86
"key escrow" methods, 87
network monitoring for
    cyberweapons, 88–91
Real Data Corpus, 87
"write-blockers," 87
Cyber arms control, possibility of, 7
Cyber Centre of Excellence (COE),
    66
Cyber deterrence, prospects for
    (American sponsorship of
    global norms), 49–77
  attribution, 55–56
    "anonymous" hackers, 55
    challenge, 50
    global norms, 55
  broad solutions, 56–60
    Domain Name System, 58
    gaps in international
        cooperation, 57
    multi-stage, multi-
        jurisdictional attacks, 57
    proxy servers, 59
    spoofing machines to mask
        geography, 58–60
    The Onion Router, 59
    Transmission Control
        Protocol/Internet Protocol,
        57
  conventional wisdom, 51
  deterrence framework, 52–55
    Air Force doctrine, 54
    information and communi-
        cation technology, 52
    PLA plausible deniability, 53
    "spoofing," 54
  framework for development,
      diplomacy, and defense,
      62–66

Air Force, 64
Computer Emergency
    Readiness Teams, 63
defense, 65–66
development, 63
diplomacy, 64–65
IMPACT, 63
International Cyber Strategy,
    62, 63
refusing aid, 62
US imperialism in cyberspace,
    perception of, 62
industrial control systems, 51
leading by example (US-based
    entities responsibility), 70
legislation, 67–70
  Congress, 67, 69–70
  efforts to eliminate cyber
      crime, 68–69
  international partnerships, 70
  minimum standards, 67–68
  non-governmental
      organizations, 67
legislative language for "victims
    of trafficking of malicious
    code," 67
linking it all together, 66–67
  Cyber Centre of Excellence,
      66
  multi-stage attacks, 66
US-based Internet
    intermediaries, 70–71
where to go from here, 71–73
  Air Force, 72
  international partnerships,
      strengthening of, 72
  White House strategy, 71
wrongful acts in cyberspace,
    60–61
  arguments, 61
  Estonia cyber attack (2007),
      61

norms of state responsibility, 60

sponsorship of "illegal" acts, 61

Cyber privateers, 6

Cybersecurity Act of 2012, 43

Cyber sovereignty, 277–289

actions by nation-states, 277

"cyber actor," 278

definition, 278–279

international law pertaining to cyber space, 280–282

confusion between perception and reality, 280

doctrine of acquiescence, 281

Outer Space Treaty, 281

routine practice, 281

social networks, 280

treaties, 281

national security implications, 282–286

e-commerce, 285

economics, 284

free speech, 284

information, 283–284

military operations, 285

norms of behavior, 283

physicality of cyber domain, 283

rationale for banishment, 284

US national security repercussions, 282

sovereignty in cyber space, 286–288

free passage, 288

indirect methods of control, 287

international waters, 287

population expectations, 286

potential implementations, 286

recognition by treaty, 286

sovereignty over cyber space, 279–280

implications of sovereignty, 280

motivation, 280

poor attribution, 279

sole jurisdiction, 279

Cyberspace Policy Review, 302

Cyberspace superiority considerations, 13–25

assessment of DoD's ability to achieve cyberspace superiority, 21–25

International Strategy for Cyberspace, 23

"machine time, 24

military capability, 22

technology undergirding cyberspace, 22

tyranny of computing cycles, 24

victory in competitive decision cycles, 23

cyberspace superiority, DoD definition of, 11

enhance capacity, 14–15

capacity recommendations, 15

diversified infrastructure, 14

"lemon laws," 14

improve capability, 15–16

capacity recommendations, 16

mission assurance, 15

symbiotic relationship, 15

increase cognizance, 16–18

cognizance recommendations, 17–18

Command and Control, 17

C2 systems, 17

DoD improvement of situational awareness, 16

Internet tools, 16

next Stuxnet attack is only a day away, 20–21

destruction of cyber-attack, 20
doctrinal perspective, 21
National Military Strategy
    for Cyberspace Operation's
    Strategic Goal (2006), 21
sophisticated threats, 20
strengthen governance structure,
    18–20
    full-spectrum cyberspace
      operations, synchronized
      approach for, 19
    governance recommendations,
      20
    Major Force Program-11, 19
    modernization of authorities,
      18
    most recent operational
      domain, 19
    National Reconnaissance
      Office, 19
Cyberstrategists on cyberlaw for
    cyberwar, perspectives for,
    211–232
    "act of war" conundrum, 214–219
    "active self defense," 218
    anticipatory self-defense
      theory, 218
    "armed attack," 216
    confusing logic, 215
    DoD definition of computer
      network attack, 217
    effects-based analysis, 216
    International Court of Justice,
      217
    "mere frontier incident," 217
    national security legal regime,
      214
    political phrase, 215
    principle of self-defense, 217
    conundrum, 212
    "cookbook" solutions, 212
cybering and citizenry, 223–225

collection of personal
    information, 223
Einstein 3, 224
emerging public attitudes, 225
incidents on impropriety, 223
National Security Agency, 223
pending legislation, 225
Planned Parenthood, 224
"terrorist surveillance
    program," 224
cybersizing LOAC, 213–214
"information warfare," 213
law of armed conflict, 212
legal questions, 211
state of war, 219–223
    CIA drone pilots, 222
    DoD publication, 223
    functional approach, 221
    fundamental targeting issues,
      220
    "incidental" losses of civilians,
      221
    law enforcement operations,
      219
    LOAC, 219, 222
    prudent targeting, legal
      mandates and, 220
    traditional definitions, 219
treaty goals, perception of, 213
Wikileaks phenomena, 211

D

Data breach, third-party
    notification, 10
DDoS attacks, *see* Distributed
    denial-of-service attacks
Deception markers, 87
Decoy, 91
Defense-in-depth, layers of, 115
De-militarized zones (DMZs), 142
Denial-of-service attacks, 84

Department of Commerce (DOC), 295
Department of Defense (DoD), 197
  cyberspace superiority, 13
  definition of computer network attack, 217
  definition of mission assurance, 123
  directive defining Mission assurance, 107
  duty to respond to hostile acts, 56
  ethics questions, 197
  improvement of situational awareness, 16
  lexicons and manuals (ontology for cyberwarfare), 38
  Strategy for Operating in Cyberspace and the International Strategy for Cyberspace, 18
  Universal Core and, 41
Department of Energy (DOE), 303
Department of Homeland Security (DHS), 128, 224, 295
Department of Justice (DOJ), 295
Department of State (DOS), 59
Descriptive Ontology for Linguistic and Cognitive Engineering (DOLCE), 39
Detect-react failure, 115
Deterrence, *see* Cyber deterrence, prospects for (American sponsorship of global norms)
DHS, *see* Department of Homeland Security
"Differential honeypots," 91
Digital policy management (DPM), 101–106
  adapting capabilities for government use, 106
  Community of Interest-based associations, 103

danger of operating on the Internet, 101
digital policy management of today, 102
  firewalls, 102
  Information Assurance, 102
  how to get involved, 106
  operations of tomorrow, 103
  operations of tomorrow require changes today, 103–104
  enterprise operation, 104
  policy sets, 104
  statements, 104
  supporting the delivery of enterprise for tomorrow, 104–105
  defining the functionality, 105
  goal of DPM team, 104
  National Security Agency, 104
  open development philosophy, 105
Digital Subscriber Line modem access, 168
Dissent in authoritarian states, Internet and, 161–191
  advancement of Internet, 162
  Arab Spring, 163
  capacity to overwhelm state coercion, 182
  data and methods, 172
  list of countries, 173
  non-democracies, 172
  decentralization, 163
  dependent variable, 172–174
  anti-government demonstrations, 172
  Cross-National Time-Series Archive, 172
  dial-up modems, 162
  dissent mobilization, 163
  distance, decentralization, and interaction, 163
  interactivity, 163

Internet and dissent, 167–169
  Digital Subscriber Line
    modem access, 168
  Internet, description of, 167
  Internet diffusion, potential
    outcome of, 169
  new repertoires, 167
  packet switching, 168
  protest costs and space, 167
  Transmission Control
    Protocol/Internet Protocol,
    168
Internet as "force multiplier," 163
Iranian example, 163, 164
Iranian protesters, 163
key argument, 163
key independent and control
    variables, 174–175
  coercive capacity, 175
  count variables, 175
  gross domestic product, 174
  Internet access, 174
  measurement of repression,
    174
  negative binomial regression,
    175
  ordinary least squares
    regression, 175
  Political Terror Scale, 175
  school enrollment, 174
  zero protest incidents, 175
likelihood of dissent inside
    authoritarian states, factors,
    163
"many-to-many" broadcast
    method, 181
Myanmar, 161
older electronic communication
    mediums, 162
results, 175–181
  "citizen journalist" data, 177
  coercive capacity, 180
  example, 176–177

incidence-rate ratios, 175
  negative binomial regression,
    175
  Political Terror Scale, 180
  predicted values, 178
  tabulation chart analysis, 179
synthesis model of dissent,
    164–167
  anti-regime protests, 166
  collective action, 164
  cultural framing, 166
  effects of opportunity and
    threat on protest activity,
    hypotheses on, 166
  falun gong movement (China),
    166
  framing processes, 166
  Information and
    Communication
    Technologies, 165
  mobilizing structures, 165
  Muslim Brotherhood (1950s
    and 1960s), 165
  opportunity and threat, 166
  political opportunity
    structures, 164
  pre-Internet example, 165
  protest movements, 167
  repertoires of contention, 166
  social change, 164
theory of Internet-mediated
    dissent, 169–171
  anti-regime protest incidents,
    171
  challenge to social boundaries,
    169
  Egypt, 169
  Facebook, 170
  Internet diffusion, increased
    dissent and, 169
  social networking application,
    170
  technical censorship, 171

Distributed denial-of-service (DDoS) attacks, 7, 241, 246
DMZs, *see* De-militarized zones
DNS, *see* Domain Name System
DOC, *see* Department of Commerce
Doctrine of acquiescence, 281
DoD, *see* Department of Defense
DOE, *see* Department of Energy
DOJ, *see* Department of Justice
DOLCE, *see* Descriptive Ontology for Linguistic and Cognitive Engineering
Domain Name System (DNS), 58
DOS, *see* Department of State
DPM, *see* Digital policy management
Duty-of-care philosophy, failure to take, 10

E

e-commerce, 285
"Economic warfare," 242, 250
Einstein 3, 224
Einstein Program, 300
ELOAC program, *see* Ethics and the Law of Armed Conflict program
Encryption, 122, 123
Environmental protection, cyberdefense as, 265–275
    adversarial nations, 266
    automated attack, 267
    concept of cyberwar, 268–269
        attribution investigation, 268
        industrial control systems, 268
        innovative *modus operandi*, 269
        spoofed actors, 268
    environmental effects of cyberwar, 269–274
    environmental cyberdefense, 273–274
    EPA superfund site, 271

fish populations, 271
"green" mission, 273
hydroelectric dams and reservoirs, 270–271
loss of legitimacy and authority, 272–273
programmable controllers, 270
public opinion and sentiment, 271–272
range of vulnerabilities, 269
SCADA systems, 269
US chemical industry, 271
    long-term damage, 267
    Three Mile Island, 266, 272
EPA superfund site, 271
e-SOS, 248
Estonia cyber attack (2007), 61
Ethics of cyber warfare, 195–209
    advantage, 195
    areas of greatest vulnerability, 200
    attribution problem, 201
    chilling scenarios, 196
    conceptual confusion, 196
    conditions for justified cyber attack, 203–204
    debates, 196
    discrimination, 199
    "double-deek" deception, 198
    formulating policy, 199
    intelligence, surveillance, and reconnaissance, 200
    inter-state conflict, 201
    "just war tradition," 199
    military necessity, 199
    NATO allies, 203
    new norms of inter-state conduct, 203
    noncombatant immunity, 199
    obstacles to analysis of military technologies, 196
    premeptive cyber strike, 204
    proportionality, 199

questions, 195–196
search for emerging norms of
    state behavior, 201
"smokestacks," 198
Stuxnet, 202
threats and vulnerabilities, 196
"unique ontology" of cyber
    objects, 205
Ethics and the Law of Armed
    Conflict (ELOAC)
    program (Oxford
    University), 197
Exploited mission, 116

F

Facebook, 6, 163, 170
Failed mission, 116
False positives, network monitoring
    and, 88
Falun gong movement (China), 166
FDDI, *see* Fiber Distributed Data
    Interface
Federal Trade Commission (FTC),
    303
Fiber Distributed Data Interface
    (FDDI), 117
Field Programmable Gate Array
    (FPGA)-based interfaces,
    117
Firewalls, 102
Firmware upgrades, 151
FIRST mechanism, *see* Forum of
    Incident Response and
    Security Teams mechanism
First-order predicate logic (FOPL),
    40
Flickr photos, 163
FOPL, *see* First-order predicate logic
Forum of Incident Response and
    Security Teams (FIRST)
    mechanism, 298

FPGA-based interfaces, *see* Field
    Programmable Gate Array-
    based interfaces
Free speech, filtering of information
    vs., 284
FTC, *see* Federal Trade Commission
Future of things cyber, 3–8
    botnets, 7
    common body of knowledge, 6
    courage, 6
    cyber arms control, 7
    cyber as a domain, 4–5
    cyber privateers, 6
    dealing with the unprecedented,
        4
    defense, 7–8
    distributed denial-of-service
        attacks, 7
    international law, 7
    Internet freedom, 7
    knowledge of threat, 5
    mankind's last great era of
        discovery, 6
    overprotected stuff, 6
    policy vacuum, 6
    privacy, 5
    private sector, what to expect
        from, 5–6
    right of self defense, 6
    structural framework, 3
    what is classified, 6
    what is truly secret, 6
    worst of all possible cyber worlds,
        8
"Fuzzing" utilities, 86

G

GDP, *see* Gross domestic product
Gene Ontology (GO), 39
Global commerce, Internet as key
    facilitator of, 11

Global norms, American
     sponsorship of, 49–77
attribution, 55–56
   "anonymous" hackers, 55
   challenge, 50
   global norms, 55
broad solutions, 56–60
   Domain Name System, 58
   gaps in international
      cooperation, 57
   multi-stage, multi-
      jurisdictional attacks, 57
   proxy servers, 59
   spoofing machines to mask
      geography, 58–60
   The Onion Router, 59
   Transmission Control
      Protocol/Internet Protocol,
      57
conventional wisdom, 51
deterrence framework, 52–55
   Air Force doctrine, 54
   information and communi-
      cation technology, 52
   PLA plausible deniability, 53
   "spoofing," 54
framework for development,
      diplomacy, and defense,
      62–66
   Air Force, 64
   Computer Emergency
      Readiness Teams, 63
   defense, 65–66
   development, 63
   diplomacy, 64–65
   IMPACT, 63
   International Cyber Strategy,
      62, 63
   refusing aid, 62
   US imperialism in cyberspace,
      perception of, 62
industrial control systems, 51

leading by example (US-based
      entities responsibility), 70
legislation, 67–70
   Congress, 67, 69–70
   efforts to eliminate cyber
      crime, 68–69
   international partnerships, 70
   minimum standards, 67–68
   non-governmental
      organizations, 67
legislative language for "victims
      of trafficking of malicious
      code," 67
linking it all together, 66–67
   Cyber Centre of Excellence,
      66
   multi-stage attacks, 66
US-based Internet
      intermediaries, 70–71
where to go from here, 71–73
   Air Force, 72
   international partnerships,
      strengthening of, 72
   White House strategy, 71
wrongful acts in cyberspace,
      60–61
   arguments, 61
   Estonia cyber attack (2007),
      61
   norms of state responsibility,
      60
   sponsorship of "illegal" acts,
      61
Global norms, cultivation of as part
      of cybersecurity strategy,
      233–264
call to discuss cyber norms,
      235–237
   commonsense ideas of
      morality, 236
   decade-old positions, 235
   global culture, 236
   national sovereignty, 237

UN group, 235
"catch-up" strategy, 234
challenge, 233
cybercrime, 252–255
    Budapest Convention on
        Cybercrime, 253
    campaign for treaty, 253
    Computer Emergency
        Response Teams, 254
    norms, 253
    prevention, 254
    strategies, 252
information and communication
    technology, 234
Internet freedom and global
    information society,
    258–259
"milieu goal," 259
military operations, 246–249
    civil-military relationship, 249
    DDoS attack, 246
    "duty to assist," 248
    e-SOS, 248
    "meat space," 248
    NATO treaty, 246
    recommendation, 247
    Stuxnet attack, 247
    uncertainty, 246
military, political, and economic
    espionage, 250–252
    anticipatory self-defense, 250
    diplomatic and political
        capital, 251
    "economic warfare," 250
    government surveillance, 252
    hackers, 251
    industrial espionage, 250, 251
    proliferation security initiative,
        251
    World Trade Organization,
        251

national positions for
    international cyber norms,
    237–243
    distributed denial-of-service
        attacks, 241
    "economic warfare," 242
    ill-prepared conference, 237
    Internet Engineering Task
        Force, 240
    law of armed conflict, 241
    "logic bombs," 242
    North Atlantic Treaty
        Organization, 237, 239
    Shanghai Coordination
        Organization, 238
    vector for dissident political
        information, 238
norms for specific cyber
    behaviors, 243–246
    Chatham House rule, 243
    principal issues, 243
    Western vision, 243
"possession goals," 259
public-private partnerships,
    257–258
    government agency, 258
    "invisible norms," 257
    "win-win" situation, 257
"reasonable deterrence," 234, 260
status quo oriented norms, 260
technological foundations,
    255–256
    fallback position, 255
    "naming and shaming," 256
    third-party certification, 256
GO, *see* Gene Ontology
Google, 6, 284
Google Maps, 182
GOTS components, *see* Government
        Off-The-Shelf components
Government Off-The-Shelf (GOTS)
    components, 116

Gross domestic product (GDP), 174, 179

H

Hacker groups, criminal prosecution of, 96
HMI systems, *see* Human-machine interface systems
"Homemade" categorizations in programs, 38
Homomorphic encryption, 123
Honeypot technology, 91
Human-machine interface (HMI) systems, 144

I

IA, *see* Information Assurance
ICANN, *see* Internet Corporation for Assigned Names and Numbers
ICJ, *see* International Court of Justice
ICRC, *see* International Committee of the Red Cross
ICSs, *see* Industrial control systems
ICTs, *see* Information and Communication Technologies
IDSs, *see* Intrusion-detection systems
IEDs, *see* Improvised explosive devices
IETF, *see* Internet Engineering Task Force
IMPACT, *see* International Multilateral Partnership against Cyber Threats
Improvised explosive devices (IEDs), 137
Incidence-rate ratios (IRRs), 175

Industrial control systems (ICSs), 51, 128
Industrial espionage, 251
Information Assurance (IA), 102, 122
Information and Communication Technologies (ICTs), 52, 165, 234
Information objects, specifying, 36
Input-output (I/O) interfaces, 112
Insider threats, 3
Instance-level data, 35
Intelligence, surveillance, and reconnaissance (ISR), 200
Intelligent end devices, 142
Intel processors, 117
International agreement
    cyberarms compliance, 84
    ineffective, 137
    international law, 281
    LOAC, 213
    major obstacle to, 94
    monitoring of, 84
    reason for needing, 88
    state accountability, 71
    stipulation, 91
    US advocacy of, 154
International Committee of the Red Cross (ICRC), 220
International Court of Justice (ICJ), 217
International Cyber Strategy, 62, 63
International Law Commission, 60
International Multilateral Partnership against Cyber Threats (IMPACT), 93
International Organization for Standardization (ISO), 255
International Strategy for Cyberspace, 23
International Telecommunications Union (ITU), 63, 89, 93
Internet

advancement of, 162
danger of operating on, 101
description of, 167
as "force multiplier," 163
freedom, 7
interconnectivity of, 9
as key facilitator of global
    commerce, 11
moves to regulate, 7
use by extremists, 224
Internet Corporation for Assigned
    Names and Numbers
    (ICANN), 50, 168
Internet Engineering Task Force
    (IETF), 240, 255
"Interoperability" problem, 37
Intrusion-detection systems (IDSs),
    142
I/O interfaces, *see* Input-output
    interfaces
IREs, *see* Incidence-rate ratios
ISO, *see* International Organization
    for Standardization
ISR, *see* Intelligence, surveillance,
    and reconnaissance
ITU, *see* International
    Telecommunications Union

J

JIEDDO, *see* Joint Improvised
    Explosive Device Defeat
    Organization
Joint Improvised Explosive Device
    Defeat Organization
    (JIEDDO), 43
"Just war tradition," 199

K

"Key escrow" methods, 87
Kill-chain, shortened, 108

L

LAN, *see* Local area network
Law, *see* Cyberstrategists on
    cyberlaw for cyberwar,
    perspectives for
Law of armed conflict (LOAC), 199,
    212, 241
Law of the Seas Convention, 7
Legacy missions, assuring, 109–115
    bottom-up mapping strategy, 112
    cost-benefit analysis, 114
    COTS, proliferation of in
        weapon systems, 113
    D4 effects in relation to extent
        and duration, 111
    example, 111
    input-output interfaces, 112
    legacy communication protocols,
        112
    mapping process, realities, 112
    mission mapping, 110
    mitigation, 110
    Operational Test and Evaluation,
        115
    permanent-and-total effect, 111
    prioritization, 110
    process-coloring, 113
    process steps, 110–111
    red teaming, 110–111
    systematic enumeration of all
        protocols, 113
    virtual circuits, 112
    vulnerability assessment, 110, 112
    vulnerability mitigation, 114
Legacy-style programming, 9
"Lemon laws" (automotive industry),
    14
Liability exposure, software
    producers, 11
LOAC, *see* Law of armed conflict
Local area network (LAN), 143
"Logic bombs," 242

M

MA, *see* Mission assurance
MAC, *see* Media Access Controls
MAEC, *see* Malware Attribute
    Enumeration and
    Characterization
Major Force Program-11 (MFP-11),
    19
Malware
  categorized, 45
  effort to share information about,
    35
  nomenclature (Symantec), 44
Malware Attribute Enumeration
    and Characterization
    (MAEC) (Mitre), 44
Markov chain, defense-in-depth as,
    115
Media Access Controls (MAC), 117
MEF, *see* Mission Essential
    Function
"Metaphysics," 47
MFP-11, *see* Major Force
    Program-11
Microsoft Internet Explorer, 172
"Milieu goal," 259
Military capability, technology
    investment, 22
Mission assurance (MA), 107–125
  assurance-in-depth, 115–117
    artificial diversity, 117
    attacked mission, 11
    defense-in-depth, layers of,
      115
    detect-react failure, 115
    environment shaping, benefits
      of, 116
    exploited mission, 116
    failed mission, 116
    Field Programmable Gate
      Array-based interfaces, 117

    Government Off-The-Shelf
      components, 116
    hallmark of mission survival,
      117
    Markov chain, 115
    pristine mission, 116
  assuring legacy missions, 109–115
    bottom-up mapping strategy,
      112
    cost-benefit analysis, 114
    COTS, proliferation of in
      weapon systems, 113
    D4 effects in relation to extent
      and duration, 111
    example, 111
    input-output interfaces, 112
    legacy communication
      protocols, 112
    mapping process, realities, 112
    mission mapping, 110
    mitigation, 110
    Operational Test and
      Evaluation, 115
    permanent-and-total effect,
      111
    prioritization, 110
    process-coloring, 113
    process steps, 110–111
    red teaming, 110–111
    systematic enumeration of all
      protocols, 113
    virtual circuits, 112
    vulnerability assessment, 110,
      112
    vulnerability mitigation, 114
  Commercial Off-The-Shelf
    components, 108
  cyber test and evaluation,
    117–122
    act, 121–122
    decide, 120–121
    DoD directives, 117
    observe, 119–120

OODA-loop construct, 118
orient, 120
"system of systems," 119
Test and Evaluation, 117
"what if" scenarios, 122
DoD directive, 107
flattening of the industrial world, 108
fractal nature of, 109
global trends, 107
kill-chain, shortened, 108
Mission Essential Function, 107, 109
Observe-Orient-Decide-Act loop, 108
public clouds, 122–123
encryption, 122
homomorphic encryption, 123
information assurance, 122
obfuscation, 123
supply chain vulnerabilities, 122
Test and Evaluation, 109
time-domain mission assurance, 123–124
just-in-time creation, 123–124
life expectancy, 123
MEF, 124
paradigm change, 123
too-little-too-late process, 109
Mission Essential Function (MEF), 107, 109
Mitre, Malware Attribute Enumeration and Characterization, 44
Moral hazard, 33

N

Natanz architecture, 142
National Cyber Incident Response Plan (NCIRP), 297

National Cyber Investigative Joint Task Force (NCIJTF), 297
National Cybersecurity and Communications Integration Center (NCCIC), 297
National Infrastructure Protection Plan (NIPP), 297
National Initiative for Cybersecurity education (NICE), 303
National Institute of Standards and Technology (NIST), 42
Common Configuration Enumeration, 45
definition of risk, 109
importance of STEM education, 303
National Vulnerability Database, 44
National Military Strategy for Cyberspace Operation's Strategic Goal (2006), 21
National Reconnaissance Office, 19
National Science Foundation Network, 58
National Security Agency (NSA), 104, 223
National Vulnerability Database (NVD), 44
NATO, *see* North Atlantic Treaty Organization
NCCIC, *see* National Cybersecurity and Communications Integration Center
NCIJTF, *see* National Cyber Investigative Joint Task Force
NCIRP, *see* National Cyber Incident Response Plan
Negative binomial regression, 175
Netscape Navigator, 172
Network monitoring for cyberweapons, 88–91

attribution, 89
behavior of cyberweapon in
    isolation, 89
decoy, 91
"differential honeypots," 91
false positives, 88
honeypot technology, 91
properties of observable network
    traffic, 90
sophistication, 88–89
targets, 88
NGOs, *see* Non-governmental
    organizations
NICE, *see* National Initiative for
    Cybersecurity education
NIPP, *see* National Infrastructure
    Protection Plan
NIST, *see* National Institute of
    Standards and Technology
Non-governmental organizations
    (NGOs), 67
North Atlantic Treaty Organization
    (NATO), 203, 237
NSA, *see* National Security Agency
NVD, *see* National Vulnerability
    Database

O

Observe-Orient-Decide-Act
    (OODA) loop, 108, 118
OLS regression, *see* Ordinary least
    squares regression
OnGuardOnline, 303
Ontology for cyberwarfare, essential
    features of, 35–48
    Basic Formal Ontology, 39
    "best practices" for applied
        ontologies, 46
    classification of entities, 36
    "conceptual model," 38
    corruption of data, 36

Descriptive Ontology for
    Linguistic and Cognitive
    Engineering, 39
DoD lexicons and manuals, 38
existing military ontologies,
    41–45
    civilian information systems,
        45
    Common Vulnerability and
        Exposures list, 44
    Common Weakness
        Enumeration list, 44
    defensive cyberwarfare, 43
    military ontologies under
        development, 43
    National Vulnerability
        Database, 44
    "sandbox," 45
    signatures, 45
    sociological difference, 42
    Universal Core, 41
    upper-level ontology, 43
    vulnerability, agent targeting
        of, 44
    XML, 41, 42
"homemade" categorizations in
    programs, 38
information objects, specifying,
    36
instance-level data, 35
"interoperability" problem, 37
malware, 35, 45
"metaphysics," 47
Ontology Web Language, 37, 40
"semantic web," 37
signatures, 45
Suggested Upper Merge
    Ontology, 39
using biomedical ontologies for
    method and content, 39–41
    first-order predicate logic, 40
    Gene Ontology, 39
    military ontology, 40

Sequence Ontology, 41
WWW search engines,
    "intelligent" searches, 37
Ontology Web Language (OWL),
    35, 37, 40
OODA loop, *see* Observe-Orient-
    Decide-Act loop
OPEC members, *see* Organization
    of Petroleum Exporting
    Countries members
Operational Test and Evaluation
    (OT&E), 115
Ordinary least squares (OLS)
    regression, 175
Organization of Petroleum
    Exporting Countries
    (OPEC) members, 181
OT&E, *see* Operational Test and
    Evaluation
Outer Space Treaty, 281
Overprotected stuff, 6
OWL, *see* Ontology Web Language

P

Packet switching, 168
PLCs, *see* Programmable logic
    controllers
Policy vacuum, 6
Political Terror Scale, 175, 180
"Possession goals," 259
Pristine mission, 116
Private sector
    attribution problem, 60
    cybersecurity triad, 293
    defense, 65
    Einstein Program, 300
    expectations, 5
    government partnership with, 18,
        95, 258
    interdependencies between public
        and, 23

Symantec malware nomenclature,
    44
what to expect from, 5–6
Process-coloring, 113
Programmable logic controllers
    (PLCs), 130, 147
Proliferation security initiative
    (PSI), 251
Protest activity, effects of
    opportunity and threat on,
    166
Provocation-response curve, 28
Proxy servers, 59
PSI, *see* Proliferation security
    initiative
Public clouds (mission assurance),
    122–123
    encryption, 122
    homomorphic encryption, 123
    information assurance, 122
    obfuscation, 123
    supply chain vulnerabilities, 122

R

RAND Corporation, 198
Real Data Corpus, 87
Red line, state declaring, 31
Remote terminal units (RTUs), 142
Repertoires of contention, 166
RTUs, *see* Remote terminal units
"Rush-to-market" mentality, 10

S

SCADA systems, *see* Supervisory
    control and data acquisition
    systems
Science, technology, engineering,
    and math (STEM) educa-
    tion, 303
SCO, *see* Shanghai Coordination
    Organization

Security-incident and event
management (SIEM)
systems, 142, 145
Self defense, right of, 6
"Semantic web," 37
Shanghai Coordination
Organization (SCO), 238
SIEM systems, *see* Security-incident
and event management
systems
Small and medium-sized enterprise
(SME), 9
SME, *see* Small and medium-sized
enterprise
Social networking application, 170
"Spoofing," 54
STEM education, *see* Science,
technology, engineering,
and math education
Strategists, *see* Cyberstrategists on
cyberlaw for cyberwar,
perspectives for
Stuxnet, 3, 85, 127–159, 202
defense, 137–153
antivirus and mobile code, 139
compromised LAN, 143
cyber security testing and
audit, 141
de-militarized zones, 142
force packaging for defense,
144
human-machine interface
systems, 144
ICSs are different from
traditional IT systems, 138
implication 1 (ICS defenders
must regularly train
together), 149
implication 2 (defenders must
be equipped to detect
deceptions), 149–151

implication 3 (embedded
control devices should
require physical access
for all firmware updates),
151–153
improvised explosive devices,
137
intelligent end devices, 142
intrusion-detection systems,
142
low-level protocols, 139
Martin Libicki was incorrect,
138
Natanz architecture, 142
patch management/change
management, 140
physical and environmental
security, 141
remote terminal units, 142
SCADA systems, 142
security-incident and event
management systems, 142
supervisory control and data
acquisition systems, 142
truth 6 (cyber weapons can
defeat even well-architected
cyber systems), 142
truth 7 (traditional IT defense
skills remain important in
ICS environments), 145
truth 8 (specialized ICS
environment knowledge is
required to defend ICS),
145–147
truth 9 (system operators are
a critical part of the ICS
defensive team), 147–149
"unassailability," 144
Windows O/S, 139
new reality, 128–132
computer network
exploitation, 130
"game-changer," 128

industrial control systems, 128
infected thumb drives, 129
malware, 128
paradigm shift, 128
programmable logic
  controllers, 130
offense, 132–133
  definition of weapon, 132
  malware purposes, 133
  "weapon effect," 132
Stuxnet and national security
  strategy, 133–137
  benefits of unleashing a cyber
    weapon may be dominated
    by risk of return fire,
    136–137
  prevention, preemption,
    and US national security
    strategy, 133–137
  truth 1 (cyber attack is
    consistent with our national
    security strategy if done as
    part of a collective action),
    133
  truth 2 (cyber attack on
    strategic targets can reduce
    casualties), 133–134
  truth 3 (cyber attack can
    achieve significant, long-
    lasting effects), 134–135
  truth 4 (cyber attacks are not
    silver bullets), 135–136
  truth 5 (cyber weapons can be
    reverse engineered to strike
    unintended targets), 136
Suggested Upper Merge Ontology
  (SUMO), 39
SUMO, see Suggested Upper Merge
  Ontology
Superiority considerations, see
  Cyberspace superiority
  considerations

Supervisory control and data
  acquisition (SCADA)
  systems, 131, 142, 269
Supply chain vulnerabilities, 122
Symantec malware nomenclature,
  44

T

TCP/IP, see Transmission Control
  Protocol/Internet Protocol
T&E, see Test and Evaluation
"Technological counterintelligence,"
  292
"Terrorist surveillance program,"
  224
Test and Evaluation (T&E), 109,
  117
The Onion Router (TOR), 59
Third-party certification, 256
Threats
  counter-, 32
  credibility, 31
  ethics, 196
  insider, 3
  knowledge of, 5
  sophisticated, risk mitigation and,
    20
  tools used to control, 82
Three Mile Island, 266, 272
TIC mechanism, see Trusted
  Internet Connections
  mechanism
Time-domain mission assurance,
  123–124
  just-in-time creation, 123–124
  life expectancy, 123
  MEF, 124
  paradigm change, 123
Token Ring, 117
Too-little-too-late process, 109
TOR, see The Onion Router

Trafficked Victims Protection Act (TVPA), 67
Transmission Control Protocol/ Internet Protocol (TCP/ IP), 57, 168
Treaty goals, perception of, 213
Trojans, 3
Trusted Internet Connections (TIC) mechanism, 299
TVPA, *see* Trafficked Victims Protection Act
"21st Century's Wild West" of cyberspace, taming of, 9–12
    college-level courses, establishment of, 9
    conflicting state laws, 11
    data breach, third-party notification, 10
    duty-of-care philosophy, failure to take, 10
    governments, 12
    interconnectivity of Internet, 9
    legacy-style programming, 9
    liability exposure, 11
    nature of interconnected environment, factors, 9–11
    "rush-to-market" mentality, 10
    small and medium-sized enterprise, 9
    stand-alone computer systems, 9
    treaties, 12
    "use at your own risk" disclaimer, 10
    weaknesses in computer programs, exploitation of, 11
Twitter, 163, 169, 183

U

UCore, *see* Universal Core
"Unique ontology" of cyber objects, 205

Universal Core (UCore), 41
US Cyber Command, 3
"Use at your own risk" disclaimer, 10
US medical systems, pending changes in, 42
US Secret Service, data breach cases reviewed, 10

V

Verizon, data breach cases reviewed, 10
Virtual circuits, 112
Voice of America, 183
Vulnerabilities
    areas of greatest vulnerability, 200
    assessment, assuring legacy missions, 110, 112
    environmental effects of cyberwar, 269
    ethics, 196
    mitigation, 114
    supply chain, 122

W

Wikileaks phenomena, 3, 211
World Bank data, 174
World Trade Organization (WTO), 251
"Write-blockers," 87
WTO, *see* World Trade Organization
WWW search engines, "intelligent" searches, 37

X

XML, 41, 42

Y

YouTube, 169

Z

Zero protest incidents, 175